D1642181

GUY BURGESS

GUY BURGESS

THE SPY WHO KNEW EVERYONE

STEWART PURVIS AND JEFF HULBERT

First published in Great Britain in 2016 by
Biteback Publishing Ltd
Westminster Tower
3 Albert Embankment
London SE1 7SP

ISBN 978-1-84954-913-4

10 9 8 7 6 5 4 3 2 1

A CIP catalogue record for this book is available from the British Library.

Set in Adobe Garamond Pro and Bureau Grotesque by Adrian McLaughlin

Printed and bound in Great Britain by
CPI Group (UK) Ltd, Croydon CR0 4YY

MIX
Paper from
responsible sources
FSC
www.fsc.org
FSC® C020471

CONTENTS

INTRODUCTION

Guy Burgess said in Moscow in 1962 that he still had 'many friends in the Establishment'. He wasn't exaggerating. During his career, he'd met three Prime Ministers, a Foreign Secretary, two Home Secretaries, a Lord Chancellor, two Chancellors of the Exchequer and a Secretary of State for Scotland – a total of ten exceptionally high-ranking individuals, eleven if we include an acting Foreign Secretary who'd been to his flat and later answered questions in the Commons about his defection. It was, and remains, unusual for a Russian spy to be quite so well connected inside the British political class.

When Burgess appealed from self-imposed exile in Moscow for his London bank account to be unfrozen, he wrote to a government minister, 'a dear' he knew from Eton and the BBC. When the minister agreed and news leaked out, it fell to another of Burgess's Eton and BBC contemporaries to defend the decision in Parliament.

In modern parlance, the Cambridge spy was a supreme networker, with a contacts book to die for: statesmen such as Winston Churchill, leading economists like John Maynard Keynes, literary figures such as W. H. Auden, Graham Greene, George Orwell and Stephen Spender, and famous actors, including Michael Redgrave and Noël Coward. He also set a gold standard for conflicts of interest, working variously, and often simultaneously, for the BBC, MI5, MI6, the War Office, the Ministry of Information and Soviet Intelligence.

Burgess was never challenged or arrested by Britain's spy-catchers in a decade and a half of espionage; a 'slob', sexually promiscuous, conspicuously drunk, constantly drawing attention to himself – how could he possibly be working for the Soviets? In fact, where there appeared to be chaos there was cunning and there were contacts.

As we researched the life and friends of Guy Burgess, we found more evidence that being an insider in 'the establishment' – the very term became common currency during the political rows that followed his defection – had helped him to spy. Our Burgess project began as a biography but became an investigation – independent of any intelligence service or government department and their inevitable spin – attempting to combine the traditions and techniques of journalism and of academic scholarship. Along the way we were fortunate to make new discoveries and new friends for the project, so that we were ready for what we knew from the start would be the big moment: the release in October 2015, after half a century, of hundreds of official files into the National Archives.

Ten thousand photographs of documents later, we are able to provide the evidence for a completely new story of Guy Burgess: the spy who knew everyone, and who used those contacts brilliantly to penetrate major British institutions, appearing to represent MI5 and MI6 when he was really working for their equivalents in Moscow. Those documents also allow us to tell the other half of the story, of how, once he made the biggest mistake of his life and fled to Moscow, those old contacts counter-attacked. Burgess the spy had been sheltered inside the establishment, but now he was kept at a safe distance outside. At one point, the great departments of state were given orders from the very top: keep him out of Britain; we don't want to have to arrest him.

We tell the Burgess story in chronological order, and then in our final chapter pull the strands together to summarise our conclusions. Our footnotes are detailed to enable readers to explore the National Archives and other sources for themselves if they wish to. To simplify the complexity of the different Soviet intelligence agencies we have called them what most people refer to them as: the KGB. With thanks to the National Archives, a dozen other archives around the world and many other helpers – all acknowledged in our footnotes – this is the story of Guy Burgess, the successful KGB spy: how he did it and how, for a long time, he got away with it.

STEWART PURVIS & JEFF HULBERT
CITY UNIVERSITY LONDON,
DECEMBER 2015

CHAPTER 1

'A NORMAL, HEALTHY, ENGLISH BOY'

A DISRUPTED EDUCATION, 1911–30

He was born Guy Francis de Moncy Burgess at 2 Albemarle Villas, Devonport, Plymouth, England, the son of a loyal servant of the Crown in the Royal Navy. He was cremated as Jim Andreyevich Elliot of No. 53/55, Apartment Block 68, Bolshaya Perogovskaya Ulitza, Moscow, USSR, wanted by the Crown as a suspected Soviet spy.

When his ashes were brought back to the family grave in an English country churchyard, the interment was carried out in secret. One family member called him 'our outlaw/inlaw'.[1] Guy Burgess wasn't just a traitor to his family, his old school, his old university and his class. He had betrayed senior ministers who found him amusing company and a useful, if unpredictable public servant. In a letter discovered during the research for this book, Burgess wrote from Moscow after his defection, 'I had no idea how much I was loathed.' The word 'loathed' was underlined twice.

The Britain that Burgess betrayed wasn't just the four nations of the United Kingdom; there was a whole British Empire with a presence in every continent across the globe. Guy Burgess's family roots went down deep into that empire: the Dominions, where Britain judged the white settlers were civilised enough to run their adopted countries; the colonies, where it was deemed the indigenous peoples were not; and the so-called 'protectorates', where the

British weren't so much protecting the inhabitants as the empire's strategic and commercial interests.

In the western hemisphere, a Burgess ancestor, William Robertson, had stumbled ashore in 1805 after a shipwreck on the coast of what was then British North America, later Canada, and fought against the Americans in the War of 1812.[2] In the eastern half of the world, when, as *The Spectator* of February 1866 put it, 'a little war has broken out in Aden',[3] a Colonel Burgess helped rout a rebellious Arab tribe. Burgess's forefathers didn't just fight for empire, they manoeuvred behind the scenes. One helped pay off the family of the Mohawk leader who fought with the British against the American revolutionaries. Burgess's own father was born in an imperial seaport – 'Steamer Point, Aden, Arabia' – and his stepfather plotted with the tribes that Lawrence of Arabia tried to unite to Britain's advantage. And they all helped keep British values alive around the world. One ancestor was the Master of Fox Hounds at the Montreal Hunt Club, the oldest foxhunting club in North America.

When Burgess was born in Plymouth in 1911, one embodiment of these imperial roots, his Canadian grandmother Maud, was on hand to help bring him into this world. Maud had been born into one of the English-speaking families that controlled business life in the predominantly French-speaking city of Montreal. In what looks to present-day genealogists like a convenient marriage between two banking dynasties, in 1880, Maud Hooper (of the Bank of British North America) married Mr William Gillman (of Grant, Gillman and Sons, later absorbed into Lloyd's Bank) who had travelled from England. Under the headline 'Fashionable Wedding', the *Montreal Gazette* reported that Maud 'looked radiantly happy under the trying ordeal' of the society wedding.[4]

'Many of the elite of Montreal' were in Christ Church Cathedral. Immediately after the wedding, Mr Gillman returned with his bride to England and they became leading citizens of Portsmouth with a financial stake in the city's banks, gas and water, and a large house with a good view of the sea. Their daughter Evelyn Gillman married a royal navy officer, Malcolm Burgess, whose own career took him and sometimes his family to various parts and ports of the empire, but on this occasion his base was the Devonport dockyard in Plymouth.

There happened to be a census just a fortnight before Guy Burgess's birth which tells us more about 2 Albemarle Villas and the people there at the time. According to the census return, the house had eleven rooms and living there were seven people, all women. Maud was helping her daughter Evelyn in the final days before she had a home birth. A 'sick nurse' is also recorded as being there possibly as a safeguard in the event of ill health. There was no mention in the census return of the 'head of family' because he was aboard HMS *Isis* at that time, anchored off the Devon Coast. Lieutenant Malcolm Burgess, aged twenty-nine, was shown as third in the pecking order of 201 officers and crew. No. 2 Albemarle Villas was an affluent household, well provided for in accommodation and staff, presumably funded by the Gillman and Hooper family fortunes rather than the naval earnings of the absent Lieutenant. Of the other women in the house, one was a housemaid, one a cook and one a maid. The word 'Burgess' is descended from the old French word '*burgeis*', which is also the origin of the word 'bourgeoisie', and his family had French Huguenot ancestors; thus his middle name 'de Moncy'.

When Guy was just nine his parents sent him away, as the English bourgeoisie did and sometimes still do, to a boarding school, a so-called preparatory school or 'prep school'. This particular preparation was to get the pupils to a sufficient standard to allow them to transfer at the age of thirteen to one of the great public schools. Lockers Park School at Hemel Hempstead in Hertfordshire, or just 'Lockers', was founded in 1874 'for the sons of gentlefolk who intended their sons for Rugby', the school where a pupil called William Webb Ellis reputedly ran with a football in his arms, thus creating a new sport.[5]

In July 1920, just before Burgess started at Lockers, a memorial window was unveiled in the school chapel to those who had died in the Great War of 1914–18. No fewer than ninety-three former pupils had been killed in action or died of their wounds during the conflict. The equivalent figure for World War Two was about fifty. Among the ninety-three names on the memorial was 'Maurice of Battenberg', a grandchild of Queen Victoria, who was killed at Ypres in 1914. Later in the war, his cousin Louis (also educated at Lockers) was among the family members who changed their name from Battenberg to the less Germanic 'Mountbatten'.

Inevitably for a family with military as well as well as banking connections, Guy Burgess's own relatives did not all survive the war. His uncle, Major Angus Gillman, was both an artillery officer and a qualified aviator. He survived one Great War retreat at Mons and then another at Le Cateau, for which he was one of the first soldiers to win a Military Cross, but he died at the Battle of Vimy Ridge near Arras and was buried in a military cemetery nearby.

The determination of much of the British political class to do everything to avoid another similar catastrophic conflict was to affect Guy Burgess's career two decades later, but in 1920 his own priority was adjusting to the immediate demands of prep-school life. One other new pupil from this period wrote that 'you must dress, wash, brush your hair and take care of yourself. Several people send children to school unable to take care of themselves and behave properly. This is making the boys' first term an almost certain misery.'[6] Subsequent evidence is that Burgess rarely got the hang of this washing and dressing business. While at Lockers, Burgess was, according to fellow pupil and later fellow Foreign Office official Stuart Hampshire, 'disgusting'. But he seems to have behaved properly enough for the school's records to show that 'he was very intelligent and tried hard', was never given anything less than an S for satisfactory and 'was often VG for very good'.[7]

At school, Burgess's hobby was reading about motoring, long before he was able to drive. From the age of nine, he subscribed to *Autocar* magazine, the 'world's oldest car magazine', first published in 1895. When *Motor Sport* magazine began, while Burgess was still at school, he subscribed to that too. When it came to participating in sport, for somebody who showed little interest in team sports in later life, he seems to have been enthusiastic and got into the Lockers First XI football team.

Lockers seems to have had a preoccupation with cake. Back in 1903, the school head had told parents, 'May I also ask you to limit the supply of cakes? At present they are reaching us at the rate of 5 or 6 a day', and a reminder followed some years later 'that some boys are receiving too many eatables from home'. A limit of one cake per term was set in 1906. It all sounds like Billy Bunter, the jovial overweight schoolboy from Frank Richards's fictional Greyfriars School.

However, there was another side to Lockers Park that seemed much more like the bullying world of Thomas Hughes's *Tom Brown's School Days*. One Burgess contemporary who remembered him as 'the scruffiest and dimmest boy in the undistinguished group' also recalled the masters as a 'repellent lot', including one who was a 'downright sadist and delighted in reducing small boys to tears', 'making one cry with fear and impotent rage'.[8] Worse would lie ahead in the next stage of Burgess's education.

Fathers like Malcolm Burgess, educated at the Royal Naval College at Dartmouth in Devon, would often send their own sons there. Until he was old enough, young Guy went to Eton for a year or, in the jargon of Britain's most famous public school, three 'halves' (terms) which make up an academic year. He won prizes for drawing. However, just after he finished that year, a traumatic event occurred for schoolboy Guy Burgess.

His father's naval career, which began in 1896 at the age of fifteen, had come to an end in 1922: twenty-six years summarised in one page of detailed notes now housed in the National Archives, which includes the comment 'conscientious but slow'. At a court martial in 1904, Malcolm Burgess had been reprimanded for neglect of duty when the signal book of a flotilla went missing from the battleship *Prince George*. There was also an early collision at sea and an inquiry judged 'sub-Lieutenant Burgess to blame, but in view of inexperience only admonished by the C-in-C to be more careful in the future'. He was then deemed 'unfit for service in destroyers'.[9] He stuck at it, however, and was praised in his service record as 'a very good officer of high zeal and ability'. He reached the rank of Commander, took his family for a year to Egypt when serving on the staff of the Rear Admiral, based near the head office of the Anglo-French Suez Canal Company, but then returned home and took retirement on health grounds.[10]

Commander Burgess, his wife Evelyn and their two sons – by now Guy had a brother, Nigel, two years younger – lived in a rambling house, West Lodge, in the Hampshire village of West Meon. It must have seemed an idyllic setting for a naval officer's retirement, close enough to Portsmouth for him to visit old navy friends and for his wife to visit family. Villagers who did domestic work at the house found Guy a difficult child, but they liked his younger brother.[11] Nigel Burgess was to have happy memories of his father: 'Very kind. He was fun. He was a nice man. He was a marvellous mechanic. Used to make things, mend things. He'd take cars to pieces and put them together again.'[12] Possibly this is where Malcolm's older son got his fascination with cars from.

On 15 September 1924, just two years after retiring, Commander Burgess died at West Lodge in circumstances that have become legendary, although there is no other source for the story than his son Guy, then aged thirteen. The official cause of death was given as 'atheroma of the aorta & valvular disease of the aortic valve'.[13] Later in life, Guy Burgess recounted how he'd heard the cries of his mother and rushed to his parents' bedroom to find her pinned down by the body of his father, who had apparently died during the act of lovemaking. According to him, he'd had to drag the corpse of his father off his mother.

There is no way of knowing if his story was true, but if it was then the immediate impact of this on the thirteen-year-old can be imagined. But harder to know is the more lasting psychological effect on him, his attitude to men and to women, and on his own sexuality. Certainly, his relationship with his mother remained very strong for the rest of his life. One person who was to witness this bond between mother and son over many of his later years was Burgess's sister-in-law Constance. 'I can't believe that it's good for a boy of thirteen to have his father removed,' she said in later years, noting that Guy became the centre of his mother's world: 'In her eyes he could do no wrong.'[14]

Malcolm Burgess left £418 to his widow, worth about £20,000 at present-day prices. Eventually, she was to leave the equivalent of £2.5 million, evidence that suggests it was her family money from the bankers – the Canadian Hoopers and the British Gillmans – that was subsidising the Burgess lifestyle.

In the finest traditions of the British 'stiff upper lip', Burgess carried on regardless of his father's death and set off for the education his father had ordained for him at the Royal Naval College in Dartmouth. In the booklet 'Practical Hints to Parents on Selecting an Outfit for the Royal Naval College, Dartmouth, Together with some Rules and Regulations to be observed by the Cadet', the gentlemen's outfitters Gieves, cautioned that 'at first sight one feels that the Royal Navy College Dartmouth is either a prison, a lunatic asylum or the house of a profiteer'. Greatly to his credit in the circumstances, the new recruit adapted well and was classified as 'excellent officer material'. He won prizes two years running for essays on naval operations, science and other subjects, such as his analysis of the military career of Napoleon.[15] But he did not like everything he saw.

One of Dartmouth's traditions was known as 'Official Cuts'. Those cadets deemed to have broken the rules were taken to the gym, spread-eagled over a boxhorse and caned with their trousers removed.[16] Some former cadets wrote of the punishment being administered by extremely fit and strong PE instructors; others witnessed it being done by fellow cadets. One estimated that most cadets were caned about half a dozen times during their years at Dartmouth.[17] As the victim was beaten for the required number of 'cuts', all the fellow cadets in that year group were paraded to watch. Burgess told how he 'rebelled against the barbarous ceremonial of corporal punishment' as 'he and three of his friends turned ostentatiously away to avoid seeing this performance'.[17] Any sanction for this act of rebellion is not recorded.

We have Burgess's own account of this episode because, in 1956, he sat down in Moscow with the former Labour MP Tom Driberg and talked about his life. These conversations formed the basis for Driberg's book *Guy Burgess: A Portrait with Background*. Burgess took the opportunity to comment on some of the vast amount of newspaper coverage that had followed his defection. As far as his time at Dartmouth was concerned, he wanted a chance to deny that he had been expelled for stealing. Driberg explained on Burgess's behalf that 'a slight defect in his eyesight was discovered, and he was told that he would therefore not be eligible for executive duties in the Navy'.[18] Burgess's mother found an old letter from the college: 'Dear Mrs Burgess, I am satisfied that Guy's eyesight must be a disappointment. If he does not take to the idea of engineering or paymaster, I can only think you would be wise to send him back to Eton.' Mrs Burgess pronounced that she had always known that he 'wasn't a thief'.[19]

Inevitably, there have been sceptics who have wondered whether the reasons given for Burgess's departure were more of a diplomatic nature than truly medical, asking why, if he had eyesight problems, this wasn't noticed when he first arrived. Dartmouth has said that eyesight deteriorating to such an extent during a cadet's training was 'a rare occurrence', but not unknown. A 1927 Admiralty document which might have cleared up the mystery is missing.

In a further twist, when Burgess had a civil service medical in 1947, he told the doctors that at Dartmouth his 'eyesight [was] not up to executive standard' and that he'd 'left [the college] owing to slight eyesight defect', but the civil service medical examiner declared that Burgess's sight was normal. Furthermore, Burgess was never photographed wearing glasses. Burgess's KGB controller Yuri Modin later wrote that, having worked closely with Burgess for many years, he never noticed the slightest defect in his vision. Modin's verdict was that Burgess loathed Dartmouth and wanted out.

So it was that in 1927, after something of a zig-zag course around the educational establishments of the British elite, Guy Burgess, by now aged sixteen, settled down for the remaining three years of his pre-university education at the institution where he would probably have been happiest all along. Burgess's housemaster during his earlier year at Eton, F. W. Dobbs, wrote to him: 'I am most awfully sorry to hear of the way your career in the Navy has been made impossible by your eyesight. I shall be delighted to have you back again.'[20] Burgess would have felt at home on his return to the most famous boarding school in the world, the seat of learning of no fewer than nineteen British Prime Ministers. He was welcomed back by old school chums from Lockers, by his old housemaster, and joined his younger brother Nigel. The brothers became 'Burgess major' and 'Burgess minor': in the Eton files, 'Burgess ma' and 'Burgess mi'. Both endured the regime whereby masters could not use the cane, but senior pupils could punish junior ones in communal mass floggings or individual acts of terror and torture with a red-hot poker. For younger boys, even washing was a stressful experience. A tin bath was provided and, two long corridors away, so was a hot tap. First-year boys were required to collect their hot water in a large can and carry it back to the bath. It didn't exactly encourage bathing on a cold winter night, according to one pupil.[21]

During his life, Burgess never showed any embarrassment that he had been educated in a citadel of educational privilege. Eton even has its own island in the Thames, Luxmoore's Garden, and Burgess would return on summer weekends to spend time lounging in a punt moored there. In Moscow, he wore his Old Etonian tie and was often seen wearing the rather more elaborate bow tie version. Burgess told Tom Driberg that, as a socialist, he disapproved of the educational system of which Eton was a part, but 'as an Old Etonian he has an enduring love for Eton as a place and an admiration for its liberal educational methods'.[22]

What Burgess loved most about Eton was what made it special. He enjoyed the access to an extraordinary range of literature, from Proust to Trollope, Browning to E. F. Benson. He was encouraged by his teachers – known at Eton as 'masters' – to draw caricatures and was taken to art exhibitions in London. One of his own etchings later turned up in a portfolio of sketches kept by a drawing master at Eton. Burgess rowed and swam and, on the extensive playing fields, took part in athletics. He was also selected for team sports such as soccer.

Eton mostly liked Burgess. In the school's then equivalent of final exams, he finished seventh out of the category of scholars known as Oppidans, with a total score of 74 per cent. He also won the Gladstone Memorial Scholarship and a Roseberry Prize, both for history.

In 1928, one master, Robert Birley, wrote to the housemaster F. W. Dobbs, who had helped get Burgess back into the school:

> At the moment his ideas are running away with him, and he is finding in verbal quibbles and Chestertonian comparisons a rather unhealthy delight, but he is such a sane person, and so modest essentially that I do not feel that this very much matters. The great thing is that he really thinks for himself...
>
> It is refreshing to find one who is really well-read and who can become enthusiastic or have something to say about most things from Vermeer to Meredith. He is also a lively and amusing person, generous, I think, and very good natured. He should do very well.[23]

Burgess began building a network of contacts that would serve him well after school. Initially it did not go smoothly. He was keen to join the exclusive

Eton society known as 'Pop' but the majority 'preferred not to have him'. He wasn't popular enough, aristocratic enough or good enough at games. Another pupil, Michael Berry, had to round up some pupils to vote for him.[24] Berry, later Baron Hartwell and chairman and Editor-in-Chief of the *Daily Telegraph*, remembered that 'at school Guy was clever; he had been the youngest boy to win the history prize and our history tutor, Robert Birley, later to be the headmaster, said he was the most brilliant student he had ever examined'.[25]

Berry was one of two Eton friends of Burgess who went on to become major figures in the British news media; the other was David Astor, Editor of *The Observer*, from the politically opposite side of Fleet Street. Some Eton boys, like the philosopher A. J. (Freddie) Ayer, became long-term friends; others, like Winston Churchill's son Randolph, were to crop up at regular intervals in the Burgess story but were never really proper friends. There was also Quintin Hogg, later Lord Hailsham, of whom Freddie Ayer wrote, 'One of the boys who beat me was Quintin Hogg, who displayed what seemed to me a more than judicial severity in the performance of the exercise.'[26]

Other Etonian contemporaries of Burgess who were to become famous Britons included: the soldier and writer Sir Fitzroy Maclean; the explorer Sir Wilfred Thesiger; the politician Jo Grimond; and cricket commentator Brian Johnston. When Burgess left Eton, he had a photograph of himself printed and gave copies to his friends which he signed 'Yours ever Guy'.[27]

Among the other curios from this period which survive are: a copy of Lytton Strachey's 1921 biography of Queen Victoria inscribed 'Guy Burgess Eton 1929 Part of Rosebery History Second Prize'; and a copy of *British Foreign Secretaries, 1807 1916* by Cecil Algernon, also marked 'Guy Burgess 1929' and full of his schoolboy annotations and observations on, for instance, British diplomacy before the First World War.

There is one other aspect of Eton life in the 1920s in which it is reasonable to assume that Burgess was a willing and active participant. Everybody at Eton knew that sexual relationships between boys were going on, but nobody dared admit it at the time for fear of expulsion. However, after Eton, the schoolboy lovers would sometimes look back with affection at their encounters.

So it was that one of Burgess's contemporaries at both Lockers Park and Eton, James Lees-Milne, remembered another, Tom Mitford:

> On Sunday eves before Chapel at five, when the toll of the bell betokened that all boys must be in their pews, he and I would, standing on the last landing of the entrance steps, out of sight of the masters in the ante-chapel and all the boys inside, passionately embrace, lips to lips, body pressed to body, each feeling the opposite fibre of the other.[28]

The pupil with whom Burgess himself was most commonly linked was David Hedley. It is not difficult to see why. Hedley was funny, handsome, a sportsman, the Editor of a school newspaper and school captain. Freddie Ayer wrote of his own couplings with Hedley: 'It was, indeed, a romantic attachment, though on my side not overtly physical. On the one occasion on which he put his arms around me and said that he loved me I was embarrassed and disengaged myself.'[29]

Burgess spent his eighteenth birthday in the North African port of Tangier, later nicknamed 'Queer Tangier'. For the first half of the twentieth century, until it formally became part of Morocco, Tangier was an international city with its own laws and attracted a diverse group of visitors and residents, some seeking respite from the restrictive sexual laws of their own countries. Even though Tangier would later gain the reputation of the world's 'first gay resort', the passenger list on Burgess's voyage to the city suggests that not everybody on board was necessarily planning to spend their time in such pursuits. The other passengers included the Countess of Galloway, a schoolmaster and his wife, a coal merchant and his wife, plus Burgess's own mother and brother.[30]

Reflecting on his schooling many years later, Burgess was keen to stress to Tom Driberg that at Eton he was 'never an odd boy out' but a 'normal, healthy, English boy'. When the General Strike of 1926 divided the country, Burgess's allegiance, no doubt like most boys at Eton, was firmly to his class: the ruling class. Burgess never sought to depict Eton as the turning point in his politics, but Driberg detected that his reading at the time suggested the first stirrings of a social conscience. *The Hole in the Wall* by Arthur Morrison was an adventure story that portrayed the life of children in the East End of London, and *Across the Bridges* by Alexander Paterson told of the author's experiences working for a charity in Bermondsey.

Burgess also remembered the visits to Eton of lecturers from the two very different ends of the social scale. One was an organiser from the dockers' trade union talking about the inequalities in Britain; the other was a diplomat from the British embassy in Berlin warning about the changes under way in Germany. That lecturer, Harold Nicolson, was to play a major part in Burgess's life, and the theme of his lecture was to be a recurring concern in the next stage of Burgess's education, at Trinity College, Cambridge, beginning in the autumn of 1930.

Before starting at Cambridge, Burgess spent part of the summer in Canada visiting a cousin in Montreal with his mother and brother. When the three of them began their journey from Liverpool to Montreal on the Canadian Pacific liner *Duchess of York*, their addresses were listed as 'c/o C. P. R London S. W.', in effect, care of the Canadian Pacific Railway office in London. But when they returned on another CPR liner, the *Duchess of Bedford*, the passengers were asked to list their 'Principal Addresses in the United Kingdom' and each Burgess gave a different address. His mother Evelyn, then aged forty, listed her occupation as 'Housewife' and gave her address as 'West Lodge, West Meon, near Petersfield', the Burgess family home where she still lived. Her son Nigel, aged seventeen, 'Student', put '47 Clarence Parade, Southsea', which was his grandparents' address. But Guy Burgess, aged nineteen, also a 'Student', wrote '7 Park Place, St James Street, London SW1'.[31]

Park Place was, and still is, in one of the most expensive areas of London, close to St James's Palace, Buckingham Palace, the gentlemen's clubs of Pall Mall and just around the corner from the Ritz Hotel in Piccadilly. What exactly was a schoolboy doing living there? In 1930, the building was divided into what were advertised as 'Furnished Service Flats', but other than that, we can find no other reference to Burgess living at 7 Park Place and no obvious reason for him giving that address.

One possible explanation lies in the name of one of the residents of 7 Park Place, listed in the electoral roll for that year: Captain Edward George

Spencer-Churchill. He was then fifty-four, a soldier, landowner and a first cousin of Winston Churchill. While at Magdalene College, Oxford, Spencer-Churchill had earned the nickname 'Juggins', sometimes defined as a simpleton. He was one of a 'set' of three men who all remained unmarried throughout their lives, known as 'Juggins, Ma and Pa' and admirers of the best-looking male students.[32] Since Burgess had no income of his own, perhaps his parents paid the rent for him to live in an expensive part of London during his holiday. More likely, Burgess had found somebody, possibly Spencer-Churchill, who let him live there for some reason. If so, the growing Burgess network was already beginning to prove useful to him, and soon Cambridge would provide an even more fruitful hunting ground for contacts.

CHAPTER 2

'A REAL RAPSCALLION'

A SCHOLARSHIP STUDENT GOES ROGUE, 1930-36

In the library of one of Cambridge's most famous colleges is a register containing the names of some its most infamous students. The Wren Library at Trinity College has many treasures, including the personal notebook of one former student, Isaac Newton, but it is a mundane-looking volume, *Admissions to Trinity College Cambridge 1913–1948*, that best helps to tell the story of Guy Burgess and the other Cambridge spies.

At the start of each academic year in that period, new students would write out their personal details. The admissions for 1 October 1930 included:

> Guy Francis de Moncy Burgess
>
> Father: Captain Malcolm Kingsford De Moncy Burgess
>
> Present Residence: West Lodge, West Meon, Hampshire
>
> Born: April 16th 1911
>
> Place of Birth: Stoke, Cornwall*
>
> School or Place of Education: Eton College, Windsor

The admissions register tells us a lot about the social elitism of the times. Of the 234 new Trinity students in Burgess's first year academic year (1930/31), no fewer than thirty had been contemporaries of his at Eton. The next most popular feeder

---

* The birth took place within the parish of Stoke Damerel, Devonport, which is in Devon. There is no explanation as to why Burgess thought it was in Cornwall

schools, Harrow and Stowe, each scored only half that number. Almost all new Trinity men – and there were only men – had been educated at public schools. There was just a handful from schools such as 'Wheelwright Grammar School, Dewsbury' or schools abroad. So Trinity College served a small sample of the tiny proportion of the general population that went to university. By contrast, figures for the education of the rest of the nation's youth show that only one out of every five children over fourteen even went to school in the late 1920s.[1]

At nineteen, Burgess was one of the older entrants at Trinity because of his circuitous route to Cambridge via Dartmouth with two stops at Eton. Most others, like a certain John Enoch Powell, newly arrived from King Edward's School, Birmingham, were a year younger. Burgess and Powell were among fourteen 'Entrance Scholars', so it is likely that the future Soviet spy and the future Conservative minister would have known of each other.

By now, Burgess was the stepson of Lieutenant Colonel (ret.) John 'Jack' Retallack Bassett DSO MBE. Five years after the death of her first husband and while Guy was at Eton, his mother, Mrs Malcolm Burgess, had remarried to become Mrs John Bassett, the widow of a naval officer becoming the wife of an army officer. She was forty-five, he was fifty-one.

It seems that stepfather and stepson did not get on. Burgess's sister-in-law Constance later remembered that Colonel Bassett

> was this sort of absolute blimp and so Guy would undo his flies a bit more and sling his tie over one shoulder and drive him absolutely mad, spill his food all down [himself] at meals. My mother-in-law [Burgess's mother] would encourage him and roar with laughter. And Jack would go out of the room.[2]

In a letter sent to a friend while he was at Cambridge, Burgess wrote that he may have to spend part of a vacation 'with my family, with whom I do not get on'. Since we know he loved his mother, this is probably a reference to his stepfather.[3] Later in life, Mrs Bassett told a family friend her husband and son 'never got on. It was always a difficult situation.' Colonel Bassett apparently 'couldn't stand Guy'.[4]

One school friend remembers Burgess saying that his stepfather was a pro-fessional gambler, which was most probably an exaggeration based on Bassett's interest in horse racing. In fact, like Burgess's own father, the Colonel had served the empire in the Middle East. He'd done a spell in the Camel Corps and as the British resident in Jeddah, the city at the heart of the conflicts that created the modern Saudi Arabia. And, like Burgess's mother, the Colonel was descended from a banking family.

With Hooper, Gillman, and now Bassett banking family money behind him, there is no evidence that Guy needed to lack for any material comforts at this time, and he was going to a Cambridge college that wasn't at a loss for funds either. Indeed, to this day, Trinity says that it 'reigns supreme as the largest and wealthiest of the Cambridge colleges'.[5]

When he walked for the first time through the Great Gate, erected between 1490 and 1535, he may well have gazed in awe at Great Court – one of Britain's most impressive quadrangles. Through a door in a corner of Great Court, Burgess would have been faced with a second great space, Nevile's Court, also known as the Cloisters. A walk down to the left-hand corner and he would be in New Court and heading for the room that was to be his home for his undergraduate years, just fifty paces from the college's punts stored by the River Cam, which runs at the back of Trinity.

Guy Burgess arrived in confident mood to study history, proudly telling people that the examiners who had awarded him a scholarship had revealed that they'd never previously awarded one to somebody who knew as little as he did. They had apparently been won over by one paper he wrote on the French Revolution.[6]

Burgess's tutor was listed as a 'Mr Winstanley'. Denys Winstanley had been a Trinity history student himself at the turn of the century and, after graduating with a double first, had become an assistant inspector of schools in Durham. Some of the children he encountered in the mining villages 'were so exceedingly stupid ... but occasionally I had glimpses of genius'.[7] Winstanley decided to return to Trinity in 1906 and, in his own words, 'I went into these rooms where I have remained ever since. I suppose like all bachelors I get selfish and in a rut.' He was too discreet to mention that he had ventured out for a spell in military intelligence during the First World War.

Under Winstanley's tutelage, Burgess got high marks in the exams at the end of his first year. His special interest was nineteenth-century England and especially Victorian literature and politics. Having heard Burgess's own account of his early years at Trinity, Tom Driberg concluded that he had 'led the ordinary life of an Old Etonian undergraduate', gaining almost automatic entry to the Pitt Club, 'where he drank a bottle of Liebfraumilch '21 (at 3s 6d!)[†] every day at luncheon'.[8] The Pitt Club has been compared to another exclusively male domain, the Bullingdon Club at Oxford. Burgess's fellow Pitt members found him bright, amusing, witty and irreverent, but in the words of one contemporary 'fundamentally destructive'.

Burgess made one change to his lifestyle while at Cambridge: the enthusiastic schoolboy sportsman abandoned all physical exercise other than swimming. He'd been advised to do this by one of his schoolmasters at Eton. Eric Powell was a keen mountaineer and an accomplished artist, particularly of Alpine scenes. At Eton he encouraged Burgess to go rock climbing and to draw. He may have even influenced Burgess to apply to his old college. When Burgess went up to Cambridge, Powell is said to have advised him: 'If you go on taking exercise now, you'll always have to, as I've had to' – a reference to the time Powell had spent at Trinity, earning a Cambridge Blue for rowing.[9]

With a successful outcome to the May exams under his belt, Burgess finished the task of designing the scenery for a production of George Bernard Shaw's comedy *Captain Brassbound's Conversion* at the ADC (Amateur Dramatic Club). The ADC is Britain's oldest university playhouse and the starting point for the careers of many of Britain's theatre directors. Given that Shaw had set Act II in a Moorish Castle and Act III in the home of a Presbyterian minister, the set designer required some ingenuity and Burgess is said to have taken the task extremely seriously. One review called his design 'not exaggeratedly realistic nor exaggeratedly stylised, but a pleasantly supportive setting for the play'.[10]

---

† In 2015's values this was equivalent to approximately £25

The ADC turned out to be a wonderful way for Burgess to widen his circle of friends. The part of Captain Brassbound was taken by a student called Michael Redgrave, who thought Burgess's sets were 'very good'. According to the future British film legend, 'Burgess was one of the bright stars of the university scene, with a reputation of being able to turn to anything.'[11]

By the time of this student production, 'Mr Michael Redgrave' – as he was billed in the *Radio Times* – had already appeared on BBC radio at least six times, reading prose and poetry and acting in plays. But in the Cambridge production he is said to have been 'acted off the stage' by the person playing the part of Lady Cicely Waynflete – Arthur Marshall. Marshall was best known as an actor in women's roles (women were not allowed to act on the ADC Theatre stage until 1935[12]), and both Redgrave and Marshall would both reappear in the Burgess story.

So too would the producer of the play, George Rylands, always known as 'Dadie' because he could not pronounce the word 'baby' as a child. Rylands had made his name as a schoolboy director at Eton and a student actor at King's. By 1931, he was a Fellow at King's College and already a doyen of Cambridge theatre, a don who both produced plays and became a magnet for new talent. Rylands said of Burgess, 'Guy could never stop chattering. He was wonderful company – full of jokes and ideas and stories and scandal and all that.'[13] He also wrote that Burgess was 'a real rapscallion and extremely talented'. A rapscallion was a rascal or a rogue, but presumably, to Rylands, Burgess was a lovable one.[14] They remained friends for life, even after Burgess defected to Moscow in 1951. In 1960, Burgess sent a contribution to an appeal for the Cambridge Arts Theatre that Rylands had helped to launch in 1936. Dadie was determined this donation should be publicly recognised and sent a message back via a mutual friend: 'How generous of Guy. I am most grateful. Of course his name must appear on any and every list like everybody else. It would not cross my mind to suppress it.'[15]

Burgess, Rylands, Redgrave and Marshall had one thing in common apart from their love of the theatre. In the parlance of the time, they were all 'homosexual'. Redgrave was bisexual, with partners as varied as Noël Coward and

Edith Evans. His wife, the actress Rachel Kempson, always understood his sexuality and wrote: 'It was probably this sensitivity in his nature that made me love him so.' They were married for fifty years until his death and had three children, Vanessa, Corin and Lynn. But Burgess, Rylands and Marshall remained firmly in the camp of what became known as 'confirmed bachelors'. Homosexuality had become, in one historian's words, a 'creed' at Cambridge; some called it 'the Higher Sodomy'. Since, it was argued, men were clearly superior to women, a relationship between two men was obviously of a different higher order than that between a man and a woman. Put more crudely by one observer of this particular scene, 'Even the womanisers pretend to be sods, lest they shouldn't be thought respectable.'[16]

The law of the land at the time was clear: homosexual acts between men were illegal (and remained so until 1967, when acts between two men aged over twenty-one were decriminalised in England and Wales). It has been estimated that a total of 49,000 men were convicted while the various laws on homosexual offences were on the statute book.[17]

Burgess's producer Rylands and his tutor Winstanley were among many Oxbridge academic bachelors later named as members of homosexual 'cells' or 'sets' by Noël Annan in 1990 in an essay called 'The Growth of the Cult of Homosexuality'. This formed a chapter in a book called *Our Age: The Generation That Made Post-War Britain*. Either for legal reasons or because of his friendship with Rylands, who was still alive, Annan concluded, 'It can safely be said about most of these bachelors that they were never guilty of any homosexual act that was criminal according to the law of the land.' But that didn't stop him writing that undergraduates had streamed through Rylands's room 'presumably for their good looks' and that 'for many undergraduates, including Burgess, he was the centre of a certain Cambridge world'.[18] He named two colleges which in the 1930s 'were full of bachelor dons'. One was his own college, King's, the other was Burgess's, Trinity.

The most striking element of Burgess's own sexuality, given the legal constraints of the time, was that he was 'out' long before 'coming out' became a badge of honour in what is now known as the gay community. The historian and diplomat, Robert Cecil, who knew Burgess, put it this way:

He had been a homosexual, of course, ever since his years at Eton; but
he had no feeling of being an outcast, because he lacked all sense of
shame. He had no particular wish to change the law on homosexuality;
so long as he succeeded in defying it, the risk involved gave an added
frisson to his exploits. He fitted excellently into the interlocking circles
on the fringes of politics, art, letters and intellectual debate, in which as
a younger man he had shone.

Burgess did not seek to hide his interest in homosexual erotica. When Robert Birley from Eton invited himself for tea with Burgess at Trinity in 1931, he found that his former pupil wasn't in his room, so Birley went inside and waited: 'I realised that something must have gone terribly wrong when I came across an extraordinary array of explicit and extremely unpleasant pornographic literature. He bustled in finally, full of cheerful apologies for being late as usual, and we talked happily enough over the teacups.'[19]

There seem to have been several overlapping strands in the sexual persona of Guy Burgess at Cambridge and beyond. At first, there was the occasional pining for a respected older man such as Dadie Rylands. Then there was 'Burgess the expert seducer', using flattery, humour and his comparatively good looks to get men into bed, as well as 'Burgess the sex counsellor', who, according to one friend, 'continued to assist his friends in their sexual lives' long after their own affairs were over. Burgess would listen to their emotional problems and 'when necessary find suitable partners for them'. One put it more bluntly: that Burgess was a combination of a father confessor and a pimp. At the rougher end of what was known as 'rough trade', Burgess pursued young working-class men, and sadism seems to have played its part too.

One of Burgess's lovers in his Cambridge years was Michael 'Micky' Burn, a bisexual man who later became a wartime commando, a prisoner of war, a poet and a *Times* correspondent. In that latter capacity, in 2003, he wrote an article for the paper recalling his affair with Burgess. The subeditors at *The Times* could not resist the headline 'Guy Burgess: The Spy Who Loved Me'.

While he was working on a history of the Brooklands motor racing circuit, Burn went to a political party in Cambridge wearing a Brooklands tie clip. Burgess – a motoring aficionado like his father – went up to him and asked how he had come by it. 'It turned out that racing cars was one of his passions. He invited me back to his rooms in College and I stayed the night. I saw him quite often during the ensuing years.'

In the *Times* article, Burn wrote of his attraction for Burgess:

> He had blue eyes and tight, wavy hair, was a good swimmer and looked menacingly healthy. I have seen his looks described as 'boyish', he did convey a dash of pertness and sham innocence, as if he had just run away after ringing some important person's doorbell. Something still clung to him of his term as a thirteen-year-old at Dartmouth. His rolling, lurching walk gave the impression that he was about to charge into somebody or something and go overboard.[20]

The article was based on private notes which Burn had typed up in 1987 on four pages of A4, which he titled 'private and confidential guy burgess etc. ... some rather random notes'. It is something of a miracle that these notes survive. Although Burn never liked to throw anything away, he does seem to have been rather careless, managing to lose a signed copy of *Mein Kampf* through a hole in his car on the very same day that Hitler had given it to him. Some of the detail in the notes was not included in the article partly, one assumes, because of space, but perhaps he also judged that readers of *The Times* may not be quite ready for some of the forensics.

In a particularly striking section of his notes, he wrote that Burgess 'liked to show me off to his gay friends':

> For example, John Sparrow, later Warden of All Souls. (I have been told that he pimped for boys for JS and kept all his letters, which were found after Guy defected ... probably lots of others too). Also the historian–don, Simpson, who had written the famous Life of Napoleon III and according to Guy been in love with Rupert Brooke; again according to Guy he thought I looked very like R. B. Also E. M. Forster, whom he asked to lunch to meet me.

Burgess was developing a tactic of using friends to make more friends among the best-known literary names of the time – and keeping their letters. It was later confirmed by MI5 that letters from John Sparrow had been found in Burgess's flat and that 'Sparrow was one of many people who were extremely worried about the possibility of being blackmailed by Burgess at the present time.'[21] One friend who later fell out with him said that Burgess never destroyed a letter and 'saw himself sometimes as a kind of Figaro figure, ever resourceful in the service of others in order to manipulate them to his own ends'.[22] Noël Annan put it more bluntly: 'Burgess could bully as well as charm.'[23]

The word 'boys', which Burn used to describe those who Burgess pimped for Warden Sparrow of All Souls, Oxford, raises the issue of their likely age. Seen through the 21st-century prism of the sexual abuse of children, it is surprising that in the first half of the previous century so little concern seems to have been given to the protection of children from their elders. It may have been an unintended consequence of the law of the land that, since all homosexual acts were illegal at the time, whatever the ages of those involved, it did not seem to matter much if those participating were under sixteen at the time or not. The homosexual literature of the period has frequent mentions of 'boys', but rarely detail on exactly how old they are. Burn himself wrote of how 'about this time I now and then used to pick up boys about Piccadilly'. That does not necessarily mean they were under sixteen, but nor does it rule this out.

As Burgess's first year at Trinity came to an end in the summer of 1931, he could look back at academic, artistic, social and sexual success: good exams results; recognition as a talented designer of drama sets; making friends at cocktail parties; sex with all comers. Micky Burn wrote that 'Guy presented Cambridge as an arcane world in which dons, fellows, professors, headed cliques like hostesses, and claques like prima donnas, stuck poisoned pens between one another's shoulder blades, and vied with one another conversationally in epigrammatic farts and counterfarts'. No wonder Burgess was so happy there.

In October 1931, Burgess began his second year at Trinity. And it was to be another successful academic one, with him earning a First in Part I of the

History Tripos. According to Julian Bell, a King's student whose first book of poems had just been published, the 'central subject of ordinary intelligent conversation' at Cambridge in 1929 and 1930 was poetry.[24] But, with every year that passed, poetry was giving way to politics. Burgess now took 'a sudden jump forward in political awareness'.[25]

The context of the times was economic depression, the failure of the old politics and a search for new solutions. After the trauma of the First World War, the 1920s had seemed to signal progress and prosperity, at least for some. New York stock prices went up and up until one Tuesday in October 1929, when some shares couldn't be sold at any price, however low. The Wall Street Crash demonstrated in spectacular style the flimsy foundations on which apparent economic success had been built. A decade of economic depression began with no obvious route back to financial stability. Maybe this was the end of capitalism, but what would take its place?

In Britain, industries closed, the queues of the unemployed got longer and the ranks of the hunger marchers from the most disadvantaged areas grew more crowded and strident. Fewer, not more, children were going to secondary school. Class differences became more, not less distinct. The political classes realigned. The Labour Prime Minister Ramsay MacDonald became the leader of a mostly Conservative National Government. Oswald Mosley resigned from MacDonald's government and founded the New Party that moved further and further to the right. Former Trinity College student Stanley Baldwin was in and out of power as Prime Minister no fewer than three times in the 1930s. It was a good time to be cynical about politics.

A Welsh student at Oxford called Goronwy Rees, who was to meet Burgess in 1932, later said of those times:

> It was the sort of general obsession of my generation, I think, which was this feeling that, during the 1930s, England was in some kind of way coming to an end. The depression had the most terrible effect on everybody, I think. And it was the depression, I think, fundamentally, which turned people like him – Burgess for instance – into, well, I suppose one has to say, traitors.[26]

In Germany, where four million were unemployed, the Nazi Party had become the second-largest party and Adolf Hitler's *Mein Kampf* was a bestseller. And, perhaps most worryingly, Japan's defeat of China in the invasion of Manchuria in 1931 had demonstrated how powerless the League of Nations was if one strong and determined country invaded a neighbour. It was, therefore, not surprising that bright young men wondered if some other form of government imported from abroad might be better. Two such models were available: Hitler's fascism from Germany, and Lenin and Stalin's communism from the Soviet Union. With Burgess's taste for extremes, we shouldn't be surprised that over the next five years he dabbled with both, but each for very different reasons.

Although there is no suggestion that any one Moscow mastermind oversaw Guy Burgess's journey from apolitical student to Soviet spy, with hindsight, KGB HQ would have been entitled to regard it as a textbook conversion and transition. Stage one was for Burgess to meet a member of the working class with whom he could talk politics. Since the students of Cambridge University lived a privileged life well away from those who suffered most in these economically stressed times, personal experiences of hardship were few and far between among the students at Trinity College. However, in his first year, Burgess was to meet one undergraduate very different from the rest.

In May 1930, the Trustees of the Miners' Welfare National Scholarship Scheme had announced that one of their annual bursaries had been won by a young miner: 'James Lees, of Sutton-in-Ashfield, Nottinghamshire, a scholarship tenable at the University of Cambridge to enable him to take a degree course in history.'[27] James, 'Jim' or 'Jimmy' Lees told Burgess,

> You will get a First because your energies are not exhausted by life, because of the class prejudice of the examiners, and because you got here easily and aren't frightened by it all. I don't have the brilliance of ignorance. I shall do ten times as much work as you and get a good Second.[28]

Burgess said that Lees taught him a lot and troubled his conscience.

Lees also provided an introduction to a man who had seen fascism on the front line and had come to his own conclusions about the appropriate response. David Haden-Guest, or David Guest as he became more commonly known, was the son of a Labour MP, Leslie Haden-Guest, and arrived at Trinity a year before Burgess.

Guest studied philosophy and mathematical logic under the renowned philosopher Ludwig Wittgenstein. In the summer holiday of 1930, he went to study at the University of Göttingen in Lower Saxony and witnessed drunken Nazi meetings in beer halls. He joined a communist youth demonstration, was arrested and reportedly went on hunger strike in solitary confinement before he was finally released.[29] This pacifist socialist returned a revolutionary Marxist. His father's party, Labour, was judged by Cambridge students of this period to have failed to respond to the challenges of the time. The Communist Party would have to lead from the front. As part of this new approach, Guest walked into the Trinity College dining hall, a magnificent example of Elizabethan architecture, proudly wearing a hammer and sickle on his lapel.

Communists at Cambridge had traditionally been more 'town' than 'gown'. The mass of the students were as yet untouched by the crisis unfolding around them and the senior communists inside the university were usually staff not students; often very distinguished staff in the form of the economist Maurice Dobb and the scientist J. D. 'Sage' Bernal. Both were long-standing and very open supporters of the Soviet Union. In the summer of 1931, Bernal made two trips to Moscow with fellow Cambridge scientists to meet their counterparts among Russian academics.[30] At a subsequent meeting in Cambridge that brought together these Marxist academics with students and Communist Party officials, Guest persuaded the national leadership that if a communist cell in Cambridge were formed, it could not only recruit students, but also work with the party members among the town's more permanent population. The former miner, James Lees, who'd introduced Burgess to Guest, was at this meeting. The Burgess–Guest relationship was not to be an easy one. According to another Cambridge communist 'they frequently clashed in argument' and as Guest was 'easily aroused, Guy would deliberately provoke him'.[31]

The cell was created in Trinity College with its base in a Marxist study group that Guest had started within what was called the University Socialist

Society, even though there were many committed communists within it working under orders from party headquarters in London. The society's communist connections weren't exactly a secret. William Rust, the first Editor of the Communist Party newspaper the *Daily Worker*, was a regular visiting speaker, but there was never anything at the university in this period that openly called itself a communist club or society.

The Socialist Society became the main vehicle for the communist recruiters. Their tactic was to attract non-party members and then, by constant dialogue, lead them to the inevitable conclusion that the only party that offered a real solution to fascism abroad and poverty at home was the Communist Party.

Among their targets were those who had joined, or might join, the rival Labour Club: nationally, the Labour Party was in bad shape after their collapse in the 1931 general election.

Some have seen the communist cell within the Socialist Society as a pyramid, with Dobb, Bernal and other dons directing operations from the top. Others have depicted them as merely observing with approval as the number of Trinity recruits in particular rapidly increased.

For some members, there was to be a striking culture clash between college lunches of 'lobster, cold pheasant and strawberry gateau, followed by Camembert cheese, Romany biscuits and finally Abdulla Egyptian cigarettes, the wine being Laubenheim hock' and then doing their 'Soc Soc' duty selling copies of the *Daily Worker* in the back streets of Cambridge.

Some recruits must have seemed very unlikely communists. The splendidly titled Francis Hovell-Thurlow-Cumming-Bruce, the grandson of a minister in Gladstone's government, went to Trinity while his identical twin brother Roualeyn went to Magdalene. Both were attracted by communism. Francis agreed to become a 'titular Communist for a while' until he was 'lying under a tree in the Bois de Boulogne reading a book by a Norwegian sociologist – it knocked the bottom out of Marxism. I was so relieved I didn't have to be a Communist anymore.'[32]

For Guy Burgess, however, reading only seems to have increased his enthusiasm for Marxism. Not that a robust intellectual such as he would sign up for an off-the-shelf, ready-formulated ideology. He set out to work out his own theory of how a modern state should work. After studying the English revolution of the seventeenth century, the Reform Bill, the French and Russian revolutions and the rise of Hitler, he concluded that those who were economically dominant exercised power. When he announced this outcome to Guest, he was told to read Lenin's *The State and Revolution*, where he would find out that someone else had come to the same conclusion rather earlier.[33] Undeterred, he read Marx's own analysis of Louis-Napoléon's capture of dictatorial power in 1851 and found that the Marxist approach to history fitted with his own thinking rather better than the conventional version taught at Cambridge.

Burgess's interest in Marxism would build as his contacts and experiences at Cambridge grew and developed.

Two young communists were important influences. James Klugman had been born Norman John Klugmann, the son of a Jewish merchant, but had decided to call himself James and to drop the final 'n' in his surname. He was educated with somebody who would become a major part of the Burgess story, Donald Maclean, at Gresham's in Norfolk, a school also attended by two other later Burgess connections, W. H. Auden and Stephen Spender.

At Trinity College, Klugman got a Double First and continued at Cambridge doing research. He summed up the mood of the times:

> We, an extraordinarily erudite and arrogant generation of Cambridge students, who thought that we were the best intellectuals, and that the intellectuals were the wisest of the community, we were still lost at the beginning of the thirties, often with immense knowledge but no philosophy, immense mental effort and activity but no purpose.[34]

Klugman could be politely direct. When asked by one right-wing tutor, 'Tell me, James, why is it that so many of our brightest students seem to be on the left?', he is said to have replied, 'Well, sir, you have to think of the common factor. And that's you, sir.'[35]

Communism seemed the answer to the challenge for those who were 'lost' and for the rich idealist young it provided some form of remission from the economic sins of their families. Klugman was the key theorist, administrator and recruiter of the communist cell at Trinity. Yet, the only mention of this period in his MI5 file is of him attending the World Congress of Students against War and Fascism in Brussels in 1934, and the file contains nothing of his work inside the university.

The other Trinity man working with Klugman was John Cornford, and together they made a powerful and persuasive double act. Cornford undoubtedly became the most glamorous of the Trinity Marxists, partly because he was a poet who went off to fight for the cause. He'd been born Rupert John Cornford, so named because his parents were friends of the poet Rupert Brooke. His mother – a published poet in her own right – was the granddaughter of Charles Darwin and his father was a professor of Ancient Philosophy at Trinity. It seemed only natural for their son to be admitted to the college from one of its feeder schools, Stowe. But, before then, Cornford spent time at the London School of Economics, where he was influenced by Frank Meyer, an American communist activist who, with Klugman, was organising groups of communist students at various British universities.

Cornford's first mentions in MI5 files were in 1933 as a result of his Young Communist League activities at LSE and then a strange episode at Cambridge railway station.

A police sergeant was called after reports of a man who was 'believed to be in possession of a quantity of cash, and in a most unclean state', 'similar to a person who had not washed for at least a week'. This turned out to be John or 'Jack' Cornford, who said he was on his way to London to renew his passport. The police interviewed his mother, who told them that her son 'associates with known members of the Communist movement'. She was not at all surprised at her son's interrogation because 'she had expected something of the sort to happen, having regard to his dress'.[36]

When the report was passed up the line, no less than the founder and first Director General of MI5, Colonel Vernon Kell, told the Cambridgeshire police that should Jack Cornford 'come under notice in connection with communist activities, I should be glad to be informed'.[37]

Somewhere between the headquarters of MI5 and the Cambridgeshire police, however, that particular baton was to be dropped, and the failure to monitor both Cornford's and Klugman's activities within the university created an intelligence vacuum that was to put the security services at a disadvantage in key moments throughout the story of Guy Burgess and the other Cambridge spies.

The problem was partly resources and partly technique. The inter-war Security Service was a small outfit: 'Even at the start of 1939 it had only thirty-six officers, assisted by 103 secretarial and Registry staff.'[38] The Special Branch officers of local police forces, who did much of the surveillance spade work on behalf of MI5, specialised in watching people enter and leave buildings, sitting at public meetings taking notes and reading the written material that communists sold on street corners. But when the activities happened within the hallowed college quadrangles such as Trinity's Great Court, which had limited public access, it would be very difficult for undercover policemen to wander freely, sit in on meetings in students' rooms and buy magazines at student-only events. Even if they could gain admittance, the likelihood was that they would stand out from the rest of the crowd.

For instance, there is no sign in MI5 files of an article Cornford wrote in a Trinity student magazine which said, 'Many of us are no longer willing to be the humble instruments for enforcing the rule of imperialism on the working class.' He wrote of the ruling class as one 'which has already been condemned by history'.[39] To boost his anti-bourgeois credentials, Cornford chewed tobacco, didn't shave, picked his nose and used a bread knife to clean under his fingernails. He was living with Rachel 'Ray' Peters, an older Communist Party activist and daughter of a Welsh miner, whom he had met and taken to Cambridge with him. Very unconventionally for these times, they openly had a child without getting married. (Believers in eugenics and/or the British class system will be interested to learn that the child also went to Trinity and got a First in history.)[40]

A striking image of John Cornford and Ray Peters in moodily lit profile was taken in a Cambridge photographic studio that seemed to have the monopoly on recording the images of the university's young would-be revolutionaries. Lettice Ramsey and Helen Muspratt were two pioneering women photographers who shared the left-wing politics of many of those who sat in their studio. Lettice Ramsey had visited Moscow and knew Guy Burgess well; she photographed him in the studio and by the river with friends. Ramsey later said of Burgess, 'All intellectuals in Cambridge were Communists at the time. We had great hopes, but then were gradually let down.'[41]

Lettice Ramsey was much more than a photographer. *The Times* later called hers 'a lifetime spent in Cambridge at the centre of the intellectual and artistic life', connecting over the years with literary figures such as Virginia Woolf and C. P. Snow. Her husband, the mathematician and philosopher Frank Ramsey, died at the age of twenty-six. She became what MI5 called an 'intimate friend' of leading Cambridge communist Maurice Dobb and soon Vernon Kell of MI5 was writing to the Cambridgeshire police asking for her to be furtively watched. A humble Detective Sergeant pointed out this would be difficult because she lived 'in a good class district with premises on one side of the street only'.

Mrs Ramsey's late husband had been a leading member of one of Cambridge's most secretive and exclusive societies, which probably explains how Ramsey and Muspratt came to take one of their most famous sets of photographs.

Entitled 'The Apostles Society 1932', the series of images shows six young men sitting and laying in various poses against a blank wall and curtain, looking rather self-conscious. They were the latest generation of students admitted to what had been founded in 1820 as the Cambridge Conversazione Society. It earned the nickname of 'The Apostles' probably because there were twelve founding members. This became the official name, although those in the know normally referred to it simply as 'The Society'. Each Saturday night one Apostle member would read an essay to open a discussion. When they graduated members could, in the jargon of the Apostles, 'take wings' to become an 'Angel'. Having reached this status, they could attend whenever they wished and were especially welcome to the Annual Dinner.[42]

In these Ramsey and Muspratt photographs, the young man who looked most unsure of where to drape his long limbs was Anthony Blunt, who, as the Trinity register recorded, had arrived at Cambridge six years earlier than Burgess:

Anthony Frederick Blunt

Father: Rev Arthur Stanley Vaughan Blunt

Present Residence: 4, Cambridge Square, London W.2

Born: September 26 1907

Place of Birth: Bournemouth

School or Place of Education: Marlborough College

One of Blunt's father's earlier postings had been as the chaplain at the British embassy in Paris and it was here that Anthony Blunt had developed a passion for French art. He won a scholarship to study mathematics at Trinity but later switched to modern languages, in which he got a First. Combining his interest in art with his fluency in French, he was elected to a fellowship in French art history and theory.[43]

Blunt certainly knew what he did and didn't like. A friend at Marlborough College, the poet Louis MacNeice, wrote that 'Anthony had a flair for bigotry; every day he blackballed another musician; he despised Tennyson, Shakespeare, the Italian High Renaissance and Praxiteles, was all in favour of the Primitives, of Ucello [*sic*], of the Byzantine mosaics'.[44] With such strong views, Blunt made an immediate impact in Saturday-night discussions among the 'Apostles' and, according to a history of the group, 'Blunt was an increasingly powerful influence within the Society from his joining until almost a quarter of a century afterwards.'[45]

Blunt was already a four-year Apostle to be reckoned with when he first met Burgess in 1931. He later recalled:

> On that occasion I did not take to him, because he began immediately to talk very indiscreetly about the private lives of people who were quite unknown to me; but as I got to know him better I became fascinated by the liveliness and quality of his mind and the range of his interests.
>
> There was no subject in which he did not have something stimulating to say and although his ideas were not always supported with full evidence or carefully thought out reasons there was always something in them to provoke thought and set one's own mind working along new lines.[46]

Blunt said Burgess could be perverse in argument and behaviour but would then apologise in such an engaging manner that it was difficult to be angry for long.

There was no doubt about the mutual intellectual attraction between the two men. Scholars are less agreed on whether this developed into a sexual relationship. Blunt's biographer Miranda Carter concluded that 'though they probably did have a brief sexual affair, neither of them cited it as the crucial fact of their relationship'. When Micky Burn typed up his notes on his time as a lover of Burgess, he recalled:

> He introduced me to Antony [sic] Blunt about whom I recall little except his appearance and that he was even then a great authority on Poussin. According to Guy, he said afterwards, 'Who was that beautiful young man?' Naturally I remember that. It never occurred to me that they were bed-mates nor that Antony was in love with Guy. 'Poor Antony' Guy said of him, 'he has no bottom' in the physical sense not the 18th Century sense of Character of course. But they were very close.[47]

It appears that Blunt enjoyed Burgess's company without necessarily believing everything he said. One of Blunt's old school friends, Ellis Waterhouse, said of Burgess, 'He used to tell us about his adventures with politicians and young boys ... and Blunt and I used to decide they were probably untrue. He was the biggest liar in the western hemisphere you know. But they were very funny.'[48]

Whatever their relationship, it was Blunt who brought Burgess into the Apostles, where he soon became a regular leader of discussions. What this offered a ferocious networker like Burgess was the opportunity to meet not just the bright young men of his own generation but also the most highly respected among previous generations of students, homosexual and hetero-sexual, Marxist and non-Marxist, in the form of the 'Angels'.

One of Burgess's own generation of Apostles was Victor, later the third Baron Rothschild. At Harrow School, Victor Rothschild was best known for cricket, scoring freely off the bowling of Harold Larwood, but at Trinity he made his name as a scientist and was elected to a fellowship for work on the fertilisation of frogs' eggs. During a long friendship with Burgess, Rothschild was to witness first-hand the very best and worst in his behaviour.

Others among his Apostle contacts were three men of note in the Burgess story who had been duly recorded in the Trinity register as arriving on 1 October 1934. One was:

John Cairncross
Father: Alexander Kirkland Cairncross, Merchant
Born: 25 July 1913
Place of Birth: Lesmahagow, Lanarkshire
School or Place of Education: Sorbonne Paris

John Cairncross took the unusual step of adding his father's occupation, 'Merchant', perhaps to make a point about his slightly humbler origins, but he omitted the fact that he'd gone from a village school in Hamilton Academy to Glasgow University before moving to Paris.

When Cairncross first met Burgess he was 'somewhat flattered by his attention', but not because of any sexual magnetism – Cairncross was enthusiastically heterosexual. What impressed Cairncross about Burgess was that he 'moved in exalted circles, was well-informed, and expressed himself with wit and ease on a wide range of issues'. However, several students warned him about Burgess, the most significant being James Klugman who, like John Cornford, was not an Apostle.[49]

The second new student in 1934 was:

Leonard Henry Long
Father: Henry Charles Long
Present Residence: 32 Bedford Terrace N7
Born: 2 December 1916
Place of Birth: Islington
School or Place of Education: Holloway County School

Leo Long's education at a state school marked him out as different from other Trinity students. He studied French and German and graduated with a series of Firsts.

The third student was from a very different background:

> Michael Whitney Straight
> Father: Willard Straight
> Present Residence: Dartington Hall, Totnes, Devon
> Born: 25 July 1913
> Place of Birth: Southampton USA
> School or Place of Education: Dartington Hall, Totnes

Straight was from a very wealthy American family. His father, who was an investment banker, died after catching influenza while serving with the US Army in France in World War One. His widowed mother met an Englishman, Leonard Knight Elmhirst, while he was studying at Cornell University, married him and came to Britain to help him create Dartington Hall in Devon. So the Hall was both the place of education and the home of Michael Whitney Straight. He was, therefore, not the average Yank at Oxbridge; indeed, his American accent was quite soft.

Among the older Apostles who'd taken their wings and become Angels – so could choose when to attend – were men whom it was extremely handy just to know and, as it turned out, were indeed to prove useful to Burgess at particular moments.

One Apostle who would help Burgess get a job after Cambridge was George Macaulay Trevelyan, who had been appointed the Regius Professor of Modern History at Cambridge by the Prime Minister Stanley Baldwin who, like Trevelyan, was a Harrow and Trinity man. G. M. Trevelyan was also chairman of the History Faculty Board during Burgess's undergraduate years.

Edward 'Eddie' Marsh had joined the Apostles back in 1894: a Trinity student whose career developed a network of contacts across the worlds of the arts, academia and politics leading to his appointment as Winston Churchill's Private Secretary in 1908. He followed Churchill from one high office to another for a quarter of a century, but retired before Churchill reached the highest office in the land. Churchill once called him 'a friend I shall cherish and hold on to all my life'.[50]

The fact that Marsh remained unmarried all his life was explained by the *Dictionary of National Biography* at one point as the result of bad cases of mumps and measles. In truth, he was more attracted to men than to women, and after one Apostles dinner at which a lot of wine was consumed some members, including Burgess and Blunt, went back to Marsh's home where a drunken orgy is said to have ensued.[51]

Of those Apostles with heterosexual appetites, notable in the Burgess story would be Dennis Proctor, a civil servant in the Treasury. An attachment to Stanley Baldwin's office came to an end when it was feared Mrs Baldwin would be upset by his imminent appearance in a divorce case involving the woman who would become his wife. But Proctor's long-term civil service career was unaffected.

These were all increasingly impressive names to mention in good company: an internationally respected historian, and two men in powerful back-room positions. However, there was one other Apostle whose name Burgess was perhaps happiest to drop into conversations for years to come. Michael Straight wrote that, at this time, Cambridge was 'dominated by the over-powering intellect of John Maynard Keynes'.[52] The economist was a King's man who was elected to the Apostles in 1903. One of his biographers, Roy Harrod, wrote that membership during Keynes's undergraduate days had a profound influence on his whole life: 'Truth was the paramount objective and absolute intellectual integrity the means of achieving it.'[53]

One truth about Keynes, that he was a predominantly homosexual bisexual, was notably absent from Harrod's biography. Other historians record that Keynes and Lytton Strachey (the biographer and literary reviewer) created a 'Higher Sodomy' partnership that dominated the Apostles for a time. The quotation about 'womanisers' becoming 'sods' is sometimes attributed to Keynes and sometimes to a lover of his, the artist Duncan Grant. Burgess was Keynes's guest at a King's Feast and present at a party Keynes held for Grant. There is, however, no suggestion of any sexual relationship between Burgess and Keynes.

Another man whom Burgess met while living in Cambridge, and who was to play an important part in his life, was George Barnes. Just like Burgess, he was a child of the empire. His father was Sir Hugh Barnes of the India Civil service and he was sent for education at the Royal Naval College at Dartmouth but was rejected for the navy because of his eyesight. George Barnes (unlike Burgess) never quite got over it; his *Times* obituary later recording that 'this fact remained a regret to him all his life'. He remained a keen sailor of small boats, was nicknamed 'The Commander' and such was his continuing interest in naval matters that, after graduating in history from King's, Cambridge, he returned to Dartmouth from 1927 as a history teacher. He arrived just as Burgess was leaving.

In 1927, Barnes married into the Cambridge academic aristocracy by taking the hand of Anne Bond, the daughter of Dr Henry Bond, Master of Trinity Hall, the college just down Trinity Lane from its younger, but larger and richer neighbour. Dr Bond was also a former member of the 'syndicate', effectively the academic publishing committee of the school books arm of the Cambridge University Press (CUP), the world's oldest publishing house. This gave him a voice and a vote on which of the books offered by his academic colleagues should be published. It also gave him influence in the appointment of staff. In the summer of 1930, on being informed by CUP that he had been appointed an assistant secretary there, George Barnes replied from Dartmouth that he 'had already heard [the news] from Dr Bond'.[54]

Barnes's job was to help look after both the creative and business sides of the publishing house, especially the liaison with CUP's operation in America, which was struggling after the Wall Street Crash. Barnes's marriage was not going so well either. His wife had discovered his relationship with a Miss Fisher. She turned for comfort to another man and wrote letters referring to her husband's 'fishering' with 'Miss F'.[55]

The recipient of over 120 letters from 1932 to 1975 from Mrs Barnes was none other than George 'Dadie' Rylands, one of Cambridge University's 'bachelor dons' who produced the play for which Guy Burgess designed the scenery. For a period in the 1930s, Mrs Barnes and Mr Burgess wrote similarly passionate letters to their mutual friend Dadie. He replied to Mrs

Barnes with equally frequent but rather more controlled letters, later making arrangements to meet at hotels such as the Savoy in London. Whether this fascinating relationship was ever consummated, we may never know.

Anne Barnes told Dadie of her husband's acquaintance, 'I don't get much fonder of the dear girl', Miss Fisher, and thereafter was getting 'young men to take me out to various meals'.[56]

One of them was her rival for Dadie's affections, Guy Burgess, and she reported 'the usual alarming drive with Guy constantly getting excited about old houses and young men and taking his hands off the wheel to admire them. He told me the latest Cambridge gossip – Humphrey Bourne and my old pal Phillips have come together – too squalid.'[57]

She gave Rylands a character sketch of Burgess's mother, Mrs Bassett, who 'longs to know actresses', and had said to Guy, 'I must have glitter.'[58]

On Sunday 10 July 1933, Anne Barnes wrote to 'My darling' Dadie in even more excited terms than normal:

> Something has just happened. Guy and I get back to Millington Rd about 5.30. The house was empty and we were making tea when I noticed a female handbag in the drawing room and various other traces of female occupation culminating in the discovery of Miss F's effects in the spare room. I warned Guy who got into a mixture of fever and giggles and then suddenly G and Miss F appeared, she full of hectic apologies and elaborate explanation as to why she was in my house. It really was funny, at least Guy thought so, but of course poor George was all stiff and embarrassed and awkward and very unfriendly to Guy. Why won't he be natural and amused at things like that?[59]

George Barnes would understandably have been embarrassed caught 'fishering' in his own home. At the time he and Burgess had no working relationship, Barnes was a junior executive in a publishing company and the eyewitness to his infidelity was just an undergraduate. That relationship was to change later, however, and with Burgess's gift for filing away evidence of people's weak points, this moment would not have been forgotten.

Anne Barnes signed off that letter to Rylands, 'Darling I want to say [all] sorts of silly things. You were so lovely, You always are my love. Always. Anne.' Soon they were on holiday together in the south of France, but she and Dadie were not alone. Guy was there too and so was Arthur 'Arty' Marshall from the Cambridge drama set, Victor Rothschild and Rylands's cousin Marnie Stanley.

Burgess's own memories of that holiday were not to be good ones. He wrote to Rylands a year later: 'The effects of Anne's feelings for you and the complications that arose from the relationship made others feel very miserable and very uncomfortable.' This was just one of the things that 'spoilt last summer for me'. It prompted Burgess to write four pages of handwritten, rambling, sometimes unintelligible, backbiting and bitching about his circle of friends. What had started as confusion about who was going on holiday with whom had escalated in Burgess's mind.

'Dear Dadie,

I was so appalled by the crisis that has arisen that it seemed to me quite essential to write you an explanation.'

Burgess hoped his forthcoming 1934 holiday would be just himself, Dadie and Arthur Marshall, but had then discovered it looked like being a repeat of the 1933 holiday because not only would Anne be joining the holiday again but so would Marnie, somebody he liked but wouldn't want to go on holiday with. He'd not been that pleased with 'Victor's behaviour' either. So he backed out of a repeat trip. Burgess then turned on Rylands, complaining that he hadn't answered a previous letter on the issue and had refused to see Burgess at Cambridge to discuss this 'crisis': 'I had thought you would know how fond I was of you and would realise how anxious I would be.' Burgess concluded:

> I know that I can behave in a way that appears inconsiderate to my friends. I know that I behaved very badly to you ... but I thought you knew and thought that affection was what mattered ... and that I do try to live up to my affection for people.

Being friends with Guy Burgess was obviously a complicated business, requiring constant 'crisis' management.

Amidst all the new friendships and acquaintances, the attractions and distractions of his undergraduate years, Guy Burgess managed to get a First in Part I of the Tripos and seemed to be in with a good chance of achieving the same high mark in Part II in his third and final year as an undergraduate. And that, according to the Burgess version of history set out in Driberg's book, is duly what happened. Driberg claims that Burgess 'was given another first in Part II of the Tripos, even though illness prevented him from completing his paper'.[60] However, the conventional view is that Burgess was given an 'aegrotat', officially defined as a degree 'awarded when a sub-standard performance, or failure to complete all papers, is officially sanctioned on the grounds of the student's ill-health'. The Cambridge University archivist supports this version of events. Burgess's degree was indeed an aegrotat, which in Latin means 'he or she is ill'. There is no sign in the files that when he graduated as a Bachelor of Arts (BA) on 20 June 1933 he was awarded a First in Part II.

Burgess, however, would not let this stand in the way of his career. In a later official form he proudly listed his accomplishments as including 'First Class Honours degree'. The exaggeration by Burgess may make the reader a little sceptical of the subsequent claim in Driberg's book that what prevented Burgess from completing his papers was insomnia, sometimes aggravated by severe headaches. Driberg explained that this was why Burgess took sedatives and that this might be the origin of newspaper allegations that Burgess was a drug addict.

One friend blamed a 'severe nervous breakdown' as 'the bright confident morning of his undergraduate days had begun to fade'.[61] Another put it thus: 'Guy thought all you had to do was work fourteen hours before the exam and have a lot of strong coffee, he cracked up on it.'[62]

Despite this setback and the disappointment, come the start of the next academic year (1933/34), Burgess was back at Trinity, but this time as a postgraduate. His pre-exam reputation as a gifted student seems to have been enough to get him fast-tracked into a chance to do research and teach undergraduates. The records show that he was now in M2 – the second room on M staircase – although more recent generations of students in room M1, including the broadcaster and author Edward Stourton, were told that they had inherited Burgess's former residence. Whichever room, Burgess commanded a wonderful front view overlooking Great Court.

The Annual Trinity Record for 1933–34 shows Burgess receiving a research scholarship although, slightly oddly, in the list of 'Cambridge University residents' for the year he was not shown under Research Scholars but under a category headed just 'B. A.'. When we asked a Cambridge archivist what this category of resident meant, we were told that 'BAs hung around Cambridge after graduating'. To say that Burgess 'hung around' would be a touch unfair, but having failed to get a first-class degree, what happened next was not the brilliant academic career everyone, including Burgess, had forecast for him. He did do some research but, more importantly, still being at Cambridge University, and at Trinity in particular, meant he could continue on to the next stage of his political journey. Increasingly over these Cambridge years, this intellectual Marxist historian was also becoming an activist on the streets of Cambridge. He would go on marches wearing a yellow Pitt Club scarf singing, 'One, two, three, four, who are we for? We are for the Working Class.'[63]

According to one of the student communists in the Socialist Society, in 1933 they set themselves two main aims. One was to form 'a big revolutionary socialist organisation', and the other to 'build a mass anti-fascist movement among students'.[64]

Part of this was the anti-war movement, a communist vehicle to try to bring together those who could agree that, whatever else they disagreed on, they were all anti-fascist. It was another tactic in the strategy to turn socialists into communists. According to Burgess, he joined the anti-war movement, and it was his membership of this which led directly to his own decision to join the Communist Party. It would be futile to campaign against war without also campaigning against the causes of war. He apparently said this to James Klugman, who told him, 'If you think like that, your place is in the party.'[65]

A Trinity history don, Steven Runciman, said of Burgess, 'Communism sat very strangely on him. But one didn't take it very seriously.' Not taking Burgess seriously was a mistake many others were to make.[66] The date on which Burgess actually joined the Communist Party is not clear; some experts have it as early as 1931 or 1932, others as late as 1934. As to who exactly recruited him, following up on the influence of Guest, Lees, Klugman and Cornford, some believe it was a job for one of the dons involved in recruiting, Maurice Dobb.

Burgess took part in one landmark anti-war movement demonstration on 11 November 1933, Armistice Day. There seems to have been a very full turn-out of Cornford and Klugman's group, emphasising their pacifist credentials to further the communist cause. They are said to have laid a wreath for the victims of the Great War at Cambridge War Memorial inscribed: 'In memory of the victims of the imperialist war which was not of their making'. Things got decidedly less peaceful in an encounter with some students from the rowing and rugby communities, which was won (somewhat ironically) by the pacifists, thanks to Burgess's decision to strap mattresses onto the beaten-up old Morris car of his friend Julian Bell and drive it at the other side. One account has it that Bell's Morris was also used as a battering ram to break through a barricade outside a college.[67] Among the other demonstrators who took part in the skirmish was a friend of Burgess's: a Canadian student of Medieval History at Trinity called Herbert Norman, who had been recruited by Cornford to the Socialist Society.[68]

Early the next year, in February 1934, Burgess joined members of the Socialist Society who set off from Cambridge to link up with the Fifth National Hunger March as it made its way from north-east England to London. By now there were about 200 members of the society and it has been estimated that about a quarter also belonged to Communist Party cells.

The students met the marchers at Huntingdon, handed over £120 they had collected for food and clothing and then joined the march into Cambridge, where female undergraduates at Girton had prepared refreshments.[69] Burgess then went to London by train to march with them again to Hyde Park. A fellow Apostle spotted him wearing a zipped up cardigan, which could be unzipped to reveal that he was wearing an Old Etonian tie. Burgess thought this would be useful if he was arrested by the police.[70]

There are also accounts of Burgess, as an activist, within his own college. One involves him booing the guest of honour at a 'Founder's Feast'; the Chancellor of the Exchequer Neville Chamberlain, who had apparently had told his audience after a very full dinner that there was no real hardship or hunger among the two million unemployed. The other depicts Burgess as a part-time equivalent of one of the Communist Party's industrial organisers, encouraging the waiters at Trinity to go on strike because they were only engaged to work during term time and received no pay during student vacations. The college authorities apparently gave way. Burgess is also said to have joined a protest by Cambridge council-house tenants against high rents, and to have helped organise a strike by busmen in Cambridge.[71]

If Burgess saw any contradiction between those encounters with the working class and the very upper-class lifestyle he lived, it doesn't seem to have stopped him enjoying the fruits of Trinity. A college magazine produced by the students in May 1934 had an account of what it called a 'brilliant party', one which 'stands out head and shoulders in our memory above the rest'. Nearly all the rich and fashionable 'Beau Monde' were there, including several Etonians. Viscount Duncannon, who had hosted the cocktail party where Guy Burgess picked up Micky Burn, was there 'looking oh! so nicely in the pink'. The magazine recorded, 'Mr Guy Burgess, not looking so fit – we all have our off-days – slipped in later, chaperoning his two young nephews who soon got into conversation with Mr John Clutton-Brock, who saw them home.' We cannot find anybody in Burgess's family tree who would have been 'his two young nephews' in 1934. Perhaps they were from an extended part of the family, or maybe there was some misunderstanding.

In a 'Who's Who' list created by Trinity students that year, the entry for Burgess is '*Honi Soit Qui Mal y Pense*' often translated as 'Evil be to him that evil thinks'.

Although the Apostles had, or affected to have, a contempt for that other university, spelling Oxford as 'oxford' with a small 'o', Burgess spent the beginning of the summer term of 1934 there making more contacts through a student he'd met called Goronwy Rees. Their relationship was building into the closest friendship Burgess had with a non-homosexual man. Almost inevitably, Burgess made a pass at Rees but discovered that he 'was as heterosexual as [Burgess] was the opposite', according to Rees. Their sexuality was not their only difference between them. Burgess was very English; he always referred to 'England', rarely Britain or any other term that acknowledged the existence of another part of the UK. Rees was very Welsh, born in Aberystwyth in a Welsh-speaking home with a Methodist minister father. He would later poke fun at his birthplace, calling his countrymen 'the intellectual leaders of their nation', creating 'a kind of smugness'. There were so many chapels – 'a Salem, a Shiloh, a Tabernacle, a Bethel and a Moriah' – that it was 'almost like walking through the Middle East'. Rees went to Cardiff High School for Boys, 'where he was able to write in English for the first time', and won a scholarship to New College, Oxford, 'where he began to lose his Welsh accent'. On All Souls' Day 1931, while Rees was still twenty-one years old, a servant from the college of the same name formally told him of his election as a Fellow, often seen as a starting point for academic stardom.[72]

Burgess would travel to Oxford to visit Rees and other friends. An Oxford student from that period later recalled that 'it was impossible to be in the so-called intellectual swim of those days without coming across Guy Burgess'.[73] Burgess stayed with Maurice Bowra of Wadham College whom he'd met through Dadie Rylands and who was to perform a similar role for Burgess at Oxford as Rylands performed for Burgess at Cambridge as an admirer of young men, well-travelled, well-read and most importantly well-connected. Bowra hosted a dinner with A. J. 'Freddie' Ayer (one of Burgess's Old Etonian contemporaries), his wife and another rising philosophical star, Isaiah Berlin, which climaxed in a dispute about a philosophical text. After dinner Goronwy Rees and Guy Burgess walked back to All Souls College and went into the common room. According to another Fellow of the college, A. L. Rowse, only half an hour later 'the junior Fellow came up to complain to me – I was senior that night – that Burgess had made a pass at him. What was I supposed to do about that? I said merely: Well, you can keep out of his way.'[74]

Burgess and Rees drank whisky and talked about the Marxist interpretation of history and the Cambridge busmen's strike.[75] Rees was left in no doubt by this first encounter that Burgess was a homosexual and a communist and would always remain so.

The two men made plans to visit Russia together that summer but Rees was unable to make the trip. Instead, Burgess went with a different Oxford student, Derek Blaikie, who, like him, was also communist, homosexual, and had suffered some kind of breakdown at the time of his final exams, in his case at Balliol College. Born Derek Edward Walter Kahn, he had changed his surname to Blaikie at the end of 1933.[76] Kahn, spelt that way, is traditionally, although not exclusively, a Jewish name. On the evening of 27 June 1934, Burgess and Blaikie boarded the Russian ship *Jan Rudzutak* at Cotton's Wharf in London's Docklands bound for Leningrad. As always with travellers on this route, the Special Branch took everybody's details and sent them to MI5. For the first time, Burgess had a file in the Security Service's records; until then, they appear to have known nothing about him from his Cambridge years that was worth typing out and inserting in the file. Burgess's return from Leningrad was logged too.[77]

The value of Burgess's old Eton contacts was demonstrated on the trip to Russia by the role of David Astor, who helped to arrange introductions ahead of the visit through his mother, Nancy Lady Astor, who had been to Russia with George Bernard Shaw. On her trip she had met Stalin who had told her that Winston Churchill would be recalled from what were then his wilderness years to face Hitler in a war.

Burgess and Blaikie had their own anecdote to underline that fear of impending war. One night of their journey, their ship having made a stopover in Hamburg, they heard the distant sound of shooting. What became known later as the Night of the Long Knives was under way as Hitler purged his Nazi rivals and other enemies. Hitler then announced himself to the Reichstag as 'the supreme judge of the German people'.[78] Such events only confirmed the view back home in the cloisters of Trinity that social democracy as practised by the British Labour Party and its Continental equivalents did not offer a forceful enough response to fascism, leaving Soviet communism as the only real alternative.

On his return, Burgess spoke to his Cambridge comrades and told them Moscow had been transformed from a Balkan town with pigs in the trams to 'one of the cleanest and best-run capitals I've ever lived in'. From the earlier accounts of an intellectually confident undergraduate student, it might appear that speaking at meetings would have presented only a modest challenge to a postgraduate Burgess. But another cell member from Trinity, Victor Kiernan, in a mostly sympathetic recollection of Burgess – 'I honour his memory' – later told a very different story of the man who had helped Klugman and Cornford induct him into the party. He emphasised the tensions Burgess suffered from:

> He smoked cigarettes all day, and had somehow imbibed a notion that the body expels nicotine very easily ... I came on Burgess one day in his room sitting at a small table, a glass of spirits in front of him, glumly trying to put together a talk for a cell meeting that evening; he confessed that when he had to give any sort of formal talk he felt foolish.[79]

This is corroborated by Miriam Rothschild, sister of Victor Rothschild, who wrote of Burgess in this period:

> One of his outstanding weaknesses was his total lack of debating ability. In those days I used to argue with him, taking a conventional Socialist line, while he wanted a bloody revolution and was a self-styled Marxist. On one occasion I reduced him to floods of tears and thereafter felt he was scarcely fair game and I hadn't the heart to bait him in general discussions.[80]

This may explain the relatively low profile of Burgess – just two passing mentions – in the best internal chronicle of the debating hub of Cambridge University militancy: the Minute Book of what, in 1928, was the University Labour Club, but by 1934 had become the Socialist Society (CUSS). The title change was the result of the endless feuding between democratic socialists and revolutionaries, with the latter, led by Cornford, firmly in control. 'Members created a precedent in Cambridge by singing the Internationale and other songs vociferously.'[81]

A definitive end date by which time Burgess had progressed from cell member to Communist Party member was provided by Anthony Blunt, who returned from a trip abroad in October 1934 to find 'all my friends ... had suddenly become Marxists under the impact of Hitler coming to power and there was this very powerful group, very remarkable group in Cambridge of which Guy Burgess was one ... he had become a totally convinced Marxist and an open member of the Communist Party'.[82]

In Blunt's mind – if not necessarily in everybody else's – Burgess was now of a status to compare him with James Klugman, 'the pure intellectual of the party', and John Cornford, 'a vehement orator', as the third of the 'individuals who dominated the movement' at Cambridge. Burgess had 'a far wider range of interest and knowledge than Klugman or Cornford'. He was 'a terrific intellectual stimulus' according to Blunt.[83]

Meanwhile, Burgess's academic career was progressing in fits and starts. In order to convert his research and teaching into a full fellowship, he needed to write a thesis. He chose as his subject the English Revolution of the seventeenth century, which is often called the Puritan Revolution although Burgess preferred 'the Bourgeois Revolution'. However, several months into the project work, he discovered that a book by Professor Basil Willey had been published that said pretty much everything he wanted to say. Burgess reviewed this 'brilliant' book in *The Spectator*: 'English historians have not as a rule been attracted to the writing of histories of English Thought, but for no period has this neglect been so marked as for the seventeenth century. And yet for no period can such a neglect be so little justified.'[84]

Burgess confided in friends that Willey's book was better than anything he could have attempted. Burgess abandoned this thesis and began another, this time on the Indian Mutiny of 1857. He soon halted that too, and with that decision came the end of his chance of becoming a Fellow at a college. He disappeared from the Cambridge records at Easter 1935. A year and a half's research and teaching had amounted to nothing much more academically than a book review in *The Spectator*. Either communism had overtaken academia in Burgess's priorities, or it had helped fill the void created by academic disappointment. Either way, his new priority was now the Soviet cause.

What was to become the final stage in Burgess's transition from apolitical student to KGB agent had begun when an Austrian called Arnold Deutsch arrived in Britain to take up a job in the Psychology Department of the

University of London. In the terminology of international espionage, a 'legal' is a diplomat, part of whose work inevitably involves reporting back to his or her homeland what they discover. An 'illegal' is somebody working as an intelligence agent in secret and without any kind of claim to be an accredited diplomat. Deutsch was one of the greatest of what became known as 'The Great Illegals'; an intellectual, multilingual, charmingly mannered man who, according to the KGB scoreboard, was eventually credited with 'the recruitment of twenty agents and contact with a total of twenty-nine' during his time in Britain.[85]

Deutsch lived in a block of flats in Hampstead known as the Lawn Road flats, where, by coincidence or design, other Soviet 'illegals' were also living in the 1930s. But there were residents who weren't spies, among them the novelist Agatha Christie. Deutsch's task in London was to execute a relatively new KGB strategy of cultivating high-achieving students at British universities on their way to jobs in the highest echelons of British public life. His forecast of the likely impact of this strategy turned out to be accurate. Deutsch believed such was the large number of communist students, and such was the turnover of the universities, that those he plucked out for KGB recruitment would pass unnoticed. And if at some point it was remembered that they had once been communists, 'this would be put down to a passing fancy of youth'. The communist students he selected would need to be turned into non-communist British government insiders for appearance or, as Deutsch put it, 'It is up to us to give the recruit a new political personality.'[86]

According to the KGB defector to Britain, Oleg Gordievsky, when Deutsch arrived he already had orders to make contact with certain students.[87] These names had, it seems, been put forward by another 'illegal' in Britain, a journalist working under the alias Ernst Henri. The 'Henri Principle', which he openly explained in an article in the *New Statesman* in 1933, was that espionage was best done in cells of five, with members working independently of other cells. If one cell was discovered, others should survive.

The man who was to turn out to be an important member in a cell of five was recorded in the Trinity Admissions Register as arriving at Cambridge on 1 October 1929, the year before Burgess:

Harold Adrian Russell Philby

Father: Harry St John Bridger Philby

Present Residence: 18 Ascot Road, London NW6

Born: 1st January 1912

Place of Birth: Ambala, Punjab, India

School or Place of Education: Westminster School

These personal details of Harold, more commonly known as 'Kim', Philby stand out on the page because he wrote in bright-blue, not the normal black ink, but his time at Trinity was of a decidedly lower profile than some of his contemporaries. He had a less illustrious academic reputation than Burgess, although Philby did at least finish his exams; he was a member of the Socialist Society, but not a leader like Cornford or Klugman. It was what Philby did when he left Cambridge that mattered most.

> On my very last day at Cambridge I decided that I would become a communist. I asked a don I admired, Maurice Dobb, how I should go about it. He gave me an introduction to a communist group in Paris, a perfectly legal and open group. They in turn passed me on to a communist underground organisation in Vienna. Matters were at crisis point in Austria and this underground organisation needed volunteers. I helped smuggle wanted socialists and communists out of the country.[88]

In March 1934, from Vienna, Philby wrote to the Cambridge University Socialist Society appealing for help for persecuted Austrian workers. Burgess and a colleague were asked to organise a fund. This may not have been very successful because, soon after, 'the Secretary read a further letter from H. A. R. Philby appealing for support'. Burgess and colleagues were to be 'instructed to work through col reps [college representatives]'.[89]

While in Vienna, Philby met an Austrian communist called Alice (Litzi) Friedman. They married and returned to England. By this time the two of them probably knew he was going to become a Soviet agent. Philby had apparently been introduced to Burgess by a Trinity economics Fellow and Apostle, Dennis Robertson.

Arnold Deutsch began carrying out his orders to recruit young British high-flyers – and successfully. In June 1934, Philby was recruited on a bench in London's Regent's Park. Burgess insisted he be recruited too. According to KGB files, Burgess told Deutsch that he was 'honoured and ready to sacrifice everything for the cause'. Deutsch gave him the code name MAD-CHEN ('Girl'; in KGB and MI5 files, names and codenames were normally spelt out in capital letters). Burgess's lifestyle must have made him appear an unlikely recruit. But Deutsch, a follower of Wilhelm Reich – the Austrian psychoanalyst whose doctrine of sexual permissiveness was becoming increasingly controversial – was also unconventional when it came to the sexual mores of the time. Burgess's rejection of bourgeois morality would have struck a chord.

To be clear about the exact date when Burgess completed the move from being a card-carrying communist to a signed-up member of the Soviet intelligence organisation, more commonly referred to as the KGB, means navigating through the kind of bureaucratic muddle which any large organisation can get into. The best guide through these particular files is a former Soviet intelligence officer, Boris Volodarsky, who said that January 1935 was when Burgess agreed with Deutsch to work for the KGB. But when Deutsch's fellow KGB agent handler, Alexander Orlov, began mentioning this new agent MAD-CHEN in reports back to Moscow in July of that year, he was challenged. Who, Moscow wondered, was this 'MADCHEN' man? Orlov, wondering if there had been some misunderstanding or whether all his reports back had been getting through, replied, 'You seem puzzled about MADCHEN ... and order [us] to break with him until you get explanations.'[90] He helpfully re-capped the story so far and explained how he and Deutsch had been tipped off about Burgess as 'a very gifted and adventurous chap for whom all doors were open' and whose 'friendship with the [Prime] Minister's secretary [Dennis Proctor] was also noted'. The KGB had noticed that Burgess was to travel to Moscow in the summer of 1934 and had thought of approaching him there but were late doing that and decided to wait until he was back in Britain (a country they had codenamed as ISLAND). KGB HQ was reassured by Orlov's recap and formally authorised the recruitment of Burgess.

Agent MADCHEN was therefore in place by the summer of 1935. These dates fit, as Burgess was giving up at Cambridge at about the same time. The KGB would soon see the weaknesses of Burgess. An early assessment of his work reports considered that he had no 'internal brakes', being 'quick to panic and prone to despair'. They also noted: 'He craves to be liked and only reluctantly acknowledges his weaknesses.' Additionally, he lied to cover up his mistakes. However, on the other hand, they were quick to realise his enthusiasm, initiative and imagination.

This file also demonstrates how Orlov was already thinking ahead about how he and Deutsch could make good use of Burgess's contacts. There were two targets in mind: Tom Wyllie, a Trinity man who had become Resident Clerk, effectively a senior duty officer, at the War Office; and Dennis Proctor, the Apostle then on his attachment to the office of Stanley Baldwin, the Lord President of the Council, and effectively acting Prime Minister during the ill-health of Ramsay MacDonald. For Wyllie, they planned to put Burgess's sexuality to good use. Orlov wrote that Burgess is 'also a cultured pederast and an adroit chap who would – according to the mysterious laws of sexual attraction in this country – conquer Wyllie's heart'.[91] The other target, Proctor, was known by Burgess to be left-wing, but Moscow thought recruiting inside so senior an office as Downing Street was rather over-optimistic.

Burgess was quick to demonstrate his value. He wrote a report on recruitment prospects and made his first approach to Anthony Blunt. Years later, Blunt recounted:

> It seemed to me and many of my contemporaries that the Communist Party and Russia constituted the only firm bulwark against Fascism since the Western democracies were taking an uncertain and compromising attitude towards Germany. I was persuaded by Guy Burgess that I could best serve the cause of anti-Fascism by joining him in his work for the Russians.

He'd been chosen, not because art historians had any inside track to state secrets, but because he was well-placed to spot future talent. Arnold Deutsch confirmed the analysis of Blunt (codename TONY) by Burgess (codename MADCHEN):

> TONY is a typical English intellectual. Speaks very highly-flown English. Looks very feminine. A pederast ... Is considerably steadier and more rational than MADCHEN. He is a simple person and without big pretensions. Can control himself, is cold and a little mannered. Is to a lesser degree connected to the Communist Party than MADCHEN. He would hardly give up his career for the sake of our work. He understands well the task he has to do for us and is ready to help us. He has a large influence on students.[92]

He was soon proved right. Blunt began contacting three of the Trinity Apostles: Michael Straight, John Cairncross and Leo Long. They all agreed to work with Burgess. Now the KGB had a proper ring, and Burgess was the linkman.

Some of the tip-offs to the KGB about Burgess's own usefulness came from Philby, and some from another Cambridge recruit, a student at the nearby college, Trinity Hall. The Admissions Register at Trinity Hall for 1 October 1931 records in its slightly different format:

'Maclean, Donald Duart: b. May 25th 1913: s/o Sir Donald Maclean, 6 Smethwick Place, London, W2: ed. at Gresham's School, Holt B. A. June 1934.'

Donald Maclean knew James Klugman from Gresham's School and he knew Burgess from the Socialist Society. They had all been on demonstrations together, such as the Hunger March and the so-called 'Armistice Day riot' when the student anti-war council were confronted by 'hearties' from the rowing and rugby clubs. Maclean even published a poem about the event. The concluding section begins with a mention of an arms manufacturer:

> Not for the sake of Armstrong Vickers
> Not for the sake of khaki knickers
> But for the sake of the class which bled

But for the sake of daily bread
Rugger toughs and boat club guys
Panic-herd with frightened eyes
Sodden straws on a rising tide
They know they've chosen the losing side.
D. M.[93]

At the time, most readers would have understood the reference to Armstrong Vickers because a number of its employees, who had been working on a contract in the USSR, were on trial for their lives in Moscow, accused of espionage.[94] Donald Maclean was different from Burgess in a number of ways. Whereas the latter rarely wrote political articles, 'Donald Maclenin', as he was dubbed, was prolific. His poem was just one of a number of political articles he wrote in the Trinity Hall magazine, named *Silver Crescent* after the college crest. He called on fellow students 'to identify with the working class', because together 'it is they who will be gassed, it is they who will be shot down'. His articles appeared to get more outspoken in the year after his father, Sir Donald, a leading Liberal politician, died suddenly while Education Minister in Ramsay MacDonald's coalition National Government.

But what the college authorities took as much notice of was that, again, unlike Burgess, Donald Maclean continued his schoolboy interest in sport, captaining the Trinity Hall cricket team and also playing for the college at rugby and hockey. Also active in college societies and with a Double First in Modern Languages, it was no surprise that his tutor called him 'one of the leading members of the College'.[95]

A handsome man, 6 ft 4 in. tall, he was noticed for his looks as well as his intellect, and was another of the glamorous left-wing students who sat for a photograph at the Ramsey and Muspratt studio. The same could not be said for a working-class bespectacled student whose time at Trinity Hall overlapped with Maclean's. Alan Nunn May, the son of a brass-founder and another recruit to the communist cause, graduated with a First in Physics, stayed on to do research and visited Russia, probably through his research connection with the Marxist physicist don J. D. Bernal.[96]

For Maclean, Burgess and Philby, their journey from the Socialist Society leftwards had resulted in them becoming part of what they preferred to see as the Comintern, the international umbrella that sat above national parties. The Communist International, founded in Moscow in 1919, sought to foster revolution by liaising with those parties offering support, guidance and often orders from Moscow. But claiming to be in the Comintern was often a cover for hard-nosed intelligence gathering and that's what they had signed up for. As the Soviet expert Robert Conquest once put it, 'One would certainly not wish to find such people in the Foreign Office, let alone the security services.' Messrs Maclean, Burgess and Philby saw themselves as part of a transnational intellectual brotherhood. Philby later wrote, 'One does not look twice at an offer of enrolment in an elite force.' Robert Cecil, who knew all three men professionally or personally, said they 'were fully conscious of their abilities and potentialities; not for them the long mornings on the street corner, selling the *Daily Worker*, nor the dreary meetings with the comrades, adopting resolutions'.[97]

The KGB soon realised, however, that there were disadvantages in recruiting from the privileged classes. One report back to Moscow said: 'Burgess is the son of very well-off parents. For two years he has been a party member, very clever and reliable (ideologically speaking), but in S's [Philby's] opinion somewhat superficial and can occasionally make a slip of the tongue.'[98]

Deustch worried about Burgess's 'personal degradation. Drunkenness, irregular way of life, and the feeling of being outside society', but couldn't ignore the value of his 'circle of homosexual friends who he recruited from a wide variety of people, ranging from the famous liberal economist Keynes and extending to the very trash of society down to male prostitutes'. Burgess did indeed know everyone.[99]

Philby later revealed that Burgess, sensing his friends' doubts about him, had been 'one of the very few people to have forced themselves into the Soviet special service'. He'd been kept out of Eton's elite 'Pop'; he wasn't going to let himself be kept out of this new highly fashionable elite by his own friends. So Burgess 'started to badger us and no one could badger more effectively than Burgess'. Since Burgess knew about Philby and Maclean's recruitment, it was thought 'he might be more dangerous outside than inside. So the decision was taken to recruit him.'[100]

The most immediate task for the KGB was to create that 'new political personality' for each of their three new recruits. Donald Maclean, who had been planning to do academic work or teaching, went straight into the Foreign Office, becoming the first of the Cambridge Five to find a job in the British civil service. Asked by the Civil Service Commission if they were 'aware of circumstances tending to disqualify him', the Trinity Hall authorities replied, 'No'. They did mention his 'rather pronounced political views', but didn't explain what these were.[101] Maclean's tutor told him that the Foreign Office might 'seem a little dull at first sight', but 'I have very little doubt that your decision is a wise one.'[102] Maclean himself told his mother that he had 'rather given up on all that' when his previous communist sympathies were brought up. Philby chose to become a foreign correspondent where the links with British Intelligence were valuable enough without being on the actual payroll.

It appears that the Soviet long-term plan for Burgess, discussed with his Soviet controllers at a café in the East End of London, was for him to penetrate the British Secret Intelligence Service, MI6, and it was a task to which he was to return later.[103] But the first step was for Burgess to resign from the Communist Party, and he struggled over the next twenty years to provide a convincing explanation for why he had done that, other than the real reason: the KGB had told him to. He could have said, as many others did, that he had become disenchanted with communism. Even by the time he talked to Tom Driberg in 1956, while still denying he was a KGB agent, his best attempt at explaining the trigger point for leaving the party was that it had been an unsuccessful attempt to persuade party colleagues of his view that colonial freedom in the British Empire was more important than political activism in Britain itself.

Burgess then began a wild lurch to the far right. He began arguing with friends from the hard and soft left. New members of the Apostles, such as a King's College historian called Eric Hobsbawm, regarded him as a traitor 'because he took care to advertise his alleged conversion to right-wing views as soon as he had gone down'.[104] It must have been a considerable blow to the

Burgess ego and psyche to forgo the kinship of the left for the uncertainty of the right. Goronwy Rees remembered, 'in circumstances of great publicity, even scandal, so far as the confined world of Cambridge was concerned, he quarrelled ostentatiously with his communist friends and even his more liberal-minded ones, and left Cambridge for London'.[105]

His former friends were inclined to assume the worst about him. At the height of a row over a disputed past debt, later partly resolved, his old Cambridge communist comrade Maurice Dobb couldn't resist linking a dispute about 27 shillings with Burgess's new right-wing views:

> As I believe now that you have adopted a new political fashion, you are inclined to treat this debt with some flippancy. I am writing to point out that this happens not to be a debit in the ordinary sense of the word, but money paid to you by other people, to be handed on, which you have kept and used for your own purposes. For this there exists a very simple & direct word. May I also point out that a good part of this sum represents pennies collected from working men, who probably have less to spend on keeping a family in a week than you probably spend on gin, in the same time.

To those he had betrayed politically, one reasonable assumption was that capitalism offered Burgess a more financially comfortable course than communism. As if to confirm this, his first paid job turned out to be providing financial advice to a very rich London family.

According to Burgess's mother, her son provided tips about stocks and shares to Victor Rothschild whom he knew from the Cambridge Apostles. 'I know he told Victor to buy some Rolls-Royce and I know he gave him some money for that.' She also said her son provided financial advice to Rothschild's widowed mother.[106] The story was strongly doubted by Rothschild's sister Miriam. Her memory was that Burgess was not a friend of her mother but got himself invited to a couple of meals and proved a good listener to her views on the gold standard. 'I never got the impression he was remotely interested in the gold standard but appreciated good cooking. And had a weakness for claret.'[107]

As for Burgess becoming a paid adviser, 'My mother was immensely and boundlessly charitable but would disguise her gifts to the people who asked her for help by plenty of adequate kindly camouflage.'

Miriam Rothschild recalled much more detail about Burgess than her brother himself ever cared to remember in later life. Victor Rothschild told one researcher, 'Because of the lapse of time neither my wife nor I feel that we have much to say which would be of use to you.' By contrast, Miriam provided a pen portrait of 'one of a crowd of clever young men who were attracted into my brother's circle of friends':

> I considered him intelligent, but rather babyish, with the slightly pro-
> truding front teeth of a thumb sucker. He was voluble to the point
> of spluttering, obviously neurotic, good looking with curly hair &
> fresh complexion and his chief attraction was vitality and rather
> boyish enthusiasm.

At this time Burgess, according to Miriam, was 'obviously clearly sincere about his sympathy for the underdog. But so was everyone else.'

In mid-1935 Burgess made an unsuccessful attempt to join the Conservative Party Research Department, which often provided an entry-level post for many aspiring Conservative politicians. Fellow Apostle Eddie Marsh wrote to another Burgess friend, Julian Bell, on 15 November 1935 saying,

> I met Guy Burgess for a couple of moments the other day; he has not got
> his job at the Conservative Central Office, but is eking out a livelihood
> by writing political reports about England for the Comité des Forges [the
> employers' organisation for the French steel industry]. He tells me that
> he still thinks that Marx is right, but that the only way that collectivism
> is likely to come to England is through the Conservative Party.

Marsh was so taken with this anecdote that when he wrote to Bell again on 26 November he told the story all over again.[108] After a short period writing articles and practising sub-editing for *The Times*, he was thanked but offered no prospects. Then, towards the end of the year, came the chance of a job inside Parliament.

In the general election of November 1935, Captain John 'Jack' Macnamara had been elected as the Conservative Member of Parliament for Chelmsford in Essex. The military title may conjure up images of elderly, splendidly moustachioed Tory MPs, but Macnamara was just thirty, a clean-shaven, handsome, slightly effeminate-looking man. He needed a secretary and personal assistant, a post which offered Burgess confirmation as a man of the far right. Macnamara was, according to Burgess's friend Goronwy Rees, 'so far to the right ... that it was reasonable to call him a fascist'. However, some of Macnamara's speeches in the Commons do not bear out that reputation, which may be explained by Burgess's claim to have written at least one of them. Working for Macnamara also gave Burgess the opportunity to see the parliamentary and political papers – including confidential ones – that passed across the MP's desk. It is not difficult to imagine where some of them would end up.

Both men joined the Anglo-German Fellowship to promote 'good understanding between England and Germany'. In reality, the fellows from this particular fellowship were mostly apologists for the Nazis. Joining Macnamara in this enterprise may have required Burgess to lie back politically and think of Moscow, but his employer's sexual politics presented no such problem. Both were enthusiastic sex tourists, travelling around Europe meeting young men.

Guy Burgess was by now a member of two elitist networks that came to dominate his life. Being part of one did not formally prevent you joining the other, but Burgess was probably one of few people with full dual membership. One was the Comintern, the Marxist high-flyers who considered themselves a cut above the average Communist Party members in individual countries. The other was what became known as the 'Homintern', a nickname created by Burgess's host in Oxford, Maurice Bowra, to apply to himself and those other men from the rich and powerful echelons of European society whose politics embraced all shades of opinion. They developed a *lingua franca* that quickly identified themselves to other members, and were experienced in furtiveness because their sexual encounters were at that time illegal and, if exposed, completely ruinous to themselves and their families.

Despite, or perhaps because of those risks, in 1936, Macnamara, Burgess, Tom Wyllie – the young civil servant at the War Office whom the KGB wanted Burgess to target – and (somewhat bizarrely) a Church of England archdeacon called J. H. Sharp went on what one writer has called a 'homosexual junket through Germany' funded by the Church of England.[109]

Macnamara was among those in Burgess's circle who did not survive Europe's armed conflicts in the 1930s and '40s. Captain Jack became Colonel Jack, promoted by Churchill to lead the new RAF regiment, but he was killed visiting his old regiment, the London Irish Rifles, on the front line during the Allied campaign in Italy in 1945.

Two of the men who helped to create the communist cell at Trinity, David Guest and John Cornford, died in the Spanish Civil War. In a letter from the front, Guest wrote, 'I have ... a lively desire to explore whole fields of theoretical work, mathematical, physical, logical ... but of course, this is not possible now – today the struggle.' He died in July 1938 at the Battle of Epro, when the British volunteers were ordered to take a hill controlled by Franco's forces.[110]

John Cornford, one of the first, if not the very first, Englishmen to volunteer in Spain, resigned his scholarship at Cambridge in October 1936 saying he was 'on the way to rejoin the unit of the Anti-Fascist Militia with which I have been fighting this summer'.[111] He was planning to write a book – 'Communism and the English Tradition' – and his publisher had noted that his new author was 'off to Spain to kill a Fascist or three'.[112]

But it was Cornford who was killed by the Fascists while fighting with Republican forces on the front line in Cordoba. The next day would have been Cornford's twenty-first birthday and Anthony Blunt told other Cambridge communists they had to be prepared to make their own sacrifices. The Canadian student at Trinity whom Cornford had recruited to the Socialist Society, and with whom Burgess had been on demonstrations, Herbert Norman, felt guilty that he hadn't signed up for Spain.

There had been a further poignant death, this one while Burgess was still at Cambridge. Eric Powell, the Eton master, artist and rock climber who had encouraged Burgess to give up sport at university, was on an Alpine expedition with three other Eton masters in 1933. Their four bodies were found, entangled in the rope which linked them together, at the foot of an 11,000 ft Swiss mountain peak. It was assumed they had slipped when their alpenstocks, the antecedents of the modern ice axe, failed to grip in the melting snow.[113]

Burgess said he had been invited by Eric Powell to join the trip but had already agreed to stay with friends in the south of France. But for that holiday booking, Guy Burgess might have ended up lying dead roped to his old schoolmaster in 1933. As it had turned out, by this stroke of fate, it was 1936, Guy Burgess was alive and well and ready to move on in his twin-track career as an English gentleman and a Soviet spy.

CHAPTER 3

'MR BURGESS IS AWAY TODAY'

SERVING MORE THAN ONE MASTER, 1936–38

For a man who lived so many double lives, it is fitting that two separate BBC departments came to entirely different conclusions about Guy Burgess – one that this Cambridge graduate was just the right person to give a talk on the radio, the other that he wasn't good enough to be allowed on the air.

Guy Burgess had a very uncertain start at the Corporation. Even getting there in the first place was a slog, but he did get a helping push. Some of Burgess's former tutors at Cambridge were trying to get him what would be regarded at Trinity as a 'proper job'. The process of making that a BBC job began on 15 November 1935, when the Cambridge University Appointments Board recommended Burgess for a post in the BBC Talks Department. The board wrote that he was a man of 'quite first-rate ability' who had been 'through the communist phase, I think'. Four days later, Burgess was considered 'worth seeing – probably for [BBC] Bristol'. Burgess accepted the interview in a letter sent from the Hyde Park Hotel, Knightsbridge.

Soon after, Sir Cecil Graves, the BBC's Controller of Programmes, received a letter from the Cambridge historian and Apostle G. M. Trevelyan. He wrote of someone who 'would be a great addition to your staff'. It continued, 'I believe a young friend of mine, Guy Burgess, late a scholar of Trinity, is applying for a post at the BBC.' He explained that Burgess had been in the running to become a Fellow in History but had decided instead, correctly in Trevelyan's view, that 'his bent was for the great world-politics, journalism etc. etc. ... He is a first-rate man, and I advise you if you can to try him. He has passed through the communist measles that so many of our clever young men go through, and is well out of it.'[1]

Professor G. M. Trevelyan may have been the Regius Professor of Modern History, but he and his colleagues' judgement on Burgess's recovery from an outbreak of 'communist measles' could not have been more wrong.

Within little over a month, the BBC had received two separate letters about Burgess, both specifically mentioning the word 'communist', both in the past tense. Burgess failed to get the job in Bristol: he was a runner-up. On the upside, the BBC thought he was 'well worth bearing in mind for the future'.[2] Later the same month, he was in the running for a job as a talks assistant working on regional programmes in Manchester. He was unsuccessful again, considered 'too metropolitan' and better suited for the Talks Department in Broadcasting House.

In 1936, the BBC established a training reserve to provide ready-trained staff to fill its future vacancies. In July, Burgess was interviewed again and stressed his keenness to get a job in the News department in London because, he told the BBC, his mother was an invalid and regional work would conflict with his commitments. This statement would have come as something of a surprise to a healthy Mrs Evelyn Bassett, but the ploy worked – Burgess was in the first intake.[3]

He listed Mr and Mrs Bassett's house at Ascot Hill, Berkshire as his permanent address, but was by then living at 38 Chester Square. Situated just off Eaton Square in the heart of London's Belgravia, Chester Square was and is a very respectable address for someone who, apparently, had been unemployed. His new near neighbours – at No. 55 – were members of the Bowes-Lyon family,[4] and, at No. 57, Alexander, Lord Dunglass (later better known as Lord Home).[5]

In the month that the Post Office first introduced TIM, the speaking clock, Burgess's address was fortunate enough to be one of the comparatively few private addresses in the entire country to have a telephone.[6]

His proposed referees for the BBC traineeship were listed as: Professor Trevelyan, J. Burnaby of Trinity College, Captain Jack Macnamara MP and P. D. (Dennis) Proctor, another Apostle and a rising civil service star, again after his involvement in a divorce case.[7] Burnaby told the Corporation that Burgess, 'after a period of enthusiastic communism during his last years here, he has now, I believe, arrived at some form of left-wing conservatism', but, significantly, he added: 'How long that will last I should be sorry to predict.' He said Burgess was exceptionally able but suffered from 'the faults of a nervy and mercurial temperament'. He concluded that by hiring Burgess, the BBC 'would be taking risks', but 'if I were in your place I should think it was worth taking them'.[8] There again was the word 'communist' in the files, and no apparent reaction in Broadcasting House at all to this, the third mention to date.

Dennis Proctor provided the BBC with unqualified praise: 'I have known Burgess for about six years, beginning when he was an undergraduate at Cambridge, and latterly I have known him well in London.' Burgess was most suitable and 'a close and penetrating observer of current politics. In fact he is one of those people whose opinion one likes to know, and attaches some value to ... and it is an opinion backed up by a pretty varied range of experience.'[9]

The 1935 Cambridge letter-writing campaign finally worked, but Burgess had only succeeded at the third attempt, and then only got in via the reserve list. On 1 October 1936,[10] he was one of twenty-two recruits in the first intake. For the next three months he learned basic studio and production skills on a salary of £260 a year.

This relatively humble beginning offered him an entry point, a passport to official events, and an opportunity to meet powerful and influential people who would confide in him their views and, sometimes, their secrets, too. While this would undoubtedly have been helpful for Guy Burgess in developing his career, it would also have been increasingly useful for his masters in Moscow, who were trying to understand what threat Britain posed to them and their international interests.

The Soviet leader Joseph Stalin believed that the capitalist world was out to get him: to stifle and kill the communist revolution. While this might now seem like paranoia, it was not without foundation. Russians easily remembered

Britain's and other countries' military interventions in the Russian revolutionary civil war, their covert scheming, economic blockades and other attempts to sabotage the Soviet project. Stalin's view was that the best way to protect the revolution from what he regarded as a permanent threat was to spread the revolution into the back yards of those countries that were trying to stifle his own. The best defence was attack: subversion and destabilisation.

The Comintern was a response to this view. It recruited and ran agents who were tasked with infiltrating themselves into the very fabric of ruling establishments. Some were sent into established media organisations because the Russians believed that they were closely and inextricably linked to the ruling elites and were powerful agents of influence. In Britain, therefore, *The Times* and the BBC were major targets, as were the principal departments of state.

The war between communism and capitalism, which Stalin believed to be inevitable, would be aided by having early and reliable inside information about the capitalists' intentions; but equally important were the efforts of agents of influence.

* * *

Just before Christmas Burgess was told that on New Year's Day 1937 he was being posted to the Talks Department. His BBC file records: 'Unfortunately his diction is bad and it is this defect alone which prevents us from recommending him as an OB [Outside Broadcast] assistant.' He was consigned to production rather than presenting, commentating or announcing[11] and as such would be firmly positioned on the other side of the microphone.

With hindsight, this was a curious decision. From recordings of Burgess's voice it's not clear what the BBC official meant about his poor diction. Unless he'd been tested when he was drunk. While Burgess's strangulated, posh, upper-class voice was, to modern ears, very like the Harry Enfield character 'Mr Cholmondley-Warner', it wasn't defective: no sibilance, no poor pronunciations and no impediments. Burgess spoke a 1936 version of RP (Received Pronunciation), no different from many of the other speakers on the wireless and like many from the elite establishment.

Indeed, we have discovered that elsewhere in the BBC Burgess *had* been deemed suitable to be a broadcaster. In exactly the same month that the BBC hierarchy was receiving letters from Cambridge dons about Burgess as a prospective recruit, another part of the BBC – the Talks Department – had already earmarked a slot for Burgess to make a broadcast. He had been seen by professional producers and had been deemed suitable to go on air.

In one of those cases where the left hand doesn't seem to know what the right hand is doing, a bright young BBC Talks producer called Mary Adams had booked young Guy Burgess for his first broadcast, which, perhaps most remarkably, was going to be about Russia.[12]

In late 1935, the Talks Department planned to broadcast a series of talks under the title of 'European Exchange', where an English perspective was voiced about a European country and a national from that country would give their own perspective on what was going on there. After some deep thought about political sensitivity, it was decided to include programmes about Russia and Germany in the series. Burgess's radio debut was planned for broadcast for either 21 or 28 December 1935. He would give an English perspective and a young Russian, who was a fluent English speaker, would talk passionately about his country.

The producer, Mary Adams, had been a research botanist at Newnham College, Cambridge, had given a number of talks on the radio in 1928 and, by 1930, had taken a part-time job with the BBC Talks Department. She was a member of the influential democratic socialist group the Fabian Society and a friend of two of its early leading lights, Sidney and Beatrice Webb, and she was married to a Conservative MP.[13]

Adams had considered several names for the English speaker in the Russian programme before deciding: 'My choice has finally fallen on Guy Burgess to take part in the Anglo-Russian discussion. I have interviewed a number of possible candidates and he seems the best.' And not a hint of any diction problems signposted.

Adams told her superiors that Burgess had

> a first in History ... did some research ... took an interest in Left-wing politics ... and before going up to Cambridge spent two years in the Navy.[14]

He afterwards worked at the Central Conservative Office and describes himself as a liberal-minded Tory ... Macmillan stock ... has been to Russia, and is a student of Russian affairs. He reviews for *The Spectator* and the *New Statesman*, and at present reports for a business agency in Paris. Have I your permission to invite him?[15]

At this point there was a significant intervention from above: W. St John Pym, the BBC's Director of Staffing and Administration, added to Adams's memo: 'Sir Patrick Gower[16] denies that he was employed at Central Office. He says that Burgess was on a short list that they considered but on discovering that he had been a communist at Cambridge they did not proceed. I feel we might get someone a little more "true-blue".'[17]

St John Pym, an important person in the BBC hierarchy, had exposed Burgess for lying but Mary Adams pressed ahead anyway. While some people embellish their CVs a little, most don't usually go as far as saying that they had worked somewhere they hadn't. Sir Patrick Gower was, after all, a senior Conservative party official, and presumably had no animus against Burgess. Burgess's claim of 'two years in the Navy' wasn't checked out, but if it had been St John Pym would have discovered that this experience amounted to the two years Burgess spent as a Dartmouth cadet – between the ages of twelve and fourteen.

Most significantly, what St John Pym had discovered about Burgess didn't get passed on to those BBC colleagues who would soon employ him.[18] Nor later, during the war, when security and suspicions about candidates' backgrounds were more important, did St John Pym, as far as we can tell, ever remember what Gower had told him about Burgess's past.

The file doesn't record exactly how Burgess came to be known by the Talks Department as an expert on Russian history and Marxism in the first place. It is just possible that Burgess's Cambridge referees might have passed his name on, but a more likely informant might have been one of his history tutors, Stephen Runciman, who had already recommended another speaker for the series. But, equally, Mary Adams was still linked to Cambridge society and may well have gleaned Burgess's name from her own contacts.

We do know that only one name was proposed for the Russian half of the programme: a young financial expert and sportsman, Gearmen Sverdloff. His name had been put forward by the Russian ambassador, Ivan Maisky, himself.

Preparations were made for the broadcast and a *Radio Times* billing was put in place for Saturday 28 December at 8 p.m.: 'European Exchange: 6 Russia. A Discussion between Gearmen Sverdloff and Guy Burgess'.

Burgess was billed as follows:

> Guy Burgess (aged 24) was educated at Eton and Cambridge, where he took a first in History. He spent two years in the navy before going up to Cambridge. He has visited Russia, and is a keen student of Russian affairs. He reviews for *The Spectator* and *New Statesman*, and at present reports for a business agency in Paris. He is very interested in politics.

This would establish a public record for Burgess.[19]

The day before the scheduled transmission, a man who knew about Burgess wrote to a reporter on the communist *Daily Worker*:

> Perhaps some notes on the English participant, Guy BURGESS, may be useful to you to have in mind.
>
> BURGESS is a renegade from the C. P. of which he was a member while at Cambridge. He is now a Conservative, and has been anxious to obtain a job at the Conservative Central Office.

The author of the letter was Derek Blaikie, the man who had visited Russia with Burgess one year earlier. With his inside knowledge of the background, but not realising the full story, the loyal communist Blaikie almost gave the game away on Burgess, and fellow KGB spy Donald Maclean, when he wrote, 'In "going over to the enemy" BURGESS followed the example of his closest friend among the Party students at Cambridge who abandoned Communism in order successfully to enter the Diplomatic Service.' Blaikie didn't mention that he himself had almost done the opposite, abandoning his own career as a diplomat to become a communist, but he concluded, on Burgess, 'If he is to speak as a representative young Englishman, he hasn't got much to show in the way of consistent principle. Yours fraternally, Derek Blaikie.'[20]

The letter never appeared in the *Daily Worker*, but because the newspaper's post was intercepted by MI5, it did find a home in Blaikie's personal file. It seems from the records that a copy was never put into Burgess's at the time.

As it turned out, Blaikie needn't have worried about the programme. A week before transmission the producer Mary Adams informed the BBC Director of Talks that 'negotiations over this discussion have finally broken down'. She explained that she had chosen a 'left-wing Tory in outlook' so as to be 'less antagonistic to communist ideology', but Burgess had scripted such leading questions as 'Was the revolutionary method the only way of remedying mistakes made by a government?' With a Soviet embassy press attaché always on hand to interfere, the Russian spokesman said he wasn't prepared to answer questions like that. Mary Adams thought, 'Mr Sverdloff can only say what he is allowed to say' and 'by mutual agreement it was considered best to cancel the programme'.[21]

As both would-be speakers had put such effort into preparing six separate draft scripts, Adams recommended that both ought to be paid for their trouble, 'if not the full fee, at any rate two thirds of it'.[22]

Afterwards, Sverdloff and Burgess were required to agree with the BBC's Director of Public Relations, Sir Stephen Tallents, the line to be taken to explain the programme's non-appearance, just in case questions were asked by the press. A press notice was issued on Christmas Eve, marked 'seen by DG', stating that, instead of a discussion between an Englishman and a Russian, it would now be between an Englishman and a Scotsman. But Sverdloff told one newspaper the BBC had 'deviated from the original basis', which had been to talk about 'the young Soviet generation, its aspirations, aims and opportunities' and introduced 'highly controversial political problems'.[23]

According to a BBC official, in a Soviet statement 'the blame for the breakdown was placed upon Guy Burgess'. How ironic that the Soviets, presumably unknowingly, were blaming one of their own side for depriving them of a propaganda success.[24]

Within the BBC bureaucracy no one ever seems to have connected Guy Burgess the anxious and waiting recruit with Guy Burgess the headhunted but eventually unneeded broadcaster. His personnel file does not mention the aborted broadcast. No one seems to have joined the dots. And no one picked up Sir Patrick Gower's information about Burgess and Conservative Central Office and his communist background. It would happen again.

By a coincidence, another young academic and a friend of Burgess's had also been recruited by Mary Adams for the very same series for which Burgess had been earmarked: Goronwy Rees. His name had been given to Adams by the journalist Sheila Grant Duff. The difference was, however, that Rees's broadcast did go ahead in late 1935 and led him to make several more over the following decades.[25]

In the autumn of 1936, Burgess was a BBC trainee in 'Talks', an important department in the BBC accounting for much of the factual programming on the Corporation's only domestic UK-wide radio station, the BBC National Programme. Talks assistants were actually producers, but relatively closely supervised ones. They organised the bookings of speakers, managed auditions, conducted rehearsals, arranged bookings of studios, edited scripts and drafted billings for the *Radio Times*. Departmental meetings were held every Wednesday afternoon: attendance was obligatory, departmental lunches were held on Tuesdays: attendance voluntary. Talks assistants were told *firmly* that they could *not* normally claim expenses for entertaining speakers.

Burgess graduated from being a trainee to a full Talks assistant, taking his first step up the career ladder that would soon see him receive more responsibility for radio programmes. His day-to-day boss was none other than George Barnes, whom Burgess had discovered 'fishering' his mistress in the Barnes family home and who knew of Anne Barnes's obsession – consummated or otherwise – with a bachelor Cambridge don.

Barnes had left the Cambridge University Press in 1935 to join the BBC, apparently at the suggestion of Sir John, later Lord, Reith. John Green, one of the BBC Talks team, later recalled that it was Barnes who had introduced Burgess to the department, and Green had 'protested to him vigorously at the time'.[26] Barnes became angry at this and cited Burgess's 'very good history degree'. He doesn't seem to have mentioned what he undoubtedly knew about Burgess's politics. Barnes had been involved in the radio series that Mary Adams had wanted Burgess to appear on but he also didn't seem to have seen Pym's serious reservations about Burgess, or he chose to ignore them.[27] Interestingly, Green also noted that 'when Burgess did arrive I was to be far more friendly with him' than Barnes was. There is no hard evidence that Burgess blackmailed Barnes into getting him the job, but nor is there much sign of real friendship either.

But while Burgess settled down to work, there were a couple of minor hiccoughs along the way. One historian who had access to KGB archives noted that one of his KGB contacts learned that Burgess had been treated for syphilis in early 1937.[28] Given Burgess's sexual proclivities this was certainly a possibility, but the disease was serious and the treatment was tricky.[29] It is true that two weeks after starting work in the Talks Department he reported sick – on 14 January 1937 (a Thursday) – and returned to work the following Monday. If the illness was a sexually transmitted disease, it is more likely that it would have been a lesser complaint.

Reading through Guy Burgess's BBC staff file, it is clear that he was not exactly a model employee. Just nine months after he had joined the training, reserve managers at the BBC were becoming concerned that some of them at least wouldn't be able to recognise him if they saw him. They wanted a photo of him for his file. After several ignored memos, things came to a head and he was told to 'take immediate steps to have one taken'.[30]

Finally he sent one, saying, 'I have already supplied two which have been rejected. Will this one do?' but adding: 'It is not easily recognisable.' The BBC administrator wrote of the new photo that 'it reminds me of him, anyway'. A colleague noted that it showed 'him sitting on the sands at Margate or some similarly unsuitable picture'. Over at MI5, there was an entry made in the files recording that, at some point in 1937, Burgess's name was 'submitted from BBC for vetting' but nothing else. When somebody looked at the file a few years later, 'there were some other traces in a P. F. [personal file] but the photographed card was quite unreadable'. So, no lasting, detailed MI5 record was created of the next stage of what was to be the extraordinarily multidimensional career of Guy Burgess, working, apart from anybody else, on their behalf.[31]

From April until June 1937, Burgess was the administrative support on a range of programmes that focused on health, food and exercise. For years it has been accepted that the programmes had the racy (for the 1930s) title *Keep Fit with Miss Quigley*. Our research shows the title was a talks series more soberly titled *Towards National Health*, and that Janet M. A. Quigley was in fact a BBC staff producer.[32] Burgess also helped out on other topics from motorcars and motorbikes (a Burgess passion) to historical and science talks. In August 1937 he produced a talk by J. E. Whittaker: 'A Schoolmaster in Russia', although few details survive in the BBC's archive to show how the talk came about, or how Burgess became involved.[33]

It is said that Burgess also produced other talks about Russia, although there is no sign of his name in the BBC's archive files about Russia dating from this particular period. There is also an undated letter from earlier in Burgess's BBC career in Christopher Isherwood's MI5 file (written on BBC-headed notepaper, but crossed out, and on which Burgess had written: 'answer please, 38 Chester Square'), showing that at some point he had tried to secure a broadcast for his friend: 'One thing is – at the moment a drive for short stories – have you anything that you would like to be read – preference is of course for unpublished stuff . . .'[34]

Like other recruits, Burgess was on six months' probation as a Talks Assistant. As the end of this period approached, the BBC considered him 'an extremely able young man. Prolific as regards ideas and a quick learner. While he has his own opinions, he is amenable to discipline & is extremely pleasant to work with.' The result was that he was 'Strongly recommended for confirmation & for service in the Talks Department.'[35]

A month later, his file shows he 'has settled into the work of Talks Department & is pulling his weight . . . we want to encourage the idea that Talks Assistants must be responsible persons, upon whom reliance can be placed to act with judgement & good sense.'[36] The result was joining the permanent Talks Department staff, getting an immediate salary increase of £40 to £300.

Around this time, Burgess was worried about his job. The exact cause is not clear, but in a letter written on BBC notepaper and sent to the Oxford economist Roy Harrod, he confessed, 'Meanwhile I am awaiting dismissal here for the story I told (or rather you told) about the Director General to the Director of Staff Administration's old Tutor.'[37] Burgess's BBC staff file shows that nothing happened: the issue never registered. It may just have been a case of nerves on Burgess's part, but it was a useful lesson that underlined the need to watch his words in future.

Almost as soon as Burgess joined the permanent staff, he challenged BBC management about his new, increased salary, which he thought wasn't enough. He got some support from his managers – 'The proposed increase in Mr Burgess's yearly salary after all amounts to less than the cost of three hours broadcast talks...' – but, after weeks of sending memos back and forth, his request cut little ice with those who set salaries and it was decided Burgess would have to wait like everyone else.

A year later, in his annual report, Burgess was described as

> brilliantly able, widely read and with a keen sense of humour he is delightful company. Has produced some admirable programmes and is always likely to do so when really interested. Seems to be rather lacking in self-confidence when faced with an awkward situation, and owing to a natural impatience with routine is inclined to make slips in matters of detail. He realises this and has improved a great deal in this direction recently.

From April 1938, Burgess's pay rose to £400.[38]

Just as he was settling into the BBC's permanent staff, some say that Burgess was tasked by Moscow with an important errand. The KGB needed him to take some money and new codebooks to fellow spy Kim Philby, who at the time was covering the Spanish Civil War for *The Times* from General Franco's side. They were to meet in Gibraltar and Burgess would have to tell Philby that Moscow wanted him to get close enough to the Spanish fascist leader to kill him. This is supposed to have happened in April 1937.[39]

This story is told in several books, including one written by Philby's Russian biographer, Genrikh Borovik, who was able to see Philby's KGB file in Moscow. Burgess's BBC file, however, shows that in April 1937, when this trip to Gibraltar is said to have taken place, he was in fact hard at work at his desk in Broadcasting House. There is no record of him being off work, either for annual leave or due to illness.

Burgess was not averse to reporting sick. He was ill for eleven days in 1937, but none of these were in April.[40] Given that the BBC's records were probably as diligently kept as the KGB's, this establishes with reasonable certainty that Burgess was in Broadcasting House during the period that he was supposed to be meeting Philby in Gibraltar.

Shipping manifests from the time also reveal that Kim Philby travelled from Britain to Gibraltar in early 1937, sailing on SS *Vandyck* on 2 February. He returned to London on the P&O steamship SS *Strathnaver* on 30 April 1937. It is likely that in the meantime he crossed into Spain, got his stories and then went back into Gibraltar.

So, who could have been Philby's courier if it wasn't Burgess? The shipping manifests show that a Mrs Philby sailed from England on the Union Castle line's SS *Llandaff Castle* on 18 March. This means that Litzi [Friedman] Philby – or at least someone masquerading as her – was probably the messenger. Kim Philby was still in Spain or Gibraltar at this time, too, so she could have linked up with him. The story of a Burgess–Philby escapade in Spain, therefore, just doesn't seem to stand up.

Over the next few months, and even while he was working on the programme with Janet Quigley, Burgess began spreading his wings at the BBC. Not only was he producing broadcasts handed to him by departmental management; he began looking for new talent himself. In April 1937, he produced a talk by the well-respected historian and *Times* journalist Roger Fulford entitled *When George IV Was Crowned*.[41] BBC files show that Burgess already knew Fulford well – they may have met during Burgess's very short sojourn at *The Times*. But certainly by the time that Burgess produced the talk they were clearly on friendly terms. Early correspondence on file is to 'My dear Guy …' and signed 'yours ever'.[42] Later, during the Second

World War, Fulford would play a role in MI5 and his relationship with Burgess would prove useful.

There was another speaker with whom Burgess worked as a producer who would go on to provide connections with British Intelligence. In early 1937 Burgess read a book that both amused and excited him. It also gave him an idea. Would the author do a talk for him? In May he wrote to the author's literary agents. The author in question was David Footman and he wrote travel books in his leisure. His day job was described as civil servant, but Burgess knew he was an officer of MI6. Burgess wrote:

> Dear Sir,
>
> I have just read your book 'Balkan holiday' with great pleasure and ask myself whether you might not be just the person to give some travel talks of a rather personal nature ... I wonder if this prospect interests you.[43]

Footman's agents told Burgess that he was interested, asking, as agents do, 'What sort of fee does the BBC pay?' They had also been asked to find out how much work the project would involve, but said that Footman would be 'pleased to meet Mr Burgess...'[44] Footman and Burgess met on several occasions to complete the preparations, including for dinner and lunch. The talk was broadcast on Monday 2 August 1937. It was called *Albania, a Fish and a Motorcar*. It proved to be a success. The Director of Talks, Sir Richard Maconachie, liked it. '[It] was, I thought, really amusing. It might be worthwhile seeing if he could do anything more on the same lines.'[45]

The full story behind Burgess's talent spotting of Footman is, however, a little more complex and a lot more significant. It appears that during the course of his Foreign Office work, Donald Maclean had encountered Footman in his capacity as an MI6 officer. Maclean passed Footman's details on to his KGB controller, Deutsch, who suggested in May 1937 that Burgess should attempt to strike up a relationship with Footman.[46] Prior to Footman's August broadcast, Burgess and he had met for lunch at the Langham Hotel opposite Broadcasting House. They got on well. Burgess subsequently told his KGB controller: 'He is an intelligent, quiet man of the English type, but quick, smart and elegant ... dressed like a Foreign Office official. Thin dark hair, dark eyes, manly face, long narrow mouth, a small back of head ... I learned something of his past.'[47]

Burgess summarised what he had learned of Footman's career: after working in the Civil Service and a spell in the private sector, Footman had re-joined

> the Civil Service, where he is working now, that is in the Passport Con-
> trol Office. We talked for a while about this organisation. The Passport
> Control Office, according to him, keeps watch over foreigners and com-
> plications in the passport service. I've checked that through another civil
> servant, Proctor. F[ootman] is always on his guard. But I think he liked
> me, and this is what I was after.[48]

Burgess also provided a pencil sketch of Footman and the MI6 officer's home address.

But what Burgess didn't know, however, was that Deutsch had had the lunch covered by one of his female agents, Kitty Harris, who was Donald Maclean's contact (and lover). Harris, who knew Burgess and Philby, observed the lunch discreetly in order to see whether he and Footman were being observed by any of Footman's colleagues, but was also able to corroborate some of Burgess's details.[49]

Shortly after the radio programme about Albania, Burgess had lunch with Footman and a senior MI6 colleague, Valentine Vivian. 'Vee-Vee', as he was known, was in charge of MI6 counter-espionage and was particularly knowl-edgeable about communism and the Soviet Union. Burgess had impressed him with his understanding of the complexities of the former and current affairs but was surprised to learn that Vee-Vee was better read about com-munist theory and trends than he was. Vivian asked Burgess to cultivate not members of the party, but non-members such as Victor Gollancz, the pub-lisher, who was 'very important and very dangerous'. Crucially, and ironically, Vivian told Burgess 'both in Oxford and Cambridge there is a secret party membership that has to be uncovered'. He also mentioned 'an underground communist organisation' in the BBC and pointedly said to Burgess that he would 'have to find out who its members are'. After this meeting, Footman told a colleague, Commander Howard, that Burgess 'was well off enough to be temporarily out of a job if required'.[50] A month later, Footman 'gave V [Vivian] details of BURGESS, explaining that BURGESS could easily get back into extreme left-wing circles in London or Paris.'[51]

Over the coming months it looks as though Footman and MI6 decided to test Burgess out.[52]

Burgess, in summing up the encounter for his KGB controller, said he was certain that Footman didn't suspect him because of 'class blinkers – Eton, my family, and intellectual. I must stress that I have always told you: "avoid people like me. We are suspect for historical reasons." Now I say, "only people like me are beyond suspicion".'[53]

However, Burgess was not able to convince Moscow to agree to some of his proposals for becoming a penetration agent within MI6. The KGB was then in the midst of the repercussions of the 'Great Purge' and they did not trust him enough. Instead, complying with Moscow's reluctance, he excused himself from taking up Footman's offer by saying that he had 'very successfully in the last five years built up a reputation for myself as a drunk, trouble-maker, an intellectual and a fascist renegade'.[54]

He then tried to interest Moscow in another scheme – this time to travel to the Russian capital to collect material for a book, but essentially using that as a cover for being an MI6 agent. Burgess was again told 'no'.

A report in Burgess's KGB file shows that inexperience led him to commit mistakes, but his controllers also recorded that they had decided to rein him in because his enthusiasm was likely to run away with itself, that he had no 'internal brakes'. He was regarded as someone who was unstable, insecure and boastful – the latter being a trait he himself admitted.

Burgess was eager to admit his mistakes, however. He confessed to telling an American 'comrade' visiting London that he was 'doing special work'. Burgess was wracked with remorse – and no doubt fearful that his friend might give the game away. As it was, the KGB forgave him this indiscretion.

Arnold Deutsch, the author of the character report, noted that Burgess 'is a hypochondriac individual and always thinks that we do not trust him completely'. Burgess 'had repeatedly tried to assure us that we are his saviours. Hence his alertness and fear of making a mistake that could bring dismissal from our work. I demonstrated my trust to him by the fact that I do not consider him a stranger, but a comrade.'[55] In a nutshell, this assessment demonstrates Burgess as eager to please, and the KGB as wilfully manipulating that insecurity for its own ends. He was, after all, a tool.

* * *

In his non-BBC/KGB hours, Burgess particularly enjoyed holding court just a hundred yards away from Broadcasting House in Yarner's Coffee House at No. 1 Langham Place (now a Starbucks). One BBC colleague, John Green, remembered:

> We used to have the most exhilarating conversations there about the pace of the world and history and interpretations of the great events, and Guy could be quite brilliant. And sometimes we were so late coming back to our offices that we were ticked off as if we want to spend all the day in Yarner's.[56]

Sometimes Burgess could 'spruce himself up and go to a cocktail party and look extremely smart', but Green's overwhelming memory was of a dirty and dishevelled figure, an eccentric-looking 'dirty don' with 'filthy habits' who left chocolate lying around, which attracted rats. Quite how dishevelled is best described in one account by Goronwy Rees of a visit to Burgess's home one summer Sunday morning. Burgess was still in bed with newspapers and books spread all around his red-, white- and blue-painted bedroom. Bottles of wine were open and there was also

> a very large, very heavy iron saucepan filled to the brim with a kind of thick, grey gruel, compounded of porridge, kippers, bacon, garlic, onion and anything else that may have been lying about in his kitchen. This unappetizing mess he had cooked for himself the previous day, and on it he proposed to subsist until Monday morning.[57]

77

In later years, when Burgess visited the Rees family home, he would attempt to flip soufflé omelettes in a pan, normally leaving the contents on a kitchen wall.

Burgess had come from a privileged background that to most people in the UK now seems alien. He had been born into a home that, like even lower-middle-class ones, had a housemaid, a cook and a parlour maid. The Burgess household in Chester Square, however, had no such luxury.

The occasions when he did spruce up were often encounters with a man Burgess had first heard speak while at Eton: Harold Nicolson. By the mid-1930s, Nicolson, then in his early fifties, had already lived a full professional and private life – indeed, very few people of that age can claim to already have been a diplomat, journalist, novelist and a Member of Parliament. He was initially elected for Oswald Mosley's New Party, but, after it turned fascist, he joined the National Labour Party of Ramsay MacDonald. What made Nicolson something of a household name was none of these achievements, however. Rather, it was the fact that, from 1929 onwards, he was a frequent broadcaster on Britain's first radio stations, such as 2LO London and 5XX Daventry, talking about a whole range of topics. For example, on the evening of 17 June 1929, both stations broadcast *A Discussion on Marriage between the Hon. Harold Nicolson and Miss V. Sackville-West*.[58] In fact, Victoria 'Vita' Sackville-West, daughter of Baron Sackville, had already been Mrs Harold Nicolson for a decade and a half by that point. If this was an unconventional billing in the *Radio Times*, then so was the marriage itself. Both had lovers of their own gender, and both knew about it. Nicolson was to be a friend, adviser and, probably, an occasional lover of Guy Burgess for the next three decades.

The two first met on 17 March 1936. Nicolson was dining with a friend, Mary Hutchinson, and, as was common in his diary, he recorded that another friend or acquaintance was present on this occasion: Maynard Keynes. Nicolson's unpublished diary shows that after the day's entry had been typed, however, another name had been added in afterwards: Guy Burgess. That suggests that Nicolson had taken the trouble to add the name of Keynes' young companion at a later stage, something he may have done only after having found out who he was. After this date, the name Guy

Burgess cropped up on a number of occasions, including dinner at the Houses of Parliament.[59]

According to author Michael Bloch, Nicolson 'gathered around him a circle of attractive, well-bred young men of literary bent'.[60] It is not difficult to imagine Burgess fitting in easily. Nicolson was not a wildly passionate man, but he possessed a vigorous libido. His son Nigel described Nicolson's view of sexual fulfilment as 'about as pleasurable as a quick visit to a picture gallery between trains'.[61]

Our study of Nicolson's unpublished diaries reveals the extent to which the two men continued to enjoy one another's company after that initial meeting. Indeed, it paints a very different picture from that of infrequent meetings and social occasions hinted at by the published ones. Some friends believed the Burgess–Nicolson relationship was also sexual – it was even suggested by Goronwy Rees that Burgess 'procured friends' for Nicolson.[62] Hints from the unpublished diaries suggest that they were correct.

Burgess dined with Nicolson and others in London's best restaurants and most exclusive gentlemen's clubs, one of which, The Reform, in London's Pall Mall, he was able to join in 1937.[63] His club offered, in particular, refreshment for the mind and the throat, with an excellent library and a convivial bar. Despite these exclusive memberships, however, the regular round of debutantes' balls of society's 'summer season' was not for Burgess, although he had been to at least one in his youth.[64]

More often he went out with friends to pubs and demi-monde clubs and drinking joints where he might pick up some passing rough trade. And, of course, there was the Homintern connection and its informal, but exclusively male drinks parties. Tom Wyllie held some at the War Office and it was at one of these, in 1937,[65] accompanied by Anthony Blunt and Harold Nicolson,[66] that Burgess met Jack (or Jacky) Hewit, a chorus boy in his late teens and then on only his second or third night in London. Hewit moved into Chester Square shortly afterwards and stayed with Burgess for most of the following thirteen years.

Cherry Hughes, a journalist who got to know Hewit very well in later life, said he felt very much in Burgess's debt for all the introductions to London society and would have a tear in his eye when he spoke of his former lover. He was hurt that Burgess lived a promiscuous sex life, having affairs with friends but also casual sex with complete strangers, but understood it was part of the game. What upset him most was Burgess's untidiness, though. Hewit was meticulously neat and regarded Burgess as a 'slob'.

One of Burgess's other lovers, Micky Burn, now added to his sexual allure what Burn called his 'political significance to Guy', the result of his appointment as a foreign correspondent for *The Times*. Burgess, he wrote, had been a 'master-flatterer from the start, when his aims were sexual'. Now the flatterer-in-chief added praise for Burn's writing as a 'softening-up stage, preparatory to an attempt at recruiting'. Burgess suggested moving in together but Burn was about to embark on a very different course: 'I wanted to learn about women and discover what my emotions towards women really were.'

The specifics of the break-up of Burgess and Burn bear testament to the risky sex lives they led. In his notes on their relationship, Burn revealed:

> About this time I now and then used to pick up boys about Piccadilly … not very many but now and then. One day I read in the *News of the World* that a male brothel had been raided and people arrested for homosexual offences. This had not occurred to me and alarmed me. So I went to Scotland Yard to see the Inspector in charge of the case and told him that I had a problem. I gave my name and address as 10, Buckingham Gate. I hoped he would advise and help. He was amazed. All he said was that he was sure I would marry and get over it. I did marry … Anyhow I told Guy this story, I vividly remember his reaction. He was rather shaken, then pulled himself together and said, Micky, that was very objective of you. After that his interest in me dwindled. I suppose, as a spy, it was not at all a good thing for him to associate so closely, let alone be in love with someone who took their problems to the police. He introduced me to Harold Nicolson, who made rather a feeble attempt to get me into bed.[67]

* * *

Early in 1938, Burgess arranged a special present for his very good friend and fellow KGB spy Anthony Blunt: the opportunity to make his radio broadcasting debut. He was signed by Burgess to give a talk about the 'winter exhibition'. On the BBC booking form and just above Burgess's signature was inserted in Burgess's handwriting, 'Mr Blunt is a reputable art critic and should be paid the maximum for this period'. The programme aired on 27 January 1938 and lasted around nine minutes. It was produced by Burgess.[68] Weeks later, Burgess arranged for Blunt to make a second talk for a series called *Forgotten Anniversaries*. The BBC wanted a talk on a forgotten art anniversary, but didn't know what, if any, had been forgotten. Could Blunt offer a suggestion? His idea was for a talk about 'the painting of the Sistine roof [*sic*] ...' which was gratefully accepted and a broadcast arranged for 21 April.[69] Blunt would not prove to be the only KGB spy Burgess produced for the BBC.

In March 1938, Guy Burgess's BBC career came to a sudden, if temporary, halt when a medical certificate arrived from a Dr Pierre Lansel in Mayfair. 'Mr Guy Burgess has been to see me this afternoon and I suggest he should have a holiday considering the state of his nerves,'[70] it read. A BBC official added the note: 'Mr Burgess is away today. It is not known when he will return.'[71]

Guy Burgess would be off work from 15 March to 27 April 1938: thirty-four days, or just under seven weeks. Half-way through, the same doctor wrote to the BBC reporting a visit from Burgess's mother, who had been looking after him in the South of France:

> She informs me that he is better, but that she did not think him well enough to return just yet. He is still in a very nervous state and suffering from insomnia. From what she tells me I feel it would be wiser to allow him to stay away for another week or so.[72]

Significantly, Burgess's mother had wanted to reassure the doctor when she saw him on 8 April that 'he is very sensible and does not go out or touch any alcohol'.

BBC managers were beginning to get anxious: they kept a check on whether

Burgess had sent a medical certificate and resolved only to pay him until the end of April. The impression is that they were gearing themselves up to suspend him, or worse, if he didn't return soon.[73]

The evidence points to a nervous breakdown. A report filed by his fellow spy Donald Maclean on 25 April 1938 to the KGB included the following: 'I heard yesterday that the third musketeer [Burgess[74]] has had a nervous breakdown of some kind and has had to go away for two months. I have not seen him myself for many months, so do not know if this is likely to be true, but I shall be sorry if it is. . .'[75]

Burgess's lifestyle couldn't have helped matters and make this a plausible explanation for his absence, but there have been suggestions that, in fact, he had been arrested for allegedly importuning in a public toilet. As one friend had quipped, 'It had to happen eventually, I suppose. Guy met his Waterloo – it was either at Paddington or Victoria station.'[76] Sources suggest he was prosecuted, but the case was dismissed due to a lack of evidence. Nevertheless, it was thought best – presumably by friends – that he leave the country for a while in order to let the dust settle. He allegedly described his brief exile as 'under a cloud no bigger than a man's hand'.[77]

The suggestion that Burgess had been charged for importuning first seems to have entered into the public domain early in 1953, when it was mentioned in a review of a book by Cyril Connolly about the then mysterious disappearance of the Foreign Office officials Donald Maclean and Guy Burgess.[78]

But, as with all other aspects of Burgess's life, he seemingly couldn't keep still for long – breakdown or no breakdown. On 9 April 1938 – right in the middle of his sick leave – he found time to send a letter to his friend, Rosamond Lehmann, on headed notepaper from the Ritz Hotel, Place Vendôme, Paris.[79] In the letter he referred to a French political activist, 'Eddy Pfeiffer', with whom he was spending half his time in Paris 'helping to form French Cabinet' – the other half being at the Ritz. France had just acquired a new French Premier, Edouard Daladier, and Pfeiffer was a close political associate. Kim Philby later described this stay as 'a nervous breakdown which he enjoyed at the Ritz in Paris, at his mother's expense'.[80]

This was not the only occasion when Burgess suddenly took time off for reasons unknown. BBC Talks colleague David Graham remembered the day George Barnes came into his office in Broadcasting House and said: 'Burgess has gone off to Istanbul or somewhere, forgetting to do the *Radio Times* billing for the next talk in the *How Things are Made* series. You have until 4 p.m. today to find a speaker and get the *Radio Times* billing written.' A local shopkeeper was apparently recruited to talk about 'How a Picture Frame is Made'.

* * *

At the turn of the year the temperature of European politics was rising as a result of a succession of crises: the Spanish Civil War; the war in Abyssinia (modern Ethiopia); and Adolf Hitler's increasingly bellicose and aggressive actions in trying to unite all of the German-speaking peoples under one government (his). Elsewhere – such as in the Balkans and central Europe – right-wing political groups were working to destabilise political systems in order to win power while Hitler encouraged them from the sidelines. In the Far East, the Sino-Japanese war grew in intensity and with it concerns about Japanese expansionism.

In London, the British Prime Minister Neville Chamberlain increasingly took personal control over foreign policy – to the disadvantage and annoyance of the Foreign Office, to whose advice he was becoming deaf. Instead, he appointed his own advisers and tasked them with executing the decisions. In France, the political system was unstable and governments short-lived. German expansionism was viewed with concern, but the will to resist it was in short supply. The United States was taking a neutral stance and keeping out of events that it felt didn't directly concern it. Meanwhile, MI6 and other national intelligence agencies pursued covert political intrigues with greater determination: all realised that the stakes were becoming more crucial by the day.

1938 was turning out to be a significant year. In March, Germany declared *Anschluss* – political union – with Austria and sent in its troops, invited by an Austrian political placeman and Chancellor for two days (just long enough to send the invitation), Arthur Scyss-Inquart. The world watched, but did nothing.

With Austria under his belt, Hitler then turned his attention to German-speaking minorities elsewhere: principally in the Sudetenland of Czecho-slovakia, where a significant number lived. Their leader, Konrad Henlein, claimed that Sudeten Germans were discriminated against, were treated as second-class citizens and were subjected to physical violence and intimidation. Hitler pledged that he would do something to help.

As the year progressed, the Nazis piled on the pressure: Hitler declared that he was prepared to go to war to protect the Sudeten Germans. Ultimately, he wanted them in a Greater Germany. Britain, France and Russia knew they had to resist what all saw as dangerous expansionism that threatened everyone. Britain and France did not want to resist to the point at which war would become inevitable. Stalin knew that his ability to resist militarily, following the ravages of his purges, was risky if he didn't have firm support from either Britain or France.

The trouble was that no one trusted Stalin, who presided over a state that had been created through revolution and which, in the face of international opposition and intrigue, pursued policies that were designed to protect its own revolution by exporting international revolution and instability to its neighbours and opponents. And Stalin did not trust either the British or the French, both of whom he saw as weak and tending towards anti-communism.

Britain and France, too, were still suffering from the longer-term effects of the Great Depression. France was weakened politically: a succession of short-lived coalition governments gave an outward appearance of a country that was ill-prepared to resist and even less well-equipped to resist militarily, notwithstanding its large military forces. This was not a misplaced perception. Britain was also weakened: it too had a coalition government and had only latterly begun rebuilding its own military forces, which had been allowed to become dangerously weakened and depleted in the decade and a half after the end of the Great War. But, importantly, many leading politicians in power in both countries simply did not possess the will (never mind the resources) to resist.

Stalin was aware of this situation. His spies in both countries were passing information to Moscow that enabled him to see that neither France nor

Britain could be relied upon to stand up to Hitler; both would make concessions to keep the peace through their own weakness. The Germans sensed it, but Stalin knew it. He also knew that Britain and possibly France might, if push came to shove, reluctantly join forces with Hitler and Mussolini and go to war against Russia.

In a timely review of the situation twenty years after the Russian revolution, in 1937, the British Foreign Office began a debate about what was the greater of the two evils: fascism or communism? While Foreign Office mandarins felt that fascism and in particular Nazism was probably the more potent immediate threat because 'they make better guns and aeroplanes', communism was perceived as the greater long-term threat because of its 'universalism' and perceived durability: fascism relied on strong leaders and when they were gone the system risked collapse if another strong leader could not be found; communism was a system where the leaders were ultimately replaceable.[81]

Stalin probably knew all about this debate since Cambridge spy Donald Maclean saw the papers while working in the Foreign Office in Whitehall and later in the Paris embassy; it is believed that they were among the thousands of pages of documents that he passed on to Moscow. In Soviet eyes, sight of the papers would have helped to convince Stalin that Britain was not to be trusted.[82]

As the Sudeten issue developed into a crisis in spring 1938, the Sudeten German leader Konrad Henlein – later shown to have been collaborating with and taking orders from Hitler's government – paid a surprise two-day visit to London, starting on 12 May. While there, he had a series of private and informal conversations with politicians, including Winston Churchill.[83]

On 13 May, Harold Nicolson gave a 'tea party' for Henlein at his apartment at King's Bench Walk in London's Temple. He'd been invited to do so by the Foreign Office.[84] He recorded in his diary that he had invited several of his fellow MPs, including Duncan Sandys and Jack Macnamara. Henlein was followed around by the press, who waited on the pavement outside Nicolson's rooms. Nicolson said that the message given to Henlein was that while Britain may support Sudeten German autonomy within Czechoslovakia, he should be under no illusion: Britain would not support him if he made demands that were unreasonable or impossible. As the party broke up, Nicolson later wrote, 'I helped this stout schoolmaster into his enormous and ungainly greatcoat', warning him as he did so that he should not let Hitler turn him into 'the Seyss-Inquart of Czechoslovakia'. Nicolson recorded that Henlein's answer was 'God forbid!'[85]

It was during this visit that Burgess was contacted by David Footman of MI6 and asked if he could perform a favour for him. Henlein was staying at London's Goring Hotel during his visit, and Footman did not want to arouse suspicion that anything was amiss by inserting one of his own staff into the hotel. He had discovered that Burgess's lover and general factotum, Jack Hewit, worked at the hotel as a locum switchboard operator whenever he was unable to find work as a dancer. Would, Footman asked, he be willing to help out? Burgess introduced the pair and Hewit later told how pleased he was to have received £10 for his services, which included noting down information about incoming and outgoing calls.[86] What is particularly interesting about this episode, however, is that it shows not only that Footman must have known about Burgess's sexuality, but that he saw how it might prove useful to the British secret service. There is, however, an element of doubt as to whether it ever happened. Analysing Tom Driberg's account of this episode, MI5 noted in carefully crafted terms, 'There is no evidence that this was done at the request of the British authorities.'[87]

* * *

Shortly after he had arranged for Hewit to snoop on Henlein's telephone calls, Burgess found out that MI6 had a vacancy for a 'Passport Control Officer'. This, he was well aware, was a cover that MI6 agents abroad often used. As a consequence, David Footman introduced Burgess to E. G. Norman, who had been MI6 station chief in Prague, which happened to be one of the main pre-war British Intelligence bases for operations against the USSR.

Burgess met Norman at the Royal Automobile Club in Pall Mall. The task proposed by Norman, however, was to find out Mussolini's attitude towards Spain, as it was looking increasingly likely that Franco's Nationalist Phalange would be the victor in the Spanish Civil War. Burgess was willing to do it and offered to ask his friend Lord (Victor) Rothschild to provide a cover job for him with the Italian branch of the family bank. Burgess had impressed, but Norman suggested a cover job as a lecturer would be more fitting.

Years later, historian Hugh Trevor Roper, who had been an intelligence officer colleague of Kim Philby's during the war, published an account in a letter in the *New Statesman* that said that Burgess had acted as a go-between for Chamberlain and the Italian Foreign Minister, Count Ciano; and that British Prime Minister Neville Chamberlain's dirty tricks specialist, Sir Joseph Ball, had been the principal organiser. He had been an MI5 officer and had worked in the Conservative research department. When this letter came to Ball's attention, he immediately threatened a libel suit and, in reaction, by all accounts, Burgess offered to give a statement supporting Trevor Roper's allegations.[88]

It was apparently at this point that Burgess mentioned to Footman that he had been a communist while at Cambridge. Rather than deter him, it had given Footman ideas about using Burgess to assist 'our boys in the anti-Communist section'.[89] If true, it is remarkable both that the admission was met with such a response and, moreover, that when Russia appeared to get into bed with the Nazis the next year, the admission was forgotten.

* * *

As 1938 wore on, the Czechoslovak crisis deepened. Hitler's demands became more unreasonable and the international political situation formed a backdrop for another of Burgess's personal enterprises. This time it was strictly BBC business, however, as he got an opportunity to produce one of his friends, the National Labour MP Harold Nicolson, on a series called *The Past Week*. George Barnes was the series senior producer and Burgess the assistant.

The first talk went on air on 4 July 1938 and the talks continued weekly until 27 September. The programme was intended to be a non-political and eclectic personal view of the week's events. But for Nicolson the parliamentarian, an expert on diplomacy, and broadcast during the tense weeks in which the Sudeten crisis developed to frightening proportions, it could hardly be entirely apolitical. The final four programmes in particular were to prove troublesome.

For the month of September 1938, during which Neville Chamberlain carried out shuttle diplomacy by flying to negotiate with Hitler three times, and which culminated in the four-power Munich Conference (Stalin's Russia was excluded),[90] the programme was to be the cause of a polite but nonetheless intense battle between the BBC and Nicolson, as they tried to agree on what should and could be said on the air about Hitler, Nazi Germany and the prospects of war.

In March 1938, Foreign Secretary Lord Halifax had had discreet words with Sir John Reith that the BBC should not rock the boat and avoid doing anything that would upset negotiations.

> I intend to speak to Sir John Reith ... making it clear that what I am saying is not an instruction from Government, but merely an expression of a desire on their part that the BBC should bear in mind the extreme sensitiveness of both Hitler and Mussolini to BBC 'Talks' and presentation of news in order that difficulties on this score should be eliminated or reduced as far as possible more especially at a time when an attempt is being made by the Government to negotiate settlements and improve relations.[91]

Indeed, Halifax had instructed the ambassador in Berlin, Sir Nevile Henderson, to make sure that it became known in the German capital that he had been personally responsible for taking programmes by Nicolson and fellow politician Leopold Amery off the air.[92] Halifax's 'advice & warning' to Reith remained in force throughout 1938;[93] the BBC, aware that the government was keeping a very close eye on its programmes, had little option other than to comply.[94] Under Halifax, 'the Foreign Office ... had almost total control over BBC output and what today looks like censorship would have in 1938 more closely resembled responsible stewardship'.[95]

The BBC was not alone. Fleet Street was also given the same 'advice'. Halifax knew most of the press proprietors socially and 'it would have been more remarkable if he had not had words in their ears'. He was also known to have 'had little time for journalists' opinions, no trust in their objectivity and was correspondingly thick-skinned about their attacks.'[96]

Harold Nicolson was one of the MPs arguing for a more resolute response to Hitler. His talk scheduled for 5 September 1938 was particularly problematic. The Foreign Office was not happy with what Nicolson was proposing to say. George Barnes had decided that the script which Nicolson had submitted should be passed on to a senior official at the Foreign Office, the head of its News Department, Rex Leeper.

Nicolson, the BBC and the Foreign Office crossed swords. Nicolson became increasingly angry at the cuts which Barnes was suggesting under pressure from the Foreign Secretary, Lord Halifax. Nicolson suggested the whole talk be cancelled but then agreed to re-write it with the proviso that Barnes didn't come into the studio for the live transmission. Surprisingly, Barnes agreed, but arranged with the announcer, Alvar Lidell, that he would fade out Nicolson's talk if he departed too far from his script. For Guy Burgess it must have been something of a relief that this battle between his two friends seemed to have been resolved without *The Past Week* ever going off the air. He kept well out of it, as far as we can tell, although he may have run messages to the Foreign Office.[97]

During what rapidly became an explosive and very tense international political crisis, Burgess also appears to have been involved in message-running of a much higher order.

In September 1938 Neville Chamberlain wanted to correspond Prime Minister to Prime Minister with his French counterpart, Edouard Daladier. Chamberlain favoured doing a deal with Germany if it would avoid war, even if it meant making concessions, while others in Britain, such as Winston Churchill, advocated drawing a line in the sand and standing up to Hitler's bullying rhetoric. The Prime Minister didn't trust the Foreign Office to convey messages, however, because he thought it would try to scupper any deal that departed from its own line on German expansionism, which was to oppose it. He needed to get his own picture of what the French government was prepared to do to resist Hitler, therefore, without officials muddying the waters.

In order to do this, it appears that a secret channel was set up through which messages could be passed between the two leaders. The French end of this back channel would be Edouard Pfeiffer, who was close to the French

Prime Minister Daladier, and Burgess was chosen to be the British messenger due to his known close association with Pfeiffer. It is not certain how the two first met – it may have been one of the forays on the European mainland that Captain Macnamara and Burgess had conducted in 1936, though, given that Burgess was a serial cultivator of contacts, it could have been through an entirely different route. One thing was clear, however: Pfeiffer was a member of the Homintern.

Burgess's biographer, Tom Driberg, said that Burgess had been invited by Pfeiffer to submit a series of articles 'to a "controlled" newspaper' (i.e. permitted under French press regulation), but that they had never been published because they had been too anti-fascist. Burgess had apparently later discovered that the newspaper in question had been financed by the Nazis.[98]

Burgess's friend Goronwy Rees described Pfeiffer as 'a peculiarly detestable Frenchman ... who seemed to me to smell of every kind of corruption' and referred to him as 'the horrible Pfeiffer, to whom nothing was important except boys and money'. He thought the bond between Burgess and Pfeiffer was homosexual.[99] And there is an oft-repeated story of a visit that Pfeiffer and Burgess paid to a Parisian male brothel that involved whips and a naked boy who was strapped to a table.[100]

Pfeiffer was a graduate of Oxford and Heidelberg universities, and a lawyer by profession.[101] He also held a senior position in the French Boy Scout movement.[102] But, more importantly, Pfeiffer was Edouard Daladier's Chief of Staff. He was a director of a socialist-radical pro-Daladier newspaper, *Notre Temps*, and a one-time secretary of Daladier's radical-socialist party. Pfeiffer moved in European radical and press circles. He was a regular visitor to the UK where his name can be found nestling among the great and the good at prestigious receptions reported in *The Times* court circular.[103]

It seems that a close associate of Neville Chamberlain, Sir Joseph Ball, was also a prime mover in setting up the channel of communication, but whenever anybody put this into print or planned to, Ball's lawyers immediately began libel proceedings.

Only written messages passed between the two Prime Ministers,[104] whose relationship was not close. Daladier was wary of Chamberlain, whom he described privately as a bull with snail's horns,[105] and meanwhile Chamberlain was afraid that if it came to a showdown, Daladier's government would not stand up to Hitler.

Accounts suggest that David Footman of MI6 was also involved in the back channel. At the British end, Burgess collected the documents and handed them over to Footman at an apartment in the St Ermin's Hotel in Westminster, which was situated just yards away from MI6 headquarters in Broadway Buildings. The letters were copied before being passed on – either to No. 10 Downing Street or taken by Burgess to Paris. Apart from anything else, this raises the intriguing prospect that MI6 just might have been spying on its own Prime Minister. Burgess, however, was more than just a messenger: 'I used to help the man I was taking them to read them – his French was not very good.' The man in question is not named, simply being described as a 'man of title' for fear of Britain's libel laws: it was Sir Joseph Ball.[106]

By helping to read the letters, Burgess was also able to take note of what they said; and it is highly likely that their contents would soon have been delivered to a desk in Moscow. The KGB's operations in London were temporarily closed at this time due to staff shortages arising from Stalin's Purges and it is widely accepted that Burgess delivered his reports – along with some produced by Kim Philby – via a contact in Paris who may have been Philby's by-now-estranged wife, Litzi Friedman, or another KGB agent-courier, Edith Tudor Hart.[107]

In mid-September 1938, Burgess, still employed by the BBC, was apparently 'still under consideration' by MI6: 'BURGESS had been to Paris (at least from 8.9.38 to 14.9.38) and gave a report on developments in France.'[108] Indeed, this note could have been referring to the 'back-channel' activities – the dates do roughly correspond to the times when Burgess reported to the BBC that he was sick and unable to go to the office.[109]

Based on the work done by Burgess at this time, it appears that he 'was finally recruited by SIS as an unpaid source' after his trips to Paris. On 26 September 1938, he had called David Footman; an MI5 note later observed: 'FOOTMAN referred to BURGESS by an SIS symbol. BURGESS' expenses for the trip were approved.'[110]

Stalin's Russia was concerned that some powerful people in Britain in particular were indifferent – happy even – about the prospect of German expansion eastwards; but equally noted that many in the British political elite worried about 'backing the wrong horse'. Ultimately, it all boiled down to which was the lesser of the two evils: fascism or communism.

If Guy Burgess's account is to be believed, the Foreign Office put a stop to the back-channel communications as soon as they were discovered. According to what Burgess told Driberg in 1956, once a senior Foreign Office official, Gladwyn Jebb, found out about it he threatened to resign, and that would have become public. Jebb, later Lord Gladwyn, was Private Secretary to Sir Alexander Cadogan, the top diplomat who ran the Foreign Office at the time; and if he knew, Cadogan would also have known, as would his political master, the Foreign Secretary Lord Halifax. Jebb, however, made no reference to the matter in his autobiography.[111]

In truth, the evidence in support of Burgess operating as a go-between with the French during the Munich crisis as well as earlier in the year with the Italians is not conclusive.[112] BBC correspondence during August and September between Burgess and Harold Nicolson shows that he was working at his desk in Broadcasting House for most of the month. However, intriguingly, Burgess's BBC personnel file does show that he was unwell on three occasions during this time: from 10 to 12 September (2 ½ working days), from 16 to 22 September (4 ½ working days) and from 30 September to 1 October (1 working day).[113] These dates are significant because they do fit around the shuttle diplomacy being conducted by Prime Minister Neville Chamberlain in the run-up to the Munich conference. Equally, it is known that both Daladier and Chamberlain were also conducting back-channel discussions with Hitler's unofficial envoys. These periods of absence would have given Burgess enough time to travel backwards and forwards between London and Paris.

But what is also significant is that during at least one of the periods of sickness (16 to 22 September), Burgess met Harold Nicolson while he was in the middle of a spell of being ill; and he did so at the BBC and in the presence of his boss, the Director of Talks, Sir Richard Maconachie. Burgess's name survives in the published version of Nicolson's diary for 19 September 1938, but for some reason Maconachie's name was omitted. After dining at the Marlborough with his friends Buck de la Warr and Walter Elliot, Nicolson made his way to the BBC. The unpublished entry reads: 'I am met by Maconachie and Guy Burgess and deliver my talk in a voice of ironic gloom.'[114] If nothing else it shows Burgess was at Broadcasting House during the hour before Nicolson's broadcast (it started at 10:05 p.m.); and, moreover, was diligent enough to forsake his sickbed for the BBC. Equally possibly, he had perhaps arrived back from Paris earlier than expected. But there is a twist.

The KGB wasn't only aware of the Chamberlain–Daladier correspondence because of Burgess's work for MI6 – it also had a source inside Daladier's own office with the codename CHANCELLOR. That source is believed to have been Pfeiffer.[115] If Burgess set a gold standard for conflicts of interest, Edouard Pfeiffer set the platinum standard, working variously for the KGB, MI6, the French intelligence services and the Nazis. Remarkably, Pfeiffer was never called to account for any of his activities. He escaped to the United States in 1940.[116]

* * *

As Nicolson's series came to an end – on the day that Chamberlain announced to a packed House of Commons that Hitler had invited him, Italian dictator Benito Mussolini and French Prime Minister Edouard Daladier to attend a political summit conference at Munich – Guy Burgess was already busy with work on his next big radio series: *The Mediterranean*.

It was planned to open with a talk by a big-hitter: Winston Churchill. He was well known but had largely been absent from the airwaves for most of the decade – except when delivering appeals for 'radios for the blind' and other worthy causes. Churchill was implacably opposed to Neville Chamberlain's foreign policy of avoiding war at all costs – appeasement – and instead argued for standing up to Hitler and not making concessions.

The talks would play a key role in Burgess's future career, according to some accounts, as the cause for Burgess resigning from the BBC, in a clash over editorial policy.

The focus of the series was on the region's role in the political develop-ment of the contemporary world and, as formulated, was intended 'to give an objective account of the interests of the various countries on the shores of the Mediterranean, showing by reference to past history how these interests took shape'. It had originated late in 1937 at a very senior level within the BBC and was designed by the Corporation to cater to the 'increased interest taken by the public in foreign affairs'.[117] Director of Talks Sir Richard Macon-achie, who wrote to various luminaries asking for advice as to who should be invited to speak, shepherded the programme.

From the BBC's perspective it was a flagship series that would go out live in prime time in the autumn schedule. The Foreign Office thought it could help to educate and inform the British public and facilitate understanding of Britain's policy decisions. Cooperation was the key, but it was an unequal partnership: a compliant and yielding BBC matched with a firm and unbend-ing Foreign Office.

Churchill's opening programme was scheduled for 6 October. In the sum-mer of 1938, Burgess was appointed the production assistant for the series, preparing speakers, rehearsing them, handling scripts and generally making everything work on the day.[118] Suggestions that Burgess played any larger role in Churchill's programme are not borne out by the files. As a result of his work on the series, Guy Burgess did get to meet Winston Churchill, but the circumstances were not at all usual.

Burgess's version of events involved the claim that he'd had some difficulty in getting his invitation to Churchill approved by the BBC (always inhos-pitable to those regarded as unorthodox by the party whips). BBC files do not support this, however. Churchill had agreed to appear, but then when Munich blew up, he said he must withdraw that acceptance. As this would 'damage the series' and because he'd 'met Churchill socially once or twice', Burgess boldly telephoned Churchill at his home at Chartwell in Kent to get him to reconsider, and was invited down to talk it over.[119] It was clearly an offer that Burgess was unable to refuse. Rather than go through complica-tions with the BBC hierarchy, it appears that Burgess simply took a 'sickie' to make time for his trip. His BBC personnel file shows that he was recorded

as being ill from midday on 30 September until some point on Saturday
1 October.[120]

There is one piece of oral history that provides an eyewitness account of
what happened next: a recording made by Guy Burgess himself. In April 1951,
the evening before he left New York (see Chapter 7), Burgess was invited to
dinner and was persuaded to record for posterity his account of the meeting
with Churchill in 1938.

Shortly after Burgess fled to the USSR, the FBI got to hear about the tape
and impounded it. Half a century later, the FBI released a facsimile copy of
the transcript. However, the tape was not released and many presumed that
it had been lost. We submitted a Freedom of Information request to the FBI
in March 2013 and in January 2014 a compact disc bearing the insignia of the
FBI archive was released to us. On it was a broadcast-quality recording of
Guy Burgess telling his story about the day that he met Winston Churchill.[121]

Until the recording was released no one outside Burgess's immediate circle in the UK had ever heard Burgess's voice. It presented, thus, a unique
opportunity for everybody to hear the person who until that date had been
the silent member of the Cambridge spies. By the time Burgess recorded it
– at the third attempt – in New York, the anecdote had become a polished
after-dinner piece. It showed off Burgess's gift for mimicry, particularly of
Churchill. It was like a short radio play in which Burgess played all the parts.

In the recording, Burgess recalled how Churchill had read him a letter
from the President of Czechoslovakia, Edvard Beneš, asking for help. Churchill seemed unsure how to reply: 'Here am I, an old man, without power
and without party, what help shall I give?' Burgess said he replied ,'Oh, Mr
Churchill, don't be so down-hearted, offer him your eloquence.' According
to Burgess, Churchill looked pleased by that and responded, 'Yes, my eloquence indeed, that Herr Beneš can count on in full.'[122]

Burgess also told how he and Harold Nicolson used to send shivers down
the spine of Sir John Simon, then Neville Chamberlain's Chancellor of the
Exchequer, over lunch or dinner at the Reform Club by imitating Churchill's
voice, saying in such a way that he could not miss a remark aimed at him:
'A man of infinite cowardice!'

In the recording, Burgess also told of how, at the end of the meeting, Churchill gave him a book he had written about the war that was coming. According to Burgess, 'He wrote in the book – and I still have it – "To Guy Burgess from Winston Churchill to confirm his admirable sentiments, Munich, September 1938". Anthony Eden refused to spoil the book by signing it subsequently actually.'

According to Burgess, the two men then went out to the car, upon which point Churchill said to him, 'This war which you and I know is coming ... if I am returned to power – and it seems likely that I shall be – if you need a job come and see me and present this book and I will see to it that you are suitably employed.'

After his meeting with Churchill, Burgess wrote a memorandum to Sir Richard Maconachie in which he reported Churchill's anger that he had been 'always muzzled by the BBC ... and that he imagined that he would be even more muzzled in the future, since the work of the BBC seemed to have passed under the control of the Government.' Burgess had added that 'WSC [Churchill] seems very anxious to talk.'[123]

Burgess soon after got a letter from an assistant in Churchill's office: 'I am desired by Mr Churchill to thank you for your letters of 1 October, and to say that he approves of the arrangement you suggest.' This arrangement appears to have been an offer from Burgess for Churchill to appear elsewhere in the series, something that never happened.

In Burgess's mind, his meeting with Churchill was a significant event because he had helped Churchill regain his resolve to fight on. The interests of Churchill, Burgess, England and the KGB in resisting fascism had at that moment perfectly coincided. But one of Burgess's BBC colleagues, David Graham, believed the meeting may not have been Burgess's idea. He remembered Sir Richard Maconachie's retirement dinner in 1945, where Burgess had said:

> Sir Richard, I think I ought now to confess that one afternoon at the height of the Munich crisis ... I was very upset at the way things were going, and – without consulting you – I rang up the Soviet ambassador, Maisky, and he said 'come and see me'. So – without consulting you, Sir

Richard – I went to see him: you may not have noticed that I was not in my office that afternoon. Mr Maisky told me to go to Churchill and call on him, in the name of British youth, to save his country, and save Europe.[124]

If David Graham's recollection was correct, was Burgess telling the truth? The evidence is inconclusive, but clues provided both by Burgess's BBC staff file and Soviet ambassador Ivan Maisky's abridged diaries leave open the possibility that there might have been a grain of truth in what Burgess had said to Maconachie.[125] On Wednesday 28 September, Maisky was en route from Paris to London. He recorded in his diary that he only reached London's Victoria station at 4.25 p.m. and rushed to the Commons, just managing to witness the aftermath of the debate in which Chamberlain had announced Hitler's invitation to go to Munich. Maisky's complete diary is as yet unpublished, but it is likely that after leaving the Commons Strangers' Gallery Maisky would have gone to the Russian embassy and prepared an urgent dispatch for Stalin about the day's events.

The next day, Maisky had a meeting with Foreign Secretary Lord Halifax, who explained the British position. Afterwards he had 'a long talk with Churchill … This was before the news came from Munich.' Churchill told him he believed that Chamberlain wouldn't make any concessions to Hitler and he also mentioned a campaign against the USSR that he believed was being waged by Chamberlain's supporters.[126] Burgess was by this time in contact with Winston Churchill's secretaries at Chartwell about the talk.[127]

On Friday 30 September Maisky went to bed at 4 a.m. He had sat up listening to the radio as news came in about the Munich agreement. Maisky rose late and met Czech ambassador to Great Britain, Jan Masaryk, who was shell-shocked. 'They've sold us into slavery to the Germans,' he told Maisky.

Burgess was at his BBC desk during that morning, but as his staff file shows, he reported sick that afternoon. It is just possible that on that Friday afternoon when Chamberlain was flying back to Britain from Munich, Burgess could have been meeting someone – Maisky, an aide, or Burgess's KGB controller – and hatching a plan to see Churchill. However, Maisky's diaries make no mention of Burgess, and there is no other tangible evidence.[128]

* * *

The Mediterranean series and the consequent meeting with Churchill came to represent – in his own mind at least – Burgess's hour of triumph. It also had two career consequences, one an internal opportunity, the other an external one. Internally, David Graham of the BBC remembered Burgess raising at a number of Talks Department lunches that the Corporation should have a diplomatic correspondent 'with direct access to FO [Foreign Office] advice, and telegrams and other classified information'. Graham goes on to explain: 'If there had been a room, in BH [Broadcasting House] … with security clearance, where properly authorised staff could study diplomatic telegrams, it could have made Burgess's work in planning and carrying out the big 'Mediterranean Strategy' talks series, for autumn 1938, much easier…'

Burgess, in this picture, no doubt, would have been one of the 'properly authorised staff'. Indeed, Graham had 'the strong impression' that Burgess 'saw himself as the diplomatic correspondent'.[129]

Graham later twigged the importance of all of this. If Burgess had 'written down the words of transcribed cipher telegrams this … would have been of first-class use to some other people he was in touch with outside office hours at the Soviet embassy'.[130] In other words, he would have been able to deliver what Bletchley Park cryptographers referred to as 'cribs': original text against which ciphered telegrams intercepted by Soviet eavesdroppers could be compared. This would have given them a key for decoding other intercepts that remained only in cipher. It was a neat idea, but fortunately it never worked out as Burgess had planned.

The other consequence of the Mediterranean series was that it brought about Burgess's resignation from the BBC. On 23 November 1938, Burgess complained bitterly to Harold Nicolson over dinner that he had been forced to cancel a talk with an admiral who was due to speak in the series under pressure from the government because he was expected to say some damaging things. When Burgess told Nicolson that he was going to resign, the latter tried to calm him down and advocated reflection, but three weeks later Burgess went ahead and resigned anyway.[131]

As with so many other aspects of Burgess's life, however, this is only one version of the story. In fact – it was probably a lie. According to David Graham, the admiral's talk was broadcast and, what's more, Burgess was happy with the BBC's handling of the episode. Certain details in Graham's version of events give it credibility. He recalled that one evening at around 8.30 p.m., 'probably Friday, November 18', he took a call from the Cabinet Secretary, not directly aimed at him, of course, but because 'apparently I was the only member of the Talks Department answering his office telephone in BH [Broadcasting House]'. The telephone switchboard operator on duty that evening had worked their way through the list of Talks Department staff, starting with Sir Richard Maconachie and continuing down in seniority until Graham answered the telephone.

> I was the only one on the spot … I picked up the phone to hear: 'Good evening, this is Bridges, Secretary of the Cabinet, speaking. I want you to stop the printing of the *Radio Times*. You are planning a talk by Admiral Sir Herbert Richmond, in your Mediterranean series for Thursday, December 1, National Programme, 8.30 to 9 p.m. This broadcast must not take place. It is of almost equal importance that it should not be announced in the forthcoming issue of the *Radio Times*, next Friday. So I can count on you to make the necessary arrangements?'[132]

At this point Graham was forced to inform Sir Edward Bridges that it was too late; the presses were already running. Bridges apologised on behalf of No. 10 – 'We ought to have read it weeks ago, but unfortunately we only got round to it this evening...' – but said that if the programme was broadcast it would create all sorts of problems for a planned Italian visit by Chamberlain and Halifax.

Ultimately, Graham remembers, Admiral Richmond's talk went ahead with one or two minor editing changes, and no diplomatic incident. He recalled telling his story to Burgess and was later surprised to learn that Burgess had passed it off as his own and exaggerated it for Nicolson's benefit at their

23 November dinner. According to Graham, Burgess had told him 'afterwards, at a departmental Tuesday lunch, that the BBC had stood up to Whitehall and Downing Street pressure very well … If it had not, Richmond (as well as Burgess) would have made no end of a stink…'[133]

On the subject of his resignation, Graham recalls him giving a rather different reason: 'Burgess surprised me by insisting that since the BBC did not agree with him about the need to have a diplomatic correspondent, he could see no point in staying on in such a dim-witted organisation.'[134]

This, however, was just yet more Burgess spin. In his resignation letter, he clearly states: 'I should like to make it clear that my reasons for taking this step do not arise out of any failure to enjoy working under the existing Director of Talks. Guy Burgess, 12.12.38'[135] and when Maconachie interviewed him about his decision Burgess confirmed that he had no 'reason to complain of his treatment'. Although Maconachie described the resignation letter as an 'unwanted bouquet', thereafter senior managers agreed to accept Burgess's resignation with what now looks like indecent haste.

Burgess's sudden departure is most likely explained by his being head hunted by MI6 in some way. The exact mechanism and details are unknown, but it is generally accepted that Burgess was approached by Footman on behalf of MI6 and jumped at the opportunity to join their ranks.[136] It seems that Burgess was 'introduced' in September 1938, three months before he actually resigned from the BBC.[137]

Equally, however, the answer may be hiding in Burgess's BBC file, in a paragraph that was crossed out only four years *after* these events, in March 1943, and can be read today. The crossed out section reveals suspicions on the part of the management that Burgess may have been jumping ship before the BBC was able to push him over the side: 'His resignation, which was voluntary, may be taken to be, to some extent at least, an anticipation of DT's [Director of Talks'] action, who had come to think of Mr Burgess as being capable of excellent work, but whose successes were spasmodic, Mr Burgess being forgetful and unmethodical.' In other words, it didn't look as though he was making the grade consistently, and might have been in line for what today would be called a final written warning prior to dismissal.

In this sense, his departure might actually have been a relief to his managers, which would explain the speed with which events progressed – on 15 December (just three day after his letter was received) that his resignation would become effective on 11 January 1939. There was no invitation to reconsider if he really was doing the right thing, no negotiations and no attempts to persuade him to stay that we know of.

If this thesis is correct, that Burgess was only leaving the BBC to avoid being sacked soon after, then it opens up the possibility that Burgess may have in fact actively sought out Footman in an attempt to engineer a position for himself at MI6.

Whatever the cause, Burgess's first spell in a proper job was coming to an end, and an intriguing new one lay ahead with a place on the payroll of one of His Majesty's Secret Services.

CHAPTER 4

I AM 'ANXIOUS TO APPOINT A MR GUY BURGESS'

BRITISH INTELLIGENCE EMBRACES A KGB SPY, 1938–41

In late 1939, a journalist called Basil Davidson enrolled for a special new unit within MI6 over lunch at Simpson's in the Strand, the home of roast beef in central London. He was told that other recruits were arriving from merchant banks and oil companies. Their new job would be subversion and resistance of one kind or another behind current and future enemy lines. Davidson was told he would be useful 'since you know the Balkans'; his expert subject was Yugoslavia.

Davidson was a little surprised, therefore, to be told his first posting would be Hungary. When he objected that Hungary was not in the Balkans, the recruiter, who was an Australian and whose knowledge of European geography may not have been up to the mark, told him there was now a war on and one should do what one was told.[1]

The MI6 unit in question was called 'Section D', and the man behind it was a Major Laurence Grand of the Royal Engineers. Not without a little ego on Grand's part, and mirroring the fact that the head of MI6 is to this day always referred to as 'C', Grand adopted the designation 'D' for himself, signing all his communications as such.[2] Some said the D stood for Destruction.[3]

Despite the initial confusion, Basil Davidson did eventually get to Yugoslavia, tasked with helping the Partisan resistance alongside James Klugman, the communist colleague of Guy Burgess from Cambridge. Burgess's own time in Section D was, by comparison, a lot less heroic and a lot more manipulative.

Major Laurence Grand had been appointed by the head of MI6 in March 1938.[4] From the outset Grand recommended that Section D should learn lessons from the IRA, from Russia and the experience gained from policing the empire.[5] Until the early months of the war it operated from St Ermin's Hotel in London. To some, it appeared amateur, to others, buccaneering. 'D Section's activities were sometimes done with scant reference to security, and alarmed a number of British diplomatic missions,' says MI6's official history.[6] However, it seemed to have a strong *esprit de corps* and Grand attracted a high degree of staff loyalty.[7]

As with other hazily defined units that were created in the run-up to World War Two, the organisation's functions overlapped with other outfits. In the area of sabotage, for example, its activities overlapped with a War Office unit called GSR, which was later designated Military Intelligence (Research): MI(R). Not untypical of the dysfunctions that characterised some of Britain's early war effort, both GSR and Section D put resources into drawing up plans to sabotage Romania's oil fields to prevent Hitler's war machine from gaining access to them, but completely independently of one another.

Grand also interpreted his brief to include propaganda – he saw it as a form of morale sabotage – but in working on that, Section D overlapped with yet another MI6 unit that was charged specifically with propaganda, a shadowy organisation called Department EH. 'EH' stood for Electra House, the building in which its offices were located on London's Victoria Embankment, also home to Cable & Wireless, a company that was covertly owned by the British government. Department EH, or, to give its official title, 'the Department of Propaganda in Enemy Countries', was set up in spring 1938 and was run by Sir Campbell Stuart, a propaganda veteran from the First World War and someone who was prepared to fight hard to protect his turf.[8] His department established a branch in January 1939 that was specifically concerned with propaganda against the enemy, called the Enemy Publicity Section.[9]

The Major, however, was not one to be troubled by overlaps: 'Grand was pretty bold in his encroachment on the field of other departments even if we judge him by the cosy standards of 1939 or 1940,' wrote the official historian of the organisation that eventually absorbed some of these units, the Special Operative Executive (SOE) after the end of the war.[10] He blamed other departments for having a lack of energy and for being confused, and they in turn quickly came to eye him with suspicion and, later, to resent his activities. Turf wars inevitably broke out and to many it appeared that, in the early part of the war, departments expended more energy in out-witting their rivals in the trenches at home than they ever did in trying to outsmart the enemy.[11]

It was into this state of affairs that Guy Burgess had been 'introduced' in September 1938,[12] although at the time he was still employed full time by the BBC. Recruitment at this time 'was on a personal basis; this was what happened in most expanding departments in the first year of the war, and was not altogether inappropriate for a small organisation working in extreme secrecy'.[13] In effect, this meant that recruits like Burgess were subjected to lit-tle if any initial vetting. Personal contacts and knowledge vouchsafed suitable candidates' reliability and trustworthiness. This was how the old-boy network operated, and it was well known 'that Section "D" was run by GRAND on a basis of direct personal dealings with each officer'.[14] Vetting was staff-intensive and time consuming and in wartime such resources were in extremely short supply. In that outfit, Burgess 'occupied a rather ill-defined role as a "bright ideas" man at GRAND's elbow'[15] and this was a weak link that he exploited without, as far as can be judged, any moral qualms at all.

Burgess was not the only Cambridge spy to capitalise on the inherent laxity of the system to the full: John Cairncross was recruited before the war first by the Foreign Office and thereafter by transfer to the Treasury and Bletchley Park without undergoing significant security checks as far as is known; like-wise Donald Maclean, who was recruited to the pre-war Foreign Office, and Kim Philby, who was recruited initially by Section D with assistance from his friend Guy Burgess.[16] Anthony Blunt, who was initially recruited by military intelligence – and then dropped due to doubts about his Marxist leanings

– was ultimately taken on by MI5, again after some behind-the-scenes help provided by Burgess and, through him, Roger Fulford.[17]

One of Section D's coups was to seize 'the bulk of Amsterdam's industrial diamond stocks (essential for machine tools) and, with the help of two Dutchmen, to bring them safely to England'.[18] Despite the occasional accomplishment, however, it was not an especially successful organisation and experienced more than its fair share of failures. Indeed, one of its sabotage operations was uncovered by Swedish police: it had been so poorly organised and the participants so poorly trained that its failure became a major embarrassment and one factor that would later undermine Grand's position.[19]

Burgess became part of the Section D story not because he was to be turned into a saboteur, but because he knew something about radio. In 1938 the British government was particularly concerned about getting its message across to ordinary Germans who, it recognised, were being fed highly partial news by the heavily controlled German media. Radio was considered to be a key resource. Grand had been involved in this area since the middle of the year and had sought help and advice from the BBC's Director General as early as July 1938.[20]

His idea was for a classic 'black propaganda' operation. Radio programmes would be broadcast in German and, crucially, would appear to be originating from a German radio station. Their message would be distinctly anti-Nazi, and designed to expose as lies the information then being served to the domestic German population by Josef Goebbels.

Another official internal history, this time of the Political Warfare Executive, recorded that Grand had been ordered by his chief (that is 'C', the head of MI6) 'to form immediately a section for the dissemination through all channels outside this country [i.e. outside the UK] of material to enemy and neutral countries'.[21]

Grand's plan originally envisaged setting up a radio station that might have become a kind of Grand Broadcasting Company, GBC, or even the 'D'BC. A variant on this theme was to get foreign stations operating close to the German border such as Luxembourg, Strasbourg and Liechtenstein to broadcast British-made clandestine content to their existing German audiences.[22]

At the height of the Munich crisis the British government had used Radio Luxembourg to broadcast in German translations of speeches by Prime Ministers Neville Chamberlain and Edouard Daladier, Czechoslovak Foreign Minister Edvard Beneš, and an appeal by President Franklin D. Roosevelt because it wanted those messages to reach ordinary German people who were being denied the facts by their own government. The pressure for the broadcasts had emanated from 10 Downing Street in the form of Sir Joseph Ball, and the broadcasting arrangements were handled by Gerald Wellesley, later the seventh Duke of Wellington. The broadcasts, which had run from the early hours of 29 September 1938, 'were discontinued' on 30 September,[23] However, as it soon became clear that Czechoslovakia had not been enough of a prize for Hitler, the idea of broadcasting the British point of view to Germany made a return to the agenda.

Chamberlain's government considered the problem of how to get its message across to ordinary Germans via the airwaves in December 1938, when Lord Halifax advised the Cabinet about use of radio stations in bordering countries: 'The programmes would be submitted to the Foreign Office in advance and careful watch would be kept over them. Any participation by the British Government in these programmes could be effectively concealed.'[24] A few days afterwards, and after the small matter of paying for it had been sorted out, the Cabinet agreed this proposal of 'very considerable importance'.

It was probably this urgency that had led to Burgess's swift, no-questions-asked recruitment. The outbreak of World War Two was just eight months away and somebody who knew about radio production was badly needed.[25] With this new, more important job he would also have been able to show his Russian friends that he was moving much closer to the centre of power. It might have been difficult to explain, however, as Section D was disguised to the outside world as a statistical unit within the War Office, called the 'Department of Statistical Research'.[26]

One of the rare mentions in Burgess's MI5 file during this period says that he 'has an important job in connection with Radio Luxembourg' but also notes that he was 'very pro-German'. That particular quality might be thought rather odd for somebody working on anti-German propaganda, but there is nothing on his file to show that the observation was ever followed up.[27]

Even before he joined Grand's outfit proper, however, Burgess filed a report to Moscow on 19 December 1938 saying, 'My first assignment from Grand was to work on the Jewish question and Palestine'.[28] He was charged with 'activating' his friend Lord Rothschild with the aim of 'split[ting] the Jewish movement' by creating 'opposition towards Zionism and Dr Weitzmann'.[29] This fissure in the Jewish opposition would enable the British to conclude a deal with Arab states, which was seen as crucial in any future war.

Meanwhile, since its inception, Grand's plan had not been progressing well, probably because at the time Section D lacked executive radio expertise. After Munich Grand again asked the BBC for help. In October 1938, the Corporation's Director of Public Relations, Sir Stephen Tallents, suggested that Grand contact someone called Hilda Matheson. She had joined the BBC in 1926 after being recruited by Sir John Reith, becoming Director of Talks soon after in the following year. Among her other achievements she had persuaded H. G. Wells and George Bernard Shaw to broadcast. She had also created *Week in Westminster* and organised the first ever broadcast political debate between politicians from the three main parties. Despite this, however, Sir John Reith had developed 'a great dislike of Miss Matheson and her works' and found her too left-wing. In 1931 she resigned from the BBC.[30]

Before joining the BBC, she had worked for Nancy Astor, who became a good friend, and through her met Lord Lothian, who became her employer after she left the Corporation. He had gone on to become Britain's ambassador to the United States, as well as becoming for a while a member of the Anglo-German Fellowship.

Early in 1939, Hilda Matheson was working with Grand and she proposed the setting up of an organisation called the Joint Broadcasting Committee (JBC). This was to be the public and legitimate cover for MI6's covert radio broadcasting activities – essentially an intelligence-led propaganda operation – and, as such, Matheson quickly set about making sure that the public appearance was in order. She also began establishing overseas contacts, starting with Radio Strasbourg, and gathered about her a group of people ('interested persons', as she called them), that appears mainly to have comprised her many (often high-profile) friends and acquaintances.

It was not long before, in addition to working for Section D, Burgess was ordered to help out at JBC as a radio producer.[31] The committee soon acquired premises just across Chester Square (where Burgess was living at the time, conveniently for him), and, by April 1939, had a list of 'distinguished members'.[32]

A glance at JBC's letter head shows that the chairman was the Earl of Rothes, and Harold Nicolson was one of the committee's eight ordinary board members.[33] Across the boardroom table from Nicolson was the woman, Hilda Matheson, who had had an affair with his wife.

She had launched his broadcasting career and that of his wife, Vita Sackville-West, but things had got a touch complicated. When Vita first went to the BBC in 1928, on one occasion she ended up staying the night with Hilda, who did not report for work the next morning. Matheson wrote to her shortly after the tryst: 'All day – ever since that blessed and ever to be remembered indisposition – I have been thinking of you – bursting with you – and wanting you – oh my god wanting you.' She was unashamed of her sexuality, telling Vita, 'What we feel for each other is all good … I cannot feel one shred of shame or remorse or regret.'[34]

The new relationship upset one of Vita's former lovers, Virginia Woolf, who told her that Hilda affected her as 'a strong purge, as a hair-shirt, as a foggy day, as a cold in the head'. These were possibly qualities that would serve Matheson well at MI6.[35]

By 1938, Hilda had broken up with Vita and was living with Lady Dorothy Wellesley, the wife of Harold Nicolson's good friend and former diplomatic service colleague Gerald Wellesley. Lady Wellesley and Hilda would stay together until Hilda's untimely death while undergoing a routine thyroid operation at the end of 1940.

All three husbands, Harold Nicolson, Leonard Woolf and Gerald Wellesley, were well aware of these relationships.

An official internal report said that one of JBC's objectives had been to 'make the English seem credible and actual human beings to the general public of other countries'. Another was to 'counteract German suggestions that Great Britain has no civilization or culture to defend'. A public leaflet emphasised that the JBC supplemented the work of the BBC, by providing news backgrounders to foreign stations as an aid to explaining the news coming out of Britain and the backgrounds of the people in the news.[36]

The SOE's official history tells how 'the political censorship imposed by commercial stations in their own interests' made it very difficult for Grand's team to persuade them to broadcast any material 'with sufficient "bite" to be of value in approaching a German audience'.[37] In other words, foreign broadcasters were reluctant to use British material that might provoke the Nazis. As a result, the JBC softened its activities and it gradually moved away from clandestine black propaganda into the realm of cultural propaganda. Instead it produced pamphlets, books, recordings and 'miniature gramophone records of violent anti-Nazi propaganda, intended for distribution with other material through D's own channels'.[38]

In carrying out these activities, however, the JBC was seriously duplicating the work done by the British Council – and its Royal Charter. So while Britain was getting ready for an inevitable war with Germany, the British Council was getting ready for an inevitable war with the committee, building up an archive of their documents that was to outlast JBC's own. The BBC was also sensitive to JBC's activities because it felt that its overseas standing could be compromised. When the nation's broadcasters of one kind or another met round the table, the BBC was always suspicious of the motives of the JBC. For Guy Burgess, however, this meant he was able to witness discussions between his former and current employers. He was at one such JBC/BBC meeting on 24 July 1939 that discussed liaison arrangements with the BBC.[39]

As war loomed in the summer of 1939 Burgess was not in the country. Taking advantage of the warm summer weather he and his close friend Anthony Blunt had decided to go on holiday in mainland Europe. The plan was to drive through France to Italy and there spend some time visiting art galleries and some of the country's architectural wonders. Things didn't go quite as they'd hoped, however. Anthony Blunt took up the story in his unpublished memoirs:

In August 1939 Guy and I went for a holiday motoring through France with the intention of going through Italy. However, when we reached Aix-en-Provence Guy found a telegram from Grand (whose section D of SIS he had recently joined) calling him back to London. We drove back to Boulogne at a furious speed, leaving the car in the care of the AA [Automobile Association] representative to be shipped to England when there was space on a boat. On the way we bought a newspaper and read the announcement of the Russo-German Pact.

Late on 21 August, it had been announced that German Foreign Minister Joachim von Ribbentrop had signed a non-aggression pact with Soviet Foreign Minister Vyacheslav Molotov. While Britain and its Western allies were preparing for war, what could have been a crucial Eastern ally against Germany had instead taken itself out of the game and effectively become a friend of the enemy, a friend of fascism. The political shock waves were extensive. Talks taking place between Soviet and British diplomats were torpedoed. British communists were suddenly in a very awkward position.

Blunt described how the news hit them: 'This was an appalling shock to both of us. The purges had been difficult enough to accept… [section deleted by Blunt] … but the pact was far harder to explain away.' Nevertheless, faithful to the Stalinist cause as Burgess was, he tried. Blunt continued:

> I have never known Guy's mind to work so fast. During the day he produced half a dozen justifications for that, of which the principal argument was the one which eventually turned out to be correct, namely that it was only a tactical manoeuvre to allow the Russians time to re-arm before the eventual and inevitable German attack.

What Blunt didn't mention was that Stalin's purges had weakened the leadership of the military forces and that they were not ready to fight a war against Germany. But, according to Blunt, Burgess 'also used an argument which he had frequently brought up in recent months, that the British negotiations which had been going on for an Anglo-Russian pact were a bluff'. This, Blunt says, Burgess 'claimed to know' because 'the delegation sent out to negotiate was of such a low calibre that they were not in a position to settle anything, and further that they had secret instructions not to reach any agreement'. Burgess later told friends he'd dined with 'his chief' who had told him that the objective was to prolong the negotiations without reaching an agreement.[40]

Blunt, who in his unpublished memoirs claims unconvincingly not to have had any independence of thought in the matter – to have been politically naïve – continued:

> That whether or not Burgess was right, I had no means of knowing, but Guy certainly believed it at the time – and no doubt passed on his opinion to his Russian contact. If it was true, or if the Russians believed it to be true, it would have been a powerful reason for negotiating with Hitler. In any case Guy persuaded himself that the pact was justified, and I accepted his reasoning, though with some reluctance.[41]

Blunt and Burgess's masters in Moscow had jumped into bed with their greatest enemy, and in doing so had turned the two men into traitors who could be working in the interests of the potential enemy should war with the Soviets ever break out. Both had started working for the Comintern because it was the only credible bulwark against fascism; now they were agents who would have to do things that would support the political creed they had regarded as so evil.

* * *

Prior to his summer holiday with Blunt, Burgess had passed several reports to the KGB. The first included his belief that the British Chiefs of Staff were convinced that 'a war between Britain and Germany can be easily won' and that the British therefore had no need to enter into a pact with the USSR.[42] Burgess reported to the KGB Neville Chamberlain's foreign affairs adviser '[Horace] Wilson's actual words: "they thought they could avoid a pact with the Russians"'.[43] It is possible that he may have obtained this information from a Foreign Office diplomat and Eton contemporary, Con O'Neill. Some of O'Neill's documents from the period were discovered in Burgess's flat after he disappeared in 1951. Most are still withheld.[44]

Secondly, Burgess relayed a conversation he had had with Grand's deputy, Montague Chidson: 'It is a fundamental aim of British policy to work with Germany whatever happens and, in the end, against the USSR.' To this Burgess added: 'Chidson told me unambiguously that our aim is not to resist German expansion to the East.'[45]

The erstwhile KGB agent also told Moscow about something else that he had learned: Britain was arranging some secret talks with Herman Goering. He conveyed to his KGB controller, Gorski, the 'substance' of a telegram sent by the British ambassador to Germany, Sir Nevile Henderson. Dated 21 August 1939, it apparently said: 'All measures have been taken for Hermann Goering to arrive under secret cover in London on Wednesday 23rd. This will amount to an historic event; we are just waiting for confirmation of this...'[46]

The proposed date for the visit was significant because on that very day it was announced that Molotov had gone to Berlin and had concluded the non-aggression pact with his German counterpart, Ribbentrop.

Of the discussions between the British and Goering – conducted through a Swedish businessman, Birger Dahlerus – historian Andrew Roberts has argued that they were maintained not altogether earnestly. They were deemed useful to convey the message that the British government was 'sticking to its guns' and as a way of bypassing 'Ribbentrop and the Wilhelmstrasse [German Foreign Office] bureaucracy, encouraging Goering in his opposition to war and slowing Hitler's plans'.[47]

It is probable that neither Burgess nor Moscow would have accepted that reasoning, even if they had been exposed to it, because Moscow would not have wanted to take the risk that British policy was sincere.

Years later Cambridge spy John Cairncross revealed himself to be the source of some of the information that Burgess had passed to Moscow:

> Guy Burgess contacted me in July 1939 and said that he was working for
> a secret British agency ... and was in touch with some anti-Nazi German generals linked with an underground broadcasting network (which

was untrue). He told me that he badly needed information for them on British intentions towards Poland, but was unable to get this from the Foreign Office…

Cairncross's career had taken him to the Foreign Office and then to the Treasury, but he nevertheless contacted some former colleagues and Burgess subsequently gave Cairncross some money to enable him to take them to lunch. One of the former colleagues was John Colville, who later became one of Prime Minister Churchill's private secretaries. Cairncross duly passed on what Colville and others told him, together with short notes on those to whom he had spoken, to Burgess and, despite Cairncross asking for these papers to be returned, Burgess never managed to do so.[48] This would have devastating consequences for Cairncross many years later (see Chapter 8).

It is not without the hint of irony that, in passing on all these reports about British intentions, Burgess had in a way played his part in helping to convince Stalin that the British were indeed not to be trusted.

* * *

Amidst the talk of Stalin and Hitler, Chamberlain and Daladier, one other name now pre-occupied Burgess and Blunt. Goronwy Rees, Burgess's heterosexual friend from Oxford, had stayed in touch during his post-Cambridge years. Like Burgess, he had been going through a similar search for a new career and so the pair had met up from time to time to drink, compare notes about their respective sex lives and talk politics. Rees had long since accepted that whenever a choice had to be made at such occasions, down to whether they would be drinking red or white wine that evening, Burgess always prevailed. Even so, as a man of the left, one thing he would challenge was Burgess's newfound enthusiasm for the far right, the reasons for which he judged to be unconvincing.

It was what Rees thought about what he called 'a rather emotional and sentimental book about the condition of the poor' that was to lead to a turning point in the two men's lives. James Handley's *Grey Children: A Study of Humbug and Misery* had been reviewed by Rees in *The Spectator* and, while the reviewer himself made no great claims for his piece, Burgess had read it and responded as if Rees had written a masterpiece. Such was his surprise at this reaction that Rees wondered if he was being made a fool of. But no, 'It shows that you have the heart of the matter in you,' Burgess responded.

'What on earth do you mean?' said Rees. It was at this moment, as they sat in Rees's flat, talking over a bottle of whisky, that Burgess suddenly said, 'There's something I ought to tell you.' He went on slowly: 'I am a Comintern agent and have been ever since I came down from Cambridge.' When Rees expressed his surprise and asked why Burgess was telling him this, he replied: 'I want you to work with me, to help me.'[49]

In Rees's version of this encounter, set out in his memoirs in 1972, he never revealed what, if anything, he had said in response to Burgess's proposal, but he did say that Burgess gave the name of another agent – 'and I don't suppose he could have named a person who could have carried more weight with me', so intelligent and upright was he. It is clear from his description in the book that the name Burgess gave him was Anthony Blunt. Rees promised never to talk to this man about it and, for the time being at least, he kept everything Burgess had told him to himself.

Despite his silence, however, the fact was that Goronwy Rees had information that could have sent both Guy Burgess and Anthony Blunt to jail. He'd kept quiet about what he knew while the Soviets had common cause with the British against the Nazis, but now, given the new circumstances resulting from the Russo-German pact, it was unclear whether his discretion could be relied on any longer.

Blunt and Burgess's best card against Rees in the event of a showdown would be to say that, when he had heard the news of Burgess's role in Comintern, he hadn't just stayed silent, but had to a certain extent gone along with Burgess's request to help him. Blunt believed there had been 'collaboration' between Rees and Burgess, and, indeed, later wrote that for a time Rees had provided Burgess with 'fairly high-grade political gossip from the High Table of All Souls, of which he was a Fellow, and where many former Fellows, some of whom occupied high positions in government or the civil service, often spent the weekend to relax from their official duties.'

He went on:

'I doubt whether Goronwy committed any breach of the Official Secrets Act, because the information he passed on to Guy did not come from official sources. But the fact remains that he did for a period collaborate with him in this way, knowing where the information which he passed to Guy was going.'[50]

The two sides – Burgess and Blunt on the one hand, Rees on the other – most likely awaited their first encounter since the news of the Molotov-Ribbentrop pact with mutual fear and suspicion. Rees later chronicled his version of what happened when Burgess broke off his holiday and returned to Britain:

> Guy appeared in my flat, having driven back from Antibes the moment he had heard the news, left his car at Calais, crossed over by the night boat … he was in a state of considerable excitement and exhaustion; but I thought I also noticed something about him which I had never seen before; he was frightened.

Rees observed how Burgess seemed on edge and 'apprehensive in his behaviour' towards him. He continued:

> When I denounced the treachery of the Soviet Union and … that the Russians had now made war inevitable, he merely shrugged his shoulders and said calmly that after Munich the Soviet Union was perfectly justified in putting its own security first and … that if they had not done so they would have betrayed the interests of the working class both in the Soviet Union and throughout the world.[51]

Rees went on to describe their ensuing conversation in which Burgess asked Rees what he intended to do. Rees says he replied that he expected to be called up for military service. He then said that Burgess asked, 'And what about me … And the Comintern?'

According to Rees, to this question he replied, 'I never want to have anything to do with the Comintern for the rest of my life … Or with you, if you really are one of their agents.' With that, Burgess said that 'the best thing would be to forget the whole thing ... and never mention it again ... as if it never really happened'.[52]

Blunt would later contend that Rees had accidentally admitted his own guilt in his account of the meeting. His own mention of Comintern certainly implied that up to that point Rees had been in on the conspiracy – 'as indeed he was', said Blunt.[53]

Whether Rees's version was accurate or embellished to suit his own ends, the fact remains that after what was doubtless a painful discussion, Burgess and Rees went to have a drink and forgot all about it, probably aided by the volume of alcohol consumed. 'That was the last drink I had with Guy before the war began,' Rees wrote later. 'We drank a great deal, as if we both knew that we were drinking the old world out.'[54]

Questions have since been raised about the veracity of Rees's account. For one thing, it was not written down until more than thirty years after the event and, according to his daughter, Rees was notoriously bad with dates.[55] There has been some suspicion that Rees was also trying to minimise his own role as a KGB agent, allegedly with the codename FLIT (FLEET in some accounts) or GROSS. Indeed, KGB files do confirm that Rees was an agent.[56]

Undeniably, during Goronwy Rees's later years in the army and MI6, he never informed the authorities that he knew Burgess had, at the very least until the 1939 Pact, been a Soviet agent until it was too late to do anything about it (see Chapter 9).

* * *

Meanwhile, in his 'day job' Burgess was showing yet more enterprise in making connections with different government departments. While working for JBC, as a Section D secondee, Guy Burgess was soon appointed JBC's liaison with the Foreign Office, we have discovered, at its own request.[57] It raises the question, however, as to just how the Foreign Office had come to know so much about Burgess and his abilities for him to become their liaison officer of choice. We can only guess that it must have been as a result of the work that he had performed for David Footman a year earlier, as well as the work that he had carried out for Section D. The upshot is that Burgess was by this stage already favourably on the Foreign Office's radar *five years before* he ultimately went to work there.

Soon after that request, and in a meeting summary written by an anonymous Department Electra House official, Hilda Matheson was said to be

> anxious to appoint a Mr Guy Burgess as Liaison Officer with our organisation. I thought that there would be no harm in his meeting the appropriate members of our organisation at Tring, after the organisation had come into being, but there was no suggestion that he should live with us or we should pay him.[58]

He didn't live with them, but he did attend meetings with their officials during the next year, so it looks as though the chemistry worked. As with Burgess's Foreign Office liaison role on behalf of JBC, this was to be yet another part of his Section D/JBC job, an additional duty; in no sense was it a different job for a different employer.

* * *

On 1 September 1939, Germany invaded Poland, and two days later Britain and France declared war on Germany. One of Section D's tasks was preparing contingency plans on how to destroy one of Moscow's economic and industrial lifelines, the oilfields at Baku in the Azerbaijan Soviet Socialist Republic. With his own focus rather more on clandestine radio, this fact may have passed Burgess by, but if he did know, the moral dilemma facing him would have been stark: should he pass the information on to Moscow? Was his allegiance to the fight against fascism or to Stalin's state, which had decided, for its own reasons, to opt out of that fight for the time being?

Remarkable as it now seems, it was only on 5 September 1939 that Section D asked MI5 to vet Burgess. Back came the reply: 'NRA: Nothing Recorded Against'. His record was clean.[59] Eleven days later, on 16 September 1939, Burgess signed the Official Secrets Act. Over nine months after Burgess had begun working for Section D, and during which time he had already had access to countless secret files and papers, Burgess's position was finally formalised.[60] With this access to MI6 files Burgess was undoubtedly able to create opportunities to learn what was going on as well as to discover the names of some people who might be of interest to Moscow.[61] It has also emerged that at roughly this time, although it is not exactly clear when, Burgess was working in some capacity with a propaganda wireless station called Radio Calais and that 'Burgess ... was in touch with ... German communists who worked in Britain'.[62]

As 1939 turned into 1940, the Russo-Finnish 'Winter War' was in full swing. Russian forces had invaded Finland on 30 November 1939 in an effort to take control of territory over which it had claimed legal rights and in order to protect Leningrad, which was close to the Finnish border. During the early months of 1940, the Cabinet considered sabotaging the Soviet oil fields to render assistance to the Finns, as well as sending up to 30,000 trained 'volunteers' to fight alongside them. It came to nothing for fear of provoking Germany to occupy Finland and Sweden.[63]

The situation was complicated, however, because, from the British and French point of view, as the Cabinet was told in early February 1940: 'So long as the Soviet [*sic*] were fully occupied in Finland, they could not be of much help to Germany; and ... it would give us an opportunity of bombing the oil supply at Baku, and thus eliminate the chances of Russia being able to spare oil for Germany.'[64] The Cabinet returned several times to its discussions of sabotaging the Baku oilfields, in collaboration with Romania;[65] and even months after the Finns had concluded a peace treaty with the USSR.[66]

If Burgess ever got to hear about the plans being considered – as well as British plans to declare war on the Soviet Union – it is a safe bet that he would have wanted to tell Moscow. One further complication in Anglo-Soviet diplomatic relations at that time was that Russian military forces were occupying the eastern half of Poland, one of Britain's allies, and the country over which Britain and France had gone to war in 1939. Britain had decided that this particular invasion did not warrant the response of a declaration of war, although files show that the government continued to mull over the question into late 1940.

Following Britain's declaration of war on Germany, Burgess continued to supply Moscow with intelligence, although contacts were difficult and mainly effected through Paris. With the conclusion of the Russo-German Pact, Russia was essentially on the German side, and Burgess was therefore passing information to what was effectively an enemy state. While it appears that whatever Section D plans Burgess encountered he passed on to Moscow, it is not, however, known if Moscow ever passed any of his material – or indeed that received from any of its other British agents – on to Berlin.

* * *

It is at this point that Burgess's professional life looks to have become very confused. By January 1940, he had left the BBC and was working for Section D, as well as the Joint Broadcasting Committee. Irrespective of whom he appeared to work for over the next two years, he was always on the MI6 payroll. (A letter from Hilda Matheson dated 23 December 1939 makes this clear. She refers to 'the section of the intelligence service for which I work...')[67] As a result he managed to inveigle himself into a number of different parts of the covert war effort. Apart from Section D and JBC, these included the War Office and the Ministry of Information, where he was listed as a member of the Foreign Division, which dealt with overseas propaganda and was headed by senior Foreign Office diplomat Ivone Kirkpatrick.[68]

This arrangement enabled Guy Burgess to take part in various Whitehall committees where he might learn something really interesting. In one such meeting we can imagine Burgess's ears pricking up considerably as the assembled group discussed the implementation of propaganda against the USSR and considered a theme that it named 'Communazism'. The meeting was held on 8 February 1940 and discussed the possibility of a broadcast discussion about the theme, something to which it returned on a later occasion.[69]

Burgess's widespread involvements inside the wartime Whitehall machine sometimes ruffled feathers, including the BBC's. In May 1940, J. M. Rose-Troup of the BBC – he had been the Director of Talks when Burgess had nearly become a broadcaster in 1935 –complained to Burgess's employers about his 'reliability'. Troup's note was passed on to Burgess by Colonel Valentine Vivian of MI6. Replying, 'Burgess asked for the opinion of Sir R Maconachie' among others in his defence. 'BURGESS claimed that his unpopularity with the BBC was "through attacking departments from the Ministry of Information".'[70]

In March 1940, Burgess was in Paris, making plans for a broadcast – in French – by his friend Rosamond Lehmann. The arrangements – if they can be called that – were vague.[71] Burgess had

persuaded Miss Lehmann to leave her children, much against her will, and go with him to Paris where he told her she was needed for work in connection with the war effort. She had no precise details from him ... He arrived carrying a diplomatic bag slung over his shoulder and they travelled together. They stayed in the Hotel Crillon and dined together that night. After air raid alarms, the following morning BURGESS took her along to the Radio Diffusion Française.

The story after that is one of confusion and chaos. He arranged a meeting for her with a radio official, which broke up because neither of them knew why they were talking to the other. Burgess later assured Rosamond Lehmann 'that all would be well', but it never was. 'BURGESS vanished only to return later and gave her a good dinner before disappearing again.' After that she decided to return to Britain and Burgess drifted out of her life.[72]

In April 1940, a new sub-section of Section D was formed called D/U. It came directly under Grand, and was described as being for 'a special purpose...'. Burgess was appointed as the assistant to this new section's head. His designation was 'D/U.1'. Later research by MI5 investigators concluded that Burgess's designation may have changed to 'D/US', although it is not clear how they established that fact. Nevertheless, the point is important because in June 1940 'D/US' wrote a memo to Colonel Valentine Vivian proposing the setting up of a school for training agents – 'selected foreigners' – who afterwards would be sent home to train resistance fighters. 'This memorandum is unsigned, but "D/US" indicates that it emanated from the SOE [sic][73] training section to which Burgess belonged ... It is reasonable to conclude', wrote an MI5 investigator, 'that "D/US" who wrote to Vivian was in fact Guy Burgess.'[74]

Shortly after writing this paper, Burgess embarked on another mysterious stage in his wartime career and began to make arrangements to go to Russia. Burgess's old friend Isaiah Berlin had been anxious to help the war effort and had offered his services to the British government, suggesting that with his Russian origin and experience he might help Sir Stafford Cripps's diplomatic mission in Moscow. Despite assistance from Harold Nicolson and Gladwyn Jebb, Cripps had not been keen to accept Berlin and little progress had been achieved. Fifty years later Isaiah Berlin recounted how soon afterwards, and out of the blue, Burgess had gone to Oxford to see him. Burgess freely admitted to Berlin that he hadn't really espoused fascism – as Berlin had believed – saying that it was connected with his work for MI6. Burgess told Berlin that he was going to travel to Moscow on MI6 business and that Berlin could travel with him if he wished.[75] Berlin had no idea why Burgess should be travelling to Moscow, however. MI5 investigators reached much the same conclusion in 1956 when they admitted that 'the reason or pretext for [this trip] has never been known'.[76]

CSS – the Chief of the Security Service – however, appears to have been told about this venture: Burgess was leaving for Moscow as a courier.[77] There is a file in the National Archives that provides some details of the visit – Burgess was to travel carrying diplomatic bags, accompanied by Berlin, presumably to provide a degree of cover for his trip.

Gladwyn Jebb and Harold Nicolson had helped with the arrangements. Burgess even found time to discuss JBC activities with the latter – by then the Parliamentary Secretary at the Ministry of Information.[78] The safer, long way round via America and Japan had been chosen, and they sailed on the SS Antonia, which left Liverpool on 9 July 1940.[79] But Berlin and Burgess never got to Russia. Shortly after arriving in Washington, Burgess was recalled. During his brief sojourn in the US, Burgess made contact with his fellow KGB spy Michael Straight and they met in the capital for dinner. They drank, spoke about Edouard Pfeiffer and the Apostles, including Leo Long, who was also one of Anthony Blunt's KGB recruits, and then Burgess said: 'By the way I have a request to make of you ... I've been out of touch with our friends for several months ... Can you put me back in touch with them?' Straight said he couldn't and wouldn't even if he could. They spoke a little more and then separated. They would not see one another for nearly a decade.[80]

After the plan was cancelled, Berlin was left to make his own way back to Britain, but 'later believed that someone in British Intelligence, perhaps Victor Rothschild, decided that Burgess was too unreliable ... to be trusted and had him recalled'. According to one account, however, it was not Victor, rather it was his sister Miriam, then living in Washington, who was the whistleblower. She had been horrified to find Burgess, whom she knew to be a communist, employed on such a mission and had warned a senior diplomat at the British embassy who cabled London and Burgess was recalled.[81]

Curiously, according to another, later account, Miriam remembered that Burgess was lodged with the British embassy's resident legal representative in Washington, John Foster. According to this version of events, Foster quickly became disturbed by his house guest's habits – including the fact that Burgess didn't appear to wear socks all the time – and swiftly pressed for his recall as he considered him unsuitable.

However, yet another, and possibly more plausible, version has come to light. As Isaiah Berlin had suspected, there is evidence that Victor Rothschild, on hearing that Burgess was en route to Russia, had spoken to Guy Liddell in MI5, mentioning 'BURGESS's unsuitability to go to Moscow'. Guy Liddell was twenty years older than Burgess and was MI5's authority on Soviet subversion in Britain. In June 1940 he became MI5's Director, responsible for counter-espionage. According to this account, 'The reason for his warning was that BURGESS as a drunkard and a homosexual might be useful material for the Russians to work on through blackmail.'[82] However, this is not conclusive. There is no evidence that the warning ever reached Burgess's MI5 file – in fact very little did until his disappearance – and Rothschild only mentioned it to MI5 in 1956. It is not clear whether MI5 checked this out with Guy Liddell, who was then still alive and in touch with his old employers.[83]

Many years later, largely out of a fear that he was more than able to fund libel proceedings, Rothschild himself was a victim 'of innuendo rather than open allegation' of having been a KGB spy.[84]

While Burgess's specific brief for his trip to Moscow is still unknown, it is curious that, a couple of weeks after returning, Burgess saw Harold Nicolson, who recorded in his diary: 'He is still determined to get in touch with the Comintern and use them to create disorders in occupied territory.'[85] Nicolson's diary is impassive as to what Burgess meant by this, and offers no comment about why he needed to establish contact with the Comintern.

* * *

Once back in England, Burgess resumed his work for Section D, but by now he had moved to an out-of-London training establishment – Brickendonbury Hall in Hertfordshire – where he devised and ran a course on sabotage. It was possibly the school that 'D/US' had recommended setting up a few months earlier. One of his fellow tutors was his old friend Kim Philby, with whose recruitment he had helped. While at the school Burgess reported to Moscow that he used the posting for 'learning the names of the agents who were sent abroad and establishing contacts with the offices of SIS and MI5 who I invited to the school to deliver lectures'.[86]

However, by this time his days were numbered. Larger political forces than even he could influence were at work. In May 1940, as a result of the disastrous campaign to save Norway, followed by the catastrophic collapse of the British and French armies in the face of a German onslaught, Britain underwent a change of political leadership. Britain acquired a new Prime Minister, Winston Churchill, and within weeks his new broom began clearing the cobwebs and clutter from the nation's war machine.

An immediate target was the overlapping secret units that were carrying on the war by unconventional means. Churchill's new War Cabinet decided on 22 July 1940 that 'the sabotage service [D]', MI(R) and Department EH were to merge under the control of Dr Hugh Dalton, the Minister for Economic Warfare.[87] A month later, the Foreign Secretary, Lord Halifax, considered that the time had come to divest himself of the responsibilities for 'D' and told Dalton, 'I consider the time has come for you to take over control of these various activities'.[88]

The upshot of this decision was that personnel in Section D were placed under new management. Like new management throughout history, it reviewed and earmarked staff either for retention – this time in a new organisation to be called the Special Operations Executive – or dismissal. In the files is a list of people who had 'been given their *congé* [the sack]'. It continues: 'There will be others to come – probably two or three more, including one BURGESS, who is now employed in the school.'[89]

It is entirely possible Burgess's recent brush with the law had something to do with his being surplus to requirements. On 10 September 1940, it was reported in various newspapers that Burgess had been arrested for 'driving a War Office Car while under the influence of drink'.

In Burgess's defence, his solicitor, Claude Hornby, told the court that his client was

> doing rather confidential work, and for a considerable period had been working over 14 hours a day. On the day in question he had driven up from the country, had been involved in an air raid and after leaving his Chief's flat he was driving a friend home when he was stopped and arrested.

Burgess had 'spent an air raid' with Eric Kessler, the counsellor at the Swiss Legation in London on 9 September. (Maybe as a result of their conversation, Burgess wrote a paper a week later in which he spoke of the 'crying need for British propaganda in Switzerland'. He also detailed Kessler's Swiss background and connections in the report.)[90]

The arresting police officer told how 'Moncy-Burgess [*sic*] collapsed into his arms, and when told he would be arrested murmured, "Right-O"'.

Remarkably, the magistrate criticised Burgess's commander: 'Judging by the rank of your chief . . . He is an older man than you and it was very wrong of him to send a young man out with the car, having given him more drink than was advisable.' Burgess, who was listed as having two addresses, was ordered to pay five guineas in costs.[91]

Whatever the reason for his dismissal, it is generally held that Burgess was sacked some time in this month (September 1940). However, newly released files at the National Archives show that he probably continued working for a rump of Section D for longer than previously thought since, according to MI5 investigators, Burgess was still writing papers during the whole of September and October 1940. For instance, on 29 September, they report that 'BURGESS was still employed by Section "D" and still managing to get a look at SIS [MI6] files'. They knew this because he wrote a note on that day about a German SIS agent, Wolfgang zu Putlitz. In the memo Burgess mentioned that 'he had had a few private words with Captain LIDDELL [of MI5]' and that the note should be passed on to him. A few days later, on 7 October, Col. Vivian did so, but said he was 'not content that SIS files should be handled by Section D'.[92] In what looks like an early reflection of the fact that MI6 and SOE had already got their relationship off on the wrong foot, he added, 'I have made arrangements to obviate this.'[93] The relationship would remain 'professional' for much of the war.

After October 1940, however, the Burgess trail goes cold. In 1955, MI5 was still trying to assure itself that 'we should ... like to be sure that he was given no other job' during November and December 1940, including 'any trace of a temporary job'.[94] The problem had been compounded by the fact that Section D's files were all destroyed. There is no evidence, however, that Burgess played any role in their destruction.

The only thing we can be certain of is that by the end of 1940, just a few months short of his thirtieth birthday, Guy Burgess had been sacked from MI6 for 'irreverence'. By now a senior figure at the Foreign Office, Gladwyn Jebb later took credit for weeding Burgess out, feeling, 'He was quite extraordinarily dissolute and indiscreet and certainly unfitted for any kind of confidential work.'[95] (Though this did not appear to prevent Jebb and Burgess from meeting socially during the war.)

Guy Burgess now needed a job ... and fast.

CHAPTER 5

'EVERYONE UNDER THE SUN'

NETWORKING AT WESTMINSTER, 1941–44

S ir Richard Maconachie, Director of Talks, was from one of the old-est of old schools of BBC executives. When he was appointed in 1936, he'd never worked in broadcasting but had a reputation as 'a master of the pen', an essential part of the BBC manager's skill set. He'd spent six years as the British Minister in Kabul and had built up what the official BBC historian, Asa Briggs, called 'a Kiplingesque dossier of deeds wrought on the Indian frontier'.[1]

Given his position, therefore, some of his staff never quite understood why Sir Richard allowed Guy Burgess to re-join the BBC. But, half a century later, the reason is becoming clearer, and it partly explains why Burgess would say of him, 'Of many chiefs in many offices in now more than one country, Maconochie [*sic*] was for me the most beloved.'[2]

A file about Burgess that was only opened by the BBC Written Archives in July 2014, from which 'papers of a confidential nature have been removed', helps tell the story of the return of Burgess to the Corporation. One memo in particular, from the BBC's Director of Staff Administration, D. H. Clarke, reported: 'Burgess resigned from the staff in December 1938 and simultane-ously or shortly after got a job in the Secret Service. He is now resigning from that and wishes to come back to us.' (Clarke was an old sparring partner of Burgess's from the days when rows about staff photos and pay rises were common.) This memo reveals that Clarke knew Burgess had been involved in hush-hush work but was for some reason under the impression that Burgess was resigning in order to rejoin the BBC, rather than being sacked.

Clarke's memo also said that Sir Richard Maconachie 'regarded him as potentially one of his best people but as you know he sat loose to his job and proved a bit of a nuisance'. It also revealed that Maconachie had

> kept in touch with him [Burgess] regularly and is anxious now to have him back on the established staff ... Burgess has assured [Maconachie] that he has grown up since leaving us and that if he comes back he will behave himself. There may be some risk in taking him back but since the risk is [Maconachie's] and he is willing to take it, I propose to agree.[3]

Maconachie, the person to whom Burgess had written the resignation note that was described as an 'unwelcome bouquet' had for whatever reason kept in close touch with Burgess after the resignation, which suggests that maybe the bouquet wasn't as unwelcome as it had appeared.

Sir Richard Maconachie was, indeed, prepared to take the risk. As far as we know, however, he was not a gambler. But he was closer to Burgess than has previously been thought. Burgess had, after all, given Maconachie's name to 'Vee-Vee' in the face of Rose-Troup's criticisms in May 1940.

Guy Burgess's MI5 file barely covers the war years. However, inside is a memorandum written by Burgess's friend, Anthony Blunt. It is dated April 1943 and is addressed to Blunt's MI5 boss, Guy Liddell: 'You asked me for a note on the position about Guy Burgess. As you know I spoke to Sir Richard Maconochie [sic] and explained to him our needs. He was entirely willing to help...' Blunt continued: 'Burgess has been working for us for some time and has done extremely valuable work – principally the running of two very important agents whom he discovered and took on.'

Blunt then went on to say:

> The reason for wanting to see Maconochie [sic] at this particular stage was that a re-arrangement of duties was contemplated in the BBC which might have deprived Burgess of the direction of a particular series of talks

which put him in a very useful position from.

ochie [*sic*] is quite prepared to arrange things so the

provided that the DG is aware of our plans for preventing.

called up. In view of the particularly delicate work which he is

the basis of these talks, it would be preferable in talking to Foote[‡]

only to mention his activities in running the two agents for us. It might

also be advisable to be a little bit vague about the exact moment at which

we asked for his reservation. This was in fact at least six months ago, but

Foote [*sic*] might resent it slightly if he realised how long this arrange-

ment had been going on without his knowledge.[4]

It looks as though the reason why Maconachie was prepared to take the risk with Burgess is because he was taking it on MI5's behalf.

This is significant because it shows that Blunt arranged for MI5 to place Burgess inside the BBC and there to have him protected by Sir Richard Maconachie. It was all dressed up as being for the benefit of MI5, but in reality it was for the benefit of the KGB that this had been arranged.

Blunt's reference to 'a particular series of talks which put him in a very useful position from our point of view' could allude to programmes which Burgess is known to have been involved in during the early part of 1943, such as *Home Guard* – a weekly talk about home defence – *Week in Westminster*, or *Industrial Forum*, which covered the industrial production subjects.

After Burgess's defection one MI5 employee (referred to only as 'BK'), but who knew Burgess, Blunt and others, mentioned to an unnamed MI5 officer that after working for MI6 Burgess 'went to the BBC where he associated with Communists and she [BK] consequently wondered whether he was really a Communist himself, or was acting as an agent for MI5'.[5] It was an interesting observation, raising the prospect that Burgess could have acted as an MI5 mole inside the BBC.

Handwritten notes in Burgess's BBC staff file record that Burgess was 'free any time' and so, exactly two years after Burgess had stopped working for the BBC and joined MI6, he was back.

‡   R. W. Foot was one of two wartime BBC joint Directors General

There are two other small, handwritten pencil memos in Burgess's BBC file that are undated and unsigned, and appear to be notes made in what was probably an interview of sorts. They are also almost certainly written by the Assistant Director of Talks, by this time George Barnes. The handwriting looks like his, but, importantly, one of the sheets features a doodle of a warship. Barnes was known to be keenly interested in naval history and had co-edited eight volumes of private papers of the fourth Earl of Sandwich, who, among other things (including being the 'inventor' of the eponymous sandwich), was a former First Lord of the Admiralty.

The two sheets, it can reasonably be concluded, therefore, are probably notes taken by Barnes in a discussion with Burgess some time around the middle of January 1941. They contain among other things a crucial line of text which sheds some light on the events of November 1938 and Burgess's resignation: 'MI applied for him to be seconded. BBC unwilling. Resigned and joined MI'. But there is also a name: 'Sir Frank Nelson'. Nelson was the boss of the part of the SOE that had absorbed Section D's propaganda arm. Barnes could call him to check out the story – Burgess had given him Nelson's phone number. Under the picture of the warship was another name at the bottom of the page, although no indication why it was there: 'M o I - Peter Smollett (26)'.[6]

George Barnes might have had other things on his mind at this time, however. A month earlier – on 20 December 1940 – Harold Nicolson, the junior minister at the Ministry of Information, saw Barnes and told him that his elder stepbrother, Jim, was 'speaking for the Italians on their wireless to England'. Nicolson felt it might 'prove awkward for him if it is learnt that the Italian Lord Haw-Haw has a brother in a high position at the BBC'.[7] After the war the Allies tried to prosecute Jim Barnes for treason, but without success.[8] As it turned out, George Barnes's own career in broadcasting was not affected by his stepbrother's.

On the other immediate matter on Barnes's mind, the re-employment of Guy Burgess, there was one hurdle to be overcome – the chance that he might be called up for military service. The Corporation began preparing the case to get his name added to the reserved list, meaning that his call-up would be deferred. The stated reason given was that he was already trained at the BBC and was therefore extremely valuable.[9] In his time outside he had 'been in constant touch with government departments', and 'Mr Burgess has to an extent not perhaps possessed by other members of the Department "the propaganda mind".' Barnes pointed out that this phrase 'was used of him to me in conversation with Mr Harold Nicolson', a nice piece of name-dropping of a government minister.[10]

For Burgess, with the return to the BBC in 1941 came the chance to produce a broadcast by another KGB spy; one he knew well and had worked with in Whitehall. They had a mutual friend, who was also a KGB spy, and Burgess would soon produce a broadcast by that spy's future wife, whose name was Aileen Furse, later Aileen Philby.[11]

This previously unknown episode in the Burgess story came to light as a result of research within the BBC's written files archive at Caversham outside Reading, in which a handwritten memorandum headed 'Mr Burgess' and signed by Barnes, Assistant Director of Talks, was found and specially declassified. In it, Burgess was told: 'I have pencilled in Harry Smollett for Friday 14 March 9.20–9.35 pm as "I was there: the Germans enter Prague March 14 1939".'[12]

Harry 'Peter' Smollett was born in Austria in 1912. His birth name was Hans Peter Smolka and his family made a small fortune from manufacturing safety ski bindings in a factory at Schwechat during the 1920s and '30s.[13] As far as is known he had first travelled to London in 1930 when MI5 opened up a file on him (PF 41490). In December 1930 the French security authorities told MI5 that they had expelled Smollett from France after he had been found photographing inside the military fortification of Fort Saint-Jean in Marseilles. In 1931, the year when Benito Mussolini formed an alliance between Italy and Nazi Germany, he was reported by Special Branch to be a 'spy in the pay of Italy', which was rather contradicted when his post was intercepted and a letter was seen in which he was addressed as 'Comrade'. He was followed and was seen photographing 'some sandwich men, a pavement artist, etc. while looking at London'.[14]

Since 1933, Smollett had been a London correspondent for the Austrian paper *Neue Freie Presse* and it is suspected that he may already have been a Comintern agent by then.[15] In London he established himself as an author and a public speaker on the Russian arctic, which he had visited and published a book about, *Forty thousand against the Arctic: Russia's polar empire.*[16] There was a vacuum of information about such regions so some observations were allowed to pass unchallenged. One history of the KGB said that the 'most ingenious fabrication in Smolka's book was his portrayal of the hideous brutality of the gulag during the Great Terror as an idealistic experiment in social reform'.[17] But Smollett's defenders say that he later recanted and openly asked himself how he could have been so blind to the evidence that was before his eyes.[18]

During the second half of the 1930s, Smollett continued to travel widely – including to the United States – writing articles about his experiences as he went. It was during this period that Smollett became a partner with Kim Philby in a short-lived London-based press agency.[19] They had met through Philby's then wife, Litzi Friedman, whom Smollett had known since childhood, and mixed with socially in London, which is how Smollett probably first met Burgess. Philby soon began making his own name reporting on the Spanish Civil War for *The Times* while Smollett became a broadcaster and got a job with the Exchange Telegraph company. Their agency may have failed, but the experience suggested to Philby that he and Smollett ought to work together again.

Decades later, Philby told his Russian biographer that Smollett was 'a hundred percent Marxist, although inactive, lazy and a little cowardly'.[20] His views about Smollett's political leanings were to some extent shared by George Orwell, whose own perception was that Smollett was a crypto-communist, a 'very slimy person'.[21]

Late in 1938, Smollett had become a naturalised British subject and changed his name by deed poll from Hans Peter Smolka to Harry Peter Smollett.[22] The publisher George Weidenfeld – also originally from Vienna – remembered the 'buccaneering' Smollett and recalled that one of his good friends was the British communist leader Harry Pollitt. He recalled a ditty about Smollett: 'If Smollett can turn into Smolka, Why can't Pollitt turn into Polka?'[23]

As war loomed, he appears to have made several attempts to get a position with British Intelligence.[24] All failed. Instead, Smollett was recruited by the British Ministry of Information (MoI), initially serving in the Foreign Division. His personal file shows that MI5 warned the Ministry against appointing him, but assurances from Rex Leeper of the Foreign Office removed this barrier and 'much to the discomfiture' of MI5, Leeper won.[25]

Undoubtedly his linguistic abilities helped him considerably. Indeed, the Ministry invited Smollett to join on the very day the war broke out (a Sunday) on a personal salary of £1,000, which placed him on almost the same income as his director.[26] Even its own ministers regarded the MoI as a hopefully short-lived wartime necessity, Harold Nicolson writing that if it 'were to become a beloved feature of our political life, then I should indeed feel that something had gone very wrong with the mental and spiritual health of my countrymen'.[27] For Peter Smollett, however, it was a beloved feature of his espionage life.

It was just at about the time that Smollett joined the MoI that Philby made his approach to work with him for the KGB. Philby's account has elements of espionage fiction: 'Listen, Hans,' he remembered saying,

> 'If in your present job you come across some information that in your opinion could help me in my work for England' – and I winked at him – 'come over to me and offer me two cigarettes. I'll take one, you'll keep the other, that will be a signal you want to tell me something important.'

Smollett was hooked, and acquired the codename ABO.[28] Shortly afterwards, Philby gave Burgess 'a wink' about Smollett, apparently, meaning that he was one with them.[29]

Smollett and Burgess had been colleagues in the Foreign Division of the Ministry of Information,[30] one of Burgess's interlocking roles at the time, and in March 1940, they had jointly authored a memorandum about a proposed radio propaganda bulletin.[31]

For some time afterwards Philby apparently fretted that his new agent ABO might give the whole game away through his amateurism. But then Philby's own amateurism had not helped either. He had recruited Smollett without bothering to ask his Russian controllers first – this was a breach of Soviet spycraft. Not only this, but Philby had also committed another infraction by revealing Smollett to Guy Burgess. This second transgression meant that there was always the possibility – no matter how remote – that, under any future interrogation, Smollett could identify *two* Russian spies. Later, as a result of his war duties, Philby was not always able to get to London to meet Smollett. So, instead, his friends Burgess and Blunt lent a helping hand and met Smollett in his place. When Moscow Centre found out, it was highly upset, not only because their permission had not been sought, but because Smollett by then knew *three* other members of the Cambridge ring.[32] As we shall see in the next chapter, Philby's action had consequences.[33]

With all this mutual background it should come as no surprise that, in 1941, instructed by his BBC boss to contact Smollett, Burgess wrote to 'My Dear Peter' and offered him twelve guineas for a talk on the radio.[34] Peter Smollett replied to 'My Dear Guy' and the programme went ahead on the subject of the Nazi entry into Prague in 1939, which Smollett had reported for a previous employer, the Exchange Telegraph news agency. The Foreign Office had helped to get Smollett out of Prague.

A search through the BBC's sound recording archive has revealed that a copy of the programme survives. The recording of Peter Smollett's voice (complete with introduction by a continuity announcer) might just be the only surviving example of a BBC radio broadcast by one KGB spy, and produced by another. Lasting just over fifteen minutes, the programme allowed Smollett to describe his impressions of Prague on the day when German troops entered the city in 1939 and occupied it. His English was polished: fluent and with a slight accent, but very confident and expressive, dramatic and well-modulated.[35] Smollett even sent in some evidence of a positive audience reaction, typed out on Ministry of Information notepaper.

Probably the most important series that Burgess produced during this second period at the BBC was the weekly political programme *Week in Westminster*, 'WinW' in BBC shorthand. Barnes instructed Burgess to take over the programme 'from Saturday, 4th October'.[36] Within eight months of rejoining BBC radio in 1941, Burgess was responsible for preparing and evaluating speakers, timing the scripts, editing them, as well keeping up to date and well-informed on parliamentary activities and issues.

Initially called *The Week in Parliament*, *Week in Westminster* had first been transmitted on 6 November 1929, but had been suspended from the outbreak of war in 1939. In its resurrected form in early 1941, the series aired initially on Friday evenings before moving to a regular slot on Saturday evenings after the popular entertainment programme *In Town Tonight*. The audience reports showed there were not significant drops when *WinW* took over the airwaves. Broadcast each week that Parliament was in session, *WinW* was an important programme and producing it an important job.[37]

While he worked on *Week in Westminster*, Burgess realised the broadcasting potential of politicians such as Douglas Houghton, John Strachey – one of his friends and a distant relation of George Barnes – and Tom Driberg, who had been elected an MP in a wartime by-election and came to know Burgess at this time. Sixty-five years later, Stella Rimington, a former head of MI5, reviewing a list of the programme's participants while Burgess was the producer, with more than a hint of incredulity in her voice, described them as 'everyone under the sun'.[38]

As a part of his work on the programme, Burgess was required to develop his political contacts within Parliament, part of which had decamped to Church House after the Palace of Westminster had been damaged by bombing. For this he was able to call on the support and assistance of his friend Harold Nicolson, particularly after the latter left the Ministry of Information and became a governor of the BBC.

Burgess produced over a hundred editions of *WinW* between 1941 and 1944 and Harold Nicolson's unpublished diaries reveal that the pair sometimes discussed the programme and potential speakers during Nicolson's visits to Broadcasting House for governors' meetings, or over a drink after they had finished. For instance, Nicolson and Burgess discussed recommending the only communist MP, Willie Gallacher, as a speaker.[39] When it was proposed, the other parties agreed because Gallacher was a good orator, knew the rules and played the game. He appeared on the programme on 12 June 1943.

The political parties delivered the weekly talk in rotation, and Burgess and his bosses preferred to draw on a relatively small pool of MPs, a number of whom appeared several times. Megan Lloyd George MP (Independent Liberal) topped the list of regulars with sixteen appearances and was considered to be one of the best performers. Lord Hailsham later recalled from his five appearances as Quintin Hogg MP that Burgess was 'a brisk, intelligent and professional producer. If he was a little given to drink and plying his customers with drink, well that was all right.'[40] David Maxwell Fyfe, the MP, lawyer, future Nuremberg War Crimes Trial prosecutor and Home Secretary, also notched up five programmes under Burgess's supervision and was regularly consulted by him. No Member of Parliament who worked with him seems to have had a bad word to say about Burgess and, indeed, many felt he had helped give them a start in becoming known to a wider audience.

There have been suggestions that Burgess's involvement in *Week in Westminster* gave him unfettered opportunities to manipulate, to decide who should address the national audience about events in Westminster. But, as always in a large organisation, things are never quite so simple.

The wartime BBC was officially and practically overseen by the Ministry of Information, whose minister from mid-1941, Brendan Bracken (a close confidante of Winston Churchill), was very active. There was also another government department with a great interest in broadcasting: the Foreign Office. The Foreign Secretary, Anthony Eden, was involved in many spheres, as well as being responsible for both MI6 and, from late 1943, MI5. In addition, there were BBC committees, the chief whips of the political parties at Westminster, senior BBC Talks Department management and a whole host of other BBC executives with a view on who should be allowed to speak to the nation about events in Westminster.

Burgess might propose, but others usually disposed. For instance, soon after he joined the programme, Assistant Director of Talks Norman Luker was asked by Director of Talks George Barnes to provide a Conservative speaker. The pressure had originated from 'upstairs' in the form of the powerful Controller (News Coordination) A. P. Ryan. On 16 October 1941, for instance, he wanted a name 'by one o'clock today' because he had been unimpressed by the previous Conservative speaker on the programme and wanted to suggest an alternative to Brendan Bracken at the MoI.[41] Burgess coordinated a list of five recommendations from colleagues: Sir Archibald Southby, Sir Derrick Gunston, Irene Ward, Alexander Erskine-Hill and Vyvyan Adams, who was Burgess's own suggestion because he had a 'fair record as reader'. The latter, whether by chance or design, also happened to be married to the person who almost turned Burgess into a broadcaster back in 1935, Mary Adams. From the surviving and incomplete list of MPs and journalists who delivered the weekly report, none of the names Burgess compiled ever made it to the microphone during the three years that he produced the programme.

There have been suggestions that Burgess was instrumental in putting on the air Hector McNeil, a Labour MP who would become a post-war Foreign Office Minister and in whose private office Burgess would work. However, memos in the BBC written archive reveal that the suggestion that McNeil should be considered for the programme first emanated from Andrew Stewart, the Scottish Programme Director (Glasgow) in 1942. McNeil had to wait eighteen months to get onto the programme, but once on air he broadcast another three times in successive months for Burgess the producer.[42] A friendship was thus formed between the two men.

There are a number of examples of times when Burgess was merely told who to invite and what to do, orders that on some occasions he seemed to ignore. In 1942, Burgess was told that the 'BBC chairman' had suggested F. J. Bellenger MP as a potential speaker. The correspondence shows Burgess wasn't keen. He described the MP as a lightweight and potentially bad for the programme. The BBC's joint Director General, Sir Cecil Graves, responded, 'Because a man is a light-weight ... it doesn't follow that he mightn't turn out a faultless broadcaster.' Burgess appeared to yield, but Bellenger did not appear on the programme while Burgess was its producer.[43]

The problem with assessing Burgess's work at the BBC, and what, if any, influence he had over the public as a result, is that every action is potentially, and invidiously, viewed through a KGB distorting lens. There were invariably times when Burgess was playing the role of diligent BBC producer, trying to make the best fist of things. Indeed, other files show that Burgess's

Talks assistant colleagues were also handling their own business in much the same way.

There have been suggestions that Nicolson and Burgess formed an exclusive coterie that proposed and disposed of MPs, and that in this Burgess was able to mastermind who spoke about Parliament's week to British audiences. However, the evidence in the BBC's files reveals just how complex and sensitive the programme was, and therefore this suggestion has no basis in fact.

However, there are one or two surviving glimpses that do show the pair working on new speakers. For example, on 8 September 1943, Nicolson wrote to Burgess about the Conservative MP Captain Peter Thorneycroft:

> Dear Guy,
> As I have often told you I don't think we take sufficient trouble to secure and train possible Conservative speakers. One of the brighter Tories is Peter Thorneycroft and it might be a good thing if you could get him and see whether he would make a good broadcaster.
> Yours ever,
> Harold

The next day, Burgess replied that he had Thorneycroft on his list. He began the letter with 'Really, Harold' and continued:

> I had a meeting with him with a view to the *Week in Westminster*. I confess that my impression, at this meeting, was that, nice though Thorneycroft is, neither his voice nor his intellect appeared likely to be an answer to the Central Office's prayer. (Even leaving out the BBC – as one so often has to do with the so-called Right). He seemed very ordinary indeed, and this is a quality which only makes for success in broadcasting when it is pushed to the point of genius. However, it looks very much as if I shall have to fall back on him so perhaps I shouldn't have said any of this.[44]

The exchange neatly illustrates not only the easy relationship between Nicolson and Burgess, but also some of the complexities of which each was aware.

Peter Thorneycroft, when he became a Cabinet minister in the mid-1950s, would reappear in Burgess's story, and would tell the House of Lords in 1989 that during his four appearances on the programme he had got to know Burgess 'very well'. Indeed, he 'knew everyone very well', he said, and 'was considered ideal in that particular world'.[45]

Probably more important for the KGB than *what* was broadcast, however, was what Burgess learned before and after the broadcast while entertaining MPs at the House of Commons, by keeping his ears to the ground, and his eyes open. *Week in Westminster* provided ample opportunities for picking up political tittle-tattle and Burgess would be able to prise more information from the unwary or those who wished to please him in pursuit of developing their public profile. He would have been able to report to the KGB not only the political gossip, but also the political mood in a way that certainly the newspapers were not able, as well as messages that Soviet diplomats might not be gathering. That didn't always mean that what was sent to the KGB was accurately translated, understood and summarised by those handling it on the way. While the KGB in Moscow was comparatively well-resourced, it was a considerable challenge to keep abreast of the dispatches sent to it.

The KGB was already aware that one of Burgess's assets was his 'wide circle of contacts' and his ability to 'make friends with almost anyone'. However, his enthusiasm could run away with itself: 'His initiative must be contained almost all the time and he must be controlled very rigidly.' If he was to be an effective agent, he must do as he was told and only go after the information and contacts that Moscow thought would be useful to it. Moscow was aware that each assignment 'should be defined in every minor detail' and that it was 'necessary to keep a watch on his private life' and all his friends.

According to one source, the material released from Burgess's KGB file shows only that the bulk of the documents that he supplied in wartime were those that he received from Section D – including weekly information bulletins 'based on Foreign Office intelligence information'.[46] But that implies that thereafter he delivered little of practical value from 1941 until he made his next career move in the middle of 1944, which seems unlikely, given

Burgess's intellectual restlessness. It is more likely that he provided character sketches of people that he met professionally while at the BBC and made notes about political conversations. Other sources do show that he was in contact with his KGB agent handler in wartime London and it is unlikely that they met simply to pass the time of day, given the inherent security risks involved. However, the reports that he made would clearly have been in a different class to the 'hot', war-related material that Philby, Blunt, Maclean and Cairncross are now known to have been passing on.

London in 1941 was described as 'easily the most productive legal residency' for the KGB. In that year alone, for instance, the British-based agents supplied Moscow with 7,867 classified political and diplomatic documents – 715 of which were on military matters, 127 on economic affairs and 51 specifically on British Intelligence.[47]

Burgess saw the opportunity to develop the flow of information still further by joining a private dining club to make new contacts. He asked his boss, George Barnes, whether the BBC would foot the bill for him and his guests: £2 a head; ten shillings for food and thirty for drink. Barnes managed to suppress his alarm and dampened it down by insisting on a drinks bill of a few shillings – wine would be off the menu.[48]

Since his return, Burgess had been a regular thorn in the sides of BBC administrators. Predictably, within minutes of sitting down again at a BBC desk, he re-launched his tilts at officialdom about his salary. At £540 per annum (some £200 greater than when he had left the BBC in 1938), he argued that in government service he had earned more (and tax free), and that if he had never left the BBC his salary would have been greater. Almost as predictably, but this time after minimal consideration, he was told in no uncertain terms that he would have to put up and shut up.

During this time Burgess was working at the Langham Hotel, just across the road from Broadcasting House. It had been converted into BBC offices. On one occasion, it seems, Burgess had wanted to collect some papers from his room there, but had found the way barred by a locked door. In May 1941, a security official wrote of the incident: 'I found that the door of Room 316 had been damaged in an attempt to force it open by using a fire extinguisher, the contents of which were spread all over the carpet outside ... The whole incident was most unsatisfactory, and I must add uncalled for.' Burgess was, perhaps, a little the worse for wear, according to BBC security staff (he had the distinct scent of alcohol on his breath) and had become angry with them, as well as arrogant and somewhat abusive.

Four days later, Burgess wrote a fulsome, if pompous and sarcastic, report about the incident. 'I am extremely sorry that any individual should feel injured by the manner in which I raised the question of getting into my room at the Langham Hotel to remove some urgently necessary papers last Thursday. Also that the Department should not in any way be injured by this.'[49]

What is perhaps remarkable about what has come to be called 'the Langham Incident' is that Burgess should have blotted his copybook so badly within months of rejoining the Corporation and escaped relatively unaffected. If he was under stress, as has been suggested, it is difficult to see from where it emanated. He was still several months away from being appointed to work on *Week in Westminster*, so it could not have been the stresses and strains of that particular job. Equally surprising is that after the incident his bosses decided to take a gamble and appoint him to the highly politically sensitive programme in which he would be expected to rub shoulders with MPs of all shades of political opinion. Perhaps his protector, Sir Richard Maconachie, helped. It is difficult to see how a behavioural problem like this could have been entirely overlooked after the first rush of memos had died down without some unseen strings being pulled.

In January 1943, it was his expenses that began to catch the eye of BBC administrators. A Mr O. Thompson felt unable to certify Burgess's expenses sheet: 'His office hours are very flexible – he is rarely here before 10.45 a.m. since he reads his papers and Hansards at home and spends most of the day out of the office making contacts.' Soon after it was the issue of why Burgess always travelled first class. He argued he had 'successfully established the principle' and saw no reason why he 'should alter my practice when on BBC business particularly when I am in my best clothes to attend a [funeral] Service'.[50] Dragged into the row, the long-suffering head of the department George Barnes decided: 'There is no case for Mr Burgess travelling first class.'

In April 1943, the Administrative Officer (Home) at the BBC, G. J. B. Allport, wrote a memo to the Controller of the Home Service headed 'Guy Burgess and the Week in Westminster'. His main concern was the money Burgess was spending in the parliamentary bar and his practice of lending out BBC secretaries to do typing for MPs. 'We shall soon get a bad name at the Treasury,' he said, and 'I cannot believe that it is not possible to do business with responsible MPs except at the bar. You will notice that the same names crop up fairly frequently, Quintin Hogg, D R Grenfell etc., while there is almost continual entertaining to Lobby correspondents.' Allport concluded: 'I do not know whether it is my business to say this, but I feel someone will be asking before long whether it would be better to have a rather older person in charge of this series.'[51]

Early in 1941, senior counter-espionage officer Guy Liddell wrote in his diary that he and four other MI5 and MI6 people, all of whom Burgess knew – Jack Curry, Roger Hollis, Valentine Vivian and David Footman – met to talk about

> building up some organisation to deal with contemporary social movements. Our objective is to collect authenticated inside information on important politico-social movements in all European countries and Great Britain and the United States ... It is suggested that [Roger] Fulford and possibly [Guy] Burgess will undertake this work in close co-operation with Footman.

It never seems to have come to anything, but the potential MI5–MI6 collaboration involving Burgess and Footman suggests that Burgess's sacking from Section D had not blemished his reputation too much.[52]

Burgess's letter of appointment to the BBC had included the line 'You agree to devote the whole of your time and attention to the service of the Corporation and to attend a duty such hours of the day or night' – in other words, the BBC wanted his full attention. However, Burgess also found time to run agents for MI5. Indeed, recruiting him for a permanent position had been considered, but, as Jack Curry, a senior MI5 officer, later wrote: 'Roger

Fulford and I were invited to meet David Footman in 1941 ... To consider a suggestion that B[urgess] should be employed under Roger ... I decided not to him employ him. My reasons cannot be simply stated but they concerned his bent and his character.'[53] It now transpires that the initiative to get Burgess recruited had been Footman's. [54]

Despite this failure to get a job in MI5, records show that Burgess's principal agent, codenamed ORANGE, was the press attaché in the Swiss embassy, Eric Kessler. Kessler was the person with whom he had shared an air raid shelter on 9 September 1940.

Kessler was a homosexual friend of Burgess and he passed on information about Nazi activity, but also gossip and other information that he picked up on the London wartime diplomatic circuit. The reception rooms and bedrooms of London's major hotels were a particularly useful hunting ground for intelligence agencies of all kinds and Burgess used Peter Pollock, his most regular boyfriend alongside Hewit who accepted that Pollock was the love of Burgess's life. Pollock's grandfather had founded Accles and Pollock, a prosperous Midlands engineering company, and was from a family of gentlemen farmers. Burgess first met him in Cannes in 1937 when Pollock was sixteen and is said to have been so struck by Pollock's beauty that he showed him off to Lord Alfred Douglas, whose own legendary looks were partly to blame for Oscar Wilde ending up in Reading Jail.[55]

Burgess arranged for Pollock to flirt with rich homosexuals visiting major hotels in London and was sometimes tasked by him with staying in touch with agent Kessler. Pollock believed his job was also Burgess's way of keeping him available in London: 'I lived in the Savoy and the Dorchester, for which MI5 or 6 – I couldn't tell the difference – paid.'[56]

Agent ORANGE produced the goods. So much so that, in March 1944, MI5 agreed to pay him a sum of money to prevent him taking up a job elsewhere (specifically, the editorship of a newspaper), such was the value of the information that he supplied from his perch in the Swiss embassy.[57] Burgess was still running ORANGE late in 1945.[58]

Burgess was not 'a salaried agent' of MI5. Instead, as an agent controller, 'His case officer had authority to pay him £10 per month. He received expenses incurred in running [name redacted, but almost certainly agent ORANGE: Eric Kessler] whom he was expected to treat handsomely.' For 1944 and 1945, Burgess received £200 in expenses.[59]

Later in the same year, the BBC producer played the role of MI5 informer using what agent ORANGE told him. Liddell recorded that Burgess had visited him to speak 'about Peter Hutton of the News Dept. of the FO who had disclosed to our Swiss contact information obtained from telegrams between Stalin and the PM'. Liddell confided to his diary:

> The fact is that all these people in the News Dept. have their pet journalists and that there is rivalry among all members of the department ... The journalists, of course, like to go to the people who will tell them most and the result may well be deplorable ... The difficulty in this case is that if Hutton is made a scapegoat our very important relations with our Swiss contact may be jeopardised.

Liddell's solution was to tell William Codrington, the person then in charge of security in the Foreign Office, that things should be tightened up generally, but in a low-key manner.[60]

Liddell's diaries, which for more than half a century were kept under lock and key in MI5's offices because they were considered too sensitive to release for public consumption, record little about whether he and Burgess, along with others, met outside the office, but there are contemporary accounts that linked the two men. For one thing, they were both members of the Reform Club.[61]

When Burgess had been rehired by the BBC in 1941, the Corporation had arranged for his military service to be deferred on account of his radio production skills, which were in short supply. However, early in 1943, the deferment lapsed, and the authorities once again asked for Burgess to put on military uniform. This time his friends and his employer were both ready to help prevent that happening. He had, by then, an MI5 code name: VAUXHALL. MI5's recruiting sergeant had been none other than his flatmate Anthony Blunt, whom Burgess had helped recruit as a Soviet spy. This renewed threat of military service is what caused Blunt to write to his boss, Guy Liddell, MI5's Deputy Director, reminding him about the 'extremely valuable work' that Burgess had been doing for MI5 'for some time' and mentioning that Sir Richard Maconachie had been a knowing collaborator in arranging things for Burgess inside the BBC. It is not hard to imagine that Burgess and Blunt had cooked up this request together. It was at this time that Maconachie had Burgess's BBC personnel file changed, and when several lines of red Xs, which we noted in Chapter 3, were typed over what would otherwise have remained an embarrassing assessment about an MI5 agent.

Burgess's part-time MI5 agent network effectively doubled as a KGB network because it was controlled – at least for a time – by one of Liddell's senior MI5 team, Anthony Blunt. Unknown to MI5, of course, Blunt the KGB agent submitted regular reports to Moscow. In one of these he said: 'There are others whom I control through Burgess.' He named the Swiss press attaché Eric Kessler, a Hungarian journalist called Andrew Revai (sometimes Revoi), who reported on 'foreign journalists', 'Hungarians generally', as well as journalists from a Swedish newspaper he represented in London. What MI5 didn't know, however, was that Kessler was also supplying information to the KGB. Burgess had recruited him for the KGB in 1938.[62] Likewise, his occasional lover, Revai, and known variously as agent TAFFY or TOFFEE, had been recruited as a KGB agent by Burgess some time before the end of 1939.[63]

* * *

In June 1941, Nazi Germany invaded the Soviet Union. Until then, Stalin had been regarded in London as the next best thing to an enemy since he was in a non-aggression pact with Hitler. Now, as the enemy of one's enemy, he was a friend, and the British Empire and the USSR were suddenly allies. In the BBC, a burst of activity was soon under way in Broadcasting House. Days after the invasion, the BBC Empire service began looking at increasing the number of programmes about Russia, and ensuring that they received a positive, but not unbridled, spin. Speakers were suddenly needed 'to reflect Russia in our programmes'. Producers were sent an invitation that ended with an injunction: 'The matter is urgent and has got to be done.'

145

In the Talks Department, George Barnes wrote, 'Everyone agrees that enthusiastic talks on the Soviet regime were not wanted...' Instead, 'Practical proposals were for talks of the simple facts type on the geography ... the peoples of the USSR and on its history (notwithstanding the obvious difficulties of getting everything except the simplest fact uncoloured one way or the other)', as well as cultural topics.[64]

Within days, Guy Burgess wrote a memo entitled 'Draft Suggestions for Talks on Russia'; 'The suggestions which follow are put down hastily, as the problem is urgent ... what follows is not intended to be in any sense a worked-out scheme.' Then, over the one and a half pages that followed, he proceeded to identify themes and suggest speakers for each. Hastily written it may have been, but comprehensive, succinct and revealing it certainly was.

The British speakers Burgess suggested can be broken down into four categories. First, there were two people – the economist and social scientist Barbara Wootton and the politician Sir Ernest Simon – who were people of the left but not communists by any definition. Then there were four experts on their subjects, who also happened to be communists or left-wing enough to be on MI5's radar, though Burgess didn't mention their political views: Three were scientists – J. G. Crowther, J. D. Bernal and J. B. S. Haldane – and the other was a friend, John Lehmann, who had written 'a certain amount of interesting stuff on Trans-Caucasia' and 'should be safe on this topic'.

So far this was a predictable list of the good and the great on the left, plus Burgess's Marxist friends. There was nobody from the centre or right. Then came two more intriguing elements. One was a category which comprised two art historians, Francis Klingender and Anthony Blunt, whom Burgess knew well and who all knew each other to be communists (the authorities were at this point unaware of this fact, however). Burgess wrote 'neither are Communists', which was, of course, untrue.

In our final, very distinctive category, was just one man. He was a historian of whom Burgess wrote: 'Christopher Hill (a Fellow of All Souls) is a Communist but is also probably the best authority in England on Russian historical studies'. This was true on both counts, but Hill's MI5 file reveals that the Security Service didn't know that he was a communist at this point

– nor did they learn of Burgess's disclosure. Although a Special Branch man watching British travellers return from Moscow back in February 1936 had noted that Hill 'looked like a Communist', it would be over a decade more before MI5 was sure he was (see Chapter 8).[65]

So what reason would Burgess have for revealing Hill to be a communist? It is possible that he didn't realise Hill's politics weren't as well-known to MI5 as they were to him, or maybe it was a diversionary tactic, since revealing Hill's communism made Burgess look whiter than white.

More importantly, perhaps, what did the episode say about MI5's failure to pick up on Burgess's revelation to his BBC bosses about Hill? For around fifty years – and particularly in wartime – a sizeable section of the BBC staff and speakers were checked by MI5 before anyone was let close to a studio, a microphone or even a desk. A number were kept away permanently. By 1952, around 5,000 of the 12,000 staff had been subjected to negative vetting, including roughly one in every ten job applicants.[66] The MI5 files from the wartime and immediate post-war period reveal many letters sent to the BBC pointing out the politically unsound views of contributors.

It was much rarer for intelligence to go the other way and for the BBC to alert MI5 to what they had discovered about somebody. However, Room 101 in Broadcasting House was the office of the resident MI5 liaison officer, and if Burgess's memorandum had ever reached him he would certainly have had cause to investigate some of the names on it more fully.

The BBC invitation to Burgess and others to nominate speakers on Russia was part of a much wider initiative to sell to the British public the new arrangement that the UK and the USSR were now friends. Yesterday's enemy – Britain contemplated declaring war on the Soviet Union in 1940 – had become today's ally. US President Lyndon Johnson famously said of political about-turns that 'overnight chicken shit can turn to chicken salad and vice versa'.[67] And so it was with relations between London and Moscow. In Britain there were concerns that if the USSR was not accepted as a true ally by the British people, any alliance would prove difficult to sustain. So there was intense activity – frenetic even – to change yesterday's offal into something more palatable for today's lunch.

One immediate step taken was to bolster inter-governmental contacts with the Soviet Union – particularly at the British embassy in Moscow, where Labour MP Sir Stafford Cripps was the ambassador – and to swiftly open up more military and cultural contacts.

Once Russia and Britain became allies, the process of sharing military and other secrets with Russia began in earnest. Very quickly, formal military liaison arrangements were established, but, remarkably, links also covered intelligence matters. The SOE soon sent Colonel Robin Guinness to Moscow – at minister Hugh Dalton's request – to act as a liaison with the NKVD (the KGB's name at that time).[68]

As one would expect, Russia's entry into the war on the British side led to a rapid change in how the country was portrayed in Britain. A scramble to publish positive images and news about Russia gripped the whole of British media, not just the BBC. Over coming months the 'less pleasant' aspects of Russia, according to a senior Foreign Office diplomat, were played down in a positive media, pro-Soviet crusade.[69]

At the Ministry of Information, Peter Smollett, who was by this time a well-seasoned KGB agent run by Kim Philby, could now see plenty of opportunities to serve both masters throughout the war.[70]

In August 1941, the MoI determined that a discrete Soviet Relations Branch should be established to handle the promotion of positive images of Britain's newest ally.[71] As the temporary head of the new unit, Smollett was tasked to draw up a list of its essential responsibilities. He identified key tasks including liaison with both the BBC and the Soviet embassy in London.[72]

Weeks after Smollett had identified liaison with the Soviet embassy as one of the new branch's key responsibilities, the process was formalised, as he became the department's head. The Minister of Information himself, Brendan Bracken, wrote to the Soviet ambassador to London, Ivan Maisky, about Smollett's appointment: 'I hope that you will find this appointment agreeable and that you will enable him to maintain close contact with your officers.' Maisky agreed, saying that 'everything possible will be done to assist Mr Smollett to maintain close contact with the Embassy here.'[73] With hindsight, that exchange is remarkable: a minister – maybe unwittingly – was essentially asking the Soviet ambassador if he would accept a KGB agent as the British government's liaison officer.

Soviet diplomats, in particular Maisky, who was the ambassador until 1943, were very much part of the political and diplomatic scene in wartime London. They knew large numbers of the establishment and Maisky's name appears countless times in the published and unpublished diaries of people in prominent positions in wartime Britain. He was in close touch with, among many others, Winston Churchill, Anthony Eden and Harold Nicolson, and his assistants frequented the salons of lesser-known members of the political and economic establishment.

But it is highly likely – in fact it would have been an accepted rule of the game – that whoever spoke to Maisky would probably have been guarded in what they said, or would have prepared themselves beforehand. Politicians talking to Maisky might give him a particular 'line', but the same politician talking to one of his own, like Burgess, might unknowingly reveal something much closer to the real view in government. In that sense, Burgess the radio producer was also an underground unofficial pollster for Maisky. There were other sympathisers, too, who would have been providing similar intelligence, but some of them have never been identified to this day. And with Peter Smollett tasked by the British government with holding officially sanctioned meetings with Maisky and his successors, the KGB had most angles covered.

Smollett's cover was helped by the fact that some British Communist Party officials were suspicious of him: they considered him untrustworthy and possibly duplicitous. Professor Norman MacKenzie, a Communist Party member until 1943, later described Smollett as 'a nasty shit'.[74] What better cover could an agent get than if those supporting the same political ideals for which he was working cast doubts on him? However, one writer on intelligence matters has argued that the Foreign Office knew perfectly well how close Smollett was in his sympathies for the Soviet Union and only gave him so much leeway. 'Smollett was a Soviet agent of influence, who was actively promoting their interests, but the Foreign Office knew where his interests lay and blocked him when necessary.'[75]

Burgess and Smollett didn't have to persuade anybody to run pro-Russian material; across the media executives were already under orders to do it. But the two KGB men undoubtedly exploited conditions for their own particular purposes too. While Burgess would have produced a few of the talks on Russia – it is not possible to be precise – his other departmental colleagues, as well as colleagues in other departments, were equally hard at work. Some of those were later revealed to be communist fellow travellers, although others, such as Eric Blair (George Orwell), leaned in the opposite political direction.

In a September 1941 list, the BBC reported back to the Foreign Office on its output on Russia:

Home Service:

21 Talks broadcast during September. One of them, a schools broadcast about Russia's Arctic territory, was delivered by Peter Smollett himself;

22 separately identified music programs, including a programme of Tchaikovsky's music

3 features and drama programs, including a 'post-revolutionary farce' titled *Squaring The Circle*;

2 variety programmes;

16 separate news talks; and

5 special 'Tanks for Russia week' programmes broadcast during 22 to 27 September.

Overseas service:

11 programs including talks on the German service, the Italian service, the Polish service, the French service, the Empire service and *London Calling Europe*.

During the war, Smollett's team at the Ministry helped to organise official British government pro-Russia rallies – including one in the Royal Albert Hall, although that was originated and managed by the ministry's Campaigns division. A programme for a 'British–Soviet Unity' event at the Royal Albert Hall on 27 June 1943, with a special goodwill message from 'Marshal Stalin', lists an introduction by the Lord Bishop of Chelmsford, a rendition of 'The Song of Stalin' (composed by Aram Khachaturian and sung by ten British choirs), a finale called 'Freedom on the March' (led by Michael Redgrave), and the event topped off with the mass singing of 'The Internationale' and 'God Save the King'. The programme points out that 'The proceedings will be filmed by the Ministry of Information'. Smollett must have been very proud. They also had a hand in BBC radio programmes about Russian themes. Thirty such programmes were broadcast to British listeners in October 1943 alone.

According to intelligence historian Christopher Andrew, probably Burgess's most remarkable coup within the BBC, on behalf of the NKVD, was to arrange for a talk on the Eastern Front in January 1942 by Ernst Henri, the journalist who had written about the usefulness of spy rings of five and was later revealed as another Soviet spy. Henri is said to have told listeners that the Soviet armed forces would triumph and used the occasion to reassure everyone, including Soviet moles, that the Soviet intelligence services were 'among the best in the world'.[76] An exhaustive search has, however, failed to locate details of Henri's programme.

Hard evidence of the involvement of Burgess or Smollett in the broadcast of 'Red Army Day' a gala event at the Royal Albert Hall, which was ordered by the Cabinet, has also been unforthcoming[77] Contributors included Malcolm Sargent, Laurence Olivier, Dame Sybil Thorndike, Marius Goring, Ralph Richardson and John Gielgud; music was specially written by Arnold Bax and William Walton; and the Internationale was played by a host of military bands and orchestras, before the political address was delivered by Foreign Secretary Anthony Eden.[78] Parallel events were held across the country.[79]

Amidst all this there were moments when BBC executives such as Sir Richard Maconachie regretted that the 'particularly disquieting symptom, as I see it, is not the demand for information about the Russian way of life, but the demand for nothing but praise of it'.[80]

On the other side of the coin, as it were, Smollett's department was also responsible for supplying information and promotional materials to the Soviet Union that would show the British Empire and the war effort in a positive light. Among other things, it produced a regular news magazine about Britain's war effort, *Britanskii Soyuznik*, which was distributed in the USSR by the Soviet government. Smollett was closely involved in selecting the stories to be included and only those likely to meet with Soviet approval were passed along.

For a time, Clarissa Churchill, niece of the serving Prime Minister and the future wife of a successor, Anthony Eden, worked as a research assistant on the production of *Britanskiy Soyuznik*. One very brief memorandum, dated 2 August 1942, refers to the departure of a member of the staff: 'Miss Clarissa Churchill will not come back and we shall therefore be grateful if you can recommend another research assistant to work in *Britanskiy Soyuznik*,' Smollett wrote.[81] There is no mention of this episode in Clarissa Churchill's memoirs.[82]

According to Anthony Blunt, Moscow had at one time given Burgess the task of wooing Clarissa, with the aim of getting closer to her uncle. As Blunt told it, Burgess was initially horrified, but then declared himself ready for the challenge.[83] Not surprisingly, what sounds like a mission impossible came to nothing.

Guy Burgess's war was turning out to involve four different elements: BBC producer (with a key element of the job now being an official pro-Russian propagandist), MI6 anti-German propagandist, MI5 agent-runner and KGB agent. Despite this seemingly full schedule, he couldn't resist a bit of political lobbying too, just as he had with Churchill after Munich in 1938.

It started when word got around that Burgess was someone who had views that were worth hearing. In June 1942, the Leader of the House of Commons, Sir Stafford Cripps, who was an early advocate of planning for the post-war world, invited several BBC producers, MPs and others to dinner and conversation. Among them was Guy Burgess, who joined his BBC colleagues George Orwell and William Empson, together with Harold Nicolson and Labour MP Lord Winster.

It may not have been quite the sparkling occasion that Burgess was hoping for, however. Orwell recorded in his diary: 'Spent a long evening with Cripps (who had expressed a desire to meet some literary people) ... About 2 ½ hours of it, with nothing to drink. The usual inconclusive discussion. Cripps, however, very human and willing to listen.'[84]

The same year, Burgess picked up on the parliamentary grapevine that Cripps was contemplating resigning from the government as the starting point of a campaign to replace Churchill as Prime Minister and to lead the country in a different political direction. Alarmed that this might not only damage Churchill's government, but more importantly the British war effort, Burgess rushed off to see Harold Nicolson for help. Nicolson recorded in his diary: 'Guy Burgess has heard from his friends who are in close touch with Cripps that the latter is so discontented with the conduct of the war that he proposes to resign ... Guy had heard all this from Luker and E. H. Carr who are Cripps' advisors.'[85] Interestingly, notwithstanding the convivial chat at Chartwell four years earlier, Burgess did not seem to think he could contact Churchill directly. Unfortunately for Burgess, Nicolson didn't feel he could make the approach either. He suggested instead that he and Burgess should go and see Nicolson's fellow BBC governor, and close friend of the Prime Minister, Violet Bonham Carter. They went to see her the same day, but it was a meeting that never made it into her (edited) published diary.[86] She passed the message on to Churchill who defused the situation and remained Prime Minister, eventually eclipsing Cripps's political career for the remainder of the war.[87]

Even though Burgess was working six days a week, sometimes twelve hours a day in his day job, with a little political lobbying on the side, he still managed to find opportunities to relax with friends in convivial company when not engaged in spare time KGB or MI5 work.

A list of those he met socially throughout the war reads like a Who's Who of wartime London and included diplomats, civil servants, politicians, writers and academics, many of whom he had met through Harold Nicolson. The Nicolson diaries record dozens of dinner dates with Burgess during the war years: on 31 January 1940, for instance, the pair dined with the then head of the Foreign Office News Department, Charles Peake; on 17 May they were in other company – at Nicolson's club; a month later they had dinner 'and then off to [Guy Burgess's] rooms afterwards where I meet Peter Montgomery ... and then back to the office.'[88] On 19 August, they met again at the Wyndham Club, shortly after Burgess's return from his abortive Washington trip, and then three weeks later it was dinner at The Travellers.

Despite this, not for Nicolson, then in his early fifties, late nights and vast quantities of alcohol. He confessed to his diary that he frequently looked to be in bed before 11 p.m., earlier if he was on fire-watching duty at the House of Commons; sometimes he went back to his office. On one occasion, in 1943, however, when the two dined together and Nicolson was scheduled to catch a train to his Leicester constituency – he fell while in the toilet and knocked himself out momentarily. Burgess came to the rescue and steadied his friend so that he could continue on his journey.[89]

If Burgess wished to prolong an evening's entertainment with or without Nicolson, he would often go on to one of his regular haunts to seek out friends and acquaintances. One favourite was the Gargoyle Club, described by the art collector and aesthete Harold Acton as 'a dinner and dance-club with paintings by Matisse hung on the walls'. The habitués included Acton, Noël Coward (a colleague of Burgess's from Section D days) and Augustus John. The actor and alcoholic Robert Newton – known to his club friends as Bobby and to post-war audiences as Long John Silver – was another member, whose outrageous behaviour appeared to cause occasional ripples. Another regular with a fondness for the bottle was the poet Dylan Thomas. Cambridge educated Wolf Rilla, a German émigré, whose father was a well-known actor, was another member. During the war he worked for the BBC and later directed some successful British television programmes and cinema films.[90] Other attendees included the writer Philip Toynbee, Donald Maclean and Gerald Hamilton, who had been immortalised – as Mr Norris – by Christopher Isherwood in *Mr Norris Changes Trains*. Stephen Spender, Cyril Connolly and the philosopher A. J. 'Freddie' Ayer, with whom Burgess was at school, also frequented the Gargoyle. Ayer told the club's historian that the Gargoyle made him 'a social figure ... I wasn't social before the war. I was an academic...'

The club's historian himself concluded that Guy Burgess 'had three ruling passions: good talk (normally his own brilliant exposition of provocative, even outrageous, propositions), sex (young, male, 'rough trade') and drink (wine, whisky and port...).'[91]

The Gargoyle was the sort of place that tolerated deviance from the strict social norms of the time – especially of the sexual kind. One evening, so the club's historian records, Burgess asked the painter John Craxton if he would like to go back with him to his flat: 'Would you like to be whipped – a wild thrashing? Wine thrown in?' The painter, reportedly terrified, was saved by Philip Toynbee.[92]

Harold Acton wrote waspishly about Burgess, whom he loosely described as one of the 'parlour pinks who talked as if nothing could be worse than the freedom they enjoyed to damn the government and the old order who had given them that freedom'. He singled out Burgess: 'The most vindictive of these was Guy Burgess ... though nobody could have been less diplomatic. Brian [Howard] confided to me that his equipment was gargantuan – "what is known as a whopper, my dear" – which might account for his success in certain ambiguous quarters.'[93]

Burgess, Howard and Hamilton would frequently move on from the Gargoyle in search of adventure in some of the seedier and less reputable Soho clubs and basement drinking dens. Brian Howard, a homosexual aesthete lampooned by Evelyn Waugh in *Brideshead Revisited*, was a poet and for the first half of the war an MI5 officer. He was a member of the Gargoyle, and Burgess was able to use his membership card as a way of gaining entrance. Those they bumped into were not always impressed. Harold Nicolson's very close friend, James Lees-Milne, wrote in his diary for 16 October 1943 how, during an evening with friends that started with drinks at the Ritz, followed by the Gargoyle, a meal at the White Tower, and more drinks at 'disreputable pubs', he had met Burgess – 'drunk and truculent, and we soon shook him off'.[94]

Months later, Lees-Milne again met Burgess at the Ritz during drinks. They went off to the Gargoyle and had dinner with Charles Fletcher Cooke MP, where they discussed sex and 'drank too much: beer and gin mixed'.[95]

Sometimes Burgess might just have wanted a night in. But even one of those wouldn't necessarily mean curling up with a copy of *Middlemarch* and a cup of cocoa. Burgess's friend Goronwy Rees wrote an elegant description of Burgess at home that has passed into Burgess folklore.

During the war years, Burgess lived in a flat at 5 Bentinck Street with his close friend Anthony Blunt and their mutual friend and lover Jack Hewit. The property was owned by fellow Apostle Victor (later Lord) Rothschild, though in his autobiography, published in 1977, Rothschild mentioned Burgess just once ('a dissolute young man with whom my mother got on very well').[96] Also living in the flat at this time was Rothschild's future wife (his second), Tess Mayor, and Patricia Rawdon-Smith (later revealed to be the woman who 'relieved' Anthony Blunt of his virginity).[97]

Rees wrote that he first went to Bentinck Street in spring 1941, just after Burgess had returned to the BBC. He remembered it as an 'oddly assorted collection of tenants', who 'sometimes gave the flat the air of a rather high-class disorderly house, in which one could not distinguish between the staff, the management and the clients'.[98] Despite this, he said that everyone seemed to have important jobs, that 'some were communists or ex-communists; all were a fount of gossip about the progress of the war, and the political machine responsible for conducting it'.[99]

Tess Mayor apparently issued a strict injunction to Burgess that no pick-ups should be brought back to the property. 'But of course he did,' wrote Rees, continuing, 'Guy brought home a series of boys, young men', most in uniform, 'whom he had picked up among the thousands who thronged the streets of London.'

In 1944, a year when Rees said he saw more of 5 Bentinck Street than in any other during the war, the antics in the house were 'rather like watching a French farce which has been injected with all the elements of a political drama. Bedroom doors opened and shut; strange faces appeared and disappeared down the stairs ... civil servants, politicians, visitors to London, friends and colleagues of Guy's, popped in and out of bed...'[100]

These impressions were apparently supported by Malcolm Muggeridge, an MI6 colleague of Kim Philby, who knew Freddie Mayor, Tess Mayor's brother. Muggeridge visited Bentinck Street only once, in 1941, but he remembered – thirty years later – that on that sole occasion he saw John Strachey, J. D. Bernal, Blunt and, of course, Guy Burgess, describing it as 'a whole revolutionary Who's Who'.

'It was the only time I ever met Burgess,' he wrote. 'He gave me a feeling such as I have never had from anyone else, of being morally afflicted in some way. His very physical presence was malodorous and sinister, as though he had some consuming illness ...'[101] Years later, Burgess made another appearance in Muggeridge's diary: in the entry for 7 January 1948, which reads: 'Dined Ralph Jarvis's. Present: character called Burgess (Foreign Office). Burgess lamentable character, very left-wing, obviously seeking to climb on the Socialist bandwagon. Long, tedious, rather acrimonious argument...'[102]

There is one other account of life in Bentinck Street, found in the unpublished memoirs of Anthony Blunt. Though his corrective may have more than an element of truth about it, however, we must remember that he also had a vested interest in downplaying any of the reported excesses, while at the same time seeking to undermine the role of Goronwy Rees as an observer, given what Rees knew and would later reveal about him (see Chapter 9).

Blunt's memoirs – still unpublished and accessible only in the British Library's Western Manuscripts room – were kept hidden completely until twenty-five years after his death. In them, he set out to question the credibility of both Rees's and Muggeridge's narratives:

> From Goronwy Rees's accounts one would conclude that it consisted of an alternation of sexual orgies and conspiratorial conversations designed to hinder the war effort. In fact the regular inhabitants were all engaged on full-time jobs – some of them very full-time indeed – directed towards the furtherance of the war effort and more often than not came back in the evening too tired to behave in the manner suggested.

Continuing to pick away at Rees as a reliable witness, Blunt wrote that 'one of the "tenants" can only remember seeing him once in the flat – though he might have come occasionally at weekends when some of the party went to the Country – but that visit stuck in her memory because Goronwy was still drunk at breakfast the next morning'. Moving on to Muggeridge's 'vivid if not altogether friendly account of his one visit to the flat during the Blitz', Blunt continued: 'Muggeridge mentions among those present John Strachey and J. D. Bernal ... Bernal was never a "Frequent" visitor and Strachey hardly ever came to the flat after the end of 1940.'

Blunt's own description of Bentinck Street and its basement presents an altogether more sober picture of life in the Blitz in the Burgess–Blunt household:

The actual occupants of that basement room varied from night to night, because there was accommodation for a large number and, as we all had a fair number of friends who might suddenly appear on leave or, given the difficulty of moving about at night, might not even be able to get hom [sic] within London, one was constantly giving shelter to those who were stranded. It is difficult now to remember – and impossible for those who did not experience it to imagine – how casual life became in this respect.

For Blunt, 'A flat, if there was no raid, or a basement, if there was one, became a dormitory, in which as many people as possible were bedded down, in single or double beds, on lie-lows or on mattresses on the floor.'

But Blunt was also at pains to demonstrate Rees's unreliability, by contrasting what he saw as mutually contradictory sentiments:

Goronwy's account of Guy's sexual behaviour at this time is also a total fantasy: 'Guy brought home a series of boys...' It is true that Guy had a number of friends who visited him regularly, but it was a rule of the house that the casual pickup was forbidden; and Guy observed this rule.

Indeed, Blunt wrote, 'Goronwy presumably based his statement on what Guy himself had told him, and he seems to have had an inexplicable belief that on the subject of sex Guy told the truth.'[103]

There was one other element to Burgess's social life alongside the 5 Bentinck Street set, the dinners at gentlemen's clubs, the Gargoyle and the Soho bars, and that was 'the Shanghai'. During the war, the Hon. David Astor, who was on Lord Mountbatten's staff and whose father, Lord Astor, owned *The Observer*, organised a dining club centred on the Shanghai Chinese restaurant in London's Soho. The club brought together 'left-leaning' journalists and literati, including Barbara Ward, George Orwell, the economist and émigré E. F. Schumacher, Guy Burgess and Peter Smollett. For Burgess the BBC producer, it was a perfect opportunity to cement relationships with colleagues such as Smollett and Orwell. It has been said that it was probably as a result of Smollett's association with the club that led Astor early in 1942 to contemplate appointing him Editor of *The Observer* in succession to the legendary J. L. Garvin. It came to nothing only because the Ministry of Information would not release Smollett.[104]

George Orwell knew Burgess as a BBC colleague and a Shanghai member, but there is no evidence that he had any suspicions about Burgess. Indeed, his name was not included on a list of communists and fellow travellers (that did include Smollett) that he drew up in 1949 while working for the British government's anti-Soviet propaganda arm, the Information Research Department (IRD).

There were others, however, who *were* developing doubts about Burgess. Yet these suspicions originated not from his friends within MI5, but his masters in the KGB.

At least three factors had precipitated the enquiry: first, Burgess's demeanour. It might have been the result of overwork. It could have been due to the conflicting demands of his three employers: the BBC, KGB and MI5. Or maybe it was just down to too many late nights, not enough sleep and numerous glasses of port. Whatever it was, it had caused Burgess's whole character to change. Instead of the person bursting with ideas that many saw him to be he had become worried and agitated.

A second factor was Kim Philby. He had confessed to his KGB controller in 1942 that Burgess had gone ahead and recruited Peter Smollett as an agent without any reference to or permission from Moscow. That was a heinous sin. Moscow liked to know who was working for it. Recruitment of agents was a lengthy and detailed process: all sorts of background checks had to be carried out to ensure that an agent was reliable and, from their point of view, trustworthy. Allowing Smollett to discover who else was in the Cambridge ring was also bad practice.

Thirdly, when it came to all five of the Cambridge ring, Moscow became very suspicious indeed. As they began looking more closely at the information that was being received from these men, they were impressed: it was good, very good indeed. In fact, the quality of the material that they delivered was so good – and so voluminous – that it appeared to be almost too good to be true. Even more worryingly from the KGB's point of view, it was consistent – too consistent for comfort.

Information supplied by one agent frequently appeared to back up information supplied by another, but had been acquired from quite different sources. Historians are often confronted by issues of varying information from multiple sources, and they have to make judgements based on the balance of probabilities involved. In the same way, intelligence analysts look to see whether their sources provide differing or even diametrically opposed information about the same subject. It is ironic that as information supplied by the Cambridge spies often coincided, rather than differed, the paranoid in KGB headquarters began to doubt its authenticity. The fact that the information frequently tallied raised suspicions that it was being manipulated by British Intelligence. Moscow became alarmed that the Cambridge spies were double agents, feeding them material that was designed to mislead Russia into making false moves. For this reason, some people in the KGB had decided to carry out a root and branch analysis of all five members of the ring, covering both the material they supplied and a thorough re-examination of their backgrounds.

When Burgess's agitated state was noticed by his London-based KGB controller during their meetings, he was given a firm talking to in an attempt to calm him down. On one occasion, when invited to unburden himself, he revealed that he was becoming distressed again about his friend Goronwy Rees.

In Burgess's mind, Rees's knowledge of his identity as a KGB agent, as well as that of one of the other members of the Cambridge Five (Anthony Blunt), meant that Rees remained a serious risk to him. From both Rees's and Blunt's accounts, it seems that the two men hardly saw each other during the first four years of the war, with the exception of occasional visits made by Rees to Bentinck Street. Rees had got married and set up home with his wife away from London and he (by then serving in Military Intelligence) and Burgess remained friends. But the fear of Rees telling the Security Service about him and the KGB continued to gnaw away at him and, in 1943, Burgess twice raised the issue with his KGB controller, on one occasion asking for permission to have Rees assassinated, and on another offering to do the job himself as he had been responsible for the predicament in the first place.

The KGB, unsurprisingly, needed time to think about that startling proposition. They started by looking into Rees. They confirmed that Burgess had recruited him without their permission and, moreover, had not passed on Rees's contact details to them. For the entire duration of Rees's time as an agent, Burgess had remained his handler and, indeed, had seemed adamant that he should continue to do so on the grounds that otherwise Rees would become nervous and suspicious. A cardinal rule had been broken – no background checks – in sharp contrast to, for instance, the methodical recruitment of Burgess himself.

As a result, a KGB unit in Moscow – led by Captain Yelena Modrzchinskaya – re-evaluated every report received from the Cambridge spies (as well as their handlers, some of whom had been shot for treason during the Great Terror) to see if they could discern any hidden hand of British Intelligence lurking somewhere in the background, manipulating the KGB into falling unwittingly into a British trap.

In some of the Cambridge spies' files that have been released by the KGB archive over the last thirty years, it is clear that part of the background assessments included 'confessions' about the individuals' character traits. Blunt, for instance, told them in an autobiographical report that he filed in 1942 that his boyfriend was Jack Hewit.[105] That was information that he had never publicly revealed during his lifetime, not even in his unpublished memoirs.

This was not prurience on the part of the KGB, but essentially a security insurance policy that the KGB would use and continually refer to in order to discern whether the intelligence supplied by the agents was all it was cracked up to be. Intelligence agencies evaluate not only the likelihood that intelligence supplied is accurate, but also analyse the backgrounds of the sources supplying the intelligence to help establish how reliable they are likely to be as individuals, how committed or how 'hooked' they are (in the case of those sources being blackmailed, solely interested in financial rewards, etc.). Such assessments attempt to establish their sources' likely motivations, and take account of the fact that tendentious information might be passed on as settlement of grudges. People prepared to betray their own countries are, by that very fact, open to suspicion as to their motivations.[106]

In Burgess's case, there is evidence that his character caused the KGB some real concern. In February 1942, a KGB officer, V. Pavlov, had written to Moscow: 'The source "MADCHEN" [Burgess] continues to work with us at present; however, he is our most dubious agent and arouses more suspicion than any other English agent.'[107] That KGB assessment had first been made about Burgess in 1937. Clearly nothing had changed in the five years since. Modrzchinskaya's unit looked carefully into his previous record. At that time the KGB was assured by his then London-based KGB handler, Kreshin:

> MADCHEN has produced a far better impression on me than that which I got from materials and characterizations at home. His distinguishing feature in comparison with other agents I meet is bohemianism in its most unattractive form. He is a young, interesting, clever enough, cultured, inquisitive shrewd person, reads much and knows much: But at the same time with these qualities he is untidy, goes about dirty, drinks much, and leads the so-called life of the gilded youth... He is well grounded politically and theoretically ... in conversation quotes Marx, Lenin and Stalin.[108]

A few months later, Kreshin, and another KGB colleague, Gorsky, wrote to Moscow:

> MADCHEN is a very peculiar person and to apply ordinary standards to him would be the roughest mistake. Having become convinced of this here on the spot as a result of all our experience with MADCHEN we cannot cite a single concrete fact which would absolutely indisputably testify to MADCHEN being a double agent.[109]

These judgements, however, were far from conclusive when it came to KGB headquarters.

It was the case of Goronwy Rees and, specifically, Burgess's wish to kill him, that most aroused suspicion and in their initial investigation of Rees's background in 1943, Captain Yelena Modrzchinskaya noted:

> Goronwy Rees, a former assistant editor of *The Spectator*, is currently an
> officer in the British Army. He is 35, the son of a Welsh clergyman, a grad-
> uate of Oxford University and a fellow of the famous All Souls College,
> where he was a friend and associate of Halifax, Lord Sutton and others
> in the so-called Cliveden group, who were also fellows of All Souls.[110]

The All Souls connection had a special relevance. Anthony Blunt, in his unpublished memoirs, dismissed Rees's spying as simply passing on the gossip from
All Souls College high table dinners. Blunt intimated that senior public servants
frequently spent the weekend there to unwind and unburden themselves before
re-entering the fray on the following Monday morning. He further had said
that such indiscretions, if Rees had repeated them (i.e. to Moscow via Burgess),
were not actionable under the Official Secrets Act. Quips made by senior civil
servants would not rock the ship of state. However, when one of their number
happened to be the Foreign Secretary, Lord Halifax, unattributable comments
and observations made about, say, Britain's foreign policy, would be of a different order. High table dinners operated on the basis of confidentiality. In
Rees's case, he would have abided by these rules and played the game: no one
in Britain would have heard any of Halifax's unguarded conversations. But it
is highly likely that people in Moscow would have done so.

Modrzchinskaya continued:

> At the end of June 1939, MADCHEN, who was linked at the time with
> Pierre,[111] recruited FLIT, without permission from the centre, on the
> grounds that FLIT apparently wanted to join the Communist Party. At
> the same time, it appeared that FLIT would be working as secretary to
> Halifax. FLIT's contacts included one [name omitted], a woman who was
> connected by marriage to the Churchill family, lived during the Munich
> period in Prague and was allegedly an intermediary between Churchill and
> Beneš. FLIT and [name omitted] were close friends of a friend of Beneš.

Research has enabled us to establish that the woman 'connected by marriage
to the Churchill family' whose name was omitted is Goronwy Rees's very

close Oxford friend Sheila Grant Duff. Her mother was a distant relative of Churchill's wife, Clementine, although the pair had never met. Between 1937 and 1938, Sheila Grant Duff, an aspiring journalist, had several meetings with Winston Churchill – some over lunch at Chartwell. She conveyed messages and gave her impressions of Czechoslovakia where she had indeed lived for over a year. Her intermediary with the Czechoslovak Foreign Minister, Edvard Beneš, was a distinguished journalist and Beneš intimate named Hubert Ripka.[112]

It was Sheila Grant Duff who had been responsible for suggesting Rees's name to BBC producer Mary Adams as a potential speaker in the 1935 European Exchange series. She and Rees shared Oxford friends who were beginning to make names for themselves, including the lawyers Herbert Hart and Richard Wilberforce, and Douglas Jay, who would become a Labour government minister under both Harold Wilson and James Callaghan.

With Rees's connections and access to the All Souls high table and, through Sheila Grant Duff, to Churchill, which undoubtedly Burgess would have known about, it is small wonder that he made Rees such a priority for recruitment.

In the end, Burgess's request to have Rees disposed of was turned down, dismissed as paranoia. He was instructed to get a grip and calm down by his KGB controller – Rees was not a danger.

There is, however, another possible interpretation of this decision. If the KGB feared Burgess was, in fact, a double agent, whose true allegiance was to British Intelligence, then what better way for MI5 or MI6 to research the KGB's methods of liquidation than for Burgess to ask for advice on assassination? If Burgess had been authorised to kill Rees, he would have been shown how. It may in this case have been safer, therefore, if Burgess was told that murdering one of his best friends was, in KGB terms, not necessary. Rees never knew that his friend had wanted to have him assassinated and continued to see Burgess socially until the latter's defection.[113]

Ultimately, the KGB's review established that the Cambridge spies and their intelligence was sound. Each was offered an ex-gratia payment for his services though, most importantly, it is likely that they never knew that their loyalty had ever been suspected by the KGB.

* * *

During Guy Burgess's second stint at the BBC, it was not only through producing *Week in Westminster* that he was able to develop a whole new network of contacts. The 250 other radio programmes he produced offered similar opportunities, as well as the chance to book old friends and acquaintances in for broadcasts

One such acquaintance was Aileen Furse, the woman fellow Cambridge spy Kim Philby was living with in London at the time. He had married the Austrian communist Litzi Friedman in 1934, but soon after Philby began working for the KGB they had separated. In 1940, he began living with Aileen Furse and they had the first of their three children the next year and eventually married once Philby had divorced his first wife in 1946.

At the end of January 1941, Burgess wrote to a contact at the Ministry of Food, John Fisher, mentioning that 'Aileen Furse (whom your Ministry has approved) is going to give two broadcasts to housewives on Community Kitchens from a personal point of view'.[114] Furse, then working in the Welfare Department of Marks and Spencer Ltd, had first been in contact with the Talks Department in 1938. Among the bundle of Furse papers at the BBC Written Archive at Caversham, there is a Talks booking form, signed by Burgess, dated 27 January 1941, showing that Furse was scheduled to give three talks (one on 'Cooking Clubs' and two untitled) for the series *At Home Today* in the next few weeks.[115] Through his radio programmes, Burgess was also able to get the inside track on a whole host of government departments that were actively battling on the home front. One such series, *Can I Help You?*, was fronted by popular broadcaster Professor John Hilton, formerly the Ministry of Information's Director of Home Publicity, and every week it helped publicise government advice and information campaigns including, crucially, how to fill out daunting and unfamiliar official forms. Burgess's duties included liaison with military and civil service officials to ensure that the programme's content would be both accurate and helpful. He might not have had access to top-secret files while working on programmes such as these, but he would have been told things that would enable him to supply lower-grade contextual information gleaned from meetings and briefings to Moscow.

But potentially just as, if not more significantly, the Hilton programme attracted thousands of letters from listeners seeking solutions to everyday problems they were facing in their wartime lives. In this era before formal opinion polls and mass observation surveys it would have given Burgess – and, therefore, Moscow – an unrivalled independent insight into British civilian morale. A sister programme for the armed forces prompted a similarly valuable postbag, this time from the military frontline.

But Burgess, as a matter of course, would also have had access to government correspondence coming into the Talks Department, including Ministry of Information morale surveys, listener research and government directives, as well as other information that would have been passed around the weekly departmental meetings.

While working on *Can I Help You?*, Burgess also had an idea for a new programme, described in a 750-word memorandum sent to George Barnes as an 'Aunt Sally' (an idea to generate reactions):

> The Citizen's daily life is becoming, in all its aspects, increasingly dependent on administrative decisions taken in Whitehall … The mass of regulations in which these administrative decisions are embodied, together with the mass of forms which confront the ordinary citizen, are hard to understand. Yet if they are not understood and acted on, there is certainly grumbling, and probably a loss to the general war effort.

Furthermore, he wrote, 'Broadcasting would appear to be far and away the best method of explaining these regulations and of coping with the increased urgent personal problems that are now confronting almost every individual in the community.'

In short, he had devised a programme strikingly similar to *You and Yours*, BBC Radio Four's classic consumer advice programme which began in 1970.

* * *

By all accounts, 27 March 1944 must have been a busy time in the office of the Permanent Under-Secretary of the Foreign Office, Sir Alexander Cadogan.

Apart from running the Foreign Office, which was at full stretch with a global war, he was also a highly regarded diplomat who had travelled with Churchill to meet both Stalin and President Franklin D. Roosevelt. However, on this date Sir Alexander evidently found time to write to the Director General of the BBC, R. W. Foot, requesting the transfer of a relatively junior member of the BBC's staff:

> Dear Foot,
> I am writing to ask if you would be good enough to consider the release from employment in your Corporation of Mr Guy Burgess, for service in our News Department.

Cadogan explained that the calls on this department were becoming extremely heavy, that they'd recently had to release two members to other work and he wanted to fill the vacancies.

> I understand that Mr Burgess of your Talks Department is interested in this vacancy and from our point of view he would be well qualified to fill it. I fully appreciate that he is doing most valuable work with the British Broadcasting Corporation and I fear that his release may inconvenience you. But as I have said our own need is great, and we should therefore be most grateful if you could see your way to facilitate his transfer to us.

This was the letter that set in train a series of events that culminated in one of the most embarrassing episodes in the history of the British Foreign Office.

Cadogan's letter seemed to merit further investigation. For instance, given that Burgess was not a senior figure in the BBC hierarchy and Sir Alexander Cadogan was very senior in the Foreign Office, was it really necessary to make such a high-level intervention as a personal letter to the Director General of the BBC? By contrast, we found other examples of transfers between the two organisations resolved at a much lower level.

Our search for an explanation reveals documentary evidence establishing that Burgess had been actively working with the head of the Foreign Office's

News Department, William Ridsdale, for some considerable time before Cadogan wrote the letter to Foot.

1943 was a year which began with the war against the Axis powers moving decidedly in the Allies' favour. Hitler's Afrika Korps was in retreat and facing defeat, the Allied bridgehead in North Africa was consolidating, and there had been a German defeat at Stalingrad. All the while Stalin placed ever greater pressure on the British and American governments to open up a second front in Europe that would divert German military resources away from Russia and deliver the war on two fronts that Hitler's high command wanted to avoid.

Meanwhile, in the Foreign Office officials were already beginning to look at what a post-war world might look like. One area considered especially important was developing a strategy for Britain's future public relations and propaganda requirements. Sir Alexander Cadogan asked senior staff for ideas and William Ridsdale, among others, replied at the beginning of March.[116]

Ridsdale thought that radio would be an important part of the future strategy. He was soon in touch with the BBC Talks Department. On 30 April 1943 George Barnes wrote to Guy Burgess: 'Please see Ridsdale, at lunch if necessary, and tell him of our project to have an occasional *War Commentary* [a regular war time radio] series on [foreign affairs]'. Barnes gave Burgess a shopping list of items for discussion: what subjects should be covered, which speakers should be approached, and would the Foreign Office kindly help by feeding speakers with information? But, knowing Burgess's legendary predilection for extravagant meals and copious amounts of alcohol, as well as imaginative expenses claims, Barnes sternly told him: 'You are not authorised to invite anyone.'

30 April 1943 was a Friday. A manuscript note by Burgess to Barnes says 'I am lunching with (vice-versa) R[idsdale] on Tuesday. This is determined by the fact that he is busy with Poland.' The note is undated, but it is highly likely that the Tuesday in question would have been 4 May.[117]

Files kept at the National Archives show that Ridsdale was indeed busy with Poland at that time. Furthermore, Cadogan and Anthony Eden were busy not only with Poland, but also with how to handle news about the Katyn massacre and help to keep it from the public's gaze, while belittling attempts by the Nazi propaganda machine to expose what it (correctly) depicted as a Russian crime.

On 7 May 1943 Ridsdale wrote to his bosses that 'the BBC feel – quite properly in my view – that they are not catering adequately in the Home Service for that large section of their public who are interested in international affairs...'[118] He proposed that the BBC should broadcast regular talks on foreign affairs using a small panel of 'expert' speakers who would prepare British and Empire audiences for the return to peacetime politics and international diplomacy.

Two days later a handwritten comment appeared on the manuscript, 'I think this is a good plan. But see the marginal notes and please speak.' It was initialled AE (Anthony Eden) and dated 9 May 1943. Soon afterwards Ridsdale noted that Eden's office had suggested to him that Harold Nicolson would be an ideal figure for becoming involved in the broadcasts.[119]

On 11 May, Burgess told Barnes about his discussion with Ridsdale, noting, 'We found ourselves in agreement.' He mentioned that some issues would be thorny, but that there was 'an inner group of diplomatic correspondents who were in direct and confidential touch with the Secretary of State. There was very little that they were not, or could not be, told or shown.' Burgess summarised Ridsdale's view that 'it was important that the BBC should give such talks as otherwise the public field was rather open (as at present) for agitation run by interested parties...'

It is worth pausing for a moment to reflect on the fascinating insight into just what was being proposed: the BBC was being offered assistance by the Foreign Office to devote programmes to foreign affairs for which the Foreign Office would (a) suggest the topics; (b) have a large say in who should present the talks (favouring speakers that it considered as trustworthy); and (c) brief the speakers.

Barnes told Burgess's line manager, Vincent Alford, that the talks should go ahead, adding, 'There is no doubt that Burgess would like to handle, but this is for you to decide. In any case, you will be in charge of the series and will decide when a foreign affairs commentary is to be included.' Soon afterwards Burgess was told: 'I would like you to give him [Alford] all the help you can from your special knowledge of the subject and of your special contacts.' Barnes probably didn't realise until much later just how special Burgess's contacts were.

In the weeks that followed memos record the preparations: selecting the subjects for talks, polishing scripts, looking for other speakers – one was apparently dismissed by Burgess for having 'a rotten voice', but former *Times* Editor and Chamberlain opponent, Henry Wickham Steed, was favoured because he might be able to inject some passion into his talk.

It is clear that Burgess remained in contact with Ridsdale intermittently during this time as a memo dated 28 May shows. Burgess proposed as a speaker to Alford a 'free Italian'. 'I believe Orlando, the charming correspondent of an Italian newspaper for this country ... known to and liked by Ridsdale. This information may be inaccurate and I have not spoken to Ridsdale about it – I will do so if you ask me to.'

Things did not go well, even with the free Italian. Barnes soon told Alford that if the first 'script is a fair sample of the information we are likely to get from the Foreign Office, the series is stillborn and should not continue'. And at that point it looks as though the project hit the buffers. There would be no more talks. Burgess wrote a note to Barnes on 23 June informing him that 'Ridsdale ... has expressed to me his great disappointment that we were suspending our broadcasts on Foreign Affairs, after our first abortive attempt ...' However, Burgess was not going to give up.

He continued:

> Since I was largely responsible for the arrangements made with Ridsdale, which lead [sic] to the experiment of this talk, I would like to state for the record, that I cannot see that the failure of this talk was due in any way to the Foreign Office. It was a bad script – badly broadcast. The responsibility for this is surely ours [sic] and the speaker's.

He went on to urge that another attempt be made because 'it seems very likely that the topic is one that may increase rather than decrease in importance in the future.'[120] The matter was quietly dropped by both the BBC and the Foreign Office.

By this stage it is not clear in whose interest Burgess had been working by defending the Foreign Office – that of the Talks Department? The Foreign Office News Department? Himself? Or the KGB?

Six months later, however, Ridsdale resurrected the subject inside the Foreign Office. With the outcome of the war looking a little more certain William Ridsdale dusted off his plans and sent a memorandum to his bosses late in December 1943, saying, 'I think the need for some constructive action on these lines is required.'[121] At the turn of the year, and with Cadogan's approval, Ridsdale invited the BBC to lunch to discuss how the proposal could be brought back to life. His note of that meeting, which is dated 10 January 1944, includes the sentence: 'I saw Mr George Barnes, Director of Talks, and his colleague Mr Guy Burgess.'[122] A manuscript note initialled by Cadogan shows that he read it on 11 Jan 1944 and Eden wrote, 'I like these ideas', signing off Ridsdale's note, with its mention of Guy Burgess, on 15 January.[123]

On 26 January 1944 Ridsdale telephoned Harold Nicolson about the proposal and the potential for him to become involved in it. A week later, on 2 February 1944, Nicolson's unpublished diary records that Ridsdale and Nicolson met over lunch at the Moulin d'Or restaurant to discuss the proposal in more detail.[124]

Crucially, Guy Burgess was also at the lunch. We know from Nicolson's unpublished diaries that in the eighteen months before Burgess started working at the Foreign Office the pair had met at least twenty-six times socially – either for drinks after BBC meetings, or for lunch or dinner.

So the plans on which Burgess and Ridsdale had collaborated during the previous summer were once again looking as though they would bear fruit. In working with Ridsdale Burgess had performed a service for the Foreign Office probably at the expense of his employer, the BBC. But significantly, Burgess had also been able to show Ridsdale his own talents, knowledge and abilities, qualities which, when the time came and vacancies arose, would help to ensure that he was the right man in the right place at the right time. In suggesting Harold Nicolson's name to Ridsdale as a suitable person to become involved in the broadcasts Anthony Eden's office had established his bona fides beyond doubt in Ridsdale's mind.

The time soon came:

> In March 1944, Burgess was invited by Mr Ridsdale, then head of the News Department in the Foreign Office, to fill a vacancy in that department. He had apparently been recommended to Mr Ridsdale by Mr Harold Nicolson, among others.[125]

To be clear, if anyone needed to check Burgess out he already had on his side at MI5 Anthony Blunt and Deputy Director Guy Liddell, and at MI6 David Footman and Vice-Chief Valentine Vivian. At the BBC he had Sir Richard Maconachie and Joint Director General R. W. Foot, and former junior minister at the Ministry of Information and thereafter BBC Governor, Harold Nicolson. What better pedigree could a candidate have?

So when Sir Alexander Cadogan wrote to R. W. Foot asking for Burgess it was not just some letter that he had been asked to sign as Permanent Secretary. It was a request for someone whose name and potential usefulness he already knew about from internal documents; and it was written to someone who equally knew about Burgess, as shown by Anthony Blunt's 1943 memorandum to Guy Liddell about Burgess and the BBC.

It is possible that Burgess's recruitment by the Foreign Office was nothing more than wartime necessity. That was how the Foreign Office explained it to ministers after Burgess defected: there was a shortage of experienced press officers, a vacancy arose and Burgess was available. However, given Burgess's track record and his close involvement with Ridsdale, as well as his friendship with Harold Nicolson, it is equally possible that he exploited the opportunities and engineered an approach by Ridsdale.

Having received Burgess's resignation from the BBC, his boss, George Barnes, tried to persuade him to stay by offering him the chance to produce the new Foreign Affairs series.[126] But it was too late: the Foreign Office – and its secrets – beckoned. There then began a negotiation about when Burgess could leave the BBC. Burgess came up with the idea that 'it should be possible for me to continue to do work for both departments while I am learning my job at the Foreign Office'. In the end that is how things worked out.

One person at the BBC was not happy that the Foreign Office had got their man. Harold Nicolson asked the BBC management in front of his fellow governors how it had come about. This was a touch rich, the management thought to themselves, because Nicolson hadn't exactly helped to keep Burgess in the BBC by supporting Burgess's appointment to the Foreign Office. Nicolson informed the Governors that had the departing Burgess stayed at the BBC he would have made 'the ideal parliamentary correspondent'.[127]

CHAPTER 6

'AN IMPORTANT PROMOTION THAT CAN BE PUT TO VALUABLE USE'

PROPERLY ESTABLISHED IN THE ESTABLISHMENT, 1944–50

On Monday 1 May 1944, coincidentally but appropriately International Workers' Day – an annual landmark in the communist calendar – a rather unkempt man with an aroma that combined yesterday's sweat, last night's alcohol and that morning's chewed garlic cloves walked into the Foreign Office. At last, he was Guy Burgess of the FO.

As part of his transfer from the BBC Talks Department to the Foreign Office News Department, the BBC agreed that for a short period Burgess could spend two hours a day at his new employer in Whitehall learning his new job. Then he would be a full-time member of staff with an open invitation to learn some of the country's greatest secrets.

Whatever uncertainty there may have been about the value of what he had reported back to Moscow so far, there is no doubt that in a series of Foreign Office roles over the next six years, Guy Burgess was a proper KGB spy. The KGB archive for this period provides the evidence for this designation, including direct quotes from his messages to Moscow.

Crucially, this period extends from the final days of Britain's wartime allied partnership with the Soviet Union through Winston Churchill's 1946

'Iron Curtain' speech into the confrontations with Stalin over the 1948–49 Berlin blockade and the outbreak of the Korean War in 1950. By then, any pretence that helping Moscow was some kind of patriotic act was long gone.

No part of government was sacred from Burgess's industry; no document that passed across his desk was considered too large or too small. In one six-month period alone the KGB reported that he had sent them over 2,000 pages of classified documents. Indeed, the sheer amount of material that he sent would seriously tax his KGB contacts in London, overloading both their supporting staff and the wireless transmitters to Moscow. And all the while he remained undetected, unsuspected and, by all accounts, totally guilt-free.

R. A. 'Rab' Butler, Foreign Office minister under Lord Halifax, had complained just five years before Burgess's arrival that 'the old Foreign Office team' of both ministers and senior civil servants 'called each other by their Christian names and had exactly the same brains'.[1] Butler was not alone in his views. In 1919, 75 per cent of diplomats were Old Etonians and criticism of the Foreign Office's tendency to fill its ranks 'too exclusively from the wealthy and well-connected'[2] was one often levelled. Seventy years on, similar criticisms have been voiced about Prime Minister David Cameron's Cabinet.

In the middle of the Second World War, the Foreign Secretary Anthony Eden, reacting to renewed criticism about the elitist character of his department, had taken a series of reforms through Parliament which included separation from the home civil service and a new scheme for recruitment. These reforms would gradually alter the character of the Foreign Office over time, but when Guy Burgess arrived in 1944, that Old Etonian tie still dominated its upper echelons, accounting for 25 per cent of the diplomatic ranks. The vast majority were still Oxbridge-educated and most had been to one of the country's major public schools.[3]

At this time, the Foreign Office did not have a monopoly on foreign policy; matters concerning the Empire were handled by the India Office, the Dominions Office and the Colonial Office. But, because there was a war on and those countries at war fell mostly within its global brief, this confirmed the Foreign Office's place, alongside the Treasury, as a major department of state. With diplomats managing tricky political and diplomatic relations with allied governments, neutrals and those in exile, the workload was heavy and staff worked long hours.

The Foreign Office News Department that Burgess joined was no exception. It had been created in 1916 during the First World War 'to keep in touch with the British and foreign press in London and to act as a channel through which official news was published'.[4] It was the only new department in the Foreign Office to survive the end of that war, and Burgess's new boss, William Ridsdale, had been there almost since its inception.

Ridsdale, whom Burgess had known well for some years, was 'small, dapper, quite sharp and often funny'.[5] A journalist on a local newspaper before the Great War, he had joined the department in 1919 after being invalided out of the army and following a spell in the Ministry of Information.[6] 'Rids' was trusted by ministers, including Anthony Eden, and by the journalists who were effectively his clients.[7] He was also trusted by Burgess. Soon after joining the department, Burgess told Ridsdale that 'he was proposing to continue to do work upon which he was already engaged with MI5'. Ridsdale later wasn't sure if Burgess had mentioned MI6 instead, but remembered telling Burgess that 'he had no objection . . . providing it did not interfere in any way with his duties'.[8]

This was not necessarily how Foreign Office insiders saw the News Department. The head of the Foreign Office's Personnel Department, E. Chapman-Andrews, was decidedly more sanguine: 'I think it is high time that a clean sweep was made of the News department,' he wrote in March 1946.[9] In his view, shared by other senior managers, the News Department was performing well below par, and even Ridsdale's future was not guaranteed.

Although the number of News Department staff had increased modestly during the war, it was still small and under pressure: on signing his temporary contract, Burgess became just the ninth member of the team. One colleague, also on a temporary contract, was the cartoonist and humourist Osbert Lancaster.

Every morning, one member of the team would get in early and read through the overnight telegrams and the Reuters news wires to create a list for the day's business. Ridsdale would give a series of press briefings as the day and events developed. *The Times*, regarded as the unofficial voice of government, got their own briefing every afternoon.[10] If off-the-record quotes were needed, the convention was then – as today – to use euphemisms such as 'diplomatic circles', 'usually reliable sources' or 'informed quarters' and so on. Burgess's role, along with his colleagues, would be to spend much of the day on the telephone answering journalists' enquiries and hoping to guide them towards the official 'line'.[11] Much the same as everyone else, he did his share of night and weekend duty, which was allocated on a rota. Out-of-hours duties were necessary in order to deal with emergencies; senior officials, ministers and others would have to be contacted, statements prepared and released to waiting journalists.

But there was also another and potentially more benign side to the Foreign Office News Department, from the press's point of view. The department's pre-war files record many instances where its officials helped journalists or their employers with arrangements for covering overseas stories, including making introductions to British embassies and consulates. As the wartime opportunities were curtailed as the war in Europe entered its final phase and territories became newly liberated, those services once again became one of its activities. It undoubtedly also helped the department to keep a watchful eye on who was planning to go where, and what they were likely to be interested in. Such activities were also likely to have been of interest to the KGB.

Foreign Office documents varied in size, complexity, longevity and secrecy; and while some would be of prime interest to Moscow, others would be deemed unimportant enough to ignore. Having access to the secret telegrams would be a bonus, and the KGB archives suggest that this is exactly what Burgess was able to supply.

Some of these were the kind of telegrams that Burgess had once proposed a BBC diplomatic correspondent (preferably himself) be allowed to see. They were either those outgoing from the Foreign Office before they had been encrypted, or incoming from British embassies abroad after they had been decrypted. Not only was the content of telegrams valuable to Moscow, so too were the full texts, including reference numbers and other transmission data. The Soviet wireless intelligence service intercepted radio messages sent by states in whom they were interested, such as Great Britain and the United States, but the vast majority of these messages were encrypted. Burgess, by supplying unencrypted copies of the telegrams that had been recorded, would enable Soviet codebreakers to work out what code had been used by comparing the two versions. Once the code was established, other messages from the same batch could then be decrypted. However, a number of different codes were used for encryption and code keys were changed daily, so Burgess needed to supply these 'Rosetta Stone' versions very regularly.

It would seem that after a while, Burgess grew more cavalier about carrying such material around with him. In February 1945, Burgess had dinner with his friend Harold Nicolson, still an MP and BBC Governor, who recorded: 'I dine with Guy Burgess, who shows me the telegrams exchanged with London and Moscow.'[12] Perhaps surprisingly, Nicolson recorded that he read the telegrams and appeared to have been unfazed by being shown an official secret document in a restaurant.

With the end of the war coming, this was a time of great upheaval in Europe. With the map set to be redrawn, countries had much to gain or lose in the final months of the conflict and the negotiations that were to follow would effectively divide Europe in two. The 'big three' allies – Britain, the US and Russia – met at Yalta in the Crimea in early March 1945 to decide the fate of post-war Europe.

KGB archives confirm that Burgess passed sample telegrams to Moscow and that action alone means that some, if not all, of the high-level exchanges between London and Moscow before the 1945 Yalta allied leaders' conference were passed on to Stalin. Hence the real value of the telegrams in Burgess's possession, and which he was so cavalier in showing to Nicolson that February, just days before the Yalta conference began. But Burgess also passed copies of British government background papers detailing the preparation of negotiating positions. Moscow knew what both Churchill and US President Franklin D. Roosevelt's pre-conference intentions were. It was a conference from which Stalin emerged the victor. Not only had he won concessions, but he had inserted some temporary but effective wedges in the bond between the two leaders.

Stalin's intelligence machine had been better served still because Burgess's fellow spy Donald Maclean – then based in the British embassy in Washington – passed to Moscow copies of top-secret telegrams exchanged between Churchill and Roosevelt before the conference began. During the conference, Stalin continued to get information from spies placed in the US delegation.[13] The immediate post-war map of Europe and the development of the Soviet bloc prove who won at Yalta.

In early September 1945, a Russian working in the Soviet embassy in Toronto approached Canadian officials and said that he wished to defect to the West. His name was Igor Gouzenko. After initial difficulties and a hair-raising intervention by Soviet security men, he was given asylum by the Canadian government. Gouzenko was a cipher clerk, but was a member of Russian Military Intelligence, the GRU. He presented the Canadian authorities with around 100 top-secret Russian documents and surprised officials by outlining to them the extent to which Western governments had been penetrated by Soviet intelligence services – both the KGB and the GRU. Over the months that followed, British and US officials were allowed to join in Gouzenko's debriefing.

Within days of Gouzenko's defection, another Russian diplomat – and KGB officer operating under the cover of Vice-Consul in Istanbul – approached his British opposite number in the city, saying that he wished to defect to the West. His name was Konstantin Volkov. He demanded money and protection for him and his wife in return for information. As a taster, he said that he was able to name agents operating within the British government machine, including one in charge of counter-intelligence. Mistakenly, as it would turn out, British officials interpreted this to mean someone senior in MI5.[14]

Volkov also told the British that he had a number of valuable KGB procedural documents, and that the Russians had recorded *all* encrypted communications between the Foreign Office and the British embassy in Moscow for the previous two years.

The embassy sent the details of Volkov's message to the Foreign Office, who passed it rapidly to MI6 where it landed on the desk of the head of its Russian Section, the man charged with countering Soviet Intelligence: Kim

Philby. With Volkov offering to expose agents working within the British government, his defection could have catastrophic implications for the entire Cambridge spy ring. Philby arranged to travel to Turkey to meet with Volkov, but most accounts show how he delayed his departure. It is accepted that this playing for time allowed the KGB sufficient opportunity to detain Volkov.

Though anxious to tell the KGB of the potential defector within their ranks as a matter of urgency, Philby judged that to do so himself could prove highly dangerous. He needed someone else to get the news to them, so he used Guy Burgess as his courier to a KGB controller in London. It is not entirely clear that Burgess would have known the details, but whether he did or not, passing on Philby's message saw to it that Volkov and his wife were quickly bundled back to Moscow. Volkov was interrogated and shot.

The actions of both Gouzenko and Volkov greatly alarmed Moscow, who recognised the threats posed to their agent networks while Western counter-intelligence agencies sought out possible spies. The KGB considered the security risks involved in maintaining contact with its agents in Britain too risky and they suspended all contact for well over a year – much to Burgess's chagrin. He spent the time doing a little moonlighting for MI5 by continuing to run his agents for them.[15] Meanwhile, it appears he was asked by MI5 to find out more about a senior Foreign Office official who they thought had some 'far from angelic' connections.[16]

* * *

In the summer of 1945 and with the war in Europe ended and the defeat of Japan expected to be just a matter of time, the US and Britain rapidly began withdrawing military forces from Germany. While the USSR also withdrew some troops it still retained over a million soldiers under arms in Germany and Eastern Europe.

Hostilities with Japan ended in August soon after the dropping of atomic bombs on Hiroshima and Nagasaki. The terrifying weapons introduced a new factor into great power rivalries. Some senior US military figures soon argued that control of atomic weapons should be internationalised since they were too dangerous to be left to nation states to develop: they were relatively inexpensive to build once the scientific knowledge had been acquired. Others argued that, in view of the weapons' power, it made sound military sense to attack the USSR with atom bombs in order to permanently prevent it from acquiring an atomic capability. Such sentiments undoubtedly played a role in influencing the latent tensions between the USSR and its former Western allies.

But US generals were not alone in expounding the logic of a pre-emptive atomic strike against the USSR. The philosopher Bertrand Russell, a future chair of the Campaign for Nuclear Disarmament, first espoused such a policy in the months immediately after the end of the Second World War. He had advocated threatening war as a means of exerting pressure on Moscow to acquiesce with plans – advocated by the US philanthropist Bernard Baruch – to internationalise the control of nuclear power and weapons, saying that one must be prepared to carry out the action threatened if a bluff was called.

Russell got into hot water in November 1948 after giving a talk at Westminster School when, in answer to a question about the chances that the UK could survive another war, he said that a decisive preventive atomic attack on Russia to prevent it from acquiring nuclear weapons was the least morally objectionable policy option available. He became embroiled in a controversy that still smoulders for some. He and his defenders blamed the brouhaha on mischievous misreporting by a section of the Fleet Street press. However, while it is less certain that he did advocate such a policy unconditionally, his later attempts to gloss over some of his statements have meant that the matter has never been firmly settled.[17]

In that highly tense atmosphere – the Russians at one stage accused the Americans 'of following in [former British Prime Minister] Mr Churchill's steps and planning a preventive war against Russia'[18] – it is hardly surprising that more emphasis was placed by the Russians on gaining insider information about the diplomatic and political intentions of governments in both Washington and London.

Part of the problem, from the USA's point of view, was that senior military and political figures in Russia thought that the USA already had a large arsenal of atomic bombs. In fact it took until the end of the 1940s for the USA to have more than a few usable weapons.

But, to the alarm of the USSR's rulers, much of the debate in the USA about bombing the USSR was carried out in the full glare of publicity. In 1946, the US Commerce Secretary, Henry Wallace, became enmeshed in controversy when he spoke about the silliness of a 'preventive war'. President Harry S. Truman was forced to go public and deny that any such policy was under serious consideration.[19] In reality, it was one option under investigation by US defence chiefs; and proponents from both sides of the argument continued to debate the issue for several more years.[20]

Unsurprisingly, Moscow became very concerned, and it was this, as much as Stalin's intention to develop a Russian bomb as a priority, that fed the paranoia. At the same time, the Americans 'showed every sign of resolute resistance to Soviet encroachment in areas marginal to Russian security – Turkey, Manchuria, Denmark, and Iran – [where] Stalin had taken a step back'.[21]

The Soviet-engineered coup in Czechoslovakia in February 1948 and the actions of the USSR in cutting access to West Berlin in early summer 1948, which led the West to respond by staging a massive and prolonged airlift to provision the besieged city, demonstrated aggressive Soviet intentions from Western policy-makers' perspectives, and led many to fear that a new world war would shortly break out. They took the absorption of Eastern European states into the Soviet sphere of influence as a further instance, regardless of whether Stalin's intention to establish a protective band of buffer states to safeguard Russia from Western attack had been clearly articulated, understood, or accepted. Within a year, the North Atlantic Treaty Organization, NATO, would be set up, providing mutual defence to member states in the event of an attack on any, backed up by US military power.

In August 1949, news that Russia had exploded its first atomic bomb made headlines worldwide. The international playing field was rapidly levelling, but it did not diminish the rhetoric. One casualty was an American general, Orvil Anderson, the commander of the US Air Force's Air War College. In September 1950, he was suspended from duty for voicing his views about preventive war, allegedly to his aviation students. Russia's possession of the A-bomb only caused people like Anderson to raise the urgency: 'Give me the order and I can break up Russia's five A-bomb nests in a week.'[22]

Western military planners had, by the late 1940s, recognised that the overwhelming size of Russian military forces still based in Eastern Europe meant that any attack launched against the West could not be contained. Therefore, Western military plans envisaged a swift military retreat to the channel ports and use of the atomic bomb to stop a war from spreading.

The UK was seen as an aircraft carrier from which US atomic attacks against Russia could be launched as, until the early 1950s, the USA did not have the capability to launch attacks from US soil. The Russians, therefore, determined that a massive attack against the UK would be necessary to deny the Americans use of the UK as a military base. But, before going this far, the Russian leadership wanted to understand how closely and systematically the US and UK governments cooperated.

* * *

'Burly, fair-haired, a keen soccer player and talking slowly in a Scottish accent',[23] Labour MP for Greenock Hector McNeil was a graduate of Glasgow University and a journalist who tried combining that career with local politics in Glasgow before deciding to focus on running for Parliament, eventually winning a seat unopposed in a 1941 by-election. After Labour's 1945 landslide election victory, the former night editor of the Scottish *Daily Express* quickly became a government minister, Guy Burgess's boss and Foreign Secretary Ernest Bevin's deputy. McNeil was, according to *The Times*, a 'disciple' of Ernest Bevin from the right of the Labour Party.

Bevin himself had been the leader of Britain's biggest union, the Transport Workers, and then the Minister of Labour in the coalition government. In later years, Burgess developed a considerable affection for him. Burgess once made an 'off-the-record' comment about American policy in the Middle East during a Foreign Office news conference and the *New York Times* had published it. Burgess wrote, 'I expected thunderbolts

– Ambassador, Wash D.C. telegraphed in fury – but was sent for by Bevin and an Under-Secretary, asked what had happened, explained and was congratulated. "A great 'elp" said Bevin.'[24] Burgess loved to parody the Foreign Secretary's 'h-dropping'.

He told Driberg of an incident where Bevin had deliberately stayed out of contact from Cabinet colleagues who were angry about a trade deal he'd done with America behind their backs. Hector McNeil's team were told by Downing Street to find Bevin, who was on a boat outside territorial waters. Burgess chronicled the scene with a cartoon of Bevin in a boat exclaiming, ''Ector needs me'. McNeil saw the drawing, wisely filled in the missing 'H' for Hector and showed it to Bevin. The Foreign Secretary then circulated it as an official Cabinet document as a way of defusing the row.

Bevin called McNeil his 'indentured apprentice'. With the Foreign Secretary so busy, McNeil regularly stood in for him. One such occasion was a peace conference in Paris attended by McNeil, Ridsdale and Burgess. McNeil was judged to have done particularly well and in 1946 was promoted to Minister of State, the youngest Privy Councillor of the day.[25]

McNeil had known Guy Burgess since at least 1943, when they had worked together on *Week in Westminster*, and, by all accounts, had great respect for Burgess's intellect, insights and imagination. In the latter part of 1946, McNeil requested that Burgess come to work in his private office in a role created for him: 'Assistant to the Minister of State'.[26] Initially, McNeil wanted 'to borrow Mr Burgess on an experimental basis from the News Department to help him with the drafting of speeches, etc.'.[27] McNeil's ministerial predecessor, Philip Noel-Baker, had employed one of Burgess's friends, Stuart Hampshire, in a similar role.[28] However, for the entire time spent working there, he remained 'on loan' and 'could revert at any time' to the News Department.[29]

Contrary to published accounts that Foreign Office mandarins didn't want Burgess to work with McNeil and would only agree if he would accept an Assistant Private Secretary as well, files in the National Archives show that this was not the case.[30] Instead, their focus was on ensuring that Treasury funding was received for Burgess's new post and that a 'new boy' could be recruited to the News Department.[31] Furthermore, the files clearly show that it was Hector McNeil himself who asked for an Assistant Private Secretary to help his overworked Private Secretary, John Rob.[32]

Meanwhile, there was progress in getting Burgess's temporary post turned into a permanent one. The process had been 'set in motion in March 1946. It progressed slowly and it was not until October 1, 1947 that the Civil Service Commission issued a certificate' showing that his application had been successful and that Guy Burgess had become a member of the permanent Foreign Office staff.[33] His grade – Executive Officer – was equivalent to the Assistant Private Secretary's grade. Burgess remained a member of the Foreign Office junior B Branch. His move to the ministerial office had not enabled him to move to the coveted 'senior' A Branch, to which all Foreign Office mandarins and aspiring mandarins belonged. However, for Burgess, this was a moment not just to advance his Foreign Office career, but to reboot his KGB one. Burgess could hardly contain his excitement at the chance to get back into proper business with Moscow.[34]

In a letter to his controller released by the KGB archive – interestingly the only one that we have come across that is in his own handwriting – Guy Burgess wrote:

> I have been offered the post of 'Personal Assistant to the Minister of State' (Hector McNeil). This offer has been made officially and for that reason and since it is I think not only an important promotion but one that can be put to valuable use I shall accept it ...We are now justified in saying that it is certainly the case that there can be <u>no suspicions</u> of any kind against me, otherwise such a central and confidential appointment would not have been sanctioned (as it has been) by the Foreign Office.

His new position would give him wide-ranging access across government and, to some extent, Burgess would have the freedom to define his own role, and perhaps even exert influence over McNeil's own direction: 'It is clear that to some extent the actual duties will depend on what is aimed at by McNeil and also, I hope, myself.' Extra keen to express to Moscow the opportunities it presented, he wrote:

> McNeil in conversation has said that routine office work will continue
> to be looked after by the Private Secretaries and that my duties will be to
> assist him in the formulation of policy by the study of documents and
> by personal contacts and conversations with other officials and also with
> politicians, both British and Foreign. There will also be opportunities for
> direct communication with the Secretary of State's office. He also wishes
> me to spend a certain amount of time in the House of Commons ... It
> would I think be wrong if I did not say that in my opinion great oppor-
> tunities are opened to us by this transfer.

He went on to list what he expected he would have access to:

> Apart from telegrams which I shall continue to see I shall hope to be able
> to see those minutes and private letters (e.g. from & to ambassadors)
> which describe the inception and formulation of policy and to be present
> at, or aware of, conversations in which future decisions are canvassed and
> discussed before being arrived at. I believe the Minister of State usually
> (and certainly a Minister of State who is on such close personal terms as
> Hector is with Bevin) is informed of all Foreign Office transactions and
> if he is, then I hope to be.

Burgess, not known for his modesty, added, 'As is known we are on excellent, indeed very close, personal terms ... it is also to some extent a personal
choice by Hector, with which incidentally Bevin, who has been consulted,
agrees.' Burgess's connections had come good, and he wanted to make sure
that Moscow knew it. One might be forgiven, though, for thinking he was
beginning to overegg the pudding: 'As I say, I think this appointment is to
one of the most desirable central positions in the Foreign Office and I should
welcome any instructions as to how to make the fullest use of it and in what
manner it can be turned to our best advantage.'[35]

It is tempting to ponder whether he was worried that Moscow might just
say no.

* * *

When word got around about Burgess's new job there was unease was among some people who knew him well. MI6 officer David Footman was reportedly not impressed[36] and Guy Liddell, the senior MI5 officer who had kept an eye on Burgess and agent ORANGE during the war, was doubtful too. On 1 February 1947, a month after Burgess had taken up his duties, Liddell wrote in his diary: 'In the evening I met ... Guy Burgess, who is now PA to MacNeil [sic] – not I venture to add a very suitable appointment.'[37] Liddell may not have thought the appointment appropriate, but he did not record that he had done anything to bring his concern to the Foreign Office's attention.

As he moved from the News Department into McNeil's office on 31 December 1946, Burgess took a few papers with him for old times' sake. He had not been senior enough to attend meetings of the Foreign Office Russia Committee, which was charged with assessing communist propaganda and considering ways to combat it,[38] however, Ridsdale and his deputy, Norman Nash, had been, and Burgess does seem to have had access to their copies of the minutes and papers, which were classified only as 'secret'.[39] In a document released by the KGB archive, Burgess writes, 'I enclose two documents from the Russia Committee, which you may keep. There is no need to return them. They are duplicates.'[40]

The likelihood is that while Burgess shared some of the workload with the private office team – led by McNeil's Private Secretary, John Rob, with support from Assistant Private Secretary Alan Horn – his duties were probably less formally defined.[41] It is possible, however, that he may have had some hand in producing the eight Cabinet papers that McNeil wrote during 1947.[42]

Burgess had achieved 'access to everything Moscow needed'. However, the documents that Burgess was able to pass, or summarise, did not answer all of Stalin's questions.

> The key question was whether the US quest for predominance among the Western allies would result in an early collision with Britain or whether, ever mindful of reduced resources, Britain would seek to harness the United States to its own advantage and therefore abrogate understandings already made with Russia.[43]

Soon after Guy Burgess's arrival at McNeil's office, he wrote to his KGB contact, whom he knew only as Max: 'I have had the splendid news from Fred (i.e. Johnson) that there is every possibility that our contact will soon be resumed.'

'Fred' was a codename for Anthony Blunt; another was 'Johnson', and a third, rather oddly, was 'Tony'. Burgess's letter dates from January 1947, directly contradicting Blunt's later protestations that he retired from active spying in 1945: Blunt was clearly still in touch with Moscow and, moreover, in touch with a KGB controller in advance of Burgess.

Having been in his new post for just a week, Burgess told the KGB that he was 'not rushing and behaving cautiously'. It was a strange new world for him, full of obstacles and dangers:

> The institution's rules are themselves new to me, and although there are documents which I would like to hand over to you (along with other things, Cabinet protocols are filed in the secretaries' room) these documents would, of course, have to be returned and I know that you are unable to do that at present. Guided by security rules, I am unable to make copies of them in the room, where three other people are working.

Burgess recognised that to serve Moscow more fully he would need to be able to pass some of the documents that were crossing his desk in McNeil's office: full text, rather than summaries. But the secretaries' room where documents were kept was not a typing pool, but where the ministers' principal private secretaries worked, all of them senior diplomats. Copying documents while sitting at his desk was just not feasible. He needed a better option.

'At the moment, I am studying the possibility of whether it is possible to take documents home for the night, but it is still too early to say whether this will be possible.'[44]

It is difficult to understate the importance of this statement. In order to be most effective, Burgess the spy needed to have access to documents that he wished to pass to Moscow. He therefore sought permission to treat the office document pool as his own lending library.

It is not known who would have been required to give that permission. It is not known, either, whether Burgess mentioned to Hector McNeil that he had been doing a little work on the side for MI5, although this is unlikely. But he might just have mentioned that Ridsdale, still his nominal boss, had been content that he could sometimes take papers home to read. Hector McNeil and Ernest Bevin might just have been aware of Burgess's request, but it would not have been a decision for politicians. More likely, permission would have come from a permanent member of the Foreign Office senior team with overall responsibility for the functioning of the ministerial offices. With its obvious security aspects, it is difficult to think that it did not at least pass across the desk of the FO's Head of Security, George Carey-Foster.§ But, to date, if any request from Burgess was authorised formally, we have been unable to discover any document in the public domain showing by whom, or crucially why, any permission might have been granted.

There was good reason for caution to be exercised over the documents passing through the private office. Many that arrived were marked 'secret', 'top secret' and frequently marked 'to be kept under lock and key'. Bevin's office in particular received top-secret reports from MI6 as well as intelligence assessments from the Joint Intelligence Committee, JIC. McNeil would have been given some access to that material, including copies of Cabinet minutes and memoranda. They were highly guarded, however. Evidence as to quite how restricted access was is provided by a Foreign Office minute written by Gladwyn Jebb. In January 1947, he took over chairing the Russia Committee. After his first meeting, he wrote to Sir Orme Sargent, the Permanent Under-Secretary, complaining that although consideration of specific Cabinet papers and minutes had been on the agenda, most of the members of the Russia Committee hadn't seen them as they were not allowed access, in spite of their all being in very senior posts.[45] Burgess gaining access to Cabinet papers and minutes therefore placed him in a highly privileged position indeed.

Document security was something that officials were aware of and did take seriously, even allowing for the fact that standards were different at

§ Throughout this book Carey-Foster's name is hyphenated. In some of the quotations his name is not hyphenated in the original documents.

that time. Britain had emerged from six years of war with a general aware-ness that documents and unguarded conversations could be very useful to an enemy. Documents were usually locked away in safes or filing cabinets at night. While later official security strictures may have enforced a rigid empty-desk policy before the lights were turned off each evening, the practice in the ministerial offices during Burgess's time was perhaps a little differ-ent. The Foreign Office entrances were staffed by doorkeepers. Once they recognised a familiar face, they usually 'nodded' officials into the building. It is unlikely that bags would have been searched as a matter of course, if at all.[46]

Burgess's friend Goronwy Rees visited him while he was working for Hec-tor McNeil. He described desks that were cluttered full of papers, and where ministerial interruptions got in the way of conversation. McNeil was, Rees wrote, 'not only Guy's superior but a personal friend. He had spoken on Guy's radio programme and the two of them had liked each other, and McNeil had considerable respect for Guy's political judgement, his fertility in ideas, and his gift for analysing concrete political situations.'[47] But, he wrote, the office possessed 'a general air of good-natured disorganization and disorder'. There he found Burgess and the minister's Private Secretary 'facing each other across an enormous desk littered with an assortment of official papers and a large selection of the daily press'. Yet within the apparent disorganisation Burgess was always able to find just the thing that he was looking for.[48]

There were also moments when ministers and senior civil servants weren't in the office, which provided opportunities for Burgess to show off to his friends. Micky Burn remembered Burgess taking him into Bevin's room and showing him a dispatch from Moscow by Isaiah Berlin about the situation of Russian writers under Stalin.

One interpretation of Burgess's plan to take the documents home for the night is that he used his MI5 work as an excuse. Alternatively, if that ruse no longer worked, it opens up the altogether more alarming prospect – from Burgess's point of view – that he (without permission) borrowed the docu-ments that he passed, therefore running the risk that he could be caught at any time without possessing any plausible explanation. If that was the case then Burgess was a thief for Stalin and, if so, it is small wonder that from that time he turned increasingly towards drink.

One document, written by a KGB officer and dated 17 May 1948, lists all the materials that Moscow received from Burgess in the previous six-month period. During this time he passed a total of 683 documents, amounting to 2,011 pages. While the report does not say what the documents were, it does mention that they were passed on to Moscow as photographic plates, by which we assume they meant negatives.[49]

Another report written by a KGB staffer also lists some of the documents sent by Burgess to Moscow via his KGB contact in London. It includes extracts from Cabinet minutes and Cabinet memoranda by Bevin, as well as extracts from the papers and minutes of something called (original English, having been translated into Russian and then retranslated back into English) the Committee on Overseas Reconstruction – a Cabinet committee – which touched on the attitude of the British government towards Germany, German industry, the German economy and German political organisation. On this occasion, Burgess passed 107 pages to Moscow.

Burgess had been able to supply his KGB controllers with unencrypted versions of telegrams ever since his time in the News Department. Reading the released material it is clear, and not at all surprising, that rather than leaving Burgess to his own devices and allowing him to decide what might interest Moscow, he was provided with shopping lists: find out about this, get details about that. This shows that Moscow did indeed take to heart Arnold Deutsch's psychological profile that said Burgess needed strict management to keep him under control. One KGB handler's report from March 1945 says clearly, 'I gave "H" [Hicks, one of Burgess's later codenames] the task of finding documents on the preparations for the San Francisco Conference. I also asked him to find material on the Anglo-French talks.'[50]

A later message showed that he had complied. Several dozen telegrams which 'HICKS' had 'handed over' were said to be 'of considerable importance. Some telegrams, for example, on oil, on the forthcoming San Francisco conference and other matters are being passed on as we requested.'[51]

Unlike the telegrams that Burgess supplied, documents were often photographed and either the negative or the undeveloped film sent to Moscow. Some may have travelled there via the diplomatic bag, but it is likely that some were transported by a KGB courier. If the documents that Burgess passed were deemed important enough, they would be translated in London, encrypted and transmitted to Moscow by radio. Given the number of documents that Burgess supplied, this inevitably placed the KGB's London station under considerable pressure.

Burgess's last London-based KGB controller – Yuri Modin, whom Burgess knew as 'Peter' – wrote that if he was translating original documents overnight before returning them to Burgess he took great care not to leave any indication that they had been touched: 'I wore gloves to avoid leaving fingerprints on the paper ... I typed the transcripts up myself ... they were put into cipher and telegrammed to the Centre, while the borrowed document was returned to the safe or desk it had come from.'[52]

Another type of material that Burgess passed was where Burgess the journalist, the contemporary observer, came to the fore. He produced witness and analytical reports: what he had heard, what he had found out and, more importantly, what he thought was happening, his predictions and views about how things would develop. In March 1945, just a month after the Yalta Conference, according to Burgess's Soviet controller:

> 'Hicks' reported that Eden [the British Foreign Secretary] said in a conversation with Ridsdale that the British government at the moment does not intend to agree to the American delegation's proposal at the Crimea conference on the division of Germany, which the Soviet delegation supported. Eden believes, and Churchill agrees with him, that the talks on the division of Germany at the Foreign Minister's meeting in Crimea offer some kind of 'opening' for avoiding making a decision on this issue.[53]

Burgess's sources were mainly his fellow Foreign Office colleagues: Hector McNeil, with whom he had many conversations, Ernest Bevin's Private Secretary and future ambassador to Moscow Frank Roberts, and diplomat Nicholas 'Nico' Henderson, later Margaret Thatcher's ambassador in Washington, DC.

In my opinion, based on two conversations with McNeil and several conversations with Nico Henderson, who is perhaps the closest of all the staff
to Bevin after Dixon,[54] (McNeil, of course, is closer to Bevin than anyone else) in my opinion, the past few months and the next few months
have been and will be a period in which decisions will crystallise and be
made which will influence international differences and which, (i.e. the
decisions) will have an effect for a very long time. At certain moments
in history diplomatic history and imperialist policy to some extent come
together and are fused. Sometimes ... history needs a jolt and sometimes
it gets one. From both sides.[55]

Burgess never lost an opportunity to update Moscow on how important he
was becoming to McNeil:

About three weeks ago Hector came over from Paris for the weekend. I think the only people he saw and had prolonged conversations
with were Attlee and Orme Sargent. Not to brag, but rather because
it is relevant here, I have to say that I was the only private individual whom he saw and he spent with me three of the 25 hours available
to him, including a night with his wife. Last Thursday (12 September)
he came back from Paris at five o'clock. On Friday 13th he spent the
morning with Bevin in Bevin's suite, breakfasted with me and departed
with his wife that evening or the next morning for the USA on the
Queen Mary.

Writing about a Russian oil deal with Persia, Burgess made sure to point out
how his position gave him influence: 'I talked to McNeil and, although he is
of the view that the concessions should not be given to the USSR, I do not
believe he will prevail. I hope to be of some service by influencing McNeil
a bit on this matter.'[56]

The opportunity for talking policy with ministers was especially important in the Foreign Office at this time because Ernest Bevin was famous for
not liking briefing papers – he preferred to argue issues out verbally with his

officials and advisers before writing his decisions in red ink and expecting his decisions to be carried out.[57]

One Burgess report demonstrates how he was able to accumulate a mix of strategic insights, political background and interesting gossip:

> In the near future Bevin will be asking the Cabinet to decide on whether to extend Great Britain's present hostile relations with the governments of the countries which he calls Soviet satellites (Poland, Bulgaria, Romania) and whether Great Britain should maintain its present policy of support for the opposition or whether the time has come to recognise Soviet influence and cease the fight against it.
>
> Bevin was greatly alarmed by the parliamentary rebellions (hence the 'conciliatory' tone of his radio address) ... British troops are now expected to be withdrawn from Greece at the same time that, under the peace treaties, Soviet troops are withdrawn from the Balkans.[58]

Some of the reports offered may have been more relevant on *Week in Westminster*, however: '"HICKS" as usual brought several telegrams ... Some of these are of interest. Hicks had also written an agent's report on the procedural conduct of debates in Parliament on the Polish question.'[59]

There were times when the ever helpful Guy Burgess felt he needed to know more about what Moscow wanted, but it was either forbidden or unwise to ask. But it didn't stop him trying:

> I have written to you an exhaustive, perhaps more than that, explanation of the situation in which I find myself. I am well aware that the rules prevent one asking what is needed and that the ruling is absolute. However, as I said, I described the situation in detail and, if you would look at my explanation, you will see that I'm faced with two problems...[60]

Moscow remained wary of what they received. A report by a Captain Kogen noted: 'There is no doubt that for perfectly clear reasons we should take a critical approach to all the material given to us by 'M' [MADCHEN, one of Burgess's KGB codenames] although this does not in the least mean that doubt should be cast on the authenticity of his information.'[61]

The task confronting even an organisation as well-resourced as the KGB was difficult. Coping with the flow of important documents from Burgess was one thing; the other was trying to place them in some wider context. The Foreign Office was, after all, just one Whitehall department dealing with the world beyond Britain's shores, and it is estimated that by 1946 it was receiving 550,000 documents in its own right, and generating a large number of its own in addition. By the time that Burgess left McNeil's office, the volume of documents received had increased to more than 626,000. Agent 'HICKS' on his own could not have provided a full picture.[62]

In April 1947, Guy Burgess, now aged thirty-six, applied for a promotion inside the Foreign Office. In the National Archives at Kew sits a file that contains his application form (referees: Anthony Blunt and Sir Richard Maconachie), the briefest of CVs (repeating his regular lie that he 'resigned' from the 'FO/MoI' to return to the BBC), a medical report (right testicle atrophied due to childhood mumps), and a BBC reference (Government Question: 'Whilst in your service, was he honest, sober, generally well conducted?' BBC Answer: 'Yes'). He was invited to fill out yet another form that showed he would be employed, if appointed, in B Branch.[63] Finally, his service record describes his performance as satisfactory and his health good. His vision was clearly much better than it had been when he had left Dartmouth all those years earlier, because there is no reference to any sight defects. His promotion came through soon afterwards.[64]

Getting from first application through to the final establishment certificate took eighteen months. It had taken so long because there were a great number of applications like Burgess's to process as temporary wartime staff queued up to become permanent. Ridsdale had mentioned it to Burgess, the papers had somehow been lost, and Burgess had to resubmit. It was all very frustrating. But on his form he notes below a blacked-out paragraph that probably deals with his time in the BBC, 'I was debarred from a commission in the Navy during the war for the reason I left Dartmouth – eyesight.'[65] This time the application was successful.[66] But it had not been an easy process for Burgess, who at times looked as though he was longing for a 'proper' permanent job.

Early in 1948, Hector McNeil's new Private Secretary, Frederick Warner, arrived in the office. Initially wary of Burgess, he soon became a good friend, unlike John Rob, the person he was replacing. Although neither knew it at the time Warner and Burgess's friendship would ultimately have a fateful impact on Burgess's espionage career. They soon became well enough acquainted to go drinking together after work and Warner quickly got to know a number of Burgess's friends, including Harold Nicolson. Warner's uncle, Christopher, had since the beginning of the war run the Foreign Office's Northern Department, which embraced Scandinavia and the Soviet Union. He had been instrumental in setting up the Russia Committee. Later correspondence reveals that whereas Nicolson was more charitable and indulgent to Fred Warner, Burgess was inclined to think him not entirely reliable: 'a charming, but very dishonest character'.[67] In a roundabout way, however, they kept in touch for many years after they first met.

Warner's arrival was fortunate. As Burgess waited for his post to become established he prodded to see if there was any progress. At various times during the waiting period, Hector McNeil and Fred Warner took up the torch on Burgess's behalf. Burgess had told McNeil the long story in July 1947 and McNeil had suggested to senior officials that someone with Burgess's intelligence should be promoted into the elite A Branch. They replied that Burgess needed more experience and would have to wait his turn. Eventually, Warner fixed things: in April 1948, he agreed with everyone that Burgess would need to serve either in an embassy abroad or in a 'political department' in London, to gain experience and thus become eligible for promotion. Political departments managed Foreign Office policy, with their work divided geographically. With experience like that under his belt, Burgess could then join the promotion waiting list.[68]

By the middle of 1948, and having been promoted to Higher Executive Officer several months earlier, Burgess should have been feeling contented. His employers had judged him, at the very least, as satisfactory, and his prospects appeared to be improving.

At this time the KGB pushed for more. A report dated 18 July 1947 and headed 'discussion of risks taken by Burgess in removing documents' shows this. A KGB agent had

> reported that we are unable to increase the frequency of the meetings, since this could place the source in great danger. V M [Vyacheslav Molotov, the Soviet Foreign Minister then in London for a Foreign Ministers' Conference] said that we should not break with the established way of working with him but make maximum use of meetings with 'H' [Hicks – Burgess] to obtain documents on allied actions. V M issued no instructions immediately before his departure.

Coming from one of Stalin's most hard-line immediate circle, the lack of sympathy and understanding for the danger to Burgess is hardly surprising.

That Burgess continued, despite the pressure, shows that he was emotionally and intellectually locked into espionage and that his ideological commitment was deep and rock solid. He was in for the duration. In recognition of his efforts, the KGB awarded him an ex-gratia payment of £200 for his travails.[69]

Some published accounts say that Burgess's performance in Hector McNeil's office was beginning to flag. According to those he steadily became more dishevelled, and his drinking increased. The warning signs were beginning to mount up. There are various stories that Burgess's health began to suffer, which on one level would hardly be surprising, given the amount of alcohol that he was apparently seen to be consuming.

For five weeks near the end of 1947, there was a 4-power meeting in London. During that time, 'Burgess passed 336 Foreign Office documents to the rezidentura and earned warm praise from Vyacheslav Molotov, who asked whether even more material could be made available.'[70]

Examples of other documents that Burgess handed over – quite apart from copies of telegrams – show the range of materials that he either sought out on demand, or acquired fortuitously. For instance, on 15 March 1948, he handed over the text of the Western European Union Brussels agreement and the record of the discussion between Hector McNeil and Paul-Henri Spaak, the Belgian Foreign Minister.[71]

That same month, Hector McNeil asked Burgess to report to him anyone operating within the Foreign Office whom he might believe to be acting suspiciously. It is not clear, however, whether this was a genuine trusting request or was the result of McNeil dropping a hint to Burgess that he should be careful. Such warnings could always be taken both ways.[72] But there is another side to this that suggests Burgess was falling under suspicion and that his antics had finally led Hector McNeil to conclude that he had to go.

Yuri Modin was surprised to learn about the hushing-up of an incident where a drunken Burgess punched the jaw of a Foreign Office colleague who ended up in hospital. The cover-up had reportedly been organised by McNeil himself, a man of whom a colleague once said 'was almost too kind and human'.[73]

Learning of this, Modin wrote that he was amazed 'even though I knew exactly the same thing might have happened in the Soviet Union'.[74] To Modin, however, Burgess's general behaviour was beginning to cause anxiety: 'The KGB lived in dread that one evening, dead drunk [Burgess] might confess everything to some stranger.'[75] However, there is no hint of any such incident in Burgess's Foreign Office file.

In April 1948 Burgess told the KGB that he would soon be required to move from the minister's office. McNeil had therefore asked him to think about his next placement: McNeil favoured the Far Eastern Department, but his KGB controllers apparently favoured the American, Northern or General departments. What KGB records do not appear to reveal is that, according to some published accounts, he was earmarked for the Information Research Department, Britain's fledgling anti-communist propaganda operation.[76]

There have been stories that from 1948 Burgess's behaviour and demeanour within the Foreign Office was beginning to irritate McNeil and to alarm George Carey-Foster, the head of the Foreign Office's nascent security department. The minister was said to be no longer able or prepared to put up with Burgess: he had to go; and he had an idea about where Burgess could be posted. A junior ministerial colleague of McNeil's, Christopher Mayhew, was a rising star in the Foreign Office. An Oxford intellectual, he had visited Russia as a pre-war student in the company of the likes of Anthony Blunt and Michael Straight, but, unlike them, he had come back staunchly anti-communist.

Following his appointment as a junior minister in the Foreign Office, Mayhew developed the idea that government ought to fight Russian communist propaganda head-on. Eventually winning the backing of Ernest Bevin and the then Prime Minister Clement Attlee, he was authorised by Attlee to set up a unit in the Foreign Office to wage an anti-Soviet propaganda war. It had to be hidden, however, because if its details became known it was expected that the Parliamentary Labour Party's more left-wing members would try to stifle it at birth.

'I now made an extraordinary mistake,' Mayhew wrote many years later. 'Hector McNeil came into my room, congratulated me on the progress the IRD was making and said that he had someone available who was uniquely qualified for IRD work.' 'Who was this candidate?' Mayhew asked. 'My personal assistant, Guy Burgess. Just your man,' was McNeil's reply. Mayhew tells how he was unenthusiastic about the slovenly Burgess, whom he had recalled lolling against the mantelpiece in McNeil's office. But his knowledge of communism and communist techniques was dazzling. He decided to try him out.

According to this version of events Burgess was transferred from McNeil's office and immediately tasked with visiting British embassies abroad to spread the word about IRD's functions and services. In hindsight, Mayhew recognised the irony of transferring Burgess to the Foreign Office unit responsible for countering communist propaganda. While the unit remained hidden from many MPs and the British public that financed it for nearly three decades, its *modus operandi* was known about almost from the outset by one of the countries against which it was pitted. But it had never occurred to Mayhew that Burgess might be working for the Russians.[77]

Burgess may have been on the team, but he was just as quickly off it again. IRD's deputy and future head, Norman Reddaway, invited Mayhew to look at Burgess's work. He was unimpressed. He made inquiries and found Burgess to be 'dirty, drunken and idle' and that was it. Burgess was passed back to McNeil's office and the Foreign Office personnel managers were tasked with foisting Burgess on to someone else.

A study of the large number of Foreign Office and MI5 files that were released to the National Archives in October 2015, however, has led us to two observations about this point in Burgess's career. The first is that traces of Burgess's time in IRD are extraordinarily hard to find. In fact nothing has so far come to light to support Lord Mayhew's account. The second is that reports about Burgess's performance while he was in McNeil's office show that he was doing a satisfactory job. Remarks made in other files after Burgess had disappeared show that a number of officials said that they had had reservations about his work, but that none were committed to paper and filed while he still worked there. Frank Roberts was Ernest Bevin's Private Secretary when Burgess worked for McNeil. He had a different view about Burgess's abilities. Describing him as 'the most wrong-headed official I have ever come across', Roberts said that, if he received Burgess's 'hare-brained schemes and ideas', he always did the opposite.[78]

When the time came for Burgess to move to a 'political' department in order to gain the crucial experience that he would need in order to qualify for promotion and transfer to the elite A Branch, his departure was delayed so that he could provide some cover for McNeil and Warner to go off to overseas meetings, provide leave cover, and then accompany McNeil and Warner to a UN meeting in Paris in October 1948.[79] However, it is possible that he was asked to spread the word about IRD (but clearly not to Moscow) when he visited Turkey in the summer of 1948. He stayed there with the Philbys for around five weeks and while there met Kim Philby's secretary, Esther Whitfield.[80]

Despite delaying his departure to assist McNeil at the UN General Assembly, Fred Warner found that 'he was no help to us at all, in fact a nuisance'.[81] There too was Sir Alexander Cadogan, Britain's ambassador to the United Nations. Uncut cinema newsreel film of parts of the meeting shows McNeil and Cadogan in lengthy conversation.[82] Burgess does not appear in the frame. Perhaps he was busy outside the conference where he passed copies of the papers and draft resolutions to a KGB contact. They were passed on to Soviet Foreign Minister Vyshinsky, who sat next to Cadogan during the key stages of the meeting.[83] The British ambassador's papers had gone straight to his Soviet neighbour via Burgess.

That same month, Burgess outlined his prospects to his controller:

> I won't do my duty if I don't tell you that I am going to work to this
> department [the Far Eastern Department] with completely different
> opportunities in comparison with those I had while working with Hec-
> tor. It is true that I am being transferred there with his support and that
> he has spoken to [Sir Esler (Bill)] Dening [the supervising Under-Sec-
> retary] and [Sir Harold] Caccia, chief of the Personnel Department,
> and given a recommendation and asked to give me important work. It
> is true but it will not mean very much. Still, we shall see. I suggest; (1)
> My being cautious and even timid in this respect until the opportuni-
> ties become clear. (2) Using to the maximum on a personal basis the
> contacts and friends, Fred, Hector and co. I know that suggestion No.1
> will be approved.[84]

Burgess did not refer to IRD explicitly in his messages to the KGB: maybe
due to the embarrassment of his being turfed out so rapidly as a result of his
behavioural problems. Alternatively, it may provide an indication that from
the early part of 1948 Burgess was not only betraying the Foreign Office, but
was beginning to deceive the KGB by airbrushing out inconvenient parts of
his own career.[85] It is equally possible, given the paucity of evidence available,
that Burgess never formally worked in the IRD at all.

* * *

Senior managers at the Foreign Office knew the pressures of the job. In 1950,
one of them, Frank Ashton-Gwatkin, spent part of his own retirement giving
a series of lectures at Syracuse University in New York State looking back on
his time as a diplomat. He told his audience that diplomats were sometimes
'finished' (i.e. burned out) well before they reached the age of retirement. In
Burgess's case it probably looked to Foreign Office managers as though he
was burning out at the age of thirty-seven.

The problem was, where could Burgess be sent next? Nowadays, someone exhibiting Burgess's alleged behaviour would be removed; things were

altogether gentler and less harsh in the tolerant 1940s Foreign Office, if you fitted into the socially exclusive mix that is.

The Foreign Office then comprised eight departments, their responsibilities divided geographically, and Burgess was transferred to the Foreign Office's Far Eastern Department. This was divided into branches, or desks, that concentrated exclusively on designated countries. Burgess was placed at the China and Philippines desk, dealing with 'general' issues. Two other colleagues dealt with 'political' issues. China was then in the closing stages of a bloody and bitter revolutionary civil war, waged between Kuomintang Forces led by nationalist and pro-Western General Chiang Kai-Shek and the communist People's Liberation Army led by Mao Tse-tung. By the time that Burgess entered the department, the war was beginning to look like a foregone conclusion. With an expected communist victory, the policy poser for Britain would be what to do about it: establish diplomatic relations or shun the country, as the Americans were signalling they would do.

It was into this politically interesting situation that Burgess sat down at the China desk on 1 November 1948.[86] He was placed under the watchful, but very acute gaze of the departmental head, Peter Scarlett. Scarlett, a highly experienced diplomat, had been interned by the Nazis for the first eighteen months of the war before being exchanged under a brokered deal. Following his release, Scarlett was made the deputy of Sir Robert Bruce Lockhart, the Foreign Office deputy secretary in overall charge of British wartime propaganda – in particular, the black sort.[87] Scarlett was not, therefore, someone who was likely to be a soft touch.

By all accounts, he developed a respect for Burgess's intellect and a mild tolerance for his behaviour and demeanour. But a review of the files generated by Scarlett's department shows not only the range of topics to which Burgess had access, but also that Burgess made some real and – from the British government's point of view – helpful contributions to the development of policy towards the Chinese communists. In many ways, his opinions and those of the Foreign Office and the Labour government were not far apart. All felt that diplomatic recognition and engagement with the communists was by far the best policy, and that America's favoured policy of isolating the communists was to be resisted.

Burgess would stay with the department for twenty-two months. During that time he had access to secret and top-secret telegrams, military situation reports and diplomatic dispatches. It is unlikely, however, that he would have had access to raw intelligence, since that would have been processed through the Secretary of State's office and by the various intelligence agencies.

Just before Christmas 1948, Burgess gave Moscow a present: his first detailed report after his move to the Far Eastern Department. He supplied character sketches of his departmental colleagues and told them:

> I can't say anything about other officials except that it has proved possible to establish excellent personal relations with them, owing not only to my abilities but also to the lucky chance that almost all of them like myself have been to Eton. Things of this kind have great importance.

He continued to provide details about the assistant head of the department, (Sir Frank) Tommy Tomlinson, who, according to Burgess, 'likes to consider himself an Etonian among radicals and he likes me as a radical among Etonians'. He warned that as a result of his move he would only have access to papers limited strictly to the Far Eastern theatre: and in particular China. Nevertheless, he expected to be able to provide a high volume. But would it be a case of never mind the quality, feel the width? His controller, Korovin, told Moscow: 'He at once advanced the idea of passing over to us at every meeting still larger bundles of documents than those he had passed over up to now, and he asked to buy a suitcase for this purpose.'[88]

After Burgess's move to the Far Eastern Department's China desk, we now know that he continued to keep in close touch with Fred Warner. This continuing relationship resulted in Burgess having access to a selection of NATO documents which he duly passed to Moscow via Anthony Blunt's inexpert camera work.[89]

The cover of a Foreign Office file (known as its 'jacket') shows when it was created, its descriptive title, who originated it, which other files (if any) it contained and, most importantly, who had seen it: each official initialled and dated it. The front cover or the immediate inside page was usually the place where comments and actions or assignments were recorded.

Those files which have been released, therefore, allow readers to see who wrote which paper and who commented on it. Reading the reports to which Burgess contributed in some way it is not surprising that his comments were considered valuable because they appear on the face of it to be reasonable, if slightly tendentious, analyses.

One example occurs within a report described as 'attitude of Yunnan in the event of a collapse of the present regime'. On the front of the file appears 'See Mr Burgess's minute', which is a page and a quarter of text written in his slightly messy handwriting. It begins by saying, 'The situation in Yunnan ... is one of political tide turning before coat turning had begun.' It continues, 'Y T Miao, the leading industrialist had, by Dec 10th ... turned against the Nanking regime of Chiang Kai-Shek.' Then, in much the same style as the dispatches he was sending to Moscow, Burgess observed,

> but whether the anti-Nanking tide will take the form of Yunnan separa-
> tion or throwing in their lot with the CCP [Chinese Communist Party]
> remained in the balance. Much wld obviously depend on what sort of
> control the CCP cld get over the bandits and what loss of face if any it
> cld itself show in the province.[90]

Burgess signed and dated his note on 26 March 1949. There is no comment on the file about his use of the term bandits, although clearly he meant the nationalists.

There are later files where it is clear that Burgess had not only seen – and initialled – telegrams and confidential dispatches, but also files containing JIC – Joint Intelligence Committee – reports. He later saw a note by Peter Scarlett that reported, via a contact in the French embassy, the possibilities of 'close cooperation between the Viet Minh and the Chinese Communists from Yunnan'. Such intelligence, if relayed to the Chinese People's Liberation Army, might have caused them to review their own security.

Burgess was also involved in other substantive tasks while in the Far East-ern Department. He appears to have had continuing access to the Russia Committee papers. As we have seen, that committee was tasked with moni-toring and countering communist propaganda worldwide. Frank Roberts recounted how Burgess 'always prepared the first draft of the China section of the Russia Committee's reports'. Interestingly, Roberts also mentioned how 'Andreas Franklin, an old China hand, who politically was extreme Right in his interpretation of Sino-Soviet relations' had had 'innumerable discus-sions on ideological problems with Burgess' on the subject and 'had never detected the slightest sign of Communist inclinations'.[91] Perhaps that is why the name G Burgess (but not G Burgess, spy) appears several times in Volume 8 of *Documents on British Policy Overseas: Britain and China 1945–1950*. There clearly were times when Burgess's and Britain's ideas coincided.[92]

Burgess possibly revealed some of his anti-Nationalist sympathies when he wrote about

> a possible comeback for Chiang Kai-shek, as sudden as his withdrawal
> on January 31, he withdrew because his support in the country as well as
> in the USA had crumbled. Were supporters to rise from the ground in
> China or in Washington he would undoubtedly try to come back. But
> there is no sign of this support being forthcoming. And indeed Chiang
> is exercising behind-the-scenes more control than the support he has wld
> logically justify, were it not for his personal history.[93]

After reading a report from a peace delegation, Burgess advised patience with the Chinese communists: 'For the time being difficulties with CCP [Chinese Communist Party] authorities may be attributed to administrative shortages rather than to a lack of good-will ... we shd continue to advise impatient commercial (and for that matter American consular) bodies to be patient...'[94]

Files held by the National Archives confirm not only that Burgess got to see JIC reports, but that he also had access to secret telegrams: for instance, military attachés situation reports, or 'sitreps', as they were known. Their great sensitivity was signalled by the stricture printed at the top:

> This is an unparaphrased version of a secret cypher or confidential code message and the text must first be paraphrased* if it is essential to communicate it to persons outside British or Allied Government services. (*Note: Messages shown as having been sent in a One-Time Pad: 'OTP' are excepted from this rule.)

A number of the sitrep telegrams were marked 'OTP' and so would have been particularly important from Soviet cryptographers' point of view if any of these 'cribs' was handed over by Burgess. They would again represent mini Rosetta stones. The subjects ranged from reports of troop movements, expected crossings of rivers, and the high standard of discipline in the communist forces.[95] Burgess also saw 'Hong Kong intelligence appreciation' telegrams, which were marked '(OTP)'.[96] The files show that he also had access to other government departments' secret telegrams, too. For instance, he saw telegrams between the Colonial Office and the Board of Trade establishing UK policy not to supply military or civilian aircraft to either nationalist or communist China. It is likely that he would have passed this information on.[97]

In May 1950, just about the time that he was being told about a job transfer, Burgess saw a file about how communist troops were being deployed to agricultural tasks. He noted, 'The policy of the extensive use of troops for productive work, particularly in agriculture is not a new one ... However, the measures described within wld seem to indicate rather strongly that no mass adventure in SE Asia is under immediate contemplation.' A month later, the Korean War broke out.[98]

Burgess stayed in the Far Eastern Department in London for nearly two years. Reading through the files, it is just possible to see that he was settling into a job where he was able to make a positive contribution to the work of his department.

But, elsewhere, there are other indications that things were not quite as they seemed. His drinking was becoming a problem. The most powerful evidence came from his friend Harold Nicolson who, after dinner with him one evening in January 1950, was deeply shocked to see the change in him and recorded in his diary, 'I dined with Guy Burgess. Oh my dear, what a sad, sad thing this constant drinking is! Guy used to have one of the most rapid and active minds I knew.'[99] Two weeks earlier, Nicolson had again met Burgess, but that time not for dinner. On that occasion too he was the worse for drink, but at least, Nicolson noted, there was some political information:

> I meet Guy Burgess who is very drunk as usual but who does give me some information as to the reasons why we recognised Mao Tse-tung. The State Department were anxious for us to do so, since it would strengthen their hands against the Republican Congress men [*sic*] whomwant [*sic*] a firm imperialist policy in Formosa. The Russians did not want us to do so.[100]

Burgess's increasingly erratic behaviour in this period was confirmed by an anecdote told by Victor Rothschild's sister Miriam, now Miriam Lane, who had known him since Cambridge days and was becoming widely known as an expert on parasitology, later nicknamed the 'Queen of the Fleas'.

Burgess telephoned her out of the blue, after having made a scene in a restaurant about maggots crawling over his fish. He wanted her help proving that the tapeworm he was subsequently suffering from was caused by the maggots. She explained there was no scientific basis for such a claim. Burgess expressed deep disappointment but added, 'Oh well, I will sue them all the same – I expect they'll pay up rather than face the publicity.'

Two other post-war episodes illustrate how those who had once been close friends with Burgess began to worry about his behaviour.

Micky Burn recalled seeing him

> in Piccadilly Circus, conspicuous in his camel-hair coat, obviously looking for a man. It was a notorious place so I thought he was running a big risk. So I tapped him on the shoulder and said, 'Don't be such a fool.' Guy said, 'Are you the police?' Anyway, I got him away and he took me to the Reform Club for a triple sherbet.

A few years later, after Burn got married, he and his wife were visited by Burgess.

Suddenly he said, 'I want to speak to you alone.' So I went out into the corridor and he wanted to kiss me and start an affair again. I said, 'You don't understand, I'm married', to which he replied, 'Don't be so pompous.' Then he said that if I ever wanted a room in which to be unfaithful he had one that he could lend me. I remember thinking that if I ever did, and I did now and then, it would not be anywhere of his. I had ceased to trust him.

Things were about to get even worse.

CHAPTER 7

'GOOD REASON TO HOPE HE WOULD MAKE A USEFUL CAREER'

CRUCIAL DECISIONS AT THE FOREIGN OFFICE AND MI5, 1950–51

In a corner of graveyard in the Moroccan city of Tangier is a simple gravestone on which can be found: 'Dean. Missed by all and sundry. Died February 1963'.

'Dean' ran a bar which seems to have been rather like a seedier version of the 'gin joint' run by Humphrey Bogart in the classic film *Casablanca*. His customers were what one writer called 'a disreputable army of refugees and deserters, spies, gunrunners, and thieves'. His true identity was probably Don Kimfull, an Anglo-Egyptian who fled London when he was mixed up in the death of an actress from a cocaine overdose in 1919.[1]

Dean (who was also a homosexual) became part of the Guy Burgess story when the two men fell out in December 1949. The incident was chronicled in perhaps one of the most extraordinary messages sent by one MI6 officer to another. 'Burgess', it was reported back to London, 'should not have pinched Harry Dean's Arab bum boy. He has created one hell of a scandal.'[2]

Nevertheless, it turned out to be just one episode in a holiday that included getting drunk on a number of occasions, offending and embarrassing a score of people, avoiding paying some of his bills, committing several security-related indiscretions – all of which culminated in an appearance in front of Foreign Office senior managers when he got back to London. Not bad for what was intended to be a holiday with his mother to recharge his batteries.

Burgess had booked a trip for the two of them to go to the Rock Hotel in Gibraltar and then onwards to Tangier, where they had holidayed some twenty-five years previously. When the pair arrived, however, he started as he meant to continue, and that meant drinking. There is little record of what his mother did, or thought, because according to all accounts she remained firmly hidden in the background. But there is evidence about what Burgess got up to, from an MI6 and an MI5 man respectively. The MI6 officer, Desmond Bristow, disliked Burgess – and it showed. His account of Burgess's activity was littered with homophobic phrases that in the 1940s and 1950s would not have seemed too out of place. The other account is drawn from the diaries of Burgess's sometime friend and acquaintance Guy Liddell, the deputy head of MI5. Despite the difference in tone, the two men shared common sources in the form of MI6 officers on the ground reporting back to London.

The trouble seems to have started when Burgess arrived at Gibraltar's Rock Hotel and discovered that he was unable to change his travellers' cheques.[3] He had with him letters of introduction from Robin Maugham and David Footman, although Footman's was never shown.[4] A later note referred to the introduction from 'one Robin Maugham, who is regarded as one of the "queer" or "Bloomsbury" fraternity and it is generally thought that Mr Burgess has similar proclivities'.[5]

MI6's man in Gibraltar, Kenneth Mills, called Bristow in London to enquire if he knew someone called Guy Burgess: 'He's here in Gib, claiming that he's a good friend of Philby, that he knows you and is personal assistant to Sir [sic] Hector McNeil, and has asked me to change money for him.' Burgess apparently told Mills that he was 'on very friendly terms with Guy Liddell ... and did I know Dick White', a senior MI5 officer.[6] Burgess then apparently made disparaging remarks about the Americans, and 'expressed great admiration for Mao Tse Tung [sic]'. Mills needed instructions. Bristow remembered saying, 'Fuck him! On second thoughts no, he'd probably enjoy that. Just chuck him out; even though he is in the FO.' Mills was told firmly not to change any money for Burgess.

When he spoke to Guy Liddell several weeks later, Mills's account was, according to Liddell's record, more low-key: 'Mills said he had never heard of Burgess until the latter rang him up' soon after his arrival, 'introducing himself as a friend of Robin Maugham'.[7] Mills told how Burgess and he discussed the question of exchange controls and currency for Tangier with an inference that Burgess was trying to surmount the £10 limit.[8] Liddell noted that 'Burgess evidently did not wish to run any sort of risk' and appears to have decided to change his travellers' cheques legally. They had later gone for a drink, after Burgess had dropped heavy hints. While Mills said he had had a Bass bitter, Burgess had knocked back three double brandies. Later, Mills took Burgess and his mother up to the yacht club 'in order that they might be introduced to various local residents'.

While still in Gibraltar, Burgess called on Mills and his wife 'and consumed quite a lot of whiskey'. He told them that he had 'met Princess de ROHAN and Mrs Oliver at the Rock Hotel, that they were extremely nice people and he hoped that Mills would look after them'. Princess Dil de Rohan was the widow of a German aristocrat and had been head of the Ministry of Information's Swiss department. Mrs Oliver was the widow of Jack Oliver, an Old Etonian and a former president of Pop, the senior pupils' society. Burgess had been a frequent wartime guest at their soirees in Pembroke Lodge in Richmond Park, until it had been destroyed by bombing in 1943.

Mills told Liddell that he later learned from Princess de Rohan that Burgess had 'spent an evening with her and Mrs Oliver in their room, where he got very drunk at their expense'. Liddell recorded that it 'was apparently on this occasion that the indiscretions took place, about which the Princess de Rohan later made a statement'. Liddell added that 'Mills, from his knowledge of the behaviour of all three, feels that it is highly probable that they were all pretty drunk and that none of them would have a very clear idea about the indiscretions of the other.'[9]

Crucially, Liddell recorded, 'Before leaving for Tangier, Burgess rang up Mills and said he was not really sure about Princess de Rohan and Mrs Oliver and that they might, in fact, be up to anything.' This was classic Burgess damage limitation: strike first and undermine someone before they can damage you.

Thereafter things started to go from bad to worse. Burgess and his mother moved on to Tangier. Still in need of money, Burgess contacted a female MI6 officer called Teddy Dunlop. She called Bristow in London to say of Burgess: 'He's rude, keeps pestering me for money and generally behaving in an appalling fashion.' Bristow advised her not to give Burgess anything. She replied that Burgess had 'gone around broadcasting the name of the Swiss diplomat who allowed the British to use the Swiss diplomatic bag to bring rare pieces of equipment and information out of Switzerland'.[10]

Dunlop told Bristow about Burgess upsetting the local ex-pats by pinching Dean's 'Arab bum boy'. Other accounts say the drunken Burgess was heard to sing in local bars: 'Little boys are cheap today, cheaper than yesterday,'[11] sung to the tune of Verdi's 'La donna è mobile'.

Soon after, Mills happened to be in Tangier having a drink with one of his contacts when he encountered Burgess, who was 'somewhat inebriated' and insisted on joining them. Eventually Mills had to tell him to go away. A while later, Mills was having lunch with the American Vice-Consul and his wife. Burgess again tried to gatecrash the occasion. This time Mills had to take Burgess outside the restaurant and tell him to get lost, which the drunken Burgess resented, although after he had sobered up he apologised for having been such a nuisance. Finally, to cap it all, Burgess arrived in the office of the local MI6 officer, parked himself 'drinking whiskeys and sodas' and generally made a nuisance of himself and prevented Mills from working. Burgess was again told to get lost. Elsewhere, it appears that a drunken Burgess had noisily spoken about a Swiss agent who passed information to the British.

Bristow's account tells how Mills took the matters up with Guy Liddell and Bernard Hill, MI5's legal adviser, but that after having heard the details Liddell had been reluctant to do anything until Hill forced his hand. Liddell's diaries make no mention of this, only saying that he would be submitting a report.

When Burgess returned to London, leaving some hotel and other bills unpaid, news of his conduct quickly followed him. MI5 received a letter

Guy Francis de Moncy Burgess.
Died 1963, aged fifty-two.

Burgess's mother, Evelyn Bassett, previously Evelyn Burgess
(née Gillman). Died 1964, aged seventy-nine.

Foreign Secretary Ernest Bevin and Minister of State Hector McNeil at a UN conference in 1938 in discussion with Gladwyn Jebb of the Foreign Office. All three worked closely with Burgess. Jebb found the defection a 'supremely distressing' business.

Kenneth Younger, returned as a Labour MP in 1951: Foreign Office Minister who'd visited Burgess's flat but never revealed the friendship when questioned in the Commons about the defection.

Sir Alexander Cadogan: the top man at the Foreign Office who hired Burgess from the BBC and later led the inquiry into the recruitment.

ABOVE: Clarissa Churchill, whom Burgess considered a 'former girlfriend' and a possible wife, with her uncle Winston Churchill and her eventual husband Anthony Eden.

LEFT: Esther Whitfield: MI6 secretary who told Burgess he could not give her the 'attention, care and interest' she would need as his wife.

BELOW: Guy Burgess on one of his holidays at a Black Sea resort. He sometimes stayed at the Sanatorium of the Council of Soviet Ministers in Sochi.

ABOVE: Tom Driberg and Guy Burgess pose for photographs in Moscow in 1956 to promote Driberg's biography of Burgess. In return for his cooperation, Driberg organised new furniture for Burgess's flat.

BELOW: Burgess's funeral. The pallbearers included (CENTRE IN GLASSES) Jeremy Wolfenden, *Daily Telegraph* correspondent, son of the author of the Wolfenden Report on the reform of the law on homosexuality and possibly Burgess's lover.

from the Defence Security Officer in Gibraltar expressing concern about Guy Burgess's behaviour. As it was official, the complaint had to be investigated formally. The letter gave a flavour of how Burgess behaved: 'Burgess appears to be a complete alcoholic and I do not think that even in Gibraltar have I seen anyone put away so much hard liquor in so short a time.' It also noted that he had mentioned a concussion that he had sustained when he 'had fallen down in the Foreign Office'. This fall would, in time, come to appear a great deal more significant than this passing mention makes it seem, and the head injury he sustained may help to explain why Burgess's behaviour had become quite so erratic. Though whether he had fallen 'in the Foreign Office' seems highly questionable, as we shall see shortly. The letter also identified some of the names that Burgess had mentioned publicly, including Guy Liddell, Dick Goldsmith White and David Footman. It also complained that Burgess had spoken in public about the relationship between MI5 and MI6 in Tangier, and what 'Passport Control Officers' did.[12]

Burgess was twice hauled in to explain what had happened to George Middleton, the then head of Foreign Office personnel. He was also seen by MI5: by his friend Guy Liddell. From Liddell's account, we learn that Middleton had accused Burgess in the first interview 'in somewhat general terms, of grave indiscretions in Gibraltar and Tangier' and had wanted 'full particulars'. At the second, 'Middleton read out to him certain more specific charges ... particularly to his indiscretions about SIS'. What Burgess had been saying about the 'neutral' Swiss diplomat who'd helped the British had got straight back to London.

Burgess told Liddell he didn't recall his 'alleged remarks in front of the Princess de Rohan and Mrs Oliver' and, intriguingly, 'nothing' about something that was clearly still too sensitive to mention nearly seventy years later: in the file it was described as an 'incident', the name of the person involved redacted.[13]

Liddell intimated that Burgess had blurted out to the Princess and Mrs Oliver exactly what Mills's role was: that he was something to do with 'passport control', a traditional cover for the MI6 head of station.[14] Burgess apparently thought of the Princess as not 'wholly outside the family, in view of the fact that she had been in charge of Swiss affairs at the M of I during the war'. He perhaps had a point here, because the Princess would have been required to sign the Official Secrets Act when joining the ministry, as Burgess had done himself.

The interview concluded with Burgess expressing concern about this 'serious accusation on his file' which he felt was 'ill-founded' but which, 'if it stood against him his career in the Foreign Office would, to say the least, be seriously blighted'. Burgess asked 'whether, in view of his explanations, the whole thing could be expunged from the record'. Liddell was unable to give any assurance because that was up to the Foreign Office, but he said he would pass on his findings in due course.

Burgess was 'admonished' by Foreign Office head of personnel George Middleton on 3 March 1950. He noted that Burgess 'continues to deny the allegations, but perforce accepts our decision'. Foreign Office Head of Security George Carey-Foster told Middleton that one of Burgess's failings 'in official circles' was that he 'talks too much and too "big".'[15] Early in January, Burgess had been vetted for a third time: the first was in 1937 for the BBC, the second in 1939 for Section D. While he again received the all-clear 'Nothing Recorded Against', this time there was a rider. Bernard Hill had written to Carey-Foster in January 1950 to say that he 'would not raise a security objection to BURGESS' appointment on strict security grounds but ... BURGESS was undoubtedly unreliable and untrustworthy'.[16]

Within days, Burgess lodged an appeal. Over the next few weeks, preparations were made for a board to review the case. Burgess was unnerved and didn't trust George Middleton, whom he suspected was playing fast and loose.

At the end of March, Guy Burgess wrote a remarkable letter which is now stored within volume one of his MI5 personal file. Addressed to his inquisitor and friend Guy Liddell, it reveals his unease about the disciplinary process and concern about the impact on his career. But the letter also represents an attempt to dissemble. Burgess informed Liddell that Middleton had read out to Burgess a letter that Guy Liddell had sent to him about the Tangier Incident. Previously, and unknown to Middleton, Liddell had told Burgess by telephone what the letter contained. Burgess thought that the text read out by Middleton was different and wanted to challenge him on it. Would Liddell give his 'permission'? Burgess threatened to launch a 'whole campaign' that would waste a lot of time, 'although not yours', he wrote, by which we can assume he was possibly hoping that Liddell might try to defuse the situation. Burgess had written personally, and so had opened it 'Dear Guy', and had closed it equally informally, signing off, 'Luv Guy'. What is remarkable about this, however, is that this was a term of affection that he normally reserved for his intimate, homosexual friends. For many years, rumours and questions have circulated about the closeness of the relationship between the two men. Does this letter provide evidence that the relationship between the pair was closer than hitherto has been admitted? Quite what MI5 Deputy Director Guy Liddell's colleagues made of the letter when it finally reached Burgess's file is not recorded.[17]

Incidentally, in trying to subvert the appeal process, Guy Burgess had also called for help from another old friend, securing an opportunity to speak officially to David Footman, despite Valentine Vivian's objections.[18]

Afterwards, the appeal process ground on remorselessly. When it concluded at the end of April, George Middleton's verdict was confirmed. Burgess's admonition stood. Burgess acknowledged it, saying, 'I would like to say how sorry I am that I have been the unwitting cause of so much bother.'[19] It was not, however, a severe reprimand, which would have been altogether more serious and damaging to Burgess's career.

At about the same time, the end of 1949 and the start of 1950, Burgess was in trouble on a completely different front. It appears that Burgess was suspected of leaking information on a number of occasions to an American journalist, Frederick Kuh, who worked for press agencies and US newspapers in Moscow, in London and elsewhere. Freddie Kuh knew lots of influential people and had a reputation for getting information out of them. His knowledge of confidential information even led some to think that he was a security risk. Indeed, both MI5 and the FBI kept a very close watch on him for many years, but never found anything incriminating. In truth, while Kuh sailed pretty close to the wind, it is more likely that he was simply a committed and industrious journalist and just very, very good at what he did.

Burgess knew Kuh through his work in the News Department, and also because they shared some friends and acquaintances, one of whom was Harold Nicolson. Burgess was believed to have passed to Kuh information about Britain's decision to recognise communist China. MI5 had even checked Kuh's subsequent cable to see what information had been passed on.[20] MI5 records reveal that apart from Burgess Kuh was in touch with William Ridsdale at around the same time, although the case officer assumed that he worked for the BBC. But Kuh's contacts also included MPs and a future US Secretary of State, John Foster Dulles, with whom MI5 had seen him lunching earlier in the year.[21]

On 26 January 1950, just one month before he became involved in the Tangier Incident and sixteen months before Burgess defected, Liddell's diary reveals that he and George Carey-Foster discussed whether Burgess should be prosecuted for Official Secrets offences. Burgess had been under some form of surveillance for some time: 'The Security Department of the Foreign Office had had doubts about the reliability of Mr Burgess since 1948',[22] and Liddell's diary recorded: 'Hill [Bernard Hill] had told him [Carey-Foster] that a prosecution under the Official Secrets Act would lie against Guy Burgess, but that for various reasons it would be undesirable to proceed.' Liddell informed Foster 'that he could be quite sure that Hill would be right on his facts'.[23]

Liddell had two reasons why 'it would be undesirable to proceed' against Burgess. First, 'that one would not wish any further publicity' about MI6's activities and second 'that counsel for the defence would be able to say, for example...' there the sentence stops because of a two-line redaction. We do not know what the redaction hides, but we think it likely that Liddell and Hill had calculated that legal discovery might reveal that Burgess had performed a number of tasks for MI5 and MI6, and that facts better left hidden from the security point of view would be brought into the open and names would be named. Quite simply, Burgess knew and had done too much, and there was concern that a sharp barrister would bring it all up in a trial in the full glare of publicity. Liddell and Hill concluded that, 'Although a technical offence was committed we never liked to prosecute in cases of this kind.'[24]

In a paragraph that Liddell might have come to regret later, however, he also committed these words to posterity:

> My own view was that Guy BURGESS was not the sort of person who would deliberately pass confidential information to unauthorised parties. He was, however, extremely keen and enthusiastic in matters which interested him and would be easily induced by a man like Freddie KUH to say more than he ought to. So far as his drinking was concerned, I had gained the impression that owing to a severe warning from a doctor, he had more or less gone on the wagon. I do not think that he often got wholly out of control but there was no doubt that drink loosened his tongue. Personally I should have thought that a severe reprimand from somebody he respected might be the answer to the present situation.

With hindsight we now see that Guy Liddell couldn't have been more wrong – Burgess had hoodwinked him absolutely. Burgess could and should have received two disciplinary admonitions, one for leaking facts to a journalist in London and one for blurting out indiscretions in Gibraltar and Tangier. Only the second had been put on record.

The published official version was that 'early in 1950 the security authorities informed the Foreign Office that in late 1949 while on holiday Burgess had been guilty of indiscreet talk about secret matters of which he had official knowledge. For this he was severely reprimanded.'[25] Burgess was, however, admonished, not reprimanded, according to Foreign Office files. In other words the judgement was less severe.

* * *

During 1949, Burgess had also been in trouble on the domestic front. He'd rented a flat at 10 New Bond Street in central London with Jack Hewit, who had now been with him for nearly a decade and a half. A solicitor for the landlords later told of problems with Burgess paying the rent, complaints from neighbours about rowdy all-male parties and fights in the night. After one such brawl, 'an ambulance drew up and Burgess, with his head and arm bandaged, was taken to hospital on a stretcher'.[26]

Burgess had also been involved in two other separate incidents that year. Precise details about the first are difficult to establish, partly because Burgess himself gave slightly different accounts in the years that followed. Essentially, it involved the now not altogether uncommon combination of Burgess and alcohol. He appears to have gone drinking with Foreign Office colleague and friend Fred Warner, at the time Hector McNeil's Private Secretary and, according to publisher George Weidenfeld, 'the most talked-about young bachelor on several circuits'. Weidenfeld thought that Burgess 'hero worshipped Fred'.[27] It was February 1949 and at some point the two had either had an argument or an over-excited conversation, at the end of which Burgess ended up at the bottom of a flight of stairs. Some accounts, such as one published later in the *Daily Express*, suggest that the injury might have occurred at Burgess's flat, though another (perhaps to save Burgess's mother some embarrassment) has the location as the Reform Club. Most accounts, however, seem to place the action at a Soho club that Warner and Burgess frequented, *Le boeuf sur le toit*. Wherever it occurred, however, Burgess sustained some sort of head injury from the fall, possibly a fracture, and was hospitalised for a time afterwards. Warner always denied that he had been responsible for causing the injury, but that didn't stop Burgess from claiming that he was.[28] The injury caused Burgess to suffer pain for a considerable time and it is likely that he was given codeine, the strong painkiller which is addictive, particularly when taken for longer than a few days. It also has side effects which can include confusion and disorientation and users are warned not to mix it with alcohol.

It is not clear whether the Foreign Office ever got to hear about the injury officially – Burgess's personal file is silent on the matter. However, the Foreign Office might have been expected to have known about what happened next. A few days, or possibly a couple of weeks after the injury, Burgess and his long-suffering mother had taken a short holiday in Ireland. One evening, while he was on his own, he appears to have met a lawyer-turned-author who also relished philosophical discussions: a former fellow of Trinity

College Dublin, Terence De Vere White, who committed the story of the encounter with Burgess to print in 1957 in his semi-autobiographical book *A Fretful Midge*.[29] In it, he wrote that Burgess was completely sober and that they discussed literature. However, within a day, he discovered that Burgess was being prosecuted.

Burgess appeared in Dublin District Court on 4 March 1949, facing charges of dangerous driving and driving without due consideration. He and his mother had just left a performance at the Abbey Theatre when the car that Burgess was driving was involved in a collision in Grafton Street. Burgess was detained.

White attended Burgess's hearing, which was presided over by the author's 'old friend' Cathal O'Flynn.[30] The story made at least two of Dublin's evening newspapers on Friday 4 March 1949: the *Dublin Evening Herald* (front-page news) and the *Dublin Evening Mail* (page five). It is likely that the Foreign Office would have got to learn about this incident because Burgess was named in full as a Foreign Office official, and his address was given as 'The Reform Club, Pall Mall'. It would have been remarkable if the British embassy in Dublin had not spotted it, although there is nothing on file at the National Archives to show that it did.

The charges were dismissed 'on a technicality' by the Justice, although he informed the court that 'in any event he would have dismissed them on the merits'. He had heard evidence from Dr Sean Lavan who had examined Burgess at College Street [Garda] station and Lavan told how Burgess 'staggered sinuously ... appeared to be limp as well as staggering' and 'looked tired and bleary-eyed'. Burgess also 'smelled of drink' and after some questions 'got rather crotchety because he did not have a cigarette and left the room to get one'.[31] The doctor concluded that Burgess had been unfit to control a motor car. *The Herald*'s report noted: 'Guy Burgess, in evidence, described the accident that had happened to him in England. After some days in hospital he persuaded his mother to come with him to Ireland...' It continued: 'In reply to the Justice he [Burgess] said he thought he was "punch drunk" from the fall...' A second physician, Dr O'Brien, examined Burgess and 'thought his expression was vague ... There was no smell of drink. He was smoking continuously, his speech was confused ...he was definitely unsteady and limp ... his behaviour was abnormal.' Dr O'Brien agreed when asked whether the abnormality could be 'due to a preceding head injury ... suffered three weeks before'.[32] In dismissing the charge, Justice O'Flynn said,

> The defendant was a man of brilliance who appeared to be over-wrought and nervous. He had a distinguished career in school and university. Whatever happened that night was not caused by drink or drugs. He did not believe that the accused had taken an abnormal amount of sedatives on that occasion.[33]

Guy Burgess's London-based KGB handler, Yuri Modin, who had access to Burgess's KGB file, would later say, when he wrote a book about the Cambridge spies in the 1990s, that in the 'Dublin incident' Burgess had 'recklessly ran over a man and killed him', but that Burgess had 'successfully pulled strings to hush up the affair'.[34] Examination of the Dublin newspapers, however, shows that Modin (or Burgess's KGB file) was undoubtedly mistaken. There had been another accident that night, but it had nothing to do with Burgess, and involved a British law student from Forest Gate, London, who was on holiday in Ireland and had been killed in Ballsbridge, near Dun Laoghaire, when the car he was driving hit a tree.[35] That story was positioned next to the one about Burgess in both newspapers.

At this point it is worth just taking stock of some of the things that Foreign Office managers would probably have been taking into account as they decided where to place Burgess on the next stage of his career. First, they knew that he needed broader experience, but that he had already committed technical Official Secrets Act offences by leaking material to a journalist, and had also risked prosecution. They might have known – although there is no evidence on his file – that he had been charged with driving offences in Dublin – potentially bringing the Service into disrepute. They also knew very well that he had committed a whole host of infractions while on holiday in Gibraltar and Tangier, for which he had been later disciplined. So, in light of all this, what did the Foreign Office decide to do with Burgess? Remarkable as it may seem, the management decided to post him to the British embassy in Washington, one of the UK's highest-profile embassies, the veritable *crème de la crème* of diplomatic postings.

For many years, this decision has been held up as either a crass error of judgement or something more sinister, such as the presence of another and still unidentified Foreign Office mole influencing Burgess's posting to Washington just as the Korean War had started. The real story, however, is a little less dramatic. In short, a vacancy had occurred for someone with Far Eastern experience and Burgess fitted the bill. The disciplinary process, after all, had not raised any suspicions that he was a spy, just someone who had little comprehension as to what the word 'security' meant. As a result, his Foreign Office bosses felt that a very sharp talking to would be enough to sort him out and decided to give him an opportunity to gain the experience he so badly needed if he had any hope of resurrecting his diplomatic career.

The vacancy had arisen in the Washington embassy in March 1950, and a cable was sent to London asking for a replacement. It was an important job, especially given the developing situation in Korea. However, its incumbent was an A Branch diplomat, Maurice Thresher. London cabled back to say that there was a someone from the Far Eastern Department who would suit, but that their grade was lower than Thresher's. Thresher was A7 and Burgess was B4.[36] The ambassador, Sir Oliver Franks, cabled back: 'He must therefore be a really good man ... I would not object to having a B4 provided the latter is really first-class and suitable for the special kind of work he will have to perform.'[37] At this stage Burgess's name had not been mentioned.

Over the next two months, and while Burgess's disciplinary appeal was being heard, there were several other exchanges between London and Washington on the subject, but the B4 officer remained unnamed.

Meanwhile in London there were some behind-the-scenes exchanges in which Burgess certainly was named. They continued the dialogue between MI5 and George Carey-Foster about Burgess's 'undoubtedly unreliable and untrustworthy' nature. On 1 March, just days before Burgess received his admonition from George Middleton, Carey-Foster had told Bernard Hill: 'BURGESS will be reprimanded, and transferred to a Consular post abroad where he will not have access to Top Secret information, as he now does'. On that occasion, Hill noted, 'Carey-Foster asked me if there were any particular parts of the world where the Security Service would not like to see BURGESS posted. Colonel Vivian and SLB said he certainly should not be posted behind the Iron Curtain, or indeed to any country within the Mediterranean area. The Foreign Office had in mind some country in South America, though SLB said it would certainly be necessary for BURGESS's conduct to be watched in his new post. This Carey-Foster said he would do...'[38] Two days later Carey-Foster confirmed in a letter to Hill that Burgess 'will be transferred in due course to a post where he will have less access to secret information.'[39]. However, less than a week later a note in a Foreign Office file shows that the Personnel Department was still thinking in terms of sending Burgess to Washington: 'The replacement for Mr Thresher we have in mind is Mr Burgess (FE Dept). This proposal to appoint him to Washington will have to be cleared with Security Dept. at an early stage.'[40]

Several weeks later Burgess's name was still fresh in a number of peoples' minds: Guy Liddell's, for instance. On 1 May he noted in Burgess's MI5 file:

Last week I met Carey-Foster at the Club, when I told him how the [Burgess] case stood. He told me that the Foreign Office had decided to send BURGESS to Washington. They had a job for him to do there in connection with Chinese affairs, and they thought that he would be better placed in a large Embassy where he would be under close supervision.

He added, 'Carey-Foster seemed a little doubtful about this decision, as indeed I was. There is certainly more opportunity for drinking and for saying the wrong thing in Washington than almost any other capital in the world!'[41] Bernard Hill read the note and returned it to Liddell with some remarks, pointing out that 'Carey-Foster stated ... that he would let us know where BURGESS was to be posted.' Clearly, that had been forgotten. Hill stressed, however, 'it seems likely that in the Embassy at Washington he [Burgess] will always have access to a large amount of secret information. One can only assume that the Foreign Office have therefore changed their minds.' Hill concluded, 'The decision as to BURGESS's employment must rest with them.'[42] Hill's note makes clear that MI5 had no power to intervene and so he washed his hands of the matter.

Seven days after Hill wrote that note the Foreign Office in London finally named the proposed Washington replacement: 'The man we are suggesting is G de M Burgess ... now working in the Far Eastern Department. Burgess has previously served in the News Department and, for a fairly long spell, as a Private Secretary to the Minister of State.'[43]

Weeks later, the senior Minister at Washington, Sir Frederick Hoyer Millar, wrote to George Middleton:

> Dear George ... I think I ought to warn you that [Cecil] Graves does not seem very enthusiastic over the prospect of having Burgess working for him, and feels that from the point of view of bottle-washing in the Chancery he will be a poor substitute ... I must say that I too have heard that Burgess – at all events before he went to the Far Eastern Department – was a bit light-hearted and unreliable.
>
> This makes it all the more important that he should ... be given a good talking to before he comes here and made clearly to understand that if he does not come up to scratch he will be turned out at short notice. This applies particularly to his work and general behaviour, but, from the distressing reports that I have heard, it might be no bad thing if something was also said to him about the necessity of his smartening up his personal appearance![44]

Weeks later, Hoyer Millar wrote again, saying, 'But are you really satisfied Burgess is the right man...?' Thresher had worked in the Far East; Burgess had only read about it. He stressed, 'I do not think that dependability has ever been claimed as Burgess's strong point' and wondered if 'it is right for us in present circumstances to run the risks involved in taking him on. Would you please look at things again ... and let us have your considered views.' He finished with, 'Ambassador has seen this.'[45]

Not wishing to give in, George Middleton insisted that Burgess was suitable for the job, but maybe the solution would be to arrange an additional secondment at a higher level to help. The embassy didn't like this idea, but eventually agreed that a First Secretary, Denis Greenhill, who had spare capacity, could help Graves out with the Far East work and Burgess could work under him. The real concern had been that if Graves had not been available, someone with senior experience would have to handle meetings in his place – possibly with US Assistant Secretary of State for Far Eastern Affairs Dean Rusk. The fear was that Burgess would be out of his depth.

Meanwhile, George Middleton was informed in a cryptic note dated 1 July that the 'Far Eastern Department had been making a little difficulty over Mr Burgess' release but we have definitely booked his passage to New York for 28th July'. It looks as though the Department had wanted to hang on to him.[46]

The final verdict was delivered by George Middleton, who by then had consulted Esler Dening in London.[47] Dening had until recently been Burgess's Supervising Under-Secretary in the Far Eastern Department. Middleton wrote to Hoyer Millar in the middle of July:

> We have carefully reconsidered the appointment in the light of the Korean crisis and what you say about Burgess himself. We still consider him to be suitable for the job ... He has a first-class brain and would have been in line for promotion ... had it not been for his unfortunate indiscretions ... It is true that he is something of a showjumper, rather than a cart horse, but I do not think that he is unreliable in his work. He has done well in the office and his handicap is being a certain lack of discretion disclosed in his private life and affairs. But we hope that we have succeeded in putting the fear of the devil into him and that he will do his very best to eradicate those faults.[48]

Three weeks later Dening happened to be in Washington on business and during his visit to the embassy discussed Burgess with Hoyer Millar and Graves and appears to have set their minds at rest.

Just before Burgess set sail from England, Sir Robert MacKenzie, George

Carey-Foster's colleague in charge of embassy security in Washington, wrote to him: 'It seems a pity that it has been decided to send him to such an important post but I will keep my eyes and ears open and let you know about any indiscretions which may come to my notice.' He continued: 'He does in fact know Kim well. They were at Cambridge at the same time and also worked together for 2 years at the headquarters of Patrick Reilly's friends [MI6].'[49]

The rationale for the decision to send Burgess to Washington, Prime Minister Clement Attlee was later told, was: 'It was decided to try him in a large post like Washington because there it would be both easier to control and judge him and less conspicuous to remove him (if need be) than in a smaller post.'[50]

As for that disciplinary record? Parliament was later told: 'Apart from this lapse his service in the Foreign Office up to the time of his appointment to Washington was satisfactory and there seemed good reason to hope that he would make a useful career.'[51] The record revealed in the Foreign Office files is not inaccurate.

There is one final twist, however, and that was, despite all the backroom discussions and machinations surrounding his appointment, Burgess wasn't at all keen on going. He was known not to like Americans very much. In an interview with George Middleton he told him, honestly, as it turned out, that he was a 'left-wing socialist' and wanted guidance 'on how free he would be to express his opinions' in the United States. 'I reminded Mr Burgess', wrote George Middleton, that 'civil servants, and more particularly "Foreign Servants" are expected to be a-political and it would be a grave mistake for him to deviate from this rule.'[52]

This benign treatment parallels that received by Burgess's future fellow absconder, Donald Maclean. During a posting to Cairo he had a fight with a colleague that left the man with a broken leg. Later he was visited by his friend Philip Toynbee[53] and at one point after drinking heavily they went on a rampage that led to them trashing the bathroom of an American secretary living in the Egyptian capital. It was the start of Maclean's alcohol-fuelled nervous breakdown. Maclean was recalled to London, required to undergo psychiatric care, but was kept on without being disciplined. After a few months' recuperation, Maclean had been 'passed medically fit' and was promoted to Head of the American Department in the Foreign Office in London.[54]

If ever Foreign Office officials had asked friends like Harold Nicolson about Burgess's political views, he may have told them what he said later, which was that 'He hated Americans'.

In the case of Burgess, however, there is new evidence that suggests that after he was told of his appointment to Washington, but before he left London, he was under some form of surveillance by MI5. Files show that MI5 had even listened to telephone calls he had made to a suspected Russian spy.

Baroness Moura Budberg had a soft spot for Guy Burgess. Born in Ukraine, she'd first been married to a Count, then briefly to Baron Nikolai von Budberg-Bönningshausen. Her first famous lover was the great Russian writer Maxim Gorky. Another was a British journalist, spy and civil servant, Sir Robert Bruce Lockhart – an associate of the so-called Ace of Spies, Sidney Reilly. It is said that she allowed herself to be recruited as a spy while in Russia as part of a deal to get Lockhart out of prison, where he was in great danger. She came to London in the 1920s and stayed. The third, and really her last companion, was the novelist and scientist H. G. Wells.

As someone with such an exotic background, it is not surprising that she captured the attention of MI5. Indeed, one suspects that she might have been a little put out if she hadn't. She had captivated not only H. G. Wells, but also part of London society, and by the early 1930s she was becoming well known – Harold Nicolson MP was an acquaintance.

Throughout the 1930s, her circle of contacts widened. In 1936, she was already well in with Duff and Diana Cooper. Alfred Duff Cooper was a rising star in politics and in the Cabinet. Diana, his wife, whose beauty was legendary and who was very active on the social scene, wrote of a 'nice dinner with HG and Bedbug'.[55]

Micky Burn was on the fringes of the Coopers' 'set'. It was through them that Moura Budberg came to know the Foreign Secretary, Anthony Eden, some time in 1936: 'She is intimate with the Duff Coopers, at whose house she meets, inter alia, our Foreign Secretary.'[56]

¶ Bedbug was Cooper's nickname for Moura Budberg

As the years wore on, Moura Budberg, who had a legendary capacity to drink almost anyone under the table without showing the least effect, began opening her house for soirées. Every week, and every weekday evening when she was in London, would be reserved for a particular 'set'. One evening was for 'the Foreign Office circle', another for 'pansy young men who were interior decorators', a third was for her circle of 'foreign acquaintances' and the fourth was kept 'for her "grand friends"'.[57] If friends turned up on the wrong day they were gently ushered towards the door and told to come back the next evening, or whenever their 'set's' next turn was.

It is not known exactly when Moura Budberg first met Guy Burgess. However, one of her friends was Hilda Matheson, who had not only given Harold Nicolson his radio debut, but had also been the lover of his wife Vita Sackville-West. Hilda had run the Joint Broadcasting Committee, had recruited Guy Burgess as a secondee from Section D of MI6, and had recruited Moura Budberg, another friend, to run its Swedish section. That had worked well until, in June 1940, MI5 intervened and her work permit was withdrawn.[58] It is likely, therefore, that Burgess and Budberg met some time during the first six months of 1940. For his part, he considered her to be 'a real nice woman'.[59]

A glance through her MI5 files shows some of her contacts. However, to make it easy, MI5 officers drew up a list or two of their own. One, dated 4 April 1950, is particularly interesting. It is a list of twenty-one names, and included are:

> Mr Huntingdon of Putnams publishing ... Mr Halpern and wife ... Commander Anthony Kimmins [of Korda films, Moura also worked for film director and producer Sir Alexander Korda] ... Miss Elizabeth Montagu [of Korda films] ... Sir Duff and Lady Diana Cooper ... Sir Gladwyn Jebb ... Miss Clarissa Churchill ... Mr Lutyens (architect) ... Mr Vernon Bartlett [the MP and former BBC and Fleet Street journalist] ... Mr Kingsley Martin [Editor of the *New Statesman*] ... Anthony Asquith [the film director and son of a former Prime Minister]...[60]

The Baroness's other contacts included Anthony Eden (by now the former Foreign Secretary but soon to wed Clarissa Churchill and then become Prime

Minister), George Weidenfeld and later Lady Antonia Fraser, who worked with Moura for a time in the 1950s. They joined many others at the weekly parties.[61] For someone with Burgess's social ambitions, an invitation to Moura's was an entry point into a whole new realm of society.

Weidenfeld, for one, 'did not hit it off with Burgess' and described his 'unpleasant habit of breaking into a conversation, sitting down, and bursting into a soliloquy without regard to the people present'.[62] In particular, he recalled a disagreement with Burgess over whether China would become a great power before the end of the twentieth century. It was at a party held by Sir Edward Marsh, Winston Churchill's former Private Secretary, and Weidenfeld remembered Burgess telling Clarissa Churchill, who was at the time known to be close to Anthony Eden, to tell Eden and 'all his Tory friends to pay more attention to the Chinese'.[63]

If the Apostles had been one of the key 'networking opportunities' of Burgess's youth, what we might call 'Moura's party networks' were performing the same role in his middle age.

MI5 was pre-occupied with trying to keep track of Moura. Her MI5 file contains two documents dating from 1950 that mention Guy Burgess. One is a partial transcript of a telephone tap from what appears to be a very widespread and long-term MI5 surveillance operation called TABLE. On 26 July 1950, probably due to the fact that he was undoubtedly readying himself to travel to the USA, Burgess telephoned Moura to apologise for being late for a soirée to which he had been invited. MI5's summary tells the story:

> Guy rang to say that he would be late but was coming along now. He mentioned that he was at EARLS COURT with TONY [in manuscript '?Tommy'] HARRIS[64] ... Baroness BUDBERG was heard to mention IVAN, but it was not possible to be sure whether she was speaking to him or about him. Later the two men could be heard giving the following address. MRS BASSETT, Flat 14, Arlington House (?)...'[65]

The inclusion of this note specifically is surprising because either it means that every telephone call was tapped – if so, Moura didn't receive many – or there is some other significance to its contents, because the note was added to the file on 11 August 1950 by the MI5 Registry, by which time Burgess was in Washington.

However, the second note in the file is even more interesting. Referred to as 'copy of note to SLB re GUY BURGESS's contact with BUDBERG', it begins, 'Reference our conversation of this morning concerning GUY BURGESS, BURGESS came to my notice in the course of an investigation into Countess Marie [*sic*] BUDBERG.' The note goes on to mention that 'she is a woman of great charm' and that her wide range of acquaintances includes 'people such as GLADWYN JEBB and DUFF COOPER,[66] to M MAISKY, the former Soviet Ambassador in London'. It also says that she 'at various times [has] been alleged to be a Soviet agent but her case has never been resolved'. The report pointed out that there was 'a renewed interest' in Budberg 'on account of her connection with a man whom we know to have been engaged in espionage with the Russians and whom we are at present investigating'.

That man was James MacGibbon, a former MI6 officer and publisher. In fact, they never managed to pin anything conclusive on to him and he was never prosecuted, but, in 2004, four years after he had died, a deathbed confession emerged confirming that he had been a KGB spy who passed British wartime military secrets to Moscow.[67]

The report continues: 'We learnt from a very delicate source that GUY BURGESS was present. It has also come to our attention that Guy BURGESS is acquainted with a certain Salomea HALPERN ... a woman who has very definite pro-Soviet sympathies.'[68] It concludes: 'There is no evidence that BURGESS was in any way indiscreet at this party, or that he notably exceeded the standard of conviviality common on such an occasion. On the other hand I am inclined to think that BUDBERG is not a desirable acquaintance for someone of his character and in his position and you may like to have this note for your information.'[69]

The significance of this is, we think, that first Bernard A. Hill had discussed Burgess and others with a colleague, just weeks after he had effectively washed his hands of warning the Foreign Office about Burgess. The copy on Burgess's MI5 file shows that it had been written by D. H. Whyte and that the main subject of the conversation had been the Halperns. The wording of the note shows that after Tangier Burgess's card was marked, although by the time it was written, 15 August 1950, Burgess was already hard at work in Washington. It shows that while he had not been entirely forgotten there is no indication that MI5 felt that it needed to follow it up with either Foreign Office Security or Carey-Foster's colleague in Washington, Sir Robert MacKenzie.

Burgess was under suspicion, but not as a *spy* – MI5 definitely did not suspect him of that – he was on their radar as someone who needed to be watched because he was a security risk.

Reading between the lines of a subsequent ministerial answer in 1951, the authorities did not dispute that they knew the previous year that Burgess had 'associations with communist circles' but they were not aware that these 'threw doubt on his reliability'.[70] That was the misjudgement that was made when sending Burgess to the United States in 1950. But the tone of the MI5 note leads us to believe that MI5 had taken a view that he was someone whose character, perhaps lifestyle, but certainly behaviour, was something on which it wished to continue to keep an eye. It was a classic case of looking to see what he did next. What is not clear, however, is whether MI5's suspicions would have been shared either with anyone else: such as the Washington embassy's security chief. It is highly unlikely that MI5 would at that stage have wished to share their doubts with the FBI because the suspicions were rooted in a low order of misdemeanour, i.e., loose talk, not spying. His patriotism was not considered to be in any doubt.

Any such news could have raised all sorts of issues that were probably considered best left alone given that the USA was then in the grip of the McCarthyite hunt for communists: reds under the beds. Of course, the risk of following such a strategy was that if matters ever got worse, a British failure to share information with the FBI could reveal a distinct lack of trust and cooperation with their American partners.

A year before Burgess was posted to Washington, 1949, the FBI enjoyed a major anti-espionage coup and shared it with the British. In the years since the closing months of the Second World War, the US signals intelligence service had intercepted a number of coded, top-secret Russian diplomatic, trade and military signals.[71] Through a combination of luck, enterprise and flashes of genius, US codebreakers based at Arlington Hall in Virginia had begun to decrypt some of the messages with help from Britain's GCHQ.

In October 1949, Kim Philby was posted to Washington. He was given a cover as a First Secretary at the British embassy, but was in reality the chief representative of British Intelligence in America.

He soon got to learn about the interception project, called VENONA.[72] He was told that two years earlier, the Americans had begun to decode enough material to establish that its government and wartime intelligence machine had been seriously penetrated by Soviet intelligence agents. There was also evidence of Soviet penetration within the British government machine. This was picked up from references to British agents' work in the US made in messages passed between the Soviet embassy in Washington and Moscow. It probably didn't take Philby long to work out that it might only be a matter of time before he and his fellow agents could come under the spotlight. He set about finding out as much as he could about the interception project and what progress had been made.

Moscow already knew of VENONA from one of their American agents, William Weisband, a signals specialist, who had told them about it in 1947. He was arrested by the FBI in 1950. In one of the ironies of the Cold War, it later emerged that the CIA didn't learn about the VENONA project until 1952, some five years *after* Moscow. The presumption is that the FBI wasn't sure that the CIA was secure enough, because its predecessor, the Office of Strategic Services (OSS), had been badly penetrated. Also, President Truman wasn't told, again, presumably because it was thought he couldn't be trusted not to let news of it slip out in his regular meetings with the head of the CIA.[73] However, as Cambridge historian Christopher Andrew concluded, 'after Weisband's arrest … [J Edgar] Hoover must have been aware that the secret they had kept from President Truman and the Agency was known to Stalin and the Centre'.[74]

In September 1949, President Truman announced that the US had evidence that the Russians had exploded their first atomic bomb. That same month, VENONA decrypts passed to the British revealed that details of the bomb had been sent to Moscow via Washington in the last year of the war by a British spy codenamed CHARLES.[75] VENONA had identified CHARLES as a British scientist working on the MANHATTAN project. FBI agents 'quickly concluded' that CHARLES was probably a scientist named Klaus Fuchs – a German-born naturalised British subject – but there was no tangible or legally usable evidence. Fuchs had been recruited in 1943 by the KGB while working on the West Coast. MI5 took a very close interest in the scientist, who was by then working in the British nuclear research facility at Harwell on a British atom bomb. In January 1950, through gentle but persistent questioning, Fuchs confessed.[76] The confession was sufficient evidence to use in his prosecution and he was duly arrested, tried and given a fourteen-year sentence.[77] There was a wrangle afterwards as to whether the FBI would be able to interview him: Hoover was insistent. Philby and others pressed the case and in May the British Prime Minister Attlee relented and two FBI agents flew to Britain to interview Fuchs.[78]

One of the problems posed by VENONA – even when it was realised that Moscow would have known about it – was that the signals intelligence 'SIGINT' source was considered to be so secret and so sensitive that it could never be used as evidence in a court. Unless spies could be persuaded to confess, or other admissible evidence could be found, no prosecution could be mounted.[79]

Philby kept a close watch and reported what he knew to Moscow, but the intelligence organisations were in a state of upheaval. In 1947, two of them – GRU (military intelligence) and MGB (the then current name for what we have been calling the KGB) – were merged under the control of the Foreign Minister Molotov. The organisations had been prised away from the grasp of Stalin's sinister and powerful security chief, Lavrenti Beria, and the control of intelligence gathering abroad was given to Russian diplomats, with ambassadors at the head. However, the diplomats were not intelligence professionals and for some time after the reorganisation things were disorganised. In some instances, intelligence officers deliberately hid what they were doing from the diplomats; in other cases there was upheaval as personnel were shuffled around or replaced.

In America, Philby had experienced two changes of KGB controller within months. He had had enough and he refused to deal with them until they could sort themselves out. So, until that time, he passed his reports and other messages to Moscow via London. The person who acted as his go-between was Guy Burgess.

Back in London, Burgess prepared to go to Washington, but realising his anti-American views made him unsuitable to join Philby at the embassy there, was trying to get another posting. He would have stayed in London if he had been allowed to, but the Foreign Office had made up its collective mind. He would be going as a second secretary and had inexplicably jumped across the divide from B Branch administrators to the A Branch senior list, according to some documents, although this is probably an error.[80]

As Burgess began packing his bags in readiness for his journey, he also sorted out where he would be living: with Kim Philby and his family.[81] His new landlord saw an internal memo which explained that Burgess's 'eccentricities' would be 'more easily overlooked' in a large embassy. He also summarised Burgess's 'past peccadillos' and warned that 'worse might be in store'. The embassy's Head of Security Sir Robert MacKenzie asked Philby what 'worse' meant – 'Goats?' Philby assured him that as Burgess would be staying with him, he'd keep an eye on him.[82]

On 30 July 1950, Burgess handed a note to Yuri Modin of the KGB via Anthony Blunt: 'As instructed, I have given "Fred" [a codename for Blunt] the most important documents I had before my departure. I am leaving in two days' time.' He had passed on a briefing which had been prepared for secret talks to be held in Washington about China and three other documents, two of which were drafts. Burgess concluded with some housekeeping details: 'I have carried out instructions on using secure code in correspondence with Fred, which I have agreed with him', and added: 'I would again press you in writing on what I asked at our last meeting, namely that in the present situation every possible secure attempt should be made for there to be contact in the USA between me and Kim.'[83] If ever that report had been intercepted, Burgess's use of the name 'Kim', rather than a codename, would have severely damaged Philby's cover. Burgess's message also shows that

Blunt was still actively working with him and the KGB at this time, albeit as a go-between.

Another KGB document reveals that Burgess wanted to bring Philby to his first meeting in Washington, but was expressly forbidden to do so. The author wrote,

> I have described in detail to 'Paul' [another Burgess codename] the conditions for establishing contact with him in the USA. 'Paul' proposed coming to the meeting with 'S' [Stanley, Kim Philby's codename]. I categorically forbade him to do so, warning that if he did that our comrade may decide not to approach. 'Paul' promised to come to the meeting alone.[84]

Earlier the report indicated that Burgess had wanted to pass on a personal note and had been told sternly to use the KGB's required format instead. He was also asked 'to recount verbally everything of importance he knew and what he thought necessary to report'.

The KGB found Burgess in a downbeat mood as he contemplated his trip to Washington, probably due to the lingering after-effects of his head injury and the pain relieving medication which had changed his personality noticeably.[85] It is also likely that he was beginning to contemplate life without close contact with his mother, his friends, and London. Two months before he went, he was apparently depressed and considering suicide. Moscow even offered him and Blunt defection as a way out, but they appear to have declined the invitation.

He put on a brave face for his farewell party, which he held at his flat at 10 New Bond Street. Among the guests were Rt Hon. Hector McNeil MP (by then promoted to be Secretary of State for Scotland with a seat in the Cabinet), Kenneth Younger MP (McNeil's replacement at the Foreign Office), Guy Liddell, David Footman, Wolfgang zu Putlitz (an anti-Nazi spy who ultimately defected to East Germany), Anthony Blunt, Goronwy Rees, James Pope-Hennessy and Jack Hewit. Three women also attended: Princess Dil de Rohan, Tess Mayor (by now married to Victor Rothschild) and Patricia Rawdon-Smith (by now married to Richard Llewelyn-Davies, an Apostle).[86]

There is no mention of anyone resembling Harold Nicolson attending.

Nicolson's diaries indicate that the relationship between the two had cooled by the late 1940s. Their last recorded dinner date was the occasion at the end of January when Burgess's drinking had so saddened him, and his name no longer appeared. A search through Nicolson's unpublished 1950 diary reveals that in the two weeks before Burgess left for Washington, every one of Nicolson's evenings was taken up with social engagements. Burgess's name did not appear once.

Someone at the party advised Burgess to be careful when in the US and to avoid discussions about communism, homosexuality and the colour bar: Burgess's riposte summarised their advice: 'Guy, for God's sake, don't make a pass at Paul Robeson.'[87]

If, as contemporary accounts suggest, Burgess was an alcoholic on his way down into ruin, that doesn't fit with the witty and lively demeanour he displayed at this event and his mischievous quip about Paul Robeson. Possibly Burgess was what is now called a 'functional alcoholic': able to hold down a job, prompt in attending appointments and dealing with other obligations – as was Burgess – yet have regular and high alcohol consumption that would class them medically as alcohol dependent. Otherwise, it is difficult to see how a downward spiralling drunk was able to make arrangements for contacting the KGB in the US, and who could still remove secret documents and pass them to Yuri Modin via Anthony Blunt without getting caught – or even suspected. The Russians have two separate phrases: people who got tiddly and tipsy, what might be called 'soaks' (все время был 'под шафе'), and those who indulge in binge drinking bouts (Страдал запоями). Burgess was probably the former, whereas Donald Maclean was by all accounts the latter.[88]

Goronwy Rees's account of the party suggests this was one of the occasions when, as a BBC colleague once recalled, Burgess would 'spruce up'. Rather than the dishevelled, unshaven, dirty and smelly Burgess, he appears to have been relatively clean and tidy. In post-war London, after all, someone of Burgess's class had high standards to maintain. A glance at contemporary photographs shows how immaculately dressed and well-manicured people were, so it is small wonder that anyone who failed to keep up those appearances would be dismissed as dishevelled and dirty.

Arthur Marshall, who knew Burgess from Cambridge amateur dramatics and a disastrous holiday in France, couldn't help but notice that when Burgess came over and sat at his lunch table in the Reform Club he was 'stinking of garlic and dirtier than ever'.

Goronwy Rees wrote of how Burgess combined 'a large and steady intake of alcohol' with 'drugs, narcotics, sedatives, stimulants, barbiturates, sleeping pills or *anything*, it seemed, so long as it would modify whatever he happened to be feeling'. Yet, Rees was astonished by the 'physical vitality' that enabled Burgess to survive the combination of drink and drugs.

* * *

All packed, Burgess made his way to Southampton and set sail for New York on 28 July 1950 on the RMS *Caronia*, a Cunard White Star Line ship that had been launched in 1947. While he would have undoubtedly liked to travel first class, he was consigned to cabin class, along with all the other diplomats. He was scheduled to disembark on 4 August and start working three days later.[89]

When he arrived in Washington he went straight to the house where Kim and Aileen Philby were living. Philby had offered to put Burgess up while he settled in and found somewhere to rent permanently. It was for the next seven-and-a-half months, however, that Burgess stayed in the basement spare room, nestling among Philby's sons' toys. By all accounts he enjoyed playing with the train set.

To some in Moscow, Burgess sharing Philby's home was very poor security: one KGB agent living with another. Burgess and Blunt had done exactly the same in Bentinck Street, and the KGB either didn't know, or if they did and issued any strictures, they went unheeded. But there was another, possibly more positive side to the Philby–Burgess ménage in Washington: at least Philby could keep an eye on him and keep him out of scrapes.

Burgess's posting had potential: if only he could impress some of his colleagues. Some of the people he would be working among would later become very senior diplomatic figures. The ambassador was Sir Oliver Franks; one of the embassy's three ministers (in effect deputy ambassadors) was Sir Frederick Hoyer Millar, who would later head the FO. One of Burgess's fellow second secretaries was Earl Jellicoe, who later became a minister in Edward Heath's government before he was sacked for sexual impropriety.

Denis Greenhill, another future Foreign Office Permanent Under-Secretary, was the First Secretary, who ended up as Burgess's immediate line manager. In his memoirs, Greenhill remembered that Frederick Hoyer Millar had exclaimed to him, 'We can't have that man. He has filthy fingernails.'[90] Despite this, Greenhill reluctantly took him on. Kim Philby called by to give Greenhill a bit of background. He told how his friend Guy 'was deserving of special sympathy and consideration', how 'Burgess had been an intellectual prodigy.' And that 'A golden future had been predicted' but that things had 'subsequently gone wrong. Brilliant promise had not been fulfilled. Burgess had unaccountably fizzled out.'[91]

When Greenhill first set eyes on Burgess, he noticed his 'tobacco stained fingers' and 'blotchy face' and a rare Old Etonian bow tie 'of which he was inordinately proud'.[92] It was not an auspicious occasion. Greenhill was a specialist on Middle Eastern affairs and with no prospect of working on Chinese affairs, Burgess was not enthused. In fact, Greenhill quickly gained the impression that Burgess was 'totally disinterested in the Middle East'.

However, embassy documents show that Burgess, at least during his first week, was on the circulation list for cables about China, so he may have continued to have some involvement in Chinese affairs after taking up his post.[93] At the end of August 1950, he drafted a report summarising a conversation about the Chinese nationalists, which was distributed within the embassy.[94] Hitherto, little other material survived to show what other issues he worked on during his posting, or even whether he had been given 'access to high level information'.[95]

Burgess's office was apparently on the same corridor where Philby and other embassy liaison officers worked, but there is no evidence to show that Burgess was assigned to work on secret intelligence matters, rather the usual diplomatic fare of organising events, handling visits and occasional policy analysis.[96]

British embassy records are incomplete as regards what Burgess actually did while posted to the embassy. There is one slender file showing that, until

29 August 1950, he had at least been involved in work about the Chinese communists and the Korean War.[97] The file has been heavily weeded, and most of the papers once kept inside are no longer there. The Foreign and Commonwealth Office confirmed that most of the papers are no longer in existence; likewise, no succeeding volumes survive.[98]

However, in August 1951, George Carey-Foster asked (Sir) Bernard Burrows, the head of Chancery at the Washington embassy during Burgess's posting, to prepare a list of all the things that Burgess had seen while at the embassy. It was released to the National Archives in October 2015 and reveals that Burgess saw 'a very large proportion of all the telegrams received and despatched here. These are the distributions normally seen by all Chancery officers.' Burgess did not, though, see any on the 'Restricted distributions', in other words highly sensitive material, because that was restricted to just a few individuals. Nevertheless, he had seen secret telegrams dealing with Formosa (Taiwan) and about 'Anglo-American relations in Saudi Arabia' as well as telegrams dealing with Germany, civil aviation, diplomatic subjects and the 'weekly political summary'. In addition, Burrows listed twenty Middle-Eastern files that Burgess had seen, covering such subjects as 'Israel-Soviet Relations', 'Korean Relief' and 'Jews'.[99] Burrows was not asked, and did not say what work Burgess had done in regard to the files.

Documents released by the FBI show that Burgess was

> an alternate member, United Kingdom delegation to the Far Eastern Commission, from August 7, 1950 to November 27, 1950. As of September 12, 1950, he was listed as an alternate on the 'Steering' and 'Reparations' committees, and as a representative on the 'Strengthening of Democratic Tendencies', 'War Criminals', 'Occupation Costs', and 'Financial and Monetary Problems Subcommittees'.[100]

The FBI agents compiling the report explained that the

> Far Eastern Commission is composed of representatives of eleven nations and was established to replace the Far Eastern Advisory Commission at

the Moscow Meeting of Foreign Secretaries in December 1945. Under its terms of reference the Far Eastern Commission has two principal functions: (1) 'To formulate the policies, principles and standards in conformity with which the fulfillment [sic] of Japan of its objection under the terms of surrender may be established.' (2) 'To review on the request of any member any directive issued to the Supreme Commander for the Allied Powers or any action … within the jurisdiction of the Commission.'[101]

The FBI even furnished recollections by US government officials who encountered Burgess during the meetings. One remarked that many of the British had been 'rather reluctant to agree with the United States', but that

> after Burgess came on the committee, he was much more co-operative with the United States … than had been the prior British representative … he had a good attitude with respect to the work of the committee, and that he seemed to believe firmly in cooperation between the British and Americans…[102]

Denis Greenhill noted that Burgess complained of being a martyr to sinus troubles and explained these had been 'caused by a blow to his head, when a colleague (Sir) Fred Warner had "deliberately" pushed him down the stairs of a London night club'.[103] Burgess had been 'at his most congenial slumped on someone else's sofa drinking someone else's whiskey telling tales to discredit the famous. The more luxurious the surroundings and the more distinguished the company the happier he was.'

He also saw Burgess as an inveterate bragger: 'I have never heard a name-dropper in the same class.' But while the list of Burgess's contacts would grow in America, 'Washington did not, however, take to him' and he did not take to it. Greenhill confirmed that Burgess often disappeared from Washington at weekends, frequently behind the wheel of his pride and joy, 'a huge 12 cylinder Lincoln convertible' which he drove 'with the fury of a Mr Toad', collecting a number of speeding tickets en route.[104]

Given Burgess's reputation for driving fast cars with less than 100 per cent attention to the rules, he might have seemed an unusual choice in November 1950 to be the chauffeur and guide for a visiting dignitary from London, Anthony Eden.

The former Foreign Secretary was now an opposition frontbencher. The main reason for his five-day visit was the unveiling of a memorial to Field Marshal Sir John Dill, the wartime Senior British Representative on the Combined Chiefs of Staff. Dill had died in Washington in November 1944 and was buried in Arlington National Cemetery, where the statue was erected. The unveiling was attended by President Truman, on schedule, notwithstanding that he had just survived an assassination attempt that morning.[105]

Eden was in Washington as the representative of Churchill's war cabinet. It would be wrong, however, to think that as a senior opposition politician he would be carrying out a full range of official duties.

In fact, apart from the memorial ceremony, his visit was a strictly private affair. Part of the reason for that was that the Labour Minister of Defence, Emanuel Shinwell, and his military big guns, were also in town. They attended the unveiling ceremony. Eden sat next to Shinwell in the fifth row. Behind them were Marshal of the RAF Lord Tedder, the current Chief of the British Joint Services Mission, Air Marshal Sir William Elliot (he was due to replace Tedder the next year, 1951), and Marshal of the RAF Sir John Slessor. Eden may have exchanged pleasantries with them, but probably little else. Shinwell and the air chiefs were in Washington for talks about US–UK defence questions, meetings of the North Atlantic Council military committee and the work of the British Joint Services Mission to Washington. With official business to conduct, the US government would have found it difficult to focus attention on Eden, no matter how illustrious his wartime record, although he did have some private meetings.

It would be interesting to know why Burgess, with those marks against his career record, was selected to chaperone Anthony Eden. It is possible that officials might have known that Burgess and Eden may have been on 'nodding terms' with one another from the time when Burgess was employed in the News Department and that Eden might, therefore, welcome a friendly face. Equally, everyone else might have been too busy. Whatever the reason, however, the Foreign and Commonwealth Office has confirmed that the papers relating to the visit have not been kept.[106]

Eden's visit had its hairy moments, largely the result of Burgess misplacing his car keys on a couple of occasions, but apparently Eden and Burgess got on well.[107] Perhaps it had been because, according to one source, they'd had 'many wartime conversations' and that had broken the ice, so to speak.[108]

They discussed German rearmament – Burgess was hostile to it. Eden confessed that Burgess's position was 'more sensible' than the one articulated at the time by Winston Churchill.[109] Whether their conversations had any lasting impact is unknown, but Eden returned from the US 'convinced that the question of rearmament would be a central consideration for some years'.[110] Burgess did perform a service for which Eden was very grateful: he engineered a reunion between Eden and his wartime American counterpart Cordell Hull, America's longest-serving Secretary of State.[111]

After Eden had left Washington he sent a letter of thanks to Burgess:

My dear Burgess—

Thank you so much for all your kindness. I was so well looked after that I am still in robust health, after quite a stormy flight to New York and many engagements since. Truly I enjoyed every moment of my stay in Washington, and you will know how much you helped to make this possible. Renewed greetings and gratitude.

Yours sincerely,

Anthony Eden

PS Incidentally that very friendly footman hadn't after all searched those evening trousers very well for I found in them those dollars and this key – so sorry! – AE[112]

In the etiquette of the day, had Eden been writing to a close friend, he would probably have begun 'My dear Guy', and if it had been to somebody who was respected, but of a lower social rank, it would have been 'Dear Burgess' – so 'My dear Burgess' was a half-way house.

During this period of Burgess's time in Washington, there are contrasting but not necessarily contradictory accounts of his behaviour at social events. At some parties it is said that he was 'an extremely difficult individual to talk to ... he usually sat in a corner and said nothing', which was most un-Burgess like. Instead of joining in, he would draw caricatures of various individuals at the party, a pursuit that was to cause some problems a little later.[113] However, at the Foreign Policy Association's Press Club bar, Burgess demonstrated his ability to 'down six highballs without turning a hair', impressed by being able to 'hold his whiskey' and held forth about China and the problems with American foreign policy.

Burgess also made some social visits outside the capital: his stepfather, Col. Bassett, had made an introduction for Guy to Emily and Nicholas Roosevelt, a distant cousin of the late president Franklin Roosevelt, who lived near Philadelphia.[114] They in turn arranged some introductions for him, including their cousins, the journalists Joseph and Stewart Alsop.[115] He promptly had a row with the former.[116]

His real pleasure was to get well away from Washington at weekends and head to New York. There he stayed at an apartment rented by Alan Maclean, Donald Maclean's younger brother, with whom he had worked for a time in the Foreign Office News Department in 1946.[117] By 1950, Alan Maclean was working in New York as Private Secretary to Sir Gladwyn Jebb, Britain's latest ambassador to the United Nations. Apparently Burgess's visits became so frequent that Jebb mistakenly thought that Burgess and Maclean shared the apartment.[118] It was Jebb who had claimed responsibility for sacking Burgess from Section D in autumn 1940, so he may have been surprised to see Burgess employed at the embassy in Washington. Burgess told Tom Driberg in 1956: 'I used to go to New York for the week-ends ... and Gladwyn and I used to cry on each other's shoulders about the American attitude to the Far East.'[119] Burgess took the opportunity to complain about the embassy's own stance on the Far East during a visit to New York by Hector McNeil's successor, Kenneth Younger, who had attended Burgess's London farewell drinks party.[120] Gladwyn Jebb made no mention of such encounters with Burgess in his own autobiography but if there was any dislike or distrust between the two it never filtered through into his wife Cynthia's post-war diary, which betrays no animus towards Burgess.

Burgess's social and sexual life and times in weekend New York were best recorded in an investigation by the FBI after his defection. Their detectives traced and interviewed many of his contacts in America and discovered that Burgess had regularly visited the Meadowbrook Club, a golf and polo club in New York which, in a throwback to an ancestor of Burgess's in North America, originally had its own hounds. In contrast, the FBI found that one of his other favourite haunts was 'the Everard Turkish Baths on 28th Street New York City (28 West 28th Street) where you could get anything you desire'.[121] The Everard had been founded in 1888 as a place for general health and fitness and by the 1930s had become a bathhouse for the more affluent New York homosexual community who re-christened it 'Everhard'.

One other FBI discovery casts a light on a more sensitive, even sentimental side of Burgess's character. At the Rackets Club in New York he would meet an American Old Etonian friend who, by 1950, was a New York stockbroker. The FBI never revealed the man's name. After leaving Eton the two men had not seen one another for quite a while then by chance had met again in New York 'some time between 1939 and 1941'. That was probably in 1940, when Burgess and Isaiah Berlin were embarked on their abortive trip to Moscow.

When the friend had been in London later in the war serving in the US Navy, Burgess had taken him to a restaurant in London. The friend noticed that most of the guests were what he called 'fairies' and asked Burgess how he knew so many men of this type. Burgess told him that he was a homosexual, but that did not end the friendship.[122] They met in New York several times, the last occasion being in the year he defected, 1951.

While out and about in Moscow several years later, Burgess took the unusual step of asking an American visitor to contact that friend in New York on his behalf. The visitor did just that on his return to America and, having alerted the FBI, they arranged to meet at the Meadowbrook Club where a message from Burgess was passed on: 'I am still wearing my old Etonian tie and hope he is still wearing the bow tie I gave him.' The rare Old Etonian tie that Burgess had so treasured and pointed out to Denis Greenhill back in August 1950 was the same bow tie that he had given to his friend in New York in January 1951.

Sentiment and sensuality apart, there were also very practical reasons why Burgess was in New York so often. Even while he was in London preparing to go to America he had been making arrangements for meeting a KGB contact in the USA. In New York, he would meet his new KGB controller, Makayev, for the first time. He took with him a message from Kim Philby. The meeting was a dry run for Philby's own meetings with Makayev.[123]

On Thanksgiving Day 1950,[124] the Philbys threw a dinner party at their house. Several of Kim Philby's important friends from the intelligence world were there, plus a couple of colleagues from the British embassy, including its Head of Security, Sir Robert MacKenzie. Among the American guests were an old intelligence friend from wartime London who was now working for the CIA, James Angleton, and someone with whom Philby was working closely on the VENONA project to decode Soviet spy traffic, Robert Lamphere, who was busily trying to establish the identities of Russian agents. For Philby, keeping on good terms with Lamphere and staying abreast of what he was discovering about Soviet spies such as himself was crucial if Moscow was going to be able to protect them.

One of the other guests, Dr Wilfrid Mann, was a science attaché at the British embassy. In reality, Mann was a nuclear scientist and the Washington representative of the Ministry of Supply's 'Atomic Energy Intelligence group which has for some time been carrying out measurements on the radioactivity of the atmosphere caused by plutonium production plants'.[125] The measurements were being conducted world-wide by both the USA and UK 'in view of the very great importance of knowing whether USSR production is appreciable compared to USA production'.

Mann was nearing the end of a two-year posting in Washington.[126] He worked closely with the British Joint Services Mission to Washington and was charged with conducting negotiations on the swapping of nuclear data with Robert LeBaron of the US Military Liaison Committee of the Atomic Energy Commission, which at the time was involved in US nuclear weapons production.[127] Mann was also involved in British attempts to circumvent what was known as the McMahon Act: a statute named after the senator who had sponsored it that proscribed the US sharing nuclear secrets with other states, including former wartime allies.[128] From Moscow's viewpoint, Mann was definitely someone whom Philby needed to know.

Back at the Philbys' Thanksgiving party the cocktails were served early and were plentiful. Dinner passed smoothly. The conversation was lively, and the evening seemed to be going well. And then Guy Burgess arrived.

There are differing accounts of what happened next, but it was noted that when Burgess entered the gathering he appeared to be in an 'aggressive' mood, but not noticeably drunk. He then proceeded to drink and to draw caricatures of some of the guests.

After a while one of the wives, a Mrs Harvey, whose husband William was a senior CIA officer, asked Burgess to draw her. When he had completed the caricature she asked him to show it to her, which he did. She was horrified with the result (he had lampooned her moderately prominent jaw and apparently depicted her in a sexually provocative pose). She was offended and the Harveys both left feeling upset and insulted. The rest of the guests stayed, but Philby was apparently in tears and angry with Burgess, reportedly saying 'How could you, how could you?'[129] The party had been about building stronger bonds between the CIA, FBI and MI6, and Burgess had effectively ruined it. In retrospect, it was fortunate for Philby that the embarrassment did not appear to drive any sort of wedge between him and Lamphere.

* * *

At the beginning of March 1951, Burgess attended a dinner and made a speech on international politics titled 'Britain: partner for peace' at the Citadel Military College in Charleston, South Carolina.[130] An FBI report reveals that 'Burgess drunk to excess during his entire stay in Charleston, and had, in fact, arrived at the dinner in an intoxicated condition. At this affair ... BURGESS made a highly contentious and unpopular speech which resulted in a serious argument.' Other information noted that Burgess 'had numerous flareups of temper in their presence and was generally disliked because of his surly attitude'.[131] Burgess later told a cadet at the college that the speech had been prepared by the British embassy and he 'was not in accord with the full text'.[132]

A day before arriving at the Citadel, however, Burgess had taken a drive with a male companion – a hitch-hiker called James A. Turck – whom he had just picked up. In the course of a few hours the car was stopped on three separate occasions for speeding while en route through Virginia.[133] In the third incident, he was briefly detained and brought before a judge and accused of reckless driving. Burgess claimed diplomatic immunity for himself and the driver, who was presumably Turck. Burgess had threatened the arresting officer with an international incident. The upshot was that early the following week – 14 March 1951 – the Governor of Virginia, John Battle, wrote to the chief of protocol at the State Department outlining the details of Burgess's exploits. However, as the British ambassador was in the UK on official business and wasn't scheduled to return until 28 March, the State Department delayed writing to him personally until 30 March.

On 16 March 1951, Guy Burgess had an invitation to go to a cocktail party. It had been set up for him not by the embassy, but by Kim Philby. The host was Kermit Roosevelt, a senior CIA officer and the grandson of President Theodore Roosevelt. Just a few years later he would be earning plaudits for the way in which he engineered the toppling of the Iranian Prime Minister, Mohammad Mossadegh, and allowed the young Shah of Persia to regain his peacock throne.

At the party, Burgess was soon introduced to Franklin Delano Roosevelt Junior, the late president F. D. Roosevelt's son and a rising politician in his own right. They began talking about US policy in the Far East and soon their differing positions led to raised voices and then to the beginnings of a passionate argument. They were separated by Kermit and a senior member of the British embassy, who was also present.

The following day Kermit walked into the office of Allen Dulles, the Deputy Director of the CIA, and told him about the troublesome Burgess. Dulles said that he already knew because his boss, General Walter Bedell Smith, ['Beetle' to his friends], had heard about it from his wife, who had also been at the party. Dulles shared with Kermit the fact that they were beginning to have doubts about Kim Philby, too, who after all had allowed this irritating Brit Burgess to lodge in his house. There is at least one account that says that Colonel Valentine Vivian, the Deputy Director of MI6, took up the question of Burgess's living in Philby's house and concluded that Philby should get rid of him.[134]

* * *

As Philby and Lamphere continued to work together on the VENONA project, details of a network of British KGB agents were beginning to emerge. Philby requested his own copy of whatever material was sent to Washington from GCHQ. He soon saw with alarm that one spy was identified by the codename STANLEY, which of course was his very own. He could rest assured, however, that at this stage he was the only person working on the VENONA project group who knew Stanley's identity.

During 1950, Lamphere worked on discovering the identity of a KGB agent who the intercepts showed had been working in the Washington embassy at the end of the war. Decrypts identified the code name HOMER.[135] Lamphere led the FBI team that carried out background checks of all of the non-British embassy employees. The time-consuming process ultimately yielded nothing. The inevitable conclusion therefore was that the suspect was British.

There had always been the danger that by carelessly dropping in words like 'Kim' or other personal details into otherwise carefully coded messages that they could be intercepted and decrypted. Burgess, Kim Philby and possibly Anthony Blunt just might then have become identifiable. From the evidence then available it did not take Philby long to realise that the agent HOMER [or Gomer] was Donald Maclean. Moscow told Philby that Maclean should remain in his post for as long as possible, but that they would make plans to rescue him before he was trapped. In April 1951, the US team decrypted two telegrams that revealed that in 1944 HOMER's wife was pregnant and staying in New York with her mother (Maclean's wife, Melinda, was American) and one telegram happened to include the date when HOMER had travelled to New York to visit her.[136] Foreign Office files show that Donald Maclean was only confirmed as the prime suspect on 18 April 1951.[137]

Philby knew that the information provided by VENONA material could not be used in a trial because it was too sensitive.[138] If Maclean was to be prosecuted, more conventional evidence would have to be gathered, or at least a confession secured, as had happened with Klaus Fuchs. For that reason, Philby and Moscow saw that there would be a delay before that evidence could be gathered and an outright move made against Maclean. That gap would provide sufficient time for Maclean to be warned and taken to safety by the Russians, but the problem was how to warn Maclean without attracting attention. The race was on to save him from certain arrest.

* * *

When the British ambassador, Sir Oliver Franks, got back to work at the end of the month, there were two complaints about Burgess for him to consider. One from the Governor of Virginia to the State Department, and one from the latter to him. Franks informed the State Department that he was consulting the Foreign Office about the action to take. But he could not see Burgess because he was playing host to his mother, who had come to visit him from England, and he was taking her on a motoring tour in a rented car. Burgess later confided to Harold Nicolson how Charleston was 'that most lovely, really lovely, of all towns', but that he had been shocked when he 'saw such notices as "for whites only"'.[139] FBI records show that they were travelling around for at least several days: first to Moncks Corner, South Carolina, then staying at the Fort Sumter Hotel, Charleston, while Burgess's car was repaired.

When Burgess returned to the embassy, Denis Greenhill remembered him working on the fallout of the sacking by President Truman of General Douglas Macarthur as Commander of the American-led United Nations Command in the Korean War. Rather oddly, this is the only occasion in Greenhill's memoirs that he recalled Burgess doing any work.

On one day that week, most probably Tuesday 17 April 1951, Burgess was finally called in to see the ambassador. He was told that the line had been crossed and his career in the embassy was finished. He was being sent home and would be invited to think about whether it would look better if he resigned from the Foreign Office rather than be sacked.

The official version, which was written some time after the event, says:

> The Ambassador reported that his work had been unsatisfactory in that he
> lacked thoroughness and balance in routine matters, that he had come to
> the unfavourable notice of the Department of State because of his reck-
> less driving and that he had to be reprimanded for carelessness in leaving
> confidential papers unattended. The Ambassador requested that Burgess
> be removed from Washington and this was approved.[140]

Sir Oliver Franks wrote to London informing him about his decision to
send Burgess back:

> If Burgess had been guilty of some really serious official or personal
> offence I would have been inclined to send him home by the first avail-
> able means and tell you that I was doing so. With the facts as they are, I
> have not wanted to do this but I must nevertheless recommend to you
> that he should be transferred from here at an early date. In other words,
> I am not summarily sending him home in disgrace, but I feel that his
> usefulness here is small and that with this speeding trouble on top of the
> rest of the story he is more of a liability than an asset to us.[141]

According to Denis Greenhill, after the meeting with Oliver Franks, Burgess
was extremely upset:

> He came straight to my room after hearing his sentence from the Ambassa-
> dor. He was boiling with rage. He had been told that he 'lacked judgement'.
> Who did the ambassador think he was to speak of him in such terms?
> ... His pride clearly had been badly hurt. When his anger died down
> he admitted he had failed in Washington ... but it would be embarrass-
> ing to tell his important friends the truth. Before he had left London he
> admitted that he had boasted of his appointment and told them all that
> soon he would be mixing with Dean Acheson and so on. Yes, he said, it
> would be awkward.[142]

With his career in tatters, Burgess booked a passage on a trans-Atlantic liner due to embark in two weeks' time. With typical bravado, he wrote to a friend: 'I am terrified that there may be a war. Very seriously and for the first time. And soon. I sail on the Queen Mary on the 1st May.'[143]

Burgess began a farewell fortnight with a week in Washington. A glimpse of how Burgess spun the inconvenient truth of his sacking is provided in an FBI report of a social engagement that Burgess and his mother attended during this time. Looking well, and without any hint of stress, he explained that 'he had applied to the Foreign Office for release from his present assignment because, as he put it, he felt he could be of greater value in the Foreign Office at London'.[144] Then Burgess travelled to New York to stay with Alan Maclean for five days to look up old friends and say his goodbyes.

Published accounts say that the KGB estimated that it would not be safe for any of its agents in London to alert Donald Maclean. But, remarkable as it sounds, Kim Philby and Guy Burgess – not the KGB themselves – developed a scheme for getting a message to Maclean.[145] The plan was finalised in New York a day before Burgess sailed for Britain. Kim Philby wrote: 'We dined together in a Chinese restaurant where each booth had "personalised music" which helped to drown out our voices. We went over the plan step by step. He was to meet a Soviet contact on arrival in London and give him a full briefing.'[146] Burgess would then contrive to get in contact with Maclean, who by this time was expected to be under surveillance. Burgess concluded that a go-between should deliver the warning. He chose Anthony Blunt.

Before Philby and Burgess parted Philby warned Burgess to be careful: 'Don't you go too,' he told him, recognising that the spotlight would be shone straight on him if Burgess, his house guest, disappeared along with Maclean.

The night before Burgess was due to sail on the Queen Mary – 30 April – he was invited for dinner and cocktails, but arrived slightly the worse for wear, probably having had drinks with friends earlier; or just possibly after his meeting with Philby in the Chinese restaurant.

After having heard Burgess tell his favourite anecdote of his meeting with Churchill at Chartwell, it was suggested that he ought to capture it on tape for posterity as it was a good tale and Burgess's mimicry embellished it well.

So that night – or in the wee hours the following morning – Burgess recorded his story. It took three attempts because nobody was able to operate the tape recorder with sufficient precision.

Until MI5's file on Guy Burgess was released the published version of how the tape had been made relied solely on the FBI's files. However, all names, except Burgess's had been redacted from the witness statement. Burgess's MI5 file names those present and provides other details. It is now clear that the recording was made in opera singer David Brynley's apartment. Alan Maclean had introduced Burgess to Brynley earlier in the month. The recording was made on Brynley's tape recorder and the other guests present were another opera singer, Brynley's friend Norman Notley, the painter James Farmer and, significantly, Alan Maclean. Knowing that Alan Maclean was present explains why there is a pointed reference to him in the recording when Burgess mentioned the book that Winston Churchill had signed for him back in October 1938: he told everyone present its current whereabouts. The New York address that Burgess gave in the recording was actually Sir Gladwyn Jebb's apartment, not Alan Maclean's. Maclean later told MI5 that the book autographed by Winston Churchill had probably been in Burgess's baggage, which he had left at Jebb's apartment. After completing the recording, Burgess departed at around 2.30 a.m. During the remainder of the party, one of the guests tried to record some music and erased the final part of Burgess's story by accident. Fortunately, weeks later, when the FBI were told of the tape, one of the guests was able to remember enough of the erased section – probably because they had heard it numerous times before – and a version of it was added to the FBI's transcript.[147]

The next day when Burgess woke, it appears that he began to wonder if he had said anything that was at all compromising in the recording. While en route to boarding the *Queen Mary* and with little time to spare, he hurriedly made a detour via Brynley's apartment and listened to the audio tape again. The FBI statement (which was probably made by Brynley) said:

> When they arrived, I questioned his motive in coming east – out of his
> way – when owing to the lateness of the hour he should have motored

to the dock. He repeated that he wished to hear again the speech that he had recorded in case there is anything incriminating in it.

They sat down and listened to the playback. 'When it was finished Burgess said "That's okay. It's an interesting story and a jolly good recording. I wish you'd send me a copy of it."' After that he dashed off to board the liner, making it just in time. The tape (see Chapter 3) was impounded shortly after Burgess's defection and was never heard in public until we secured a copy from the FBI in January 2014.[148]

MI5's summary of David Brynley's statement makes no mention whatsoever of Burgess's frantic dash to review the tape before the *Queen Mary* set sail.

While the identity of Brynley might have been redacted by the FBI Brynley had in fact been named as the person responsible for the tape recording in an interview with him published by the *Daily Mirror* on 1 November 1952, the day after questions had been asked about the recording in the House of Lords.[149] Much later Alan Maclean told MI5 how he had tried to get hold of a copy of the tape because it could 'offer an extremely good money making opportunity' but he said Brynley had 'stuffily' told him that he had given the tape to the FBI and that was the end of the matter.[150]

There is a coda to this story. James Farmer was questioned by telephone shortly after Maclean had been interviewed by MI5's top interrogator, W. J. 'Jim' Skardon. Farmer corroborated Maclean's account of how the recording had been made. At the end of the conversation Skardon noted in the file, 'I warned James FARMER that I should seek him out if he so much as mentioned this matter to anyone else, and he promised that he would not talk about it.' It is not clear if Skardon's threat was an isolated example, or whether as a matter of course all witnesses were placed under similar pressure to keep quiet.

The journey home in Cabin B-130 with two other passengers passed uneventfully, save for Burgess picking up a young American medical student called Bernard Miller whom Burgess promised to introduce to medical friends in London, although evidence for this is scant. When the liner docked in Southampton, Burgess was met by Anthony Blunt and they travelled to London together. While Burgess had been in the process of leaving the US, Blunt had been in contact with Donald Maclean and had developed the strong impression that he was beginning to fall to pieces.[151]

* * *

Once back in the UK, Burgess embarked on a round of visits and meetings. Details of these, however, are partial. After arriving in London from Southampton, he first returned to his New Bond Street flat, from where he made a telephone call to someone in America that cost £7.[152] He then got in touch with his friend Michael Berry, who owned the *Daily Telegraph*, regarding the prospect of a job.[153] Burgess spent the night at Blunt's flat.[154]

The next day he travelled to Sonning in Berkshire to stay the night with his friend Goronwy Rees and his family. The following day he returned to London and met the writer Cyril Connolly for lunch. That afternoon, Burgess called Maclean's mother, and asked for a private telephone number that he could use to contact her son.

Burgess then went to the Foreign Office where he had a meeting with the Personnel Department. According to the official version, 'he was asked to resign from the Foreign Service. Consideration was given to the steps that would be taken in the event of his refusing to do so.'[155] The files show that there was some doubt that he could be sacked and persuading him to resign was the preferred option. If that failed, the next step would be 'premature retirement'.[156] Denis Greenhill had observed Burgess agonising over writing what he described as 'a personal letter' to Maclean: 'He spent weeks on this letter and in the end showed me a messy draft ... I do not know whether the letter ... was ever sent.'[157] A copy of the letter was handed by Burgess to his former Far East department head, J. H. Shattock, who passed it on to the Permanent Under-Secretary a month after Burgess had disappeared.[158]

It was probably in this first week back that he had lunch with Michael Berry to discuss the prospects for a job on the foreign side of the *Daily Telegraph*. Berry's subsequent account of this meeting over a glass of vintage port was that Burgess tried to impress him by showing him a top-secret document he'd drafted in Washington, but Berry was 'appalled when I read it.

His writing had certainly gone to seed … So I felt relief when he went, because I no longer had to find him something to do.' Gladwyn Jebb did not agree: he had read the letters (there was more than one) and felt they were 'well written and the general view … was quite moderately expressed'.[159]

Burgess remained in London on 10 May.[160] Although Col. Bassett had told his friends the Roosevelts that he believed Burgess had been out of London for most of the time since returning from America and had only returned on Saturday 12 May.[161]

Burgess later told Tom Driberg that he met Donald Maclean in the Foreign Office, where they had talked on a sofa outside the latter's office in case his room was bugged. Burgess finally got to talk about a memorandum on foreign policy that he'd long laboured over and was relieved that Maclean agreed with it. Maclean told him: 'I'm in frightful trouble. I'm being followed by the dicks.'[162]

On the day in question, 15 May, MI5 had no record of this meeting in the Foreign Office. However, they did observe Burgess and Maclean have lunch together. They had met in the Reform, but because the dining room was full they went further along Pall Mall to Burgess's other club, the RAC. Burgess then returned to the Reform where he dined with Peter Matthews of the Foreign Office News Department that evening.[163]

At a second lunch a week later, Maclean said – according to Burgess – that he thought he was in trouble because of indiscreet remarks he had made in the office praising Soviet policy. Asked by Tom Driberg in Moscow in 1956 if this was when Maclean had first mentioned going to Moscow, Burgess replied: 'No, that was the third time we met. Donald suddenly said: "Look here, Guy, I think I'm going to clear out and go to the Soviet Union. Will you help me? The trouble is, I can't even buy a ticket. They'd be on to me at once, wouldn't let me leave the country."'[164]

Burgess's answer to Maclean, according to Driberg, was that he'd be leaving the Foreign Office anyhow, probably couldn't stick the *Telegraph*, so why not help Maclean? He specifically refuted the suggestion that Maclean had to persuade him – 'I did it because I thought he was right.'[165] There is no other eyewitness account of this meeting because the only other person involved,

Donald Maclean, never wrote or spoke publicly about his defection. But we can be sure Burgess, as a former spin doctor himself, would have refined and polished his version before going public with it via Driberg.

The more logical and likely scenario is that the two men, one now known to be a KGB spy and one still undetected, debated their options and made their decisions. But, according to Anthony Blunt's unpublished memoirs, the KGB inevitably had a hand. Blunt wrote:

> At the first meetings between Guy and his Russian contact the discussions were entirely about Donald's escape and no mention was made of Guy's going with him, but at a later stage I remember Guy coming to see me at Portman Square … those in control of his contact had decided that he should go with Donald, on the grounds that Donald was not in a fit state to carry out the complicated arrangements which had been made … In fact I have no doubt that the suggestion was made by Guy himself. He realised that his career in the Foreign Office was ruined, and although his hopes of getting a job on the *Daily Telegraph* from his friend Michael Berry … I doubt whether he was counting on this. In fact he knew he was finished and decided to get out, not taking into account the consequences that this action might have for his friends. For Donald to disappear was going to cause trouble enough, but the two of them to vanish would require a great deal more explaining and would lead to a much fuller investigation.[166]

The most authoritative timetable of Burgess's meetings with Maclean is probably MI5's because they had officers following the latter.

The two met four times before they disappeared on 25 May. They spoke to one another on the telephone on 14 May, but there is no record of what they discussed. The first time they met together was for lunch on 15 May at the Reform. They next met a week later on 22 May in the evening in the Grosvenor Hotel smoking room, where they were together for an hour. The next day, 23 May, they met for lunch at Queen's restaurant. That was a strange event, however, because soon after sitting down at the table Burgess got up and walked out and had a drink in a nearby pub. He returned to the restaurant and a few minutes later left for a drink in a different pub, before returning to the restaurant again. Soon after the pair left together and parted. Each time Burgess went to a pub he appeared to be on edge and was muttering to himself, while drinking quickly. MI5 concluded that Burgess's strange behaviour was his way of checking whether they had been tailed. The next day the pair were spotted leaving the Reform Club after lunch.

Burgess was also in touch with David Footman on four occasions. On 8 May they lunched at the Reform and dined together on 11 and 21 May, also at the Reform. Their last contact was when they spoke together on the telephone on the morning of 25 May. Burgess saw Fred Warner twice: at Burgess's flat on either 15 or 16 May and at the Reform on 21 May where Burgess introduced Warner to Bernard Miller. Burgess saw Peter Pollock most. They had lunch at the Reform on 16 May, and dinner, again at the Reform, on 24 May where Pollock was also introduced to Miller. Burgess spent his last ever weekend in Britain at Pollock's farm from 18–21 May. Burgess only appeared to meet Blunt twice: for lunch on 7 May and at the Reform on 23 May. Burgess must have visited his mother in between his social engagements, but there is no record when.[167]

One of Blunt's students at the Courtauld Institute of Art was Brian Sewell, later to become the art critic of the *London Evening Standard*. In his memoirs, Sewell remembered that he'd often seen Burgess leaving Blunt's study on the first floor and, on one afternoon in May 1951, 'we fell into step and he suggested a drink'.

They ended up drinking something 'sweet and pink through straws' in a milk bar in Baker Street. With the precision that became a hallmark of his art criticism, Sewell 'contemplated the egg on his tie and savoured the tobacco on his breath'. There followed a dinner and a visit to Burgess's 'club' which was not the Reform or the RAC but 'some cellar haunt where I was more or less compelled to dance with him – more food stains and foul breath, and an overwhelming discomfort at the very idea of doing such a thing. I fled.'[168]

On the afternoon of Thursday 24 May 1951, Burgess paid his last ever visit to Eton, where he had tea with the headmaster, (Sir) Robert Birley.[169] That evening, after returning to London, Burgess called Stephen Spender. The call was taken by Spender's wife. Burgess asked for Auden, who was staying with them, but Mrs Spender forgot to pass on the message to Auden, who was in any case out. The next day Burgess again tried to get hold of him. Whatever his intention it came to nothing because Auden only received the messages during the weekend, by which time Burgess had already disappeared.

* * *

Friday 25 May 1951 was the day of departure. A detailed account of Burgess's day comes from the *Daily Express*, at the time the pre-eminent daily chronicler of the Burgess and Maclean saga, which had hired Burgess's friend Jack Hewit. In their 1955 book *The Great Spy Scandal*, the *Express* team said that Burgess told friends he would be going on a holiday with his new friend from the *Queen Mary*, the young American Bernard Miller. They would leave on a ferry at midnight from Southampton for a long weekend. Miller was put up at a hotel and Burgess stayed in the New Bond Street flat with Jack Hewit, who told the *Express* that Burgess had phoned somebody in America. He didn't know who but we can assume it was Philby (Burgess later left without paying for the £7 call).

On the Friday of the ferry booking, when Hewit took Burgess a cup of tea in bed they arranged to have a drink that evening before he left for France with Miller.

Other details are taken from the detailed timeline that MI5 pieced together in the years immediately following Burgess's disappearance. Some of the details are based on observation by MI5's watchers. At 8 a.m., Burgess telephoned David Footman. Two hours later he called Anthony Blunt. He then 'called at Continental Booking Office, Victoria. Booked two tickets, himself and MILLER (said MILLER might not travel).'

Afterwards he called at a car hire firm in Jermyn Street, booking a car to be delivered to the Reform Club at 2 p.m. The *Daily Express* established that he paid £25 cash in advance for the beige Austin A70.[170]

At 2 p.m., the car was duly delivered and an hour later he met Bernard Miller at the Reform. At 5 p.m., the two went shopping to Gieves in Saville

Row, and then they went to Burgess's flat, arriving at 5.30 p.m. By 6 p.m., Burgess was back at the Reform, but alone. He was last seen talking to 'a tall man' on the club's steps at 7 p.m. MI5 estimated that it took him thirty minutes to get to Maclean's house at Tatsfield. Burgess's habit of driving fast would have been a useful skill, although 1951's London rush-hour traffic would have died down by then.

From various sources it appears that Maclean was getting through that Friday with every outward appearance of unruffled normality. It was his birthday and he planned to leave the office promptly at 5 p.m. He had also been allowed leave for the following morning (at that time diplomats, like many other office workers, worked on Saturday mornings). As for Maclean's next movements , he left by taxi from the Foreign Office at 5.45 p.m., carrying a cardboard box. At Victoria station he had a drink, and boarded the 6.10 p.m. train to Sevenoaks. That was the last that anyone from MI5 saw him.

When Maclean arrived home he went to his bedroom and threw some things into a suitcase. He told his pregnant wife Melinda, who had cooked a special birthday meal for him, that he had to go away for a couple of days' business, and that as he would be travelling that night, could an extra place be laid for a colleague, Mr Roger Styles, who would be driving to collect him? He couldn't say any more because the work was sensitive.

Shortly afterward, Mr Styles appeared at the door. He sat down and dined with the family and then motioned that time was advancing and that they should think about leaving. Goodbyes were said and Styles and Maclean got into the car and drove at a furious pace to Southampton, where they were to catch the packet-boat, SS *Falaise*, which was sailing for the French port of St Malo at close to midnight. Roger Styles was a name that Guy Burgess had concocted from two Agatha Christie detective stories.[171] Burgess and Maclean arrived at the dockside at the very last minute, dashed up the gang-plank and were safely on board the ship that would take them away from England forever. Spotting that the car – a cream Austin A70 – had been left on the quayside, someone yelled after them, 'What about the car!' Burgess apparently called back, 'OK, back on Monday!'

They never came back to Britain alive. From St Malo they travelled via

Paris to Switzerland, picked up false passports from the Soviet embassy, and took a flight to Stockholm via Prague, where they left the aircraft and, once behind the Iron Curtain, their progress to Moscow was a less nerve-racking journey. Whether Burgess thought that Prague was where he would bid farewell to Maclean or whether he always knew he was in for the full journey, the KGB wouldn't be taking any chances – he was going to Moscow.

On the Saturday morning, 26 May, Anthony Blunt had phone calls from Bernard Miller, wondering what had happened to his weekend away with Burgess, and from Jack Hewit, who was concerned that Burgess usually called in after a night away. Both were agitated. Blunt remembered: 'I tried to calm them down, saying that I imagined he had gone off, on the upside of an impulse on some escapade, but they remained alarmed and Jack telephoned to many of Guy's friends to find out if they had seen him.'[172]

By the Sunday evening all Burgess's friends were alerted and concerned. Goronwy Rees had now heard from his wife about a strange telephone call that she'd had from Burgess on the Friday morning, in which he spoke about doing 'the right thing'. Rees concluded 'on a hunch' that Burgess had gone to Russia. He rang David Footman at MI6, who was – with Burgess – a godfather to his son, told him his conclusion and asked Footman to ring someone in MI5, which rather reluctantly he did. Blunt was then telephoned by Goronwy Rees who told him what he'd done.

So forty-eight hours after that midnight sailing to St Malo, MI6 knew they'd gone, MI5 also knew and now the KGB would know that they knew. But Burgess and Maclean were well on their way.

They were now the 'Missing Diplomats'.

* * *

All that weekend everything had been calm. Queen Mary had celebrated her eighty-fourth birthday, Prince Charles had taken her a gift of flowers and the King's health was improving after a mild attack of influenza. Richard Chapman had won the British Amateur Golf Championship at Royal Porthcawl.

The first hint of trouble came on Monday 28 May, when it was noticed that Donald Maclean was not at his desk. MI5's watchers had not seen him arrive on his usual train. It took some time to establish that he hadn't been given a day's leave.

That afternoon, a Foreign Office contemporary of Burgess's at Trinity, Lord Talbot de Malahide, told George Carey-Foster that Maclean had 'generally been regarded as a Communist at Cambridge'.[173]

The following day, Tuesday 29 May, there was still no sign of Maclean. It was on this day that MI5 first noticed that Guy Burgess was nowhere to be seen either. Dick Goldsmith White of MI5 saw Carey-Foster at the Foreign Office. In the hours that followed, officials began reporting the news to a very small band of senior officials. The Permanent Under-Secretary, Sir William Strang, was told what had happened at 1 p.m., Foreign Secretary, Herbert Morrison, was informed at 4 p.m.

That afternoon the Home Secretary was asked to alert Immigration Authorities, telling them to stop the pair if they were seen. At this stage fewer than half a dozen of the most senior figures in the Foreign Office knew. Guy Liddell, Dick Goldsmith White and Carey-Foster saw Leonard Burt, Head of Special Branch, at 3.30 p.m. He agreed to put his officers on alert alongside immigration officials. Everything was to be kept hush-hush. Meanwhile, the Foreign Office contacted Melinda Maclean and tried to persuade her not to alert the police.

Around 6 p.m. Carey-Foster and Dick Goldsmith White arranged a progress meeting. They called for Burt to join them, but he had gone home for the day. He was contacted and whisked back ready for an 8.30 p.m. meeting. It was then that reports were received that the missing diplomats had been seen boarding a weekend cruise on the SS *Falaise*. They had failed to re-board the ship before it left St Malo. Attention was quickly focused on France. A search was finally under way.

The following day, White was in Paris dealing with the French police. Alerts were sent to a number of Western European MI6 stations, and selected consulates. But, still, everything was to be kept ultra-secret.

On 30 May, it was decided to rush Alan Maclean back to London. Gladwyn Jebb, Britain's ambassador to the United Nations, was instructed to deliver Maclean to the airport, make sure that he got on the first available flight and not to answer any questions. A glance at Patrick Reilly's draft telegram to Jebb shows either that he habitually had a gigantic scrawl, or that he was tense when he wrote it. Lord Talbot de Malahide's original pencil cypher has been preserved in the file.[174] It was also agreed that the FBI should be informed about the disappearance. But a telegram was sent to Washington telling the embassy: 'You should do your best to prevent FBI informing State Dept. and Attorney General or other authorities of security aspect, since it is not repeat not yet established and there may be some quite different reason.' It continued: 'If they are inclined to do so, report immediately.'[175]

All the while this very small band of senior diplomats and security officials tried to act as though nothing was wrong; it was business as usual.[176] Only two years later, after Sir William Strang retired, was his successor, Sir Ivone Kirkpatrick, told that Burgess had been a long-term spy and that 'Maclean was under suspicion before he disappeared ... This is still a closely guarded secret.'[177]

MI5 and Foreign Office files covering the first few weeks of the search reveal that it took officials some time to grasp what had happened. Guy Burgess was at first an enigma. Only slowly did it dawn on the officials that he was probably a spy, too. Whereas the initial focus had been on Donald Maclean, as the more senior of the two, once the penny dropped, attention turned to Burgess as well. It was at this stage, after the initial shock had subsided, that a piecemeal plan of action was put together. People would have to be found and questioned, records checked, movements established to create a timeline.

The press would have to be informed, but so too would the Americans and Britain's other allies. They would need assurances that British security was not compromised and ramshackle.

By the middle of June, MI5 had a pretty good idea where the pair had gone, but were reluctant to allow that fact to become public. Signals intelligence (SIGINT) radio traffic analysis had provided the answer. MI5's Deputy Director Guy Liddell recorded in his diary on 12 June that

> GCHQ reported an increase in the volume of traffic between London and Moscow as from 25th May, the day BURGESS and MACLEAN left. Two or three days later there was an increase in the traffic from Berne,

and about the 4th or 5th Junean [*sic*] increase of traffic from Prague. These increases may, of course, have no connection with the departure of BURGESS and MACLEAN, but on the other hand they may be significant.[178]

In the weeks to come that fact did not pass entirely unnoticed. But, by some still unknown route, however, it seems that Fleet Street reporters had nevertheless got wind of a story.

It looks as though there had been a leak from the French Sûreté to a *Daily Express* reporter in Paris. On the morning of 7 June 1951, the *Express* broke the story, emblazoning it with a banner headline stretching across the top of the front page: 'YARD HUNTS 2 BRITONS "On way to Russia" From Foreign Office'. No names were mentioned, but it was clearly well-informed: 'Scotland Yard officers and French detectives are hunting for two British Government employees who are believed to have left London with the intention of getting to Moscow.' It continued: 'According to a friend, they planned the journey to "serve their idealistic purposes." One report says that the two men were employed by the Foreign Office, and there is a possibility that they may have important papers with them.'

That morning, Guy Burgess's mother, Mrs Eve Bassett, called some friends about the story. She asked Anthony Blunt: 'You don't think that thing in the *Express* about two Foreign Office people trying to get through to Russia could be Guy, do you?' He said he hadn't seen the story. In a question that reveals her knowledge of her son's friendship with Guy Liddell at MI5, she then asked, 'Guy would know whether it was our Guy wouldn't he?' Blunt agreed.[179]

Meanwhile, in the Foreign Office it was acknowledged that the time had finally come for it to inform the press: it issued a tight-lipped statement confirming the story, but releasing little additional information, apart from the diplomats' names.

That lunchtime the breaking news was carried in the BBC's 1 p.m. Home Service news bulletin. The story had finally broken over thirteen days after Burgess and Maclean had boarded the SS *Falaise* at Southampton and sailed into the night.

The Foreign Office has announced that two members of the Foreign Service have been missing from their homes since May the 25th (nearly two
weeks ago). They are Mr D. D. Maclean and Mr G. F. de M. Burgess.
The statement says all possible enquiries are being made. It is known that
they went to France a few days ago. Mr Maclean had a breakdown a year
ago because of overstrain, but it was believed he had fully recovered. The
statement ends by saying that as they are absent without leave, both men
have been suspended with effect from June the 1st.

It wasn't the lead story: it was in the middle of the bulletin and followed
reports about the King's birthday honours and that morning's Trooping
the Colour.

Having heard about the 1 p.m. radio news bulletin Mrs Bassett was soon
on the phone again. The MI5 officer tapping the family phone noted that
at 2.17 p.m. there was an 'outgoing call from Mrs Bassett to BBC to ask for
the news item to be read to her. They complied.' Now she was sure it was
her Guy. She called her younger son, Nigel, to tell him 'that according to
the wireless Guy was one of the two people who had disappeared'.[180] Nigel
agreed to find out some more details. Shortly afterwards she spoke briefly to
Blunt who was by that time at Burgess's flat.[181]

It is worth pausing for a moment to note this significant fact. On the day
that the news broke, and was broadcast on the radio, Blunt was at Burgess's
flat with MI5 officers, including R. T. (Ronnie) Reed and another sleuth
called Holmes. That appears to have been the first occasion on which MI5
visited the flat, notwithstanding the fact that Burgess had been 'wanted'
by the security services for over a week. It sounds as though the search was
supervised by Anthony Blunt, who presumably still held some sway, being
an ex-MI5 officer and a personal friend of Deputy Director Guy Liddell.
Published accounts tell how Blunt had earlier visited the flat and removed
'sensitive' documents before MI5 carried out its search. But there was still a
large cache of papers: a transcript of a telephone call from Holmes to Dick
Goldsmith White, conducted just minutes before Blunt spoke to Mrs Bassett, shows that Holmes told White that 'A. B. was willing for the stuff to

be taken away on his, HOLMES', promise that a car could not park out-side'. Holmes told White 'to avoid using the guitar-case'. A mailbag was used instead.[182] The papers found in the flat included confidential minutes, a 'Cypher/OTP Telegram'; an emergency 'OHMS pass stamped by "Com-munications R. D., London"'; and the 'courier's passport' dated 1 July 1940 that Burgess used for his journey to Washington: 'signed by Halifax … "Mr G F de Moncy BURGESS proceeding to Moscow via USA and Japan and returning to London, charged with despatches…"'. Among other Foreign Office documents were 'lists of personnel of H. M. Embassy, Moscow, and of Military Mission to USSR' that Burgess might have been taking with him on his abortive journey to Moscow. The bundle of documents has not been released to the National Archives.[183]

An hour after Eve Bassett had spoken to him at the flat, Anthony Blunt called her and the conversation included:

Mrs Bassett: 'Did they find anything at the flat, or anything?'

Blunt: 'No.'

Mrs Bassett: 'Oh, I'm so thankful.'[184]

Not surprisingly Blunt didn't tell her (or MI5) that he had got to the flat first.

By now the London evening newspapers were on the streets.

The Evening News headline was: FOREIGN OFFICE RIDDLE; the story occupied roughly a third of the broadsheet's front page. The tabloid *Even-ing Standard*'s headline was FOREIGN OFFICE NAME TWO MISSING CHIEFS and it devoted about half its front page and some of its back page to the story. *The Star* gave it a little less space – MI5 SEEK TWO WHITE-HALL MEN – and continued its report on page two, where it took around a quarter of a column.

Fleet Street had immediately grasped the implications: secrets, and possi-ble defection to Russia (not confirmed in the Foreign Office's press release). The following morning the story was front-page news in all of the national dailies. It would there for much of the next week. A flavour of how the story was understood by Fleet Street editors is revealed by some of the head-lines: MESSAGES FROM PARIS DEEPEN MYSTERY OF THE LOST

DIPLOMATS (*Daily Mirror*);[185] DIPLOMATS: CABLE PUZZLE (the *Daily Express*); ALL-EUROPE HUNT FOR TWO BRITONS (the *Daily Telegraph*); MISSING FOREIGN OFFICE MEN IN PARIS? (*Manchester Guardian*); HUNT FOR DIPLOMATS WIDENS (*News Chronicle*); PARIS CLUE TO LOST OFFICIALS (*Daily Graphic and Sketch*). *The Times*, then still the newspaper of record, carried its story on page four, its Home News page. It was still a master of restraint and the story was titled 'SEARCH FOR TWO DIPLOMATISTS' and was written by 'Our Diplomatic Correspondent'.[186] For the communist *Daily Worker* the story was 'FOREIGN OFFICE IN A TURMOIL'.[187]

The stories that followed the headlines showed that Fleet Street's editors not only knew a big story when they spotted one, but that they were not slow in putting journalists on to the trail. The *Daily Express*, then still under the ownership of Lord Beaverbrook and under the editorial control of the formidable Arthur Christiansen, put its best and most combative journalists on to the story including ace crime reporter Percy Hoskins. Other titles deployed considerable resources, too.

Reviewing the initial coverage some sixty-five years later it is interesting not only how little information the BBC news programmes reported, but how much of the story Fleet Street's ferrets managed to reveal within hours.

Fleet Street very quickly began piecing together the backgrounds of the two men, a task that was probably helped by the fact that a number of Fleet Street reporters would have remembered Burgess from his Foreign Office News Department days.

By the time the newspaper reading public had digested the front pages along with their breakfast on 8 June, they would have learned many of the salient facts. These included that Donald Maclean was a senior FO figure and head of the department dealing with American affairs, and that he had suffered a nervous breakdown the previous year, and had worked in Washington during the war.

As far as Burgess was concerned, the same readers would have learned that he was expert and interested in China, that he was an Old Etonian, that he was a member of the Reform Club where his favourite topics were 'politics and art on a very intellectual level'.[188] They would also have learned of his stint in the Foreign Office News Department, and that he had at one time been a special agent in a hush-hush job. Reports said he was very talented but erratic, and that he was anti-American, while mentioning that he had worked in the Washington embassy, but had recently returned following a disciplinary issue. Readers were also informed that Burgess had been a special assistant to the former FO Minister of State, Hector McNeil.

Writing in the *Manchester Guardian* from New York, Alistair Cooke paraphrased one British embassy official as saying that 'Burgess's recall last month had nothing to do with any suspected defection to the communist cause. They described him as being "a little left of centre" but not an earnest or intellectual man.'[189] One newspaper even identified, but only partially correctly, Burgess's stepfather as Colonel 'R D' Bassett. The *Daily Mirror* had established that both men were members of the Gargoyle Club.[190]

But, significantly, by the close of play on 8 June two other names had been placed into the public arena: Burgess's friends Professor Anthony Frederick Blunt, CVO, the surveyor of the King's pictures, and Goronwy Rees. *Daily Graphic* reporters had already picked up the story about Burgess's telephone call to Rees shortly before the disappearance and that it had been taken by Rees' wife.[191]

Despite this glut of information, however, there was also concern in Fleet Street that something was not quite right about the story. While the theme was picked up by several newspapers, the *Daily Mirror*'s Bill Greig raised his concerns in a front-page article. It is worth quoting this at length because in a very economic style he raised many of the questions that would dog the Burgess and Maclean story for years to come.

Under the headline 'The nonsense of a hush-hush hunt', Greig wrote (we have retained the article's occasional use of bold type):

> The Foreign Office took a strange and dangerous decision in the mystery of the vanished diplomats.
>
> It decided NOT to take those steps which would most quickly and surely lead to the discovery of its two missing officials.

There can be few newspapers in France or Britain not anxious to assist in tracing the men.

In a few hours yesterday tens of millions of men and women could have learned through those newspapers what the men looked like … **The Foreign Office decided against this step. It has detailed descriptions. But it refused them to all comers.**

Pointing out that the safety of the men themselves may be involved, I made a formal request last night for photographs. This was refused.

I was told that the decision to withhold photographs and descriptions had been taken 'at the highest level'.

The FO action in this case is as hard to understand as the disappearance of the men.

Thirteen days passed after it was known that the men had disappeared before the news was given out. Even then the step was taken only because the news had leaked out and had to be admitted.

Greig then turned the knife that he had already stuck into the FO. Accusing it of 'tortoise-like caution', he wrote, 'The facts are that the FO has no clue as to what has happened.' He even suggested that they might have been kidnapped. He finished by pressing the point that if descriptions and photos had been published earlier it '**would have meant a watching eye in every street, in every hotel, in every café, on every train…**' He accused the FO of not taking 'the obvious steps to find the missing diplomats' and concluded with the challenge 'Parliament may want to know why.'[192]

As the news was breaking in London, Sir Roger Makins, Donald Maclean's boss, noted, 'Mr Penfield of the American Embassy telephoned this afternoon to enquire about the reported disappearance of Mr Maclean and Mr Burgess. I read out to him the communique which has been issued to the press.' He assured Mr Penfield that the diplomats hadn't 'taken any official papers with them'. He mentioned Donald Maclean's 'recent breakdown' and said that Burgess had been sent back 'in disgrace'.[193] The American embassy had learned about what would become one of the biggest spy scandals of the early Cold War by reading about it in the newspapers.

As the story remained front-page news over the days that followed, more facts emerged, and pictures of Burgess and Maclean were published by most newspapers on 9 June, along with brief descriptions. Newspapers reported questions being asked in the Cabinet, and finally, a few days after the news had leaked out, there was a statement to Parliament given by Foreign Secretary Herbert Morrison, although he said that he could only reveal scant details. But, with every fact gained, a new question emerged. It was a process that would roll on for decades.

* * *

A study of the Cabinet minutes shows that the first discussion about the men's disappearance took place on 11 June 1951, four days after the news had been broken by the BBC.[194] Until then, only the Prime Minister, Foreign and Home Secretaries had known about it. During that Cabinet meeting, Burgess's old boss, Hector McNeil, then the Secretary of State for Scotland, was present, but the Cabinet Secretary's notes show that he made no contribution to the short discussion.[195]

The British embassy in Washington told the Foreign Office that the disappearance of Burgess and Maclean had 'inevitably created a major sensation here'. A wire service story from the United Press agency was forwarded reporting that the CIA and the State Department were 'highly disturbed' by the news. Clearly American officials were briefing against their allies saying 'the two men should not have continued to occupy posts in the British Foreign Office'. It was pointed out that 'in the State Department repeated drunkenness, recurrent nervous breakdowns, sexual deviations and other human frailties are considered security hazards, and persons showing any one or more of them are dismissed summarily'.[196] Inevitably such a culture clash had immediate consequences.

General Walter Bedell Smith, the Director of Central Intelligence, told Sir William Elliot, the chairman of the British Joint Services Mission in Washington, that he would have to 'withdraw CIA support for improved intelligence co-operation and for extended atomic cooperation in general', although the State Department maintained a softer line. British diplomats described the situation as 'obscure, gloomy, but not necessarily hopeless', but prospects for a joint US–UK atomic test at Eniwetok Atoll, which had been under discussion, were suddenly 'dim'.[197] The Chiefs of Staff in the British Ministry of Defence told the chairman of the British Joint Services Mission in Washington that he may have to give the US British atomic data 'without reciprocity', recognising that they would be 'giving up one of our strongest cards in the negotiations for collaboration'.[198]

Back in London a former British diplomat who would have been sacked long before if the American policy on 'sexual deviation' had been followed at the Foreign Office wrote a letter to his wife. Harold Nicolson was 'upset by the Maclean–Burgess business'. He hated 'my old profession being made a fool of and degraded' and was 'really sorry for Anthony and all Guy's friends'. When Nicolson's son Nigel later published the letter he provided some annotations to the text. The sentence about 'Anthony' became 'I am really sorry for Anthony [Eden] and all Guy's friends'. Those at the very top of politics appeared to have cause for concern. Why Harold Nicolson should have singled out Anthony Eden for a special mention is never made clear.

The letter ended with Nicolson reflecting on a conversation with his other son, Ben. 'I do not think that Ben would be as terrified as I am by someone betraying his COUNTRY, but it is terrible to him to think of someone betraying his friends. So I feel a little easier about it. But what a curious mystery it all is!'[199]

CHAPTER 8

'THIS PECULIARLY BRITISH FIELD OF COUNTER-ESPIONAGE'

AND THEN THERE WERE FIVE SPIES, OR WAS IT SIX OR SEVEN? 1951 ONWARDS

At four o'clock on Saturday 15 September 1951, a young, short, dark, rather sporty-looking man drove up to Broadcasting House in London in a maroon sports car, alongside a fair-haired young lady. He then got out of the car and pushed some books into the arms of a BBC commissionaire. He said he was going on holiday and would be away for some time so he thought he had better return the books. The commissionaire handed them in at reception.

It was discovered that these were books that Guy Burgess had once borrowed from a BBC library and, in classic Burgess style, had never returned. A fellow commissionaire – to whom we will always be grateful for the colourful detail he reported – sent a note up through the BBC hierarchy with a perceptive comment from a Mr Hopkins that 'This is interesting.'[1]

Another BBC report on the incident concluded, 'You may wish to pursue this as I understand that the Foreign Office are anxious to ascertain the whereabouts of Mr Burgess and it might be helpful to them.' Since Burgess was long gone to Moscow, although this hadn't been confirmed at this point, and since the description of the man in the car doesn't resemble Burgess, we can only wonder who exactly this sporty young man was, how he came to possess Burgess's overdue library books and why, exactly, he took the trouble to return them.

Among the belongings Burgess and Maclean had left behind on the ferry to France were some clothes. Burgess's stepfather, Colonel Bassett, and Donald Maclean's brother, Alan, met up at Waterloo station and went through the items, sorting out whose they were. Among them was 'a revolting pair of socks, which were quite stiff with sweat'. Alan Maclean thought they were Burgess's, the Colonel was sure they were 'your chap's'. The socks ended up in a bin.[2]

Burgess's stepfather was becoming 'rather difficult to handle' according to MI5 officers who visited him and Mrs Bassett. 'The Colonel was formerly some sort of a judge in the Sudan and has been accustomed to a form of rough and ready detection – combined with execution.' Inspired by the lost property he'd divided up with Alan Maclean, the Colonel, 'possessed of a keen detective instinct', had been to the shop in Savile Row where the items were bought to go through old bills and ledgers with no immediately obvious benefit to the investigation.[3]

His younger stepson Nigel considered himself a bit of an authority on detection too having previously worked for MI5 monitoring the Communist Party. He told the Security Service that in his expert opinion 'it was most unlikely that an organisation of the capability and resources of ours should have produced so little information' about the whereabouts of his brother. He suspected they did know more but didn't want the Americans to know what they'd discovered.[4]

But Nigel Burgess's main task, having long had to suffer the friction between stepfather and stepson which he believed was encouraged by his mother, was now to try to manage the elderly couple as best he could. By July 1951 Eve Bassett was 'in an hysterical state' according to friends; she would probably have been even more hysterical if she had known that MI5 was listening to every phone call in and out of her home and opening all the letters arriving at 14 Arlington House, SW1. Among these was an encouraging note from Victor Rothschild's wife, Tess, hoping 'that very soon the mystery will be cleared up and we shall all welcome him home again'.[5]

There were some in society who hoped the suggestion that Burgess and Maclean were Russian spies was all some awful mistake. Among them was the wife of the British ambassador to the United Nations in New York. Cynthia Jebb, wife of Gladwyn Jebb, had a special interest because her husband knew both men well and Alan Maclean was one of his team at the UN.

In August 1951, Cynthia Jebb wrote to her mother:

> We have been much concerned about the 'missing diplomats' particularly because Alan Maclean is the younger brother of Donald. The latter is extremely tall and good-looking, quite spectacular in fact and had a breakdown last year and got into the hands of the brilliant and dissolute Philip Toynbee who seems to have influenced various other people, such as Ben Nicolson, Harold's eldest son ... It is, of course possible and likely that Burgess is playing this sort of role? And that the whole thing is a great debauch and not political. But it is all very unpleasant whatever the outcome is.[6]

The first the Jebbs had heard about the defection was a message that didn't actually mention Burgess. It was a top-secret cypher from the Permanent Secretary at the Foreign Office, Sir William Strang, sent on 30 May. The cypher numbers were still in the file released to the National Archives in 2015. 'Donald Maclean has disappeared,' it began. The next sentence was drafted as 'His wife is expecting baby soon and is very worried' but was deleted and replaced with 'We fear he may have had another breakdown.'[7]

When the situation had clarified just a little, Gladwyn Jebb sent over from New York two handwritten notes to Strang marked 'Strictly Personal'. One said, 'If the French police cannot track down the couple's whereabouts it certainly looks rather sinister to me. The companion is in any case a pretty deplorable character. Of course it may be that they both got tight and met with some accident.'[8]

It appears that to the top man at the Foreign Office, this was all a touch informal from the British ambassador to the UN, the tone rather more suited to Lady Jebb's personal diary.

Strang sent a cold, typed reply, copied to the Head of Foreign Office Security: 'I have your manuscript letters of June 1st and June 4th. I am sorry that I cannot add anything to what has been said in the official statement we issued ... I am sorry to have to be so reticent.'[9]

But a further Jebb letter was already on its way:

> I always regarded Mr B as about the most unreliable man I ever met ... I believe that there is still no proof at all that they have defected: but frankly I fear the worst. The red youth: the 'breakdown': the apparent homosexual aspect all point in one direction. We can only hope that this is not so.[10]

In subsequent, only slightly more cautious correspondence later that month, Jebb wrote that Burgess had been a deplorable selection for the Foreign Office and he took his share of the blame for not getting rid of him, but 'one never wants to blacken somebody's character if one can help it and to say nothing is often the line of least resistance'. In other letters Jebb looked in danger of trying too hard to cover his back over what he called this 'supremely distressing' business.[11]

Demands for information and explanation from Strang's team came from their political masters at Westminster and from the press, mostly based in those days in Fleet Street. In the files there are scribbled Downing Street briefing notes beginning 'Prime Minister' [Clement Attlee] and ending 'What's your view?' preparing him for awkward questions from MPs and checking what should be said in statements to the press.[12]

There are also constantly changing drafts of documents as the truth began to sink in. In one draft the words 'Absences may therefore be due simply to indiscipline' were crossed through. But there were pressures, too, on the people who were meant to catch spies, the Security Service, MI5 – and not just in London. American officials wanted to know how many British government employees had spied for Russia on US sovereign soil. MI5 sent orders to their people in Washington: 'You should do your best to prevent FBI informing State Dept. and Attorney General or other authorities of security aspect [to the disappearance of the two men] since it is not repeat not yet established and there may be some quite different explanation.'[13]

From Washington came a constant stream of pertinent questions from men like Robert Lamphere of the VENONA decryption project at FBI headquarters, one of which was, why exactly had Burgess been travelling through the United States on his way to Moscow with Isaiah Berlin in 1940? They dug out the file, including a note by a Mr Maclean that 'Mr Berlin is intolerable', but when the British embassy responded with 'we have been unable to discover the precise nature of the mission' it was perhaps not surprising that Mr Lamphere 'does not seem to be completely happy with this reply'.[14]

As a result of all the pressures, the Foreign Office and MI5 began probably one of the biggest catch-up operations Whitehall had ever seen. They discovered many painful facts about themselves in the process, including the fact that a KGB officer had once told colleagues at a conference not to worry about British security 'as they were asleep'.[15]

'B.2.Investigation Plan' was MI5's four-page 'outline of arrangements' for the way B.2 branch was going to find out as much as possible about the past of Burgess and Maclean. What is significant about it half a century on is that Burgess took up three of the four pages despite Maclean being the more significant diplomat. That was because, 'Maclean is said to have been a man who kept to himself, and much less is known about his circle of friends.' What MI5 had unearthed about Burgess's circle by mid-June 1951 would ultimately lead to the eventual discovery of a number of other spies, but what they found out about Maclean led nowhere in particular. The file is more evidence that whoever made the decision that Burgess should escort Maclean to Moscow, the KGB paid a heavy price in agents for getting this one man 'home'. Had Maclean gone alone the wider damage might have been minimal. Presumably Moscow decided he wasn't in good enough shape to make it alone.[16]

Much of the work in June 1951 was done by reviewing files and questioning those who knew the two men. MI5 even asked 'C' at MI6 if he had any objection to tracking down 'D', Lawrence Grand, to see what he remembered of Burgess in Section D. 'C' didn't.[17]

One of MI5's top interrogators, Jim Skardon, was sent to Stafford Prison with photographs of Burgess and Maclean to talk to Klaus Fuchs, the German-born British physicist who the previous year had confessed to passing information to the Russians from the American, British, and Canadian atomic bomb project during and shortly after the Second World War. Fuchs said he didn't know the missing men. Skardon concluded, 'I am sure that FUCHS was quite truthful about this.'[18]

Rather late in the day, MI5 sent people to Cambridge to try to find out what on earth had been going on there two decades earlier. One report back said, 'I visited Cambridge on 8th, 11th and 12th October with the object of seeing what useful material on communism during the early '30s could be gleaned from open sources in Libraries.' The man discovered a listing in an old copy of *Cambridge Review* for the 1931 production of *Captain Brassbound's Conversion*, with a mention of Burgess's scenery. Also there was a review of a book entitled *Conservatism in England* by F. J. C. Hearnshaw. The review 'was obviously written by a Communist and was signed 'G. F. De M. B.'. This discovery was confirmation that some relevant written material had existed at the time that had evidently not been on Cambridge Special Branch's reading list.[19]

The search for information about 'G. F. De M. B.' went much wider afield. MI5's men in Africa called in on the British 'colony' in Tangiers and interviewed various men, at least one of whom was 'reputed to be a sexual pervert'.[20]

Another task was to find 'any knowledge of the ballet dancer with whom BURGESS was said to have been in contact while in Washington'. Burgess had been seen with her at 'the old Balalaika Club'. The embassy couldn't locate her.

In the reports back to MI5 headquarters there would be the occasional nice words about Burgess, such as he was 'efficient and helpful at *The Spectator*', but normally the anecdotes were about drink and driving: his taste for alcohol and for speed and the unfortunate moments when the twain met with him at the wheel. More suspiciously, there were examples of his extraordinary curiosity about the precise role of military and security colleagues.

MI5 discovered yet another Burgess London club, 'The Thursday Club', based at Frascati's Restaurant, where you brought along a guest – 'If the guest was up to the standard of membership he would be entitled to join in his own right at the next meeting. If he [the member] heard nothing he considered himself to have been blackballed.'[21]

There were unexpected sources. Hungarian émigrés pointed out a Burgess friendship with George Mikes, author of *How to be an Alien*. An Englishman travelling in northern Afghanistan told somebody he probably didn't realise was an MI5 contact that he'd been a fellow communist at Cambridge.[22] A man who'd rented to Burgess the room at Chester Square thought the key to his character 'was a desire to be important'.[23]

'A letter from the House of Commons' passed on a memory of a 'Cambridge circle well-known for their left-wing views, and Burgess was the most erratic and rabid of them all'.[24] But a former colleague from the Foreign Office News Department was 'absolutely certain that having known Burgess six years, he is not a Communist or fellow-traveller'.[25]

The more they looked into his background the more questions there were. Why had a London marketing and advertising business paid Burgess £300 in 1939? It was especially suspicious because its office in China was said 'to have been used as a channel for Soviet intelligence payments'. It turned out the payments to Burgess were made on behalf of Section D of MI6.[26] Why had Burgess 'occasionally deserted his usual intellectual circle and disappeared on visits to the slum area of London docks'? Were these visits 'made in order to contact Soviet agents'? Nobody seems to have mentioned they could be as much to do with sex as with spying.[27]

In later inquiries MI5 did follow up a report from a source who 'is a reliable reporter and is himself a patient of Dr Harkness' of 12 Wimpole Street, W1 that the doctor 'had apparently treated Guy BURGESS professionally' in 1948. Dr Harkness was 'a specialist in V.D. and other sexual disorders' and therefore knew 'a great deal' about 'the extent and prevalence of homosexuality' and that 'it is practised by many leading personalities and public figures'.[28]

MI5 talked to a lady who 'does for him at 10, New Bond Street, Flat 3', Burgess's 'daily char'. She surfaced wanting to know about the money he owed her and revealed that she was 'also employed at Broadway [MI6's offices] in a similar capacity'. MI5 was reassured to be told that Burgess had never asked her about her cleaning job at MI6 or asked her 'to undertake any mission there'.[29]

The Burgess 'network' was getting bigger all the time. The Special Branch reported that, 'At a dinner table a very well informed man Mr X. said one man who knew Burgess well was Lord Killanin' who as Michael Morris had been an Eton contemporary of Burgess. Killanin later became the President of the International Olympic Committee.[30]

Inevitably, as well as interviewing, at which it counted itself as something of an expert, MI5 used other techniques in its information-gathering. Intercepting letters was a tried and tested way of producing genuine leads, but also occasional amusing distractions. In the post for Burgess at the Reform Club they found a letter from an old friend, Brian Howard, writing to him on 19 June 1951 from Austria:

> Dear Guy,
>
> I cannot conceive what you and Donald are up to, but doubtless there is some explanation or other.
>
> Whatever it may be, please rest assured – as they say – of my friendship and my sympathy which will never fail you, no matter what happens.[31]

How very loyal of a friend to assume that after whatever Burgess had been 'up to' he would eventually return safely to the bar at the Reform.

MI5 also made a lot of 'T.Cs' – telephone checks. One of their first priorities was tapping the home phone of Burgess's mother and his friends Anthony Blunt and Goronwy Rees. Lists of calls were compiled and some conversations were transcribed. When MI5 didn't know the person at the other end of a call, the names of the subscribers at that number would be tracked down.[32]

On 28 June 1951, MI5 took stock of what they'd done over the past month.

There were so many telephone checks operating that they'd had to suspend some because of the pressure on staff. They continued the checks on one of what were to become known as the Cambridge Five, Kim Philby, but suspended for a time those on another, Anthony Blunt. In one file it was properly pointed out that he was by now 'the Keeper of the King's pictures'. MI5 also sent the Special Branch a list of ten people, including Philby and Blunt, they wanted watching for any sign that they tried to leave the country during the summer.[33]

The bulk of the work had been simply talking to people. By July, the internal scoreboard showed thirty-four known friends and relations had been interviewed by MI5 and twelve on their behalf by the FBI. There were over eighty other 'miscellaneous reports and rumours' followed up by various services.

Perhaps more fruitful were the interrogations of those closest to Guy Burgess, in which MI5 tried to list as many of his circle as they could. One lover, Jack Hewit, gave them the names of Spender, John Lehmann, Rees, Isherwood, Auden, Tom Wyllie and Brian Howard. Hewit said these men 'used to foregather at Chester Square for long and earnest discussions on political affairs'. MI5's interrogator, Jim Skardon, found Hewit 'a loathsome creature' and 'was glad when the interview was over'.[34] Another lover, Peter Pollock, added the names of the art critic Ellis Waterhouse, Isaiah Berlin and Victor Rothschild, and talked of the 'Bentinck Street ménage' of Burgess, Tess Mayor and Pat Rawdon-Smith. Pollock also mentioned that he 'had been to Tom Wyllie's parties at the War Office'.[35] He'd first met Burgess and friends at those Chester Square discussions on politics, but he 'was so very young at the time' he didn't understand what was going on.

The police were also tipped off about an eighteen-year-old French student living in London who had been invited to parties which were 'in the main, attended by individuals with homosexual tendencies', where he had been introduced to Auden and Spender.

They talked to the young American, Bernard Miller, who recounted his tour of Burgess's favourite London haunts such as the Gargoyle and the Reform and had gained the impression that Burgess's politics were in line with 'present British Labour government policies'. Indeed, a young American visitor might have been excused for not fully understanding how a socialist at the Foreign Office differed or otherwise from what the British press constantly called a socialist government.

A search for whatever had happened to Tom Wyllie led to the discovery he had been in a 'dipsomaniacs home' and had died from tuberculosis and alcohol at the age of thirty eight.[36]

The interrogators who seemed to have had the most fun were those who went to interview Moura Budberg who, one colleague had earlier remembered, 'at various times has been reported to be a Soviet agent but her case has never been resolved'. The MI5 officer assigned to the case reported back: 'When I rang Mura [sic] she invited me to her flat for the same evening (June 20th) at 6.00 p.m. Contrary to expectations I was not alone with Mura.' It was one of Moura's party nights – just four other people on this occasion, but all very happy to give him their views on Burgess and Maclean. On another occasion, an MI5 officer dined with Budberg 'at the Sherry Bar in Pelham Street' and when that closed 'we then adjourned to my flat where Mura remained until 2.00 a.m. Our talk was very frank' – as well it may have been after a night out with Moura.[37]

Fred Warner had sent a handwritten statement from Moscow: he hadn't defected, he had been posted to the British embassy. He named their mutual friends – including Harold Nicolson, Hector McNeil, Sheila McNeil 'for whom [Burgess] had a great admiration', Arthur Marshall, Noël Annan and David Footman. Warner told how Burgess had pestered him about getting a promotion and how it had been 'a contributing reason to using [Warner's] influence to bring [his career move] about ... there really was no need for his presence in the M/S [Minister of State's] office and I arranged with the minister that Burgess should leave without replacement'. He mentioned Burgess's head injury, that he had helped until medical attention had been arranged, but denied any responsibility. He also mentioned that Peter Scarlett had formed a positive view of Burgess in the Far Eastern Department. He had last seen Burgess shortly before he disappeared.[38]

In the weeks that followed, others said that Warner was closer to Burgess than he cared to admit.[39] Months after Warner's statement, Jim Skardon interviewed him. Warner said that he had written his statement in 'great haste' and wanted to clarify and correct some of the details. He said Burgess was never drunk in McNeil's office ('tipsy once') because McNeil had threatened instant dismissal if he was. Burgess didn't go to conferences with McNeil, instead handled 'mundane' arrangements badly. Burgess had only gone to one: the October 1948 UN meeting in Paris.

Warner then gave Skardon some more details about the head injury. The venue was a pub. They had drunk heavily in an upstairs bar and, after 'good-natured jostling' Burgess had ended up injured at the bottom of the stairs. Warner also told Skardon that he had met Anthony Blunt with Burgess, but felt that Blunt had resented his influence.[40]

Hector McNeil himself offered 'very little new information about Burgess' according to the notes of his interview at the House of Commons in June 1951. He was then the Secretary of State for Scotland in the final months of Clement Attlee's Labour government. The notes do not suggest it was a particularly rigorous interrogation. McNeil had 'realised some time ago that he [Burgess] was an extremely unreliable character' who had not been allowed to have 'access to Defence papers on important matters'. He had 'particularly asked Burgess if he had any Communist or fellow-travelling leanings', presumably not the kind of question a minister would ask one of his team without due cause, but 'Burgess had told him that he had no such tendencies'. McNeil was much better informed on Burgess's private life and said Blunt would know even more.[41]

Among the testimonies there were some that were just plain wrong. The former BBC Controller of the Home Division, Sir Richard Maconachie, told Patrick Dean of the Foreign Office that it was Hector McNeil who had come to see him and asked for the transfer of Burgess to the Foreign Office. Since McNeil didn't work there at the time and was just a backbench Labour MP, Sir Richard was obviously getting a bit muddled. However, Dean, who would have known that, did nothing to correct Maconachie's statement before sending it to MI5. Maconachie's own priority was to ask if there was anything in the records that showed him recommending Burgess to the Foreign Office because in fact he'd been 'reproved' by the BBC Governors for 'letting such a brilliant young officer leave the BBC'. He was told there wasn't.[42]

One of the longest but not always totally honest accounts was that of 'Morgan Goronwy REES of Falcon House, Sonning, Berkshire' signed on

6 June 1951. It was a detailed and, from what was subsequently discovered, largely accurate account of Burgess's life and times as far as Rees knew them from Cambridge to Washington. Where it was unconvincing was when he explained how Burgess 'wished me to help him in carrying out his work' for the Comintern but had never got round to asking Rees 'to obtain or provide any information for him'. The best explanation Rees could offer for Burgess's curious lethargy was that 'owing to Burgess's strange personality I was never quite certain whether he was what he professed to be or whether I was indeed myself what I was supposed to be in this strange combination'. Strange indeed.[43] It was not surprising that MI5 concluded they had not been told 'the full extent' of Rees's association with Burgess.[44]

From the interrogations in May and June 1951, MI5 was able to produce by early July a 'note of further action to be taken'. On the version released to the National Archives in 2015, there are forty-four names listed, but some further names, probably three, were redacted for some reason. Under each name the document summarised what had already been done and where more interviews were needed.

Anthony Blunt and Kim Philby were among an eclectic mix of familiar names from the Burgess story as well as some totally new ones. What is striking about the list released in 2015 is the absence of Harold Nicolson, although one name which was redacted appears in the alphabetical slot where Nicolson could have been. If it was redacted, why his name still needed to be kept secret in 2015 when he died in 1968 is not clear.

Also absent from the list was Kenneth Younger MP, McNeil's replacement as Minister of State at the Foreign Office who had gone on to become the acting Foreign Secretary for a time when Ernest Bevin fell ill in 1950. Younger had been at Burgess's farewell party before his departure to Washington and had been mentioned to MI5 by two people, including Rees, who said Younger was 'the most important' in Burgess's eyes of 'several influential persons' he thought sympathised with his views on foreign policy.[45]

While MI5's list was being drawn up in June 1951 Younger answered questions in the House of Commons about Burgess's defection on behalf of the Foreign Secretary, Herbert Morrison. He was attacked by Conservative MPs including Anthony Eden, when in their view he appeared to imply that there were others in the Foreign Office with the same views as Burgess. Neither Younger nor Eden mentioned that they knew Burgess.[46]

It is also noticeable that Victor, Lord Rothschild, was listed but, by comparison with the others, nothing much appears to have been done about him at this point, and there is only a note that he is a 'possible source of further information about BURGESS'.[47] It would be four years before he offered Dick Goldsmith White of MI5 a statement 'in the nature of self-insurance, for the future, when such people as yourself and Guy [Liddell] may not be around' setting out his version of events.[48]

By October of 1951, the information about all those listed had been distilled into what was called a 'secret cross reference' of material relating to Burgess. It was a grid where just eight people were listed and mapped against events in Burgess's life. Some were referred to by codenames of one kind or another and others by their own names.

The first name on the grid was Paul Hardt, which was the name adopted by Theodore Maly when he came to Britain in the early thirties from central Europe as a KGB 'illegal' and helped in the recruitment of the Cambridge spies. By 1951, he was dead, having been executed in Moscow in September 1938 in one of the purges of the time.[49]

The next name was 'Peach', which MI5 had adopted as a codename for Philby, then Burgess himself under his own name, followed by 'Curzon', an MI5 codename for Maclean, 'Blunden', a not very secretive name for Blunt, and 'Raleigh', their name for Goronwy Rees.

The two other names in the grid were mostly covered up, but in one place the name 'Klugmann' can be seen, the original spelling of the Cambridge communist activist James Klugman. As to the identity of the eighth man in the grid, his name was covered up more successfully, but some points about him are still visible and from them we have been able to establish who he was.

According to the grid, in 1933 he was in Yugoslavia working for 'H.M.V. Co' and doing 'casual work for SIS'. By 1935, he had returned to London, 'joined SIS', and then in subsequent years 'recruited BURGESS as outside agent'.

The man who fits this bill is David Footman, MI6 officer and author, whom Burgess turned into a broadcaster and who then turned Burgess into an MI5 'outside agent'. Footman had lived and worked in pre-war Yugoslavia, where he had been MI6's man in Belgrade. The book he wrote in 1935 which prompted Burgess to commission Footman's first broadcast had the secondary title of 'Visiting Macedonia, Serbia and Croatia'. He even spoke Serbo-Croat and broadcast in this language for the BBC in wartime transmissions to the Balkans.

A review of mentions of Footman's name in other documents reveals how an invitation from him to Burgess led to a top-secret document ending up in Burgess's hands. It was Burgess at his most cunning and, knowingly or otherwise, Footman had initiated it. In 1949, Footman had recommended 'roping in Guy Burgess' as a speaker at a high-level Military International Affairs Study Group at Oxford University.

The list of people who attended remains secret, which hints at their seniority. Footman said, 'Even if he did not speak BURGESS would be an excellent recruiter and his profound knowledge of Marxism and Far Eastern conditions most useful in discussions.' He added that Burgess 'should be able to land Anthony BLUNT' to talk about Soviet ideology and art. Burgess did give a talk on communism in the Far East, but Blunt couldn't attend.

During the event, Burgess found out that a handbook on Russian forged documents written by a top expert on Marxism, Robert Carew-Hunt, was being issued on the basis that it should not be distributed 'outside Head Office'. The handbook was particularly sensitive because it dealt in part with the authenticity of the so-called 'Zinoviev letter' published by the *Daily Mail* four days before the 1924 general election, which was purported to be a directive from the Comintern to the British Communist Party calling for communist agitation to be stepped up.

Burgess went up to Carew-Hunt and asked if he could see the handbook because 'the Minister of State had instructed him to prepare a paper on Russian forgeries'. It was sent to Burgess on the stipulation that he returned it, but he never did.

Now, with Burgess long gone, that former Minister of State, Hector McNeil, was questioned and 'stated that he had never seen' the document.

Reviewing the evidence, Ronnie Reed of MI5 wondered how Burgess had found out about the handbook in the first place. 'The number of persons present who were aware of this document was not large and included FOOTMAN for certain.'[50]

This was not the work of some drunk staggering from one shambles to another. Burgess had used a contact to get into an important event and procured a very sensitive document by citing the name of a minister. Further investigations into what had happened at this joint MI5–MI6 event at Worcester College revealed that one of the other visiting speakers was a defector from Soviet military intelligence, Nikolai Borodin. When he had finished his talk and left, some in the audience attacked his credibility. MI5 remembered that 'those who were forefront in the attack upon Borodin were BURGESS, REES and FOOTMAN'.[51]

In other documents, Reed wrote that 'one of BURGESS's closest friends was David FOOTMAN of the Foreign Office, and I suppose we ought to confine ourselves to saying just this and no more' and elsewhere noted that someone 'had never seen a man [Footman] closer to the verge of a complete nervous breakdown'.[52]

From the available evidence in those official files which have been released Footman remained a lower-profile figure in the investigation compared with 'Peach' (Philby), 'Blunden' (Blunt) and 'Raleigh' (Rees).

This was despite an intervention by the writer Rebecca West, who contacted the Director of Public Prosecutions on 8 June 1951 to say that she had known Burgess for some years and that he and Footman were part of a 'group with Foreign and War Office connections who I have long been certain were Communists'. She had first met Footman in 1935 in Yugoslavia, where he was working for MI6, and in 1941 she concluded that he was trying to convert her to what became known as 'Titoism'.[53] She told the DPP that she had 'seen Sir Orme Sargent [PUS, Foreign Office, 1946–49] about this very matter some time ago, but had had scorn poured on her information'.[54]

MI5 files later revealed that 'David FOOTMAN resigned from MI6 because of his association with Burgess'. This confirmation was prompted by a letter they intercepted from Burgess to his mother asking, 'Is David F all right? ...

I am very worried I may have caused him trouble – and others too.' Burgess was absolutely right.[55]

A suitable solution was found to the Footman problem. He was offered a fellowship at the newly founded St Antony's College, Oxford, which specialised in modern international studies. The first Warden, Sir William Deakin, who enjoyed the company of former intelligence officers, said he wanted a Soviet expert who was free of any commitment to Marxism, and Footman was appointed.[56]

* * *

Harold Nicolson wrote in his diary on 7 June 1951:

> If I thought Guy Burgess was a brave man, I should imagine that he had gone to join the Communists. As I know him to be a coward, I suppose that he was suspected of passing things on to the Bolshies, and realising his guilt, did a bunk ... I fear that all this will mean a witch-hunt.

Jack Hewit told Anthony Blunt that 'now the persecution would start'.[57] That 'witch-hunt' or 'persecution' was to take nearly thirty years of suspicion, cover-ups, rumour, betrayal, leaking and eventual exposure before it was certain that, in addition to the two 'missing diplomats', there had been a 'third man', then a 'fourth man' and, eventually, allegations of a further man in a 'ring of five'.

The hunt for information about Burgess, Maclean and any other British KGB spies was becoming a race between the authorities and the media. The press, especially the *Daily Express*, was too good at discovering facts for the government's liking. There were regular official investigations into suspected leaks. How, for example, had the *Express* found out the men were missing in the first place? The embassy in Paris reported that Sam White, Paris Correspondent of the *Express*'s sister paper, the *Evening Standard*, got it from a French official who'd seen the official alert. White was questioned by the police for alleged bribery but not charged.[58]

During an inquiry into another leak, MI5 was told it had originated from 'Percy Hoskins' bar' – the London flat of a *Daily Express* correspondent which was a 'rendezvous for civil servants, police officers and officers of the Security Service'.[59]

The security services and their political masters had a particularly complicated task. Whitehall's model attitude for a government minister during an espionage crisis can best be summarised in the words of a Prime Minister one decade later. When Harold MacMillan heard of the arrest of John Vassall, a Soviet spy in Whitehall, he told MI5, 'I am not at all pleased. When a gamekeeper shoots a fox, he doesn't go and hang it up outside the Master of Foxhound's drawing room: he buries it out of sight. But you can't shoot a spy as you did in the war. You have to try him. Better to discover him, and then control him, but never catch him.'[60]

The defection of Burgess and Maclean created a chase for other foxes that was taking up an enormous amount of government, MI5 and, indeed, Fleet Street time. Some of the guilty were, in Macmillan's terminology, 'controlled' – but none were ever tried. Other chases turned out to be a waste of time. Burgess himself was often to blame for setting the foxhounds running and a few of the hunted didn't help themselves.

Two writers with whom Burgess was in contact during his time in America were W. H. Auden and the poet, novelist and essayist Stephen Spender. In those stressful hours before Burgess set off with Maclean, he had made that phone call to Spender, hoping to speak to Auden, who was staying with him on his way to Italy. Auden wasn't there and the message wasn't passed on. Inevitably a bad case of crossed lines ensued and it played out in the press after the Reuters news agency got on to the story. Spender said he'd passed a message on from Burgess to Auden, who'd told him, 'Burgess must be drunk'. Auden denied receiving such a message from Spender about Burgess. No wonder an MI5 man got a bit confused, regretting that 'for the moment I cannot put my hand' on telegrams from MI6 that might clear up 'these divergent views'.[61]

Auden then gave an interview to the *Daily Express* and ended up being reported as saying that he knew that while Burgess worked in the Washington embassy he was a communist, and that Burgess had talked to him about the atomic bomb spies Klaus Fuchs and Alan Nunn May. Auden immediately complained that some of the *Express* report was invented.

There was then an even more significant development, involving Spender and two other friends of Burgess.

Rosamond Lehmann and her brother John were two of the four children of Rudolph Lehmann, a Cambridge oarsman, writer, Editor of *Punch* magazine and a Liberal MP at the turn of the century. They both followed in their father's footsteps to Cambridge and into careers as writers. Burgess had nominated John Lehmann on his list of speakers about Russia for the BBC.

MI5 knew John Lehmann as far back as the mid-1930s as a communist fellow-traveller, literally doing long-distance errands for party members. MI5 called him 'a young, effeminate, type of fellow' and found his friends included 'drummer Fred' Turner of the 3rd Battalion Coldstream Guards to whom he was sending money regularly but still being asked by Fred for more.[62] MI5 had prevented Lehmann from being recruited by the BBC during the war, despite pressure from Harold Nicolson and senior Foreign Office mandarin Sir Ivone Kirkpatrick, among others.[63]

MI5 probably also knew Rosamond Lehmann's second husband Wogan Phillips, later Britain's only hereditary Communist Party peer, Lord Milford, who went off to the Spanish Civil War to drive an ambulance. This caused their marriage to fall apart and Rosamond Lehmann subsequently had an affair with Goronwy Rees. He would openly visit her family home, and played with her children. Burgess, who was then a BBC producer, would be invited along too, would swim in the nearby river, smoke, drink and talk literature and left-wing politics. While at Girton College, Cambridge, Rosamond observed that 'it seemed everyone was a homosexual or was pretending to be one', but even she thought Burgess was overstepping the mark when he 'expressed his hopes of seducing the gardener's handsome son. I forbade it. "Oh Rosie, Rosie", he cried, "Can't I?" "No," I said.'[64]

More significantly, Rosamond Lehmann also remembered one dinner alone with Goronwy Rees when he revealed that Burgess had just confided to him that he was a Comintern agent and had asked Goronwy to join him. Rees cautioned her, 'If you ever mention that I've told you, I'll kill you.'

She later wrote: 'My main feeling was: "Oh this explains Guy's extraordinary volte face; his (to me) most unacceptable and inexplicable dallying with the Anglo-German Fellowship etc. He has been ordered to do this as a cover."'

With her affair with Rees long over (by 1951 she had just finished another with Cecil Day-Lewis), she now felt sufficiently released from her bond of confidentiality to tell her brother John. What she had not anticipated was that this story would end up in the *Daily Express*. John Lehmann wrote to Stephen Spender warning him that 'someone you know very well' was 'absolutely sure' that Burgess was a spy. The letter ended up in the hands of the *Daily Express* who promptly published the contents, including John Lehmann's name.[65]

Years later, two mysteries were solved; Burgess told Spender the reason he'd tried to speak to Auden was that he wanted to borrow his home on the Italian island of Ischia after delivering Maclean to Prague.

Spender explained he'd shown the Lehmann letter to a *Daily Express* reporter on the condition that he wouldn't quote from it. Some hope.[66]

MI5, alerted by the press reports, got one of their top interrogators, Jim Skardon, to interview John Lehmann. Why hadn't he passed his information about Burgess on to the authorities? Lehmann said he tried to do this via Harold Nicolson, pillar of the establishment, but Nicolson 'found himself unable to assist owing to a heavy list of engagements'.[67] There is no record of whether MI5 followed this up by asking Nicolson himself what he meant by this extraordinary statement.[68]

In terms of informing the British public, the press was winning the race hands down. The Foreign Office and MI5 deliberately kept what they discovered a closely guarded secret. However, a 1953 memorandum by Lord Talbot de Malahide shows that the Foreign Office had adopted the classic policy of never confirming nor denying details. The press might discover new information, but the Foreign Office would not confirm its accuracy because it had not supplied it. Talbot's memorandum reveals that a principal reason for this approach was to keep secret the way in which Maclean had been discovered. Talbot wrote:

> [I]t is most important to conceal from the Russians our knowledge of
> [the VENONA] material. They cannot, of course, now prevent us from

extracting what we can from it. But if they knew we were doing this, they could take defensive action which would probably ruin any chance we still have of making use of the knowledge we obtain this way.

He continued: '[I]it is to safeguard this basic piece of information that we have concealed the fact that Maclean and Burgess were under investigation before they disappeared.'[69]

In September 1952, not much more than a year after the defection, the *Sunday Times* published the first articles about Burgess and Maclean to be written by a fellow member of what the author called 'the governing class'. An MI5 officer was deputed to go through the article looking for clues.

Cyril Connolly knew Burgess and Maclean socially, and even spoke to Maclean on the day of the defection. He was a man who liked to spend his mornings in his bed and his bath, before a little light literary criticism. His 'personal and intimate study' of the two men gave readers, including those in MI5, new insights into the 'missing diplomats' they had heard so much about. Burgess was 'cynical and argumentative, avidly curious, yet sometimes vague and incompetent'. He was also 'immensely energetic, a great talker, reader, boaster, walker, who swam like an otter and drank ... like some Rabelaisian bottle-swiper whose thirst was unquenchable'. Maclean was seldom heard to talk politics; 'Guy never seemed to stop'. Connolly believed, 'If traitors they be, they are traitors to themselves.'[70] His not-for-publication views were even stronger; Burgess was 'a ruthless, scheming exhibitionist'.[71]

Over at MI5, not only were they discovering facts from news organisations which put their political masters, and thus them, under more pressure, but they were getting a very hard time from the Americans. In the MI5 files of this period there is a consistent theme best encapsulated by the sentence, 'We do not wish to encourage the FBI to direct a lot of questions at us about our progress in this peculiarly British field of counter espionage.'[72] One MI5 officer recorded with relief that the DG (Director General) 'seems to have been successful in keeping (J. Edgar) Hoover quiet'.[73]

The fact that Auden and Spender had homes in America and knew Burgess in Washington only increased the concern of the FBI. They wanted to know the outcome of the MI5 interviews with Auden; they pressured the British embassy; an interim report was promised.

Homes were searched, friends were interviewed, letters were intercepted and phones were tapped, particularly that of Cyril Connolly. He was referred to as 'one of that off clique in the Reform Club'. A conversation about Connolly overheard on a train was reported back. Unaware of most of this, Connolly and his friends gossiped away on the phone about each other.[74] When these MI5 files were eventually released to the National Archives, some sections were still blacked out. But other names were visible, people who had cropped up simply by association: the artist Lucian Freud, the poet Louis MacNeice, the journalist Robert Kee.

Jim Skardon interviewed William Ridsdale, Burgess's former News Department boss, only in December 1952. The questioning was constrained by a 'charter' imposed by Lord Talbot de Malahide three days previously. Ridsdale claimed he had not known Burgess until he 'joined the News Department in 1943 [sic]' and that Peter Hutton had 'recommended' Burgess. This was the same Peter Hutton whom Burgess had reported to MI5 in 1941 for loose talk. Ridsdale said that he was not fond of Burgess: 'BURGESS was not a particularly good member of his department. He was slovenly and irresponsible, and it was never possible to assign him any task of importance.' He later corrected himself, saying, 'it was just possible that he had made the acquaintance of BURGESS earlier' but, if so, 'it was merely a casual acquaintanceship of no significance'.[75] By the time Skardon interviewed Ridsdale, MI5 had visited the BBC and had read the files and spotted Ridsdale's name there, alongside Burgess's.

Skardon allowed Ridsdale to read copies of the documents found in Burgess's flat as his name was prominent, as well as Peter Smollett's, whom Ridsdale described as 'a bad boy'.[76]

Skardon thought it possible that Ridsdale had been worried because he had known the missing pair better than he cared to admit. In the end Skardon concluded that 'RIDSDALE is of no particular security interest'. In other words he was a dupe rather that a spy.

MI5 spent most time on the two men who had always been top of their list; Blunt, formerly of MI5, and Philby, still a serving officer in MI6.

Blunt had signed a one-page statement on 6 June 1951 in which he adopted a clever patriotic strategy – whatever Burgess had been up to that looked suspicious appeared to have been done 'in highly cloak and dagger style' on behalf of His Majesty's Secret Services. So, he argued, contacting 'old Communist friends' was somehow part of Burgess's job at the Joint Broadcasting Committee, carrying communications to Pfeiffer had been done 'on behalf of Chamberlain', and he and Burgess had abandoned their holiday in the South of France on hearing the news of the German–Soviet pact because Burgess 'would be needed by his organisation'. *Which* organisation wasn't spelt out.[77]

One senior MI5 officer, Ronnie Reed, wasn't convinced by this. He noted that, as with his verdict on Goronwy Rees, MI5 had not been told 'the full extent of their association with Burgess'.[78]

But four days later one of his bosses, Guy Liddell, concluded after dining with Blunt: 'I feel certain that Anthony was never a conscious collaborator with BURGESS in any activities that he may have conducted with BURGESS on behalf of the Comintern'.[79]

Among the thousands of pages of official documents now in the National Archives are two sides of closely typed A4 paper, headed 'Interview with Anthony BLUNT on 9.5.52', which suggests that Jim Skardon was not always a great MI5 interrogator.

> BLUNT adheres to the story he told in his statement that he was not informed, as was Goronwy Rees, by BURGESS that the latter was working for the Comintern. He agrees that this is a surprising fact, but does seek to explain it by saying that whereas Goronwy REES was clearly interested in politics, BLUNT was much more interested in art and to a lesser degree in people.

He concluded, 'I am left with the strong impression that whatever BLUNT knows he has passed on to the authorities.'[80]

And so, in the case of Blunt, the matter largely rested for a decade.

In the case of Philby, or 'Peach', one of the earliest messages from MI5 London to MI5 Washington after the defection was summarised in the index as 'Telegram to SLO Washington with latest inf. re Burgess and warning re Philby'.

The telegram itself, on which someone confusingly scribbled 'NOT SENT', said, 'Suspicion now thrown on whole circle BURGESS's acquaintances who include PHILBY. "C" has been informed of this.'[81]

Kim Philby had already anticipated such a message. After all, as Burgess's landlord in Washington he was the obvious candidate for the role of the 'third man'. He sent a telegram to 'C', Sir Stewart Menzies, in which he said that Burgess was so undisciplined and irresponsible that it was scarcely conceivable that he could have been involved in any clandestine activity. This would become a familiar response among senior people who had known Burgess.

But then he had second thoughts on his tactics and decided on what can only be described as a master-class in disingenuous dissembling. Given that Burgess was by now in Russia there would be no harm in shopping his KGB colleague; after all, surely no spy would do that to a fellow agent. A copy of his memo to 'C', passed on to MI5, said it came 'from C's representative in Washington'. Philby was still in a job.

His memo said he'd been 'piecing together' a 'few isolated facts' about Burgess's time in Washington. Burgess had a sunlamp and a camera, he worked late at home after office hours, he travelled frequently to New York, he even owned a copy of a book by Stalin. The man who was too irresponsible to be a spy was suddenly transformed into somebody who 'had available the essential requirements of an espionage agent'.[82]

Philby followed it up with a four-page, closely typed statement to MI5 in which he appeared to be trying to be as helpful as possible without telling them anything that might incriminate himself. He was happy to list Burgess's 'incredibly wide range of acquaintances'; the 'intellectuals' included 'E. M. Forster (one of Guy's particular heroes), Somerset Maugham, H. G. Wells', and among the Cambridge friends were the photographer Lettice Ramsey and Anne Barnes. He also offered the insight that her husband George, by now the Director of BBC Television, was 'one of the very few people whom Guy positively disliked'.

But when it came to anything to do with Russia, Russians or communists, Philby's excellent memory failed him. The only communists he remembered from Cambridge were the three usual suspects, Guest, Klugman and Cornford, whom he confused with a fourth, Maurice Cornforth, to create a hybrid 'John Cornforth'. Of Burgess's trip to Moscow: 'I can remember nothing of any significant contacts made in Russia', only Burgess's 'comments on the Regency architecture of Leningrad'.[83]

It was a bravado performance, good enough to keep 'Peach' from arrest but not good enough to save his job. In December 1951, Kim Philby was subjected to a hostile cross-examination by former MI5 officer Helenus Milmo QC. 'Buster', as he was known, led an 'official inquiry' into whether Burgess and Maclean had been tipped off. He concluded that 'Philby is and has been for many years a Soviet agent and that he was directly and deliberately responsible' for warning the pair. While he felt there 'is no room for doubt' he also admitted that 'there is no evidence in law to prove the source' of the tip-off.[84]

In October 1955, the Prime Minister Harold Macmillan was forced to make a statement: 'I have no reason to conclude that Mr. Philby has at any time betrayed the interests of his country, or to identify him with the so-called "third man", if indeed there was one.' Eleven months earlier the *Daily Mirror* had been making enquiries of the Foreign Office about Philby, but had been met with silence.[85]

Philby himself gave a press conference to issue his own denial and he was filmed being interviewed by an unnamed reporter with a North American accent.

Q 'Would you still regard Burgess, who lived with you for a while in Washington, would you still regard him as a friend of yours? How do you feel about him now?'

A 'I consider his action deplorable. On the subject of friendship I prefer to say as little as possible as it is very complicated.'

Q 'Was there a third man? Are you in fact the third man?'

A 'No I was not.'

Q 'Do you think there was one?'

A 'No comment.'

Nowhere in the different film versions of this encounter did the reporter ever ask Philby what he meant by 'this deplorable action' by Burgess – was it spying or defecting, or simply bad behaviour? No wonder Philby looked pleased with himself at the end of the interview. It had hardly been a grilling.[86]

At the Foreign Office the top diplomat had floated a different option for dealing with the 'third man' in 1952. Sir William Strang wrote of Philby: 'If we want to avoid embarrassment, the best course would be to let him slip away.' And that, as much by accident as by design, is how it worked out a decade later.[87]

MI6 helped to find Philby a job, working for David Astor's *Observer*. He took up his place in the Middle East press corps, which was stationed in those days in the relatively peaceful and cosmopolitan city of Beirut. In January 1963, MI5, who'd received new information on Philby, sent Nicholas Elliot, an MI6 officer, Eton contemporary of Burgess and long-term friend of Philby's, to confront him. As soon as Philby saw Elliot arrive he told him, 'I rather thought it would be you.' After their conversation, Elliot didn't arrest or detain Philby in any way. He returned to England and didn't attempt to contact him again for two weeks. Not surprisingly, Philby decided that pleasant though the life of a foreign correspondent had been in Beirut, it was now time to make for Moscow.

Nowadays one suspects that a confrontation with a suspected Russian spy would be preceded by a 5 a.m. knock, a smashing down of front doors and side windows and a ubiquitous police helicopter hovering overhead with live TV capability. Even allowing for the very different times of 1963, it does seem remarkable that Philby was offered such an easy escape. This led to the theory that perhaps it had been decided at a high level that a defection, embarrassing though it undoubtedly would be, would at least avoid the need for a trial and the unpredictable revelations that might accompany it. On the other hand, by 1963, the British government had learned that it was possible to prosecute spies and keep the press away: the trial of KGB spy George Blake was conducted mainly *in camera*, but after he had made a confession. In Philby's case, it is not clear how much of a confession he had actually made; nevertheless, the press was finally able to confirm Philby as the 'third man'. It would be a long time before they could confirm a fourth.

Politics inevitably played its part throughout the Burgess and Maclean affair, and particularly among the political friends of the two men. Lady Violet Bonham Carter, née Asquith, was the daughter of the Liberal Prime Minister Herbert Asquith and a Liberal politician in her own right. Her father's old friend and loyal supporter was Sir Donald Maclean, father of the 'missing diplomat'. She had met Guy Burgess through Harold Nicolson and on 21 July 1952 she wrote to *The Times* complaining about what she called 'a recent and flagrant violation of what, I hope, may still be called the ethics of journalism'. This was 'the repeated invasion of the privacy' of the families of Burgess and Maclean. Her son-in-law, Jo Grimond, who had been at school with Burgess, raised the matter in the Commons. Another Eton contemporary of Burgess, David Astor, spoke up for Maclean's wife in *The Observer*.

Three years later, in September 1955, *The Spectator* columnist Henry Fairlie cited these interventions when he wrote in his 'Political Commentary':

> I have several times suggested that what I call the 'Establishment' in this country is today more powerful than ever before. By the 'Establishment' I do not mean only the centres of official power – though they are certainly part of it – but rather the whole matrix of official and social relations within which power is exercised. The exercise of power in Britain (more specifically, in England) cannot be understood unless it is recognised that it is exercised socially.[88]

Fairlie wrote of how the 'representatives of the "establishment"' had moved in after the Burgess and Maclean defection, and that the effect 'may be traced in the columns of the more respectable newspapers at the time'. This wasn't the first time the term 'establishment' had been used by Fairlie and others, but this was the moment it entered the mainstream.

One unintended consequence of the defection of Burgess and Maclean was that it seemed to become a badge of honour for a politician to be able to say that he or she *didn't* know them. In a House of Lords debate in 1955, Viscount Astor, brother of David Astor, somewhat proudly announced that he was 'one of the few people who never knew Guy Burgess'. 'By all accounts he was one of the most amusing and clever conversationalists there was, who charmed a great many people. But he was a drunken, dirty and a sexual pervert.'[89]

There is no reason to disbelieve Viscount Astor when he said he never knew Burgess, though it is worth bearing in mind that when, in 1963, he denied having sex with Mandy Rice-Davies during the Profumo scandal, she memorably replied, 'Well he would, wouldn't he?'

Henry Fairlie specifically accused David Astor's *The Observer* and *The Times*, which was then owned by yet another Astor, John Jacob Astor V, of being the agents of the establishment.

Two decades later, *The Times*, by then under the ownership of the Canadian proprietor Roy Thomson, tried to make a break with the past and made a terrible mess of it. On 15 June 1977, the paper ran the front-page headline: 'Fourth Man in Inquiry on Philby, Burgess and Maclean'. The by-line was 'by Peter Hennessy', who subsequently became Baron Hennessy of Nympsfield, a respected English historian and academic specialising in post-war British politics. His 1977 story claimed that 'Inquiries by *The Times* have now established that Mr Donald Beves, a wealthy Cambridge don, was suspected by security circles of having played a crucial role' in the transformation of Philby, Maclean and Burgess from Cambridge undergraduates to Soviet agents. Not so much the fourth spy as the man who helped recruit the three. Beves had died in 1961, so was not around to answer his accusers.

Considering the prominence that the story was given on page one of *The Times*, it was perhaps surprising to read, further into the paper, that 'the evidence against Beves amounted to strong suspicion, but fell short, and still falls short, of conclusive proof'. Instead, the story relied on phrases such as 'his name cropped up at several points in connection with the three traitors'.

Friends of what Hennessy tactfully called this 'much loved, old-fashioned type of unmarried don' displayed their outrage in the correspondence columns of the paper. George Rylands regarded the story as 'some kind of extraordinary fabrication'. The few who knew of Blunt's role in the Cambridge spy ring may have spotted the coincidences that could have led *The Times* to the wrong man: Cambridge don, five letters, begins with the letter 'B'.

Two weeks after his articles on Beves first appeared, Peter Hennessy wrote a letter to his own paper: 'I wish to retract in full the grievous allegation they contained about his involvement in the Philby/Burgess/Maclean affair. In doing so I accept personal responsibility. I would like to apologise unreservedly to the family, friends and former colleagues of Donald Beves for the harm and distress caused.'

So if Beves wasn't a spy or a recruiter, were there any more spies in the Cambridge 'ring'? Over the next decades, painstaking work by MI5's top investigators led to private confrontations, secret deals and only lately, and belatedly, public exposure by the media. As in any good spy thriller, betrayal played its part.

Betrayal number one was by Michael Straight, the American who had been recruited to the KGB by Anthony Blunt at Cambridge to work with Burgess. Ironically, Straight betrayed Blunt so that he too could get a job almost as prestigious as his, who, as Surveyor of the Queen's Pictures, was in effect head of her art collection. In 1964, Straight was nominated as President Kennedy's chairman of the National Endowment for the Arts. He knew he would face a vetting by the FBI, so he decided to get in first and tell them of his past and Blunt's role in it. The FBI passed on the news to Arthur Martin, an MI5 man they had worked with on the Burgess and Maclean defection inquiry. In April 1964, Martin put the allegations to Blunt, who reportedly paused theatrically before replying, 'It is true.' His confession was undoubtedly influenced by the fact that Martin had been authorised to offer him immunity from prosecution and a guarantee of confidentiality in return for his cooperation.

In his unpublished memoirs, Blunt wrote that he felt 'immense' relief and handed over 'all the information that I had about the Russian activities ... I also believed, naively, that the Security Service would see to it – partly in its own interest – that the story would never become public. I therefore went back to my own work not only relieved but confident.'[90]

Betrayal number two ended Blunt's relief, and was partly at the hands of Goronwy Rees, who had first told MI5 about Blunt in 1951, but had not been entirely believed. Over the years, he had developed a strong dislike of

Blunt, remembering how at the time of Burgess's disappearance Blunt had persuaded him not to reveal his suspicions about Burgess because it was 'not the act of a friend'. He also grew increasingly frustrated that thanks to the guarantee of confidentiality and immunity from prosecution, Blunt's career seemed unaffected by his treachery.[91]

It was to be a case of 'revenge is a dish best served cold'. In 1978, more than twenty-five years after Burgess's defection, Goronwy Rees met Andrew Boyle, a journalist who somehow managed to combine creating and editing the BBC's *World at One* radio programme with a successful career as a biographer. Boyle had been tipped off about Blunt by intelligence officers and Rees told him what he needed to know. Rees heard from Micky Burn that he too had met Boyle at a local pub and learned that 'our friend AB had actually confessed to him but it was deemed too much of a scandal to do anything about it'. Presumably Rees reasoned that if Blunt was no longer denying that he'd been a Soviet spy, why not let the world know at last? Rees was dying and hard-up, what was there to lose? He'd even get to share some of Boyle's earnings from articles.

Boyle's 1979 book *Climate of Treason* did not name Blunt, instead referring to him as 'Maurice', which was the title of a novel by E. M. Forster about a gay academic. *Private Eye* magazine saw no need for such restraint and named him unequivocally. His crimes were no longer confidential, but the guarantee of his immunity from arrest remained. Or, as *Private Eye* put it, 'While lesser mortals received sentences of 10 to 20 years for handing over documents, and a key traitor such as George Blake was jailed for 42 years, "Maurice" was able to confess and walk away.'

Listing all the clues in Boyle's book that pointed to 'Sir Anthony Blunt, adviser for the Queen's Pictures and Drawings', the magazine concluded, 'It is clear that as far as Andrew Boyle and Fleet Street are concerned, the Blunt truth is that "Maurice" = Sir Antony Blunt.'

Professor Sir Anthony Blunt KCVO went from a respected art historian to a man named by Prime Minister Margaret Thatcher as a KGB spy. He was stripped of all honours and when he entered a cinema in London was booed until he had to leave. Goronwy Rees watched the news of the Prime

Minister's announcement on television in hospital. When pictures of Blunt came up on the screen, he said, 'Got you, you swine.'[92]

Blunt gave a series of interviews calling Burgess 'one of the most remarkable and intelligent people he had ever known', who could also be 'extremely wrong-headed'.

Blunt died of a heart attack in 1983. When asked how he'd coped with the strain over the years, he pointed to a glass of whisky and replied, 'With this and more work and more work.'[93] Eric Hobsbawn, who knew him well from the meetings of the Cambridge Apostles, past and present, wrote that Blunt, a man with an 'elongated, elegant, supercilious face', had such 'ruthless self-control that he spent the day of his public exposure, besieged by the hacks and the paparazzi in the house of a friend, quietly correcting proofs'. His partner John Gaskin, who had first tried and failed to kill himself by jumping eighty feet off a balcony in 1980, ultimately succeeded when he threw himself under a train in 1988.[94]

All the familiar elements which had contributed to the eventual naming of Blunt, the betrayal of a spy by a friend, a 'confidentiality' deal with MI5 that didn't hold, and, crucially, the helping hand of the fourth estate, were reprised for the unmasking of more Cambridge spies.

In 1979, back at *The Times*, the Editor was still sore about his wrong 'Fourth Man' story about Donald Beves. William Rees-Mogg, who went on to become Baron Rees-Mogg, chairman of the Arts Council and vice-chairman of the BBC, had told colleagues that in the face of 'a lot of stick' he had gone back to his source, who told him 'it was absolutely right about Beves'. However, Rees-Mogg accepted there was an alternative theory that Beves had been a recruiter for MI6 not the KGB.

The sister paper of *The Times* was the *Sunday Times*. Once parts of rival newspaper groups, they had been brought together by Roy Thomson. But two very different cultures remained. When Blunt was named publicly as 'the fourth man', Phillip Knightley led a team of no fewer than thirteen *Sunday Times* reporters in following up the story.

He remembered back to a conversation with Rees-Mogg earlier in the year. The Editor of *The Times* had told him the story of how Sir John Colville, who had been a Private Secretary to Sir Winston Churchill, had been contacted some years before by MI5 and asked if he could tell them the name of a man he had dined with on a certain day in October 1939. As Colville had kept his diaries, he could. The reason MI5 wanted to know was that among the papers Guy Burgess left behind when he defected was a note naming somebody who appeared to be one of his informants and who had lunched with Colville on that particular day. It was an interesting tale that potentially led to a fifth man, even though there was a major gap in it: the name of the man, Burgess's informant, Colville's lunch guest.

With all the papers chasing follow-ups on Blunt, Knightley expected *The Times* to be running the story of what Colville had told Rees-Mogg, but they didn't. So he rang Colville himself. Colville confirmed what Rees-Mogg had told Knightley, but wouldn't name the man. It was enough to give the *Sunday Times* a front-page news story: 'Churchill's Man Reveals Yet Another Spy'. When Rees-Mogg still didn't respond, the *Sunday Times* decided that, if the Editor of *The Times* wasn't going to try to track down the still unnamed man, they would.

Knightley had kept notes of the clues Colville had given Rees-Mogg about the identity. For example, the man had worked at the Foreign Office and then the Ministry of Supply. Two *Sunday Times* reporters, David Leitch and Barry Penrose, went to the Civil Service Library and after looking through thousands of names came up with the only one that fitted. Colville was called and, perhaps caught by surprise, confirmed it. Penrose went to knock on the door of the man's home in Rome.

On Sunday 23 November 1979, a front-page headline ran: 'John Cairncross, Ex F.O. Confesses To Sunday Times. I Was Spy For Soviets'.

The next day *The Times* followed up the story with a rather less direct headline: 'Official who spied for Guy Burgess may have been Cambridge Blunt recruit'. At the *Sunday Times* Phillip Knightley wrote a memo to his own Editor, Harold Evans, 'to set down how we came to scoop *The Times* twice on its own story'.

Like Blunt, Cairncross thought he had a deal with the authorities to keep his treachery secret. He'd been questioned after a document found in

Burgess's flat by MI5 had been traced to him. The secretary of one of the MI5 men working on the case recognised the distinctive handwriting in the notes as being that of a former colleague in the Civil Service. It was Cairncross's handwriting.

John Cairncross had not been on MI5's 1951 list of forty-four Burgess contacts, nor the grid of eight suspects, but in March 1952, as a 'Civil Servant with Comm. connections', his phone was being tapped. MI5 heard a strange call to a man called Karl who wanted to make a film about the missing men. Cairncross 'thought it should show a complete victory smashing Russian attempts to get hold of Allied secrets' – a very optimistic spin on events.

The next month he had to face a much more realistic scenario when it was clear MI5 had something on him in the notes Burgess had left behind.

He was called in and questioned by Jim Skardon, who produced the handwritten notes. In Cairncross's own words 'he handed it to me and I froze as soon as I recognised my own writing'. His mind went back to July 1939 when Burgess had asked for his help as a former Foreign Office man in understanding Britain's policy on Poland. Cairncross argued with MI5 that giving 'not very confidential details' to a friend working in military intelligence at the time was not an offence. But Skardon had another piece of paper waiting. It was a letter 'from a source in Cambridge' which said that Cairncross had been a communist at Cambridge. 'There was no doubt in my mind as to the source – it was Blunt,' Cairncross later wrote.[95] It was yet another betrayal by a Cambridge spy that did it for Cairncross.

In his autobiography, published posthumously, it was clear that tags such as the 'Fifth Man', the 'Ring of Five' and the 'atom spy' really got to him. He saw himself not as a member of a spy ring but 'an independent and voluntary agent, using the KGB as a channel to the Russians'. He pointed out that Kim Philby had said 'we were recruited individually and we operated individually. Burgess was the only one who knew all the others and he maintained the links with all of us.'

If Philby and Cairncross were right, this provides an extra dimension to the importance of Burgess as 'the spy who knew everyone' and it points to the significance of others who, while not in the inner circle, were also known to Burgess.

Men like Leo Long, who nearly a decade before Cairncross was named publicly, had himself been described as 'The Fifth Man' by the BBC's *Panorama* programme. Leo Long certainly fitted what was by now becoming the stereotypical Cambridge spy. He was at Trinity, had become a communist because of the rise of fascism, was influenced by John Cornford and James Klugman and joined the Apostles. He knew Burgess as 'a sort of Dylan Thomas figure, revolting, larger than life, always drunk, a creature from a different world'.

What set Long apart from the rest of his contemporaries, however, was class: 'I was a working-class boy from a secondary school. My father was often unemployed. It was a very poor background.' And there was timing; he wasn't recruited as a spy while at Cambridge but afterwards while working in military intelligence during World War Two. As was by now the fashion, Long had made a full statement to MI5 in 1964 but was never arrested or charged.

Burgess's hasty retreat from London to Moscow and the disorganised files he left behind created one more paper trail, this time to a Cambridge graduate of a previous generation.

Viewers of British television in the 1970s may remember a scientist called Dr Magnus Pyke who presented science programmes such as *Don't Ask Me* with bouts of enthusiastic arm-waving.[96] Magnus Pyke's cousin, Geoffrey Pyke, was also something of a boffin, but also a suspected spy connected to Burgess by documents found in his New Bond Street flat after the defection. By then, Pyke was dead; he had committed suicide in 1948 by taking an overdose of phenobarbitone after a deterioration in his mental health.

What intrigued MI5 most was a typed-up account of a wartime meeting where Pyke had explained how he had been working since May 1940 on a plan to paralyse German-occupied 'water-power stations and oil wells'. He would build a new machine, a 'snow tank' which commandos would drive up mountain slopes to put out of action power stations in German-occupied Norway and other locations. Lord Mountbatten, who was Commander of British Combined Operations, was enthusiastic enough to commission experiments in the mountains of North America. Pyke emphasised that the Russians should be brought into the plan as soon as possible.

So who had typed up the account of this important meeting? Pyke himself? Maybe Burgess? There was one peculiarity that led MI5 elsewhere. Every time the letter 'm' was typed, it appeared lower than any other letter.[97] This allowed MI5 to work out that the typewriter belonged to the ubiquitous Hans Peter Smolka, aka Peter Smollett, journalist turned broadcaster turned Head of Soviet Relations at the Ministry of Information and, most importantly, a key contact of Burgess and the KGB.

But were there yet more people who were never in the inner circle, maybe never dealt directly with KGB handlers, but had still passed on information intended for Moscow?

More than fifty years after Burgess defected, yet another Marxist student from the 1930s, this time from Oxford University, was named as another agent. He was the man whom Burgess had even recommended to the BBC as a speaker on Russia and even revealed was a communist. However, MI5 was never sure until much later that he was such, let alone an agent. Yet again, there was to be a Smollett connection.

In 2003 it was *The Times* that reported:

> One of the most influential historians of the 20th century, who went on to be Master of Balliol College, Oxford, stands accused today of taking a dark secret to his grave: he was a Soviet mole.
>
> Christopher Hill, who died last week aged 91, concealed his membership of the Communist Party to serve first in Military Intelligence, then at the Foreign Office, during the Second World War.

The source for this story was the British academic Professor Anthony Glees. He explained that in 1985 he'd done a deal with Hill, who'd confirmed to him that he had been 'a Communist agent of the NKVD/KGB' in return for Glees agreeing not to publish this fact during Hill's lifetime.[98]

When the MI5 files on Hill were released in 2014, one newspaper concluded 'How MI5 watched the wrong Marxist academics'. However, our more lengthy study of Hill's pre-war and wartime files has revealed that he was something of a serial applicant for secret intelligence work whose communist views were never detected when he was vetted at the time. There is no doubt that Hill was a secret party member in the mid-1930s. Another covert member at Oxford in that period, Jennifer Hart, has written of how he suggested she should recruit Isaiah Berlin to the party, but she knew Berlin well enough to realise this would be impossible.

The parallels between Burgess and Hill are striking; they were both Oxbridge students who had become communists, but the authorities didn't seem to know that because neither man had told them. Both travelled to Russia, both had done wartime work in military intelligence and other secret or secretive government bodies and by 1944 they were working in the same government department. The Foreign Office list for that year shows a G. Burgess in the News Department, which handled 'the supply of information to the British and Foreign Press', and a J. E. C. Hill in the Northern Department, dealing, in part, with the Soviet Union.

Re-enter Peter Smollett, at the Soviet Relations Department of the Ministry of Information, who'd invited the Communist Party to nominate people to help with his work. The party put Hill's name forward. Smollett wrote to the BBC suggesting that for a forthcoming talk on Russia in the series *The Allies*, 'Major J. E. C. Hill of the Foreign Office could probably do this very well'.[99]

Smollett is also believed to have been involved in the publication in 1945 of a book called *Two Commonwealths* by K. E. Holme, which was published in London in the series 'The Soviets and Ourselves'. It compared the British and Soviet 'Commonwealths', presented a glowing picture of the Soviet system and in particular set out to reassure British readers that they need not feel threatened by the long-term ambitions of the Soviets. The author's name, Holme, is the Russian for 'hill'. The initials K and E are the first letters of the Russian equivalents of the names Christopher and Edward. Thus 'K. E. Holme' equalled 'C. E. Hill'.

Smollett's name just kept cropping up in the Burgess story. In 1951, an observant MI5 officer reviewing the BBC's personnel file on Burgess had noticed; 'When Burgess was interviewed before being re-engaged in January 1941 no proper record of the interview was made for his file. There is simply a series of fairly inexplicable pencil notes on a small sheet of paper. At the bottom of it is a written note – "M. of I. Peter Smollett (26)".' This suggests that in addition to Blunt having had a hand in the return of Burgess to the BBC, Smollett may have been involved too.

When we began this project, we had a hunch that Smollett was a much bigger figure than had ever been realised. We wondered if the BBC had a file on him at their Written Archive Centre near Reading. They did, and it was declassified for us.

Then, in 2015, MI5 released the personal file PF39680/V2 on 'SMOLLETT/ SMOLKA, HARRY PETER' to the National Archives, who said the subject of the file had been 'assessed to have been implicated in Soviet espionage between (at least) 1930 and 1945'. The records didn't mention the fact that, like Maclean, Philby, Blunt and Cairncross, he was awarded an honour for his services to the Crown, in his case an OBE in 1944, but they did fill in a number of important gaps.[100]

After the war, Smollett returned to Austria, initially as a correspondent and then ran a factory previously owned by his father and lived 'in some affluence'. The discovery in 1951 of papers in Burgess's flat typed with the same distinctive 'dropped' letter 'm' as the notes of Geoffrey Pyke's wartime meeting on snow tanks had reawakened MI5's interest in him. Described as 'racy accounts of conversations with senior Government officials', to a modern-day reader these papers look more like a Whitehall insider newsletter recording appointments, policy papers and office gossip. There appears to have been no follow-up with Smollett then and he continued running his business in Austria.[101]

Five years later, in September 1961, Smollett, who'd recently renewed his British passport, decided to make his first return visit to London for five years, staying with his wife at the Savoy Hotel at a cost of ten pounds per day. The BBC's diplomatic correspondent, Thomas Barman, who was a former Moscow reporter and may have known Smollett 'on the road', was invited to have dinner with him. He tipped off the head of the government's covert propaganda arm, IRD, and the news was passed to MI5 that Harry Peter Smollett was in town again. Finally, MI5 decided this would be their chance to talk to him about Burgess, those documents and the business he'd run with Kim Philby.

Before interviewing him, they wanted to hear the phone calls to and from Room 387 at the Savoy Hotel, so they took out a warrant on the grounds that Smollett was 'suspected of being a Russian spy and is known to be a contact of Guy BURGESS. It is desired to learn as much as possible about his present activities.'

The interrogation took place on 2 October 1961 and, unusually, the whole twenty-page transcript of MI5 confronting a suspected spy was put in the public domain sixty years later, complete with what read almost like stage directions such as: 'S. (having his cigarette lit)'.

The interrogator was Arthur Martin, and just as his colleague Jim Skardon had been a decade before with Anthony Blunt, he was facing a wily fox. What was different on this occasion was that this suspected spy was sitting in a wheelchair. Smollett explained that he had an incurable illness – 'creeping paralysis' – and although his wife didn't know it, 'this may not last very long now'. He had just celebrated his forty-ninth birthday.

Martin's opening gambit was to confront him with the documents from Burgess's flat. Smollett explained that Burgess had told him that he worked for MI5 and had asked him to supply notes on any interesting conversations. The implication was, 'How could I say no to a man from MI5 just like you?'

After a gentle ramble through Smollett's CV, Martin again came to a crunch question, this time about Kim Philby's communist first wife:

A.M. Well, now, tell me about LIZZY? PHILBY married LIZZY FRIEDMAN as she was then.

S. FRIEDMAN, yes I knew her as KOLMAR(?)

Again, Smollett's tactic was to accept the obvious facts and almost challenge his interrogator to make more of it. Yes, he had known Lizzy Friedman for most of her life, and he'd had a business partnership with Kim Philby but found him too right-wing politically. As for his own politics, he'd been a communist fellow-traveller but had now severed his communist links.

Martin sent in a report that

> SMOLLETT, even in his present paralysed condition, is a forceful personality with a quick, shrewd mind. He said nothing that was demonstrably false but in the interrogator's opinion, he was probably lying when he described the circumstances which led him to write the 'BURGESS documents', and that he could have been lying when he described his relationship with PHILBY. His claim to have lost his Communist faith should therefore be treated with reserve.[102]

It was decided there was not enough evidence to charge Smollett with espionage, and he went back to Austria leaving, in MI5's words, 'as much doubt as ever about the truth of his involvement in the BURGESS story'. But, of course, 'his doctors give him only a year or so to live'.

As it turned out, Smollett lived for nearly twenty years more, dying as late as 1980. The man in the wheelchair spent two decades peacefully at home, a rich man. As Smollett was wheeled out of his MI5 interrogation in 1961, heading back to a comfortable and affluent retirement in his native city, how his old friend Burgess, sitting in Moscow, would have envied him.

* * *

Looking back on the whole post-defection search for more spies, is the number five, as in 'The Cambridge Five', the appropriate number? At the time of Blunt's public exposure, William Rees-Mogg of *The Times* told colleagues, 'I think that there were about 20 in the Cambridge ring.'[103]

If we take as the criteria for membership of the 'ring' that they had to be Cambridge students from Trinity College or Trinity Hall whose time at those colleges overlapped, who knew at least one of the others and who for a period of their lives worked for the KGB, we can certainly add Leo Long and Michael Whitney Straight, because they admitted it later. That gets the total to seven.

It seems legitimate to add Alan Nunn May, the Trinity Hall physicist and contemporary of Maclean's, who was later convicted in a British court of passing secrets of the atomic bomb to the Soviet Union. There was also Arthur Wynn, a Trinity graduate of a similar period, posthumously named in 2009 as KGB 'Agent Scott', who on moving to Oxford University had recruited spies there.[104]

Of those against whom allegations were made but never confessed or were tested in a court, one could add the name of the Trinity student from Canada, Herbert Norman. After Cambridge he had cut his links with left-wing groups and joined the Canadian diplomatic service. In 1957, while ambassador to Egypt, he was recalled to Ottawa to be questioned about his communist past at Cambridge. He jumped to his death from the roof of the block of flats where he was living.

This leaves one of the men who formed the communist cell at Trinity in the first place and who also was never arrested. John Klugman devoted his life to the communist cause and as a result was the subject of constant scrutiny by MI5. As an SOE agent in Yugoslavia in World War Two, when he vetted possible agents, he allegedly sent the best ones to Tito's communist partisans and the worst ones to the right-wing Nationalists. But a much more direct allegation against Klugman came from one of the Cambridge Five, John Cairncross, in his autobiography published posthumously in 1997. He'd stayed in touch with Klugman after Cambridge and, in 1937, arranged to meet him in Regent's Park. Klugman introduced him to a man called 'Otto' who, as Klugman promptly disappeared from the park, began explaining to Cairncross how he could help the struggle against Hitler. 'Otto' was in fact Arnold Deutsch, the KGB's star recruiter of Burgess, Philby and Maclean. Klugmann had the KGB codename MAYOR and provided regular reports on potential recruits.

The files on Burgess and Maclean show that MI5 checked out and dismissed a theory that Klugman was involved in getting the two men to France.[105] There was also a mention that 'James KLUGMAN of well-known fame has been said by REES possibly to have introduced BURGESS to the espionage network' but MI5 couldn't prove this.[106]

However, they did find one eyewitness to an attempted recruitment of a potential Foreign Office informer by Klugman and Cornford. It provided a belated but revealing insight into Cambridge student life of the 1930s in which Burgess was a player and which MI5 completely missed at the time. A Cambridge communist described only as 'D', who'd decided to leave the party because he wasn't convinced about their opposition to the Nazis, recounted what happened when he told Klugman.

> KLUGMAN asked what career he hoped to follow and D explained that his family had always destined him for the Diplomatic Service. KLUGMAN said that was just the place where they wanted undercover members, but D was adamant and threw his card down on the table. At this CORNFORD accused him of wanting to join the Trotskyist reactionaries and the meeting broke up in anger.[107]

So, by our calculations, there were at least eleven men who fit our criteria: Burgess, Blunt, Philby, Maclean, Cairncross, Straight, Long, Wynn, Norman, Nunn May and Klugman. Only one of them, Nunn May, ever spent a day in a British prison.

Those caught up in the aftermath of Burgess's defection ranged from the guilty who should have gone to jail to those who were innocent if a touch naïve. According to the official scoreboard four years later 'so far, there have been four cases in the Foreign Service in which an officer's political activities and associations have led to his leaving the Service altogether. In about half a dozen other cases it has been considered prudent to move officers to other work of less importance to the national security, or to accept their resignations.'[108]

These were all in Burgess's own word 'wounded' directly or indirectly by what he and Maclean had done. The impact on one of the innocents would trouble Burgess for the rest of his life.

Her name was Esther Whitfield and she worked for MI6 as Kim Philby's secretary. She had also been his mistress and drinking chum. When Philby was the MI6 man in Istanbul in the late 1940s and his wife Aileen was in very poor health he still found time to take Esther out to dinner with friends.

She wrote of how 'in the middle of this Aileen crisis on the Thursday evening ... Kim (v.drunk) and I (modestly sober) got back from drinks at about 11'.[109]

She first met Burgess in the summer of 1948 when she was living with the Philbys in Istanbul. Burgess stayed with them for five weeks and he 'showed considerable interest in her, speculated freely about her feelings for him. At the time I took this for another flight of fantasy on his part and paid little attention to it', according to Philby.[110]

When she moved to London in September 1948 she saw Burgess frequently over a period of six months.

Whitfield's letters reveal how she cared for him. 'Guy what have you been doing?' began one letter after she was told by somebody 'at the office' that he had broken his arm. 'Guy dear, horrible old conference' started another when he was sent away just as she had hoped to meet up with him in London. She suggested, what nowadays would be called 'guilt shopping', *Mousseline*, *Arpege* or *Indiscretion* from the perfume counter.[111]

When Philby moved to Washington in 1950 to become MI6's man there, Esther Whitfield went too as his secretary and set up home in the attic of his house. She was unaware that within a few months Burgess would be moving to the American capital as well and be living in Philby's basement.[112]

In Philby's words Burgess's 'relations with Miss Whitfield developed'. There was talk of marriage. 'I gather that he did make a definite proposal on one occasion.'[113]

On 18 May 1951, Esther Whitfield wrote a six-page letter, put it in an air-mail envelope, stuck on two 15 cents stamps and posted it in Washington marking it as 'From E. Whitfield, British Embassy, Washington, DC.' It was addressed to 'Guy Burgess Esq, The Reform Club, Pall Mall, London SW1'. He would have received it after he'd been to the Foreign Office to discuss his future but just before he and Maclean left the country.

In this letter her style, rather like Burgess's, was to abbreviate words so that, for example, 'which' would become 'wh.'. She began, 'Thank you so much for letter wh. I was glad to get. But you didn't say how the office was & whether they were cross. I am glad it will be alright about Michael Berry.' This was presumably a reference to the job on the *Daily Telegraph* which Burgess told people he'd been promised. She prepared him for his interview there:

> Dear I do hope you are not getting drunkers. And when you go to Michael Berry do be clean (nails, hand, face etc) & clothes & no bottle on the desk. You will not believe me but people do not repeat not want that sort of thing with their staff. He may say I think you are wonderful but no one is going to pay a large salary unless they produce something in return. So don't be conspicuous unnecessarily (you are quite enough on your own).

The most significant and poignant part of the letter is about their relationship. She told Burgess that Kim Philby didn't know about the letter he'd sent her, especially 'the private part'.

> I felt you wanted me to as you had always wanted me to talk to Kim – but I couldn't so somehow. So lovey if Kim thinks you have behaved badly as regards me, I am afraid at the moment I can do nothing to justify it. As far as I am concerned it is quite alright – nothing in our relationship has been exactly traditional. I am quite happy taking it in all its contexts. I think you are probably right about it all. It is not so much the actual bed but everything – the attention, care and interest – that it engenders that I myself wd want and that I don't think you wd give. Being a woman I cd give all that without the bed, but for a man I suppose it is different and all those things only come as a result of the bed. How mis and badly circumstanced everything is. But I suppose nothing wd be more mis than being unhappily married. I wd far rather keep you always as a good and loving friend. Guy there is one thing I wd like to know about this bed. Has it always been like that with you or is it recent or is it just me? I hope this is not a very impertinent question. I know you will not take it as such and to know the answer wd somehow be a great help to me. So if you can please tell me the truthful (real truth) answer it will tidy it up in my mind whatever the reason. And there is one other thing I will ask of you dear, that it is not to mention it either by words or implication to anyone.

Later in the letter she wrote 'I miss you horribly lovey' and she ended, 'Dear sweet, bless you and lots of love. Esther. Please destroy this letter at once. Not leave around. Luv to yr. mother'. Inside the envelope she wrote again 'PLEASE destroy this letter'.[114]

Burgess didn't destroy it. He did leave it lying around. After he defected MI5 went through those of his belongings that remained in his flat after Blunt got there first. They found the letter, read it and Ronnie Read of MI5 wrote a note: 'It is a personal letter which she asks BURGESS to destroy immediately. The letter shows that they were on very close terms.'

This very personal letter became item 133a in one of Burgess's MI5 files which had once been so slim but were now becoming voluminous. All six pages can now be read by anybody anywhere in the world via the internet.[115]

Esther Whitfield, 'with whom BURGESS was on intimate terms', was name number five on one MI5 list of Burgess's acquaintances. Could she have helped Burgess discover that Maclean had been found out and alert him? Guy Liddell wrote in his diary, 'BURGESS might have made it his business, either by keeping his eyes open or by interrogating Kim's secretary, Esther WHITFIELD with whom he has for some time been conducting a desultory affair. Kim was emphatic in his defence of Esther Whitfield.'[116]

The MI6 secretary produced a concisely written, well-typed, five-page document about Burgess for her ultimate boss, Sir Stewart Menzies, 'C' of MI6. She admitted she'd been 'close friends' with this 'extremely erratic and irresponsible person' with a 'very lively mind and an attractive personality' but no mention of marriage ever having been discussed. With hindsight she was suspicious about how inflexible he'd been about ever postponing one of his regular trips to New York and how, when talking about the possibility of another world war, he'd said, 'Oh, of course, if there is another war, I might be put in prison.'[117]

Her career in MI6 was over. Her family remembered her coming back to London 'rather suddenly'. She never married and went to live in Rhodesia. The final days of her 'good and loving friend' would be sadder, lonelier and colder.

CHAPTER 9

'I HAD NO IDEA HOW MUCH I WAS LOATHED'

SETTLING INTO THE USSR, 1951–56

In June 1951, the month after her son Guy went missing, Mrs Evelyn Bassett got a telegram from him: 'Terribly sorry for my silence,' it read. 'Am now embarking on long Mediterranean holiday. Do forgive all love Guy boy.' The telegram had been sent from a post office on the outskirts of Rome by a man who wrote his name as 'Walter Parodi, Albergo Flora – Roma'. It turned out there was no such person registered at that hotel but 'the handwriting was continental in style'.[1] Then letters in Burgess's handwriting began arriving for her. These had been posted in London. Christmas cards followed.[2]

So where exactly was 'Guy boy' and how was he sending these telegrams, letters and Christmas cards? Far from living it up in some plush Mediterranean resort, Burgess was actually staying in what he called a 'dreary provincial town', which was 'permanently like Glasgow on a Saturday night in the nineteenth century'.[3]

Burgess could have ended up in worse places in the world than Kuybyshev, now known as Samara, the sixth largest city in Russia. It wasn't exactly a gulag. During the Second World War, when Moscow was in danger of falling to the Nazis, large parts of the state bureaucracy were moved the 500 miles to Kuybyshev along with a bunker for Stalin.

Also transferred to Kuybyshev were large sections of Stalin's military production, after which it became what was known as a 'closed city', which was extremely difficult, even after the end of the war, for Westerners to visit. Burgess and Maclean were completely isolated there. Presumably the Soviet authorities decided that this was the best place for the two 'missing diplomats' to stay missing.[4] They provided the men with what Burgess called 'beautiful flats, looking out over the (Volga) river' plus servants and a car. Maclean took a job in a language institute but Burgess refused – 'I wouldn't. I did nothing.' Burgess never learned Russian properly, later complaining that a lesson 'always completely exhausts me' and that 'I am really am too old to learn a new language'.[5]

The authorities in Kuybyshev probably did not plan for Burgess's encounters with the citizens of 'this horrible place'. He explained some years later that he had been 'walking along a street when a thug saw the watch on my wrist and knocked me down'.[6] He lost all the teeth on one side of his face. He once told a visitor who hadn't noticed this injury, 'Oh but you must have.'

A different version of the encounter came later from a Reuters correspondent in Moscow, John Miller. He wrote that the Soviet authorities had offered Burgess male lovers but that he preferred to find his own. The first time Burgess went out in search, he was beaten up. Dentures were made for the gap where his teeth used to be but according to Miller they were stained and uneven and Burgess hated them for the rest of his days.[7]

The British authorities had no idea exactly where Burgess and Maclean were until 1954, when the Third Secretary at the Soviet embassy in the Australian capital Canberra sought political asylum from the authorities there. The man claimed to have joined one part of the KGB, the NKVD, in 1933 and to have been the controller of another, the MGB, in Australia since 1951.[8]

What Vladimir Mikhaylovich Petrov revealed to his interrogators was summarised in a telegram from Australia to London:

1. Source has so far produced following information on BURGESS and MCLEAN [sic].

(a) N.K.V.D recruited them as students and targeted them into Foreign Office.

(b) Moscow valued them highly and when BURGESS and MCLEAN considered Security Services were on their track M.G.B. ordered their withdrawal.

(c) Escape arrangements handled by KISLITSYN now M.G.B officer under PETROV in Canberra. These included planning trip over Czech border.

(d) BURGESS and MCLEAN brought out valuable Foreign Office information and are now living in Kuibyshev.

2. Source states he was given para 1 (a) by KISLITSYN.

So the key but unsuspecting source was MGB officer Kislitsyn, who had helped Burgess and Maclean get to Moscow, and on being posted to his new role in Australia had been reminiscing with his new boss Petrov about the story of the two defectors, not knowing that Petrov would himself defect to the other side and tell the West.[9]

Debriefing the Petrovs was not easy. Mrs Petrov was not happy about the defection, still had some sympathy with the Soviets and was, according to an MI5 report, 'putting the brake on Petrov's talk ... Situation needs careful handling if Petrovs are to be successfully milked.'[10]

It was time for MI5 to prepare Burgess's family for the bad news that there was now more than rumour and surmise against him. They had been complaining about a lack of information, but this was not the kind they were hoping for.

Guy's brother, Nigel, 'was undoubtedly very shocked by the information and for a moment was silent. He soon recovered his composure, however, and said that he knew sooner or later something of this sort was bound to happen, and he only hoped to goodness the revelation about his brother would not be too damning and would not show that he was a spy or any such thing.' The MI5 officer, H. I. Lee, could only assume that he 'guessed the worse'. Lee had been a friend of Nigel Burgess since his days in MI5; by now Burgess was an advertising agent, so Lee was able to confirm what

Nigel Burgess told him, that the brothers had never been on close terms and 'never got on well together'.

Nigel's priority was now to move his mother, who was 'still entirely convinced of her son's innocence', into a hotel to avoid 'the horde of newspaper reporters who were likely to descend upon her'.[11]

The story broke in the British press in April 1954. When Whitehall officials tried to find out from the *Daily Express* where they got their information from they were told that, since the Australian government were going to have to pay for the upkeep of the Petrovs for the rest of their lives, they had decided to sell the story to the highest bidder to raise funds. The British officials were understandably sceptical about that version of events.

It was to be a full year and a half before the British government published its own version of Petrov's revelations in Paragraph 23 of the twenty-eight that made up 'Report Concerning the Disappearance of Two Former Foreign office officials'.

This was the British government's first attempt to tell any of the story of the 'disappearance' and it came out four and a half years after the event. One key sentence – 'Petrov states that both Maclean and Burgess were recruited as spies for the Soviet Government while students at the University' – marked the first time the British government had admitted in public that the two men were spies. As to what exactly Burgess and Maclean were now doing in Russia, the British government said only that 'they were used as advisers to the Ministry of Foreign Affairs and other Soviet agencies'. There was precious little else new in the document and no evidence that Burgess had been considered a spy until he left the country with Maclean. The report said that when Burgess was appointed to his post in Washington there was nothing on record 'to show that he was unsuitable for the public service'.

All this time, Burgess had been trying to persuade the Soviet authorities that he should be allowed to go public with a statement of why he was in their country. He wanted to write a letter to *The Times* but the authorities wouldn't allow it. He wanted publicity; they didn't.

Three months after the British government statement, the Foreign Manager of the *Sunday Times*, Ian Fleming, was sitting at his desk happily continuing his day job despite the success of his first three James Bond spy novels. A cable arrived from one of his correspondents, Richard Hughes, who had just a short time to run on a visa allowing him to be in Moscow. Hughes had been beaten on a big story and was keen to get back into Fleming's good books. He arranged an interview with the Soviet Foreign Minister, Vyacheslav Molotov, and had the bright idea of using the opportunity to put in a bid for an interview with Burgess and Maclean, who'd still not been seen in public.

As he finished talking with Molotov, Hughes handed over a memorandum about the visit to Britain the Foreign Minister was about to make with the Soviet leaders Bulganin and Kruschev. Hughes suggested to Molotov they would be constantly asked about the two diplomats so 'you would be wise to produce Burgess and Maclean with some sort of agreed explanation before you leave Moscow'. Just as important, Hughes argued, this should happen before he left Moscow, effectively giving Molotov a deadline of 5 p.m. that Saturday – when his visa was due to expire.[12]

At 7.30 p.m. on the Saturday, Hughes got a call asking him to go to Room 101 at his hotel, the National. His deadline had passed with no response and he assumed the invitation was to a farewell drink with the hotel manager. When he arrived, he found five men sitting around a white-clothed table surrounded by Victorian-style bric-a-brac. Sidney Weiland of Reuters was waiting there with two Russian correspondents and two other men he'd never seen before.[13]

> One of them, a tall, good-looking man in a blue suit and a red tie, got
> up and said 'I am Donald Maclean'. I registered some surprise and con-
> sternation and even alarm at this, he nodded. Then the man sitting next
> to him, shorter but just as debonair and quite as contented looking said,
> 'I am Guy Burgess.' 'Gentlemen', I said, 'this is the end of a long trail,'
> and they laughed.[14]

Burgess had finally persuaded the Soviet authorities to let him meet the press. He opened a leather briefcase and handed out four copies of a typed, three-page, 1,400-word document headed 'Statement by G. Burgess and D. Maclean'. The two men did not read it out and when the reporters started asking questions Maclean said that everything was explained in the statement. But the reporters did get a little more out of Burgess. Asked if he and Maclean were employed as advisers on Soviet foreign policy, Burgess said, 'You won't find me by sitting outside the Foreign Office. The fact is I don't want to have correspondents trying to follow me around.'

One reporter complained that the two men weren't 'playing fair' by not answering questions properly. Burgess told him, 'Now don't try to tell me that. I have given out too many statements to the press in my life not to know what I have given you fellows. We just don't want to add to our statement.' Richard Hughes observed that Burgess was affable, smiling and clearly enjoyed being the spokesman for the two, whereas Maclean seemed content to sit back, smoke and let him.[15] No photographs were allowed.

The main thrust of their written statement was that 'we neither of us have ever been Communist agents' and that they had gone to Russia to try to achieve 'better understanding between the Soviet Union and the West'. They each offered a summary of their career written in the third person. Burgess's included the lines:

> Neither in the BBC or the Foreign Office nor during the period that he was associated with the secret service and also MI5 itself did he make any secret from his friends or colleagues either of his views or the fact that he had been a Communist. His attitude in these positions was completely incompatible with the allegation that he was a Soviet agent.

According to his version of events, months before he left Washington he had decided to leave the Foreign Office and get another job. Surely, he argued, no agent would do that. As to why they had both ceased their open communist activities after Cambridge, this had been because 'we thought, wrongly it now clear to us, that in the public service we could do more to put these ideas into practical effect than elsewhere'.[16]

Hughes rushed off to file his copy for the next day's *Sunday Times*. The front page proclaimed that Hughes was 'the only representative of any newspaper in the world invited to the disclosure'. The reporter from the Communist

Party newspaper *Pravda* (*Truth*) who was there clearly didn't count. On the Monday morning the correspondent from the *Sunday Times*'s stablemate, *The Times*, reported rather sadly that he lived next door to the hotel room where Burgess and Maclean had handed out their statement but at the time he'd been on an aeroplane.

The British ambassador in Moscow, Sir William Hayter, was caught up in the Soviet charm attack before the Bulganin–Khrushchev visit to London when he was invited to become the first British envoy to speak on Soviet television. In his broadcast on 19 March 1956, Sir William expressed the hope that the two leaders would 'not be the only Soviet visitors to our country'.[17]

He got what must have been a most unexpected letter in response from London SW1. It began: 'My son is Guy Burgess and he is most anxious that I should visit him in Moscow.' Mrs Evelyn M. Bassett was writing because she'd heard that in his broadcast Sir William had said 'too few British subjects come to the USSR'.

Evelyn Bassett wanted to know, 'Would it be troublesome if I came? And could I be prevented from returning for propaganda purposes? And could my presence be used in any way by the Russian authorities to put pressure on Guy?' She didn't want to be the cause of any fresh trouble to the British authorities 'but naturally I long to see my son again. I am not very well and getting old.'[18] She was in her early seventies. Her son told her he 'did not know whether to laugh or cry loudest at your initiative and cleverness'.[19]

Mrs Bassett was becoming a bold letter writer. In 1954, she'd written to the then Foreign Secretary Anthony Eden, asking, 'Can you possibly tell me anything? I know Guy met you in Washington, and I know he knew Mrs Eden [the former Clarissa Churchill] ... Guy is not a traitor, he feared America was heading for war – it was unfortunate he saw D. Maclean again.'

There was a P.S.: 'I feel I should not bother you, but I am so unhappy.'[20]

Eden's office replied three days letter saying there was no news – 'Mr Eden asks me to say that he sympathises deeply with your distress and regrets that there is nothing to tell you.'[21]

Now, in 1956, Mrs Bassett awaited Sir William's reply 'with much anxiety'. He thought it most unlikely that she would be prevented from returning to the UK but he gave her fair warning that if that were to happen 'we should not be very favourably placed to help you'.[22] As it turned out, Mrs Bassett was able to visit her son during a summer holiday that year at the Black Sea resort of Sochi and returned safely without embassy help. She 'adored' the trip to Sochi but was never well enough to make another trip to Russia. She would never see his Moscow flat so her son sent her a sketch plan of the layout. If they were ever to meet again in person he would have to travel to Britain.[23]

Guy Burgess followed up his press statement with two very different initiatives. Burgess the romantic phoned one of his former lovers, Peter Pollock, who was now a Hertfordshire farmer. 'I was terrified,' Pollock said afterwards. 'I thought MI5 would be listening in.'[24]

Then Burgess, ever the former Foreign Office spin doctor, placed an article in a British newspaper. He responded to a cabled request from the News Editor of the *Sunday Express* with a message that he had prepared an 800-word article 'containing some personal experiences and developing Moscow statement'. He demanded that it would have to be published unchanged or he would take up one of the many other media offers he'd received. Alert to any suggestion that he might be cashing in on his new status, he proposed that the fee – 'the highest reasonable normal sum' – should be paid to the Royal National Lifeboat Institution; his mother took that as a nod towards his Royal Navy days at Dartmouth. The RNLI declined to accept the contribution: 'We do not accept money from traitors.'[25]

Burgess duly filed his copy on time, eleven words short of the 800-word target and it was published just one week after his Moscow statement with Maclean. There was none of the 'personal experiences' he had promised the *Sunday Express*. Instead, it was predictable stuff; emphasising how much he wanted to help 'East–West relations in general and Anglo-Soviet relations in particular'. He claimed he was already doing what he could 'to convince my friends here' that an understanding between the two sides was possible.

The following month, one of the *Sunday Express*'s main rivals, the Sunday paper known as *The People*, hit back with an exclusive which readers would have found a lot more interesting than Burgess's views on foreign policy. Certainly the headline – 'GUY BURGESS stripped bare!'– would have grabbed their attention.

It was the first of what the paper called 'a profoundly disturbing series of articles' and began: 'For 20 years one incredibly vicious man used blackmail and corruption on a colossal scale to worm out Britain's most precious secrets for the rulers of Russia.' It went on: '...men like Burgess are only able to escape detection because THEY HAVE FRIENDS IN HIGH PLACES WHO PRACTISE THE SAME TERRIBLE VICES.'[26]

Over five weeks of Sunday paper sensation all the 'appalling facts' of the story were laid out. The author was anonymous, but the articles were dripping with clues as to who he might be. For example, he was Burgess's 'closest friend'; they'd met in 1932 while he was a fellow at 'one of the most famous Oxford colleges'; he'd worked on 'the Conservative journal, *The Spectator*'; and now occupied 'a high academic post'. With so many fingerprints on the articles it was not surprising that MI5 turned up on the author's doorstep the next day. But it took 'Peterborough', the diarist of the *Daily Telegraph*, a full two weeks to 'detect Mr Goronwy Rees, Principal of University College of Wales, Aberystwyth, as author of a strange series in *The People*'.[27]

In a paper owned by one of Burgess's oldest friends, Michael Berry, Peterborough observed that 'the series is not at all the scholarly analysis one would expect from a Principal. For the most part it consists of gossipy jottings ... It is difficult to imagine why Mr Rees should be taking up his pen again after so long a silence.' Rees's tabloid demolition of Burgess was rather different from what he told the *Daily Mail* at the time of the defection in 1951. Then, Burgess had been one of the nicest and most patriotic Englishmen he knew. He mentioned that Burgess was the godfather to his son[28] and declared, 'To my knowledge he is not a Communist.'

Peterborough fact-checked one line in a Rees article, that Burgess had kept a copy of the Kinsey Report on sexual behaviour in the safe of the Foreign Secretary, Ernest Bevin. He found 'the flaw in the story – perhaps symptomatic of a good deal else – is that the Foreign Secretary does not have a safe'. Peterborough correctly observed that the names of other well-known people were described in the articles 'sufficiently for easy identification by their acquaintances. Mr Rees is careful to acquit them of knowledge of Burgess's activities. But a little mud always sticks.'

Among those being habitually covered in mud was Guy Liddell, who'd left MI5 in 1953 after being passed over for the top job. He went instead to a much less prestigious security job at the Atomic Energy Authority. Rather unwisely he asked to see J. C. (James) Robertson at MI5 and offered the opinion that there was 'doubt as to whether BURGESS in fact had ever been a spy in the full sense of the term'. Robertson 'thought it right to tell him that there was no reasonable doubt about this'.[29]

In one article, Goronwy Rees had also referred to one of Burgess's fellow Comintern agents, described only as 'X', who was 'one of Burgess's boon sex companions and he holds a high position in public life today'. That sounded like a reference to Anthony Blunt. The *Telegraph* diarist was left wondering (along with most readers, one can only assume), if Rees knew so much about all this, why had he never reported Burgess to the authorities?

Rees's employers wondered too. The University College of Wales, Aberystwyth, set up an inquiry, Rees admitted he was the author, offered his resignation and it was accepted. He also resigned as a member of the body which was reviewing the law on homosexuality and other sexual offences of the time, the Wolfenden Committee.

When his daughter Jenny got to read the articles many years later, 'a shiver ran up my spine as I tried to imagine what could have driven my father to commit such a self-destructive and extraordinary act of folly'. Even the *People* journalists who'd worked with him on the articles weren't clear. The Deputy Editor, Nat Rothman, also a qualified lawyer, later told Jenny Rees that he had remembered thinking it was a 'very strange thing' for her father to be doing – 'Why on earth has he come out with this now?' he thought. He seemed to have 'some terrible guilt feeling,' Rothman recalled. He especially couldn't work out why Rees wanted the articles to be anonymous; it seemed cowardly and it was that in particular, he thought, that 'put people's backs up'.

Intriguingly, the Aberystwyth University inquiry concluded that the common assumption, including that of Burgess, that *The People* had sensationalised

Rees's articles was not correct. In fact, the paper had edited out 'long passages dealing with homosexual promiscuity which were shocking in the extreme'.

There were stories at the time of Rees struggling with money and unpaid bills and he is said to have been paid £2,700 by *The People*. The University inquiry concluded, though, that his primary motive was not commercial but 'in a very large degree ... self-regarding ... that it was in his own interests as well as in the interests of others, to discredit Burgess completely, even at the cost of exposing himself as embarrassingly compromised and surprisingly gullible'. However, his daughter recalled her parents saying later that he *had* done it for the financial reward, which had been enough to buy a home to get away from Aberyswyth.

Rees's best attempt to explain himself, in his own book *A Chapter of Accidents*, was that Burgess's reappearance in Moscow had triggered his own guilt at not informing the authorities that he knew Burgess was a spy.[30]

Many of Burgess's friends were angry at Rees at the time and their outrage went on for years. Stuart Hampshire 'wrote a very angry letter to Rees'. Harold Nicolson was 'sickened'. Maurice Bowra wrote from Oxford suggesting Rees plant 'Judas trees' around his college. Isaiah Berlin was 'horrified' and while visiting Moscow told a friend of Burgess, 'Give Guy my warmest love, and tell him that none of us are speaking to Goronwy.'[31]

Michael Berry wrote that Rees had 'smeared' people and could not be counted on to be loyal to his friends. Rees met up with the economist Roy Harrod at a wedding and Harrod asked how he was getting on having been sacked. Rees replied that he was in a new business venture but short of capital, to which Harrod responded, 'Oh well, Goronwy, that ought not to give you any bother; you only have to write a few articles for a newspaper.' They subsequently had to be separated by wedding guests.[32]

When Rees published his book, almost sixteen years to the day after the first article appeared in *The People*, Roy Harrod, by now Sir Roy, returned to the attack: 'Guy was such a charming, cultivated, civilised and loveable person. I cannot bear to think of the memory of him being sullied. Your account presents him as half drunk, half sex debauchee. Could anything be further from the truth? It really is too bad of you.'[33]

Burgess's own reaction was initially anger – 'Goronwy alone cannot have been responsible for such nauseating lies'[34] but 'if he really did write the articles of his own free will I could of course ruin him'.[35] But eventually he was forgiving. On receipt of one of Harrod's updates about Rees, he summarised his own feelings in bullet points:

1. He was such an old and dear friend & such mistakes can & must be forgiven.

2. I was convinced that he would suffer much more than I for what he did – as he did.

3. I was devoted to Maggie & the children & feared they would suffer – as they did.

4th & most important, I had a hunch that Goronwy was acting under some pressure or other apart from the pressure of his own internal strains. Somehow or other I suspect he was got at to do what he did in order to blacken an individual (me) who still presented some dangers to the Anglo-American Establishment.

On one occasion, when Harrod passed Burgess's feelings back, Rees replied:

As for Guy I think forgiveness is a strange word for him to use in this case, but so far as it means anything I am glad that he should feel it. But really after sixteen months of almost continuous pain, one really doesn't mind much what anyone thinks of one.[36]

Rees never reached out to Burgess. He told Harrod: 'Guy wrote to me once but I didn't reply ... This is now an old and still painful story.'[37]

The allegation by Rees that annoyed Burgess most was that he had once made love to Maclean. 'The idea of going to bed with Donald Maclean!' he exclaimed. 'It would be like going to bed with a great white *woman*.'[38]

Burgess's reappearance in Room 101 of the National Hotel in Moscow, which had partly prompted Rees's 'self-destructive' action, was to be the last time Burgess and Maclean were seen together. A few years later, Burgess would be telling people 'I don't see him very often' and 'we were never close friends'.[39] The way Burgess told it, he worked for the Foreign Literature Publishing House, while Maclean worked for a 'sister institution', the Foreign Languages Publishing House. Burgess's employer published foreign books in the original languages; Maclean's published Soviet works in foreign languages. Burgess didn't speak Russian, whereas Maclean did and even his children, who had joined him in Moscow, went to a Soviet school. Burgess became happy to socialise occasionally with the Western news correspondents; Maclean did everything to avoid them.[40]

It is likely that for Maclean, having spent so long with Burgess in isolation in Kuybyshev, it was a good idea for the two men to settle into very different lives.

The only journalist they both spoke to was one of the small press corps of Western journalists committed to the communist cause who, unlike reporters from the 'guttersnide press', as Burgess called them, had long-term visas. The *Daily Worker*'s man in Moscow, Sam Russell had attended 'jolly' social evenings at Burgess's flat where he was entertained by the spy's Russian lover playing the balalaika. Soviet files show Burgess trying to help Russell get meetings with Soviet leaders.

Russell's relationship with Maclean, however, was even closer. The intelligence services intercepted letters from Maclean's mother, Lady Maclean, who regarded him as 'a most wonderful link between our two families. We like him <u>so</u> much and can talk about anything so easily.'[41] On one occasion, when Russell's wife was packing a trunk to send to her husband, she included 'roller skates & football' for the Maclean family.[42]

Russell, Burgess and Maclean had one jointly mourned mutual friend, John Cornford. To the Cambridge communists Cornford was one of their inspirational leaders who went off to fight with the International Brigade in the Spanish Civil War. Russell remembered Cornford as a comrade in arms, was alongside him when he was wounded – 'he came back with his head bandaged, looking very romantic' – and was nearby when he was later killed. Incidentally, Russell himself was wounded and left for dead on the battlefield until a friend went back for him. Afterwards, unable to fight, he covered the war for the *Daily Worker* instead.

Although Russell seems to have been on good terms with both Burgess and Maclean, the *Daily Worker* always had a problem with how to report their defection. In 1956, the paper ran a front-page editorial which said, 'the Burgess-Maclean way of working for an understanding is not our way – is, indeed, not a Communist way'. The battle should be fought by British citizens in Britain, they thought. Possibly concerned that the defection might be used as a reason for action against the Party, the *Worker* declared there was nothing 'in the Burgess-Maclean episode to justify the suggestion that the Communist Party is a conspiracy or that it is concerned with infiltrating into Government departments'. Subsequently the paper rarely published anything about the men's life in Moscow. For his political soulmates in Britain, Burgess was becoming an inconvenient friend.

He tried to keep his spirits up, however, admitting to a friend: 'Even if one is quite deceiving oneself at least the illusion of doing something in the uncomfortable near perilous situation we are in keeps one's morale high.'[43] In addition to his work at the Foreign Literature Publishing House, Burgess told a friend he was 'working under the Ministry of Foreign Affairs here in quite a good position'.[44]

Confirmation that this was indeed true came half a century later when a former colleague there wrote an article for a Russian Foreign Policy Journal. Boris Piadyshev told of working at the Ministry's Information Committee which had been split off when Stalin's consolidation of all intelligence, information and propaganda services had proved too unwieldy. The committee regarded itself 'as a place for high fliers – both in the quality of the Cadre and the intellectual product that it put out'. On Piadyshev's first week he met a man who introduced himself as 'Burgess, Guy Burgess' and worked in the office next door. He helped the Russians practise their English and talked about English football and English beer but 'unfortunately he was never able to fit into a new environment'.[45]

So far in his life, the wealthy Guy Burgess had never owned a property; he'd always rented. After he'd left 10 New Bond Street in a hurry, 'a notice to quit' arrived promptly in the post from a solicitor.[46]

Now he had a new landlord: the Soviet government, and the rent was free.

He was provided with a dacha in a country village about an hour's drive from the capital and a three-bedroom flat in one of the capital's more pleasant areas, in a block near the Novodevichy convent with a view of the Moscow River. Initially, the furniture was standard Soviet issue (for which Burgess apologised incessantly to visitors) but he gradually replaced it with Scandinavian imports. There was also an old upright piano on which he would pick out with two fingers some hymns he remembered from Eton, and a large library of classic English literature.

The Soviets even laid on, or at the very least didn't object to, a live-in lover for Burgess, 'Tolya', whom everybody assumed reported back to the KGB. Burgess is said to have met him in a favourite pick-up toilet near the Metropole Hotel, and Western correspondents who met him described Tolya Chishekov as a 'dark, handsome' former coal-miner from Ukraine, 'short, cheerful, broad-shouldered'.[47] He sometimes answered the door to them in bright blue pyjamas.[48] The only photograph of him and Burgess together betrays a certain mutual affection in their faces.

Burgess would report with pride to friends that Tolya had passed an exam on his 'Instrument' – the Russian Bayan accordion – and was playing in factory concerts for a living. But, he admitted, 'I do rather wish he had chosen a <u>different</u> Instrument.'

Burgess's surviving friends in Britain would arrange to have some things which he needed shipped to Moscow. Hampers from Fortnum & Mason would arrive several times a year and Burgess would tuck into the pate and chocolate biscuits. Books would be sent from Heywood Hill's bookstore in Mayfair so that he could add to his large collection and Mr Heywood Hill himself wrote to say he would 'be delighted to open an account for you'. Burgess sent Peter Pollock a list of thirty-two authors of fiction and non-fiction, everything from 'A. Trollope. Any novels not in Barchester series' to 'D. Scott Moncrieff. The Vintage Motor Car'.[49]

He kept up to date on British news through subscriptions to *The Observer* and *The Spectator* and on motoring matters through *Autocar* and *Motor Sport*.[50]

There was, of course, an extraordinary amount of alcohol (and time to drink it) available. One visitor found Burgess 'alert in the morning' but 'of the evening, getting a bit sizzled on vodka'. But he also once discovered Burgess drunk, 'reeling and chortling' in the middle of the afternoon. For this, Burgess received 'a bit of a talking to' from the boss at his office.[51]

Despite his initial reluctance to meet up with them, Burgess would provide British correspondents with plenty of material for their articles and memoirs. Nora Beloff of *The Observer* once danced with him on holiday in Sochi. Ian McDougall of the BBC recalled dinner at the National Hotel when Burgess 'unceremoniously removed his shirt-complaining of the heat – it was a Moscow July at its sultriest – and revealed a very hairy chest'.[52]

McDougall once told a British diplomat in Budapest that Burgess was 'living with a lady who he describes as his wife and who is a motor mechanic'. A message was passed back quickly to a sceptical MI5.[53]

James Mossman of the *Daily Mail* remembered Burgess rushing off to the bathroom to be violently sick, and also a lunch after which Burgess insisted on accompanying him to a French press reception. Reporters gathered round as he sounded off about British foreign policy. A French general walked out in disgust.[54] Suddenly Burgess said: 'Chaps, I desperately need to urinate. Must I do it in the fireplace?' Mossman decided to beat a retreat with Burgess in tow.[55]

British diplomats in Moscow were partly safe from such incidents; they were told 'your staff should withdraw at once from any function at which Burgess and Maclean are detected'.[56]

Guy Burgess often contacted British visitors to Moscow. Stephen Spender got a phone call at his hotel from Burgess at 1.15 a.m. Later that morning Burgess turned up at his door. Spender later recalled:

> As soon as he arrived, and I asked him how he was, he said, 'I love living in this country. It's solid and expanding like England in 1860, my favourite time in history, and no one feels frightened.' But a few minutes later, while we were talking, he waved in the direction of a corner of the ceiling and said, 'I suppose they're listening to everything we're saying.'[57]

Spender noticed that Burgess 'seemed quite nervous and never stopped walking up and down the room'.

As Burgess's hand motions had expressed, KGB listening devices were never far away and MI5 also had ways of finding out what Burgess told his visitors once they got back to Britain. In 1959, the actor Michael Redgrave visited Moscow with the Shakespeare Memorial Theatre Company to play Hamlet. MI5 believed Redgrave was a communist and kept a close watch on him, so they were particularly interested when he agreed to meet his old Cambridge drama club colleague without telling the British embassy. This meeting came about, according to Redgrave later, because when the Theatre Company's plane landed in Moscow 'from amongst the press corps waiting to photograph us on arrival an English journalist took me aside and said he had a message for me: "Guy Burgess wants to know if you would agree to meet him."'

On the first night of *Hamlet*, according to Redgrave, Burgess 'swept into my dressing room... He had been crying. "Oh, Michael! Those words, those words! You can imagine how they carry me back. Magic!"' Burgess lurched past Redgrave and, with 'what looked like practised accuracy, was sick into the basin'.

The next day, Burgess gave Redgrave lunch at his flat; a pot of pate de foie gras and an inedible hare, badly cooked by the housekeeper. As Redgrave left, Burgess told him: 'Write to me, it's bloody lonely here, you know.'[58]

Somebody Redgrave spoke to afterwards briefed the British embassy on what Burgess had told Redgrave about his defection to Moscow.

> Burgess had more than once told him that he, Burgess, had considered that he had done his bit (or words to that effect) in delivering Maclean to the Russians. Burgess also said that he himself had not intended to go on to Russia once he had introduced Maclean to persons whom he met 'at a certain place'. Burgess said that in spite of his wishes he had been forced to continue his journey and ended up in Russia.

An MI5 officer noted that this was an 'extremely interesting report which confirms the information we had already obtained'.[59]

As a result of the Theatre Company's visit, Burgess made a new friend and wrote about her to his mother: 'The Queen in *Hamlet* who I met for the first time is a very good actress, very pretty, not v. young, called Coral Browne

(Mrs Pearman).' Coral Browne was forty-five, was Australian by birth and had emigrated to Britain at the age of twenty-one. She was married to the actor Philip Pearman.

According to another member of the company, Eileen Atkins, it was Browne, not Redgrave, who'd provided the wash basin for Burgess's stomach expulsion. 'He was very, *very*, drunk. He tried to get into Michael Redgrave's room but Michael utterly refused to see him then. Somehow, Burgess got into Coral's dressing room, which is where he was sick in the sink. And she looked after him.'[60]

Her encounter with the 'missing diplomat' was to become part of the Burgess legend when it formed the basis of Alan Bennett's play *An Englishman Abroad*, later made into a BBC drama film starring Alan Bates as Burgess and Coral Browne as herself. Burgess's own version of their meeting was in a letter to his mother, which told how Coral Browne had been to lunch, there'd been more 'fine gossip' and she'd stayed

> long after it was clear even to me she had to be off! I do love gossip …
> I hope I made rather [*sic*] friends with her – but you never can tell with
> stage people – anyhow she had very kindly promised to buy me some
> suits (I haven't had any for 8 years and wear and tear is beginning).[61]

To Browne herself, Burgess wrote:

> It was a great pleasure to gossip with you all. The Comrades, tho' splen-
> did in every way of course, don't gossip in quite the same way about quite
> the same people and subjects.[62]

Burgess told his mother Coral Browne was 'a dear – but people often think of actors and actresses when it is in no way reciprocated'. As if to prove that indeed theatrical folk are not entirely to be trusted, Coral Browne's version of their lunch as told to British newspapers highlighted 'pretty foul food', Burgess's ill-fitting dentures and his obsession with talking about 'this and that "pretty boy" he had known at Cambridge'.[63]

Whether or not his affection for her was fully reciprocated, Coral Browne became extremely useful to Burgess, ordering and having delivered not only suits but also Homburg hats from Lock & Co. Hatters in Piccadilly. Burgess had one further request, however, which he put in a letter to her:

> What I really need, the only thing more, is pyjamas. Russian ones can't be slept in – are not in fact made for that purpose. What I would like if you can find them is 4 pairs (2 of each) of white (or off white, not grey) and Navy Blue Silk or Nylon or Terrylene [*sic*] – but heavy, not crêpe de chine or whatever is light pyjama. Quite plain and only those two colours... Don't worry about price... Gieves of Bond Street used always to keep plain Navy blue silk. Navy and white are my only colours, and no stripes please.[64]

Browne not only followed up his 'no stripes please' requests, but made her own suggestions to him about people he could meet in Moscow, such as Paul Robeson, the black American singer, actor, civil rights activist and communist sympathiser with whom she'd had an affair, but, unknown to Browne, about whom Burgess had made a quip before leaving London for Washington years before.

Even for an inveterate name-dropper like Burgess, meeting such a giant figure as Robeson was a daunting prospect. He replied to Coral Browne:

> In spite of your suggestion, I found myself too shy to call on him. You may find this surprising but I always am with great men and artists such as him. Not so much shy as frightened. The agonies I remember on first meeting with people I really admire e.g. E. M. Forster (and Picasso and Winston Churchill – but not W. S. Maugham). H. G. Wells was quite different but one could get drunk with him and listen to stories of his sex life. Fascinating. How frightened one would be of Charlie Chaplin.[65]

In all, at least a dozen visiting Britons met up with Burgess in Moscow, including Eton contemporaries such as Randolph Churchill, university friends such as Michael Redgrave, politicians including Konni Zilliacus MP and writers like James Morris (later Jan Morris), who thought Burgess 'often got in touch with visiting actors and actresses, journalists and authors – the sort of people, I suppose, least likely to rebuff him'. He and Burgess had champagne and caviar and agreed to go to the Bolshoi ballet, though, in a rather odd turn of events:

> We arranged to meet outside the theatre door and when I got there he was waiting for me on the steps. I waved a greeting as I approached him through the crowd, and he waved a response, but by the time I reached the door he had vanished. I never saw him again.[66]

Our research into Burgess's other (mostly less well-known) visitors in Moscow has revealed a whole new network in his life - not one that compares with the significance of the Comintern and the Homintern, but that does illustrate his continuing contacts across the British left.

The connection between these visitors was that they had all been a part of Mass Observation, a social research organisation which from 1937 to the early 1950s, systematically recorded the attitudes and everyday lives of people in Britain.

The originators of Mass Observation, or M-O to its historians, all had links to Burgess. Geoffrey Pyke, the wartime 'boffin' whose notes on a top-secret meeting were found in Burgess's London home after his defection, Charles Madge, who knew him from Cambridge, and Tom Harrisson, who had done a radio talk with the working title *Art and the Ordinary Chap*, produced by Burgess.

No fewer than five other former 'Mass Observers', as they became known, took the trouble to meet up with Burgess at various times in his self-imposed exile.

Ralph Parker was a journalist in Moscow for the *Daily Worker* and other communist papers around the world. Burgess once said of him: 'We all think he's an agent but we can't make out whose side he's on.' MI5 and MI6 files on 'our old friend' and 'renegade journalist' Ralph Parker suggest there was understandable confusion throughout his career. He definitely worked for British SOE, yet also had links with the KGB. He also had interesting old friends who'd worked for both sides; in 1958 he stayed in London with Cedric Belfrage of MI6 and the KGB, and in 1962 he stayed in Vienna with Burgess's fellow wartime propagandist and spy Peter Smollett, who had returned to Austria after his unexpected London interrogation at the end of the previous year.

Parker invited to Moscow Julian Trevelyan and his wife, Mary Fedden, both artists. When they arrived by boat in Leningrad they are said to have been handed a note, 'Come and see me the moment you reach Moscow. Guy Burgess'. The meeting does not seem to have gone well. Trevelyan's son described it as an 'unsettling day' for the visitors.[67] Trevelyan himself wrote to his friend Bertrand Russell, 'We lunched with Guy Burgess who seemed rather homesick.'

Among the Mass Observer Five, one name stands out as the most intriguing. It was the BBC producer who back in 1935 had suggested Burgess broadcast for the BBC and, coincidentally, went on to do the same for one of the best known broadcasters in the history of the Corporation, David Attenborough. She knew Burgess at the beginning of what seemed a promising career; now she would see him again in exile.

Mary Adams, as wartime Director of Home Intelligence at the Ministry of Information, monitored domestic morale. Which is how she came to work with M-O. After the war she returned to the BBC and then worked for the Consumers' Association. According to her daughter Sally, Mary Adams, the widow of Conservative MP Vyvyan Adams, was 'a socialist, a romantic Communist'.

In September 1958 she was among a British delegation attending the congress of the International Scientific Film Associations in Moscow, on which the British embassy kept a special watch because it believed the association was 'and is slightly penetrated by Communists'.

Half of the dozen-strong British delegation, including Adams, had security records, PFs or Personal Files, at MI5.

While in Moscow, Adams and another former 'Mass Observer', Hugh Gibb, went to see her 1935 protégé for dinner. Burgess thought their visit was evidence that, 'I seem to be not quite so unpopular as I thought' with 'v nice people like Mary Adams'. Indeed, Burgess had to end the letter to his mother because 'I must go and meet Mary Adams. She dines here but doesn't know way.'[68]

Hugh Gibb, who was subsequently debriefed by MI6, told how later on in the Moscow visit he was in his hotel bed with suspected malaria when Burgess phoned and said he might look in for a few minutes, although he was desperately busy. Burgess arrived at 2 p.m. and stayed until 10 p.m., 'by which time he had gone through a whole bottle of vodka and several bottles of beer'.[69]

The fifth visitor connected to Mass Observation was Tom Driberg, who, when the Editor of the William Hickey column in the *Daily Express*, had devoted nearly all its space one day to the launch of Mass Observation in 1937 and subsequently went to work with M-O.

So what are we to make of the five Mass Observers and their meetings with Burgess in Moscow? One expert on M-O, Tom Jeffrey, called them 'explorers, upper middle class young men who felt that it was their duty to make contact with, and to get to know, the working class'. Julian Trevelyan said M-O 'partly resolved for myself the problems that beset all my generation in the years before the war'.

The symbolism of the Moscow meetings would seem to be that those who had the opportunity to work with or for M-O had found it a therapy for their class guilt – a therapy that Burgess, by following the Comintern's directions for his career, had never been able to undertake. His visitors seem to have gone away sad for a once kindred spirit and very relieved that they had not chosen the path he had. Presumably he would have enjoyed their company, but he may also have reflected on their freedom to travel compared with his.

The meeting with Adams and Gibb in Moscow in 1958 stimulated Burgess to get in touch with an American friend and possibly one of his early lovers at Cambridge: 'I've been seeing Hugh Gibb this week and he spoke so much of you that I thought I would write.' The recipient of the letter had registered at Trinity the year before Burgess as John Evans Hunter. He was probably the first and last Trinity student educated at 'Hollywood Union High School, Hollywood, California'. His father, Thomas Hayes Hunter, was a Hollywood director of silent films who billed himself as 'The Greatest Director of His Time' and in 1927 suddenly moved to Britain, made more movies and sent his son to Cambridge. 'Jack' Hayes Hunter, as his son later became known, built a career as a film screenwriter, agent and occasional actor. He was homosexual and his partner, Michael Ronan, had served time in a British jail because of his sexuality.

Burgess wrote to 'Dearest Jack (or, as we once said, dearest Boy)'. He quoted another of his former lovers, Peter Pollock, who had 'told me I have no idea how much I was <u>loathed</u> ... Certainly in the press I am treated as a combination of the worst features of Wilde, Crippen & Byron.'

When we were being shown this previously unknown letter by the nieces of Hunter's partner, Michele Emrick and Katherine Ronan, there was a further unexpected bonus. Out of a file of documents fell a printed programme for a student play. Jack Hunter had been a keen member of the Amateur Dramatic Club (ADC) at Cambridge and had kept the programme for the 1931 production of *Captain Brassbound's Conversion*. The programme confirmed that 'G. F. de M Burgess' had designed the scenery, but revealed that among the ten 'Brassbound's Men, Arabs, Bluejackets' was also 'G. F. de M Burgess'.

Weary travellers who called in on Burgess sometimes left even wearier. In his own words, Burgess 'behaved inconsiderately' towards the novelist Graham Greene and 'bored him and exhausted him by keeping him up – the temptations of parish pump gossip were too great – but I have everything important that I need except that, so greedily and ruthlessly sought it – and he had been up 65 hours out of the last 72!'[70]

Burgess then asked Greene to send Moura Budberg, the Baroness MI5 had been watching and listening to, a bottle of gin of his behalf. 'I hear and fear she needs it,' wrote Burgess. 'Such a real nice woman and how she must miss Connie Benckendorff [a relative of her first husband], one of the best people to sit up all night with I ever knew.'

Not everyone who was visiting or passing through Moscow was willing to have a meeting or sit up all night with Burgess, however. Isaiah Berlin, for one, passed up the opportunity to reminisce about their abortive visit to Moscow via North America in 1940.

But there were also those for whom a visit would have been too expensive, especially Jack Hewit, who wrote to Burgess about how he'd lost jobs because of his connection with Burgess.

'Do not think that I do not know and did not anticipate that was has happened would happen when I left' came the reply from Moscow. 'I would still do the same again for the reasons which I did it'. Burgess said that he'd realised that of all his friends Hewit, 'as not being upper class, were likely to be persecuted most by our delightful class system'. He explained that immediately he arrived in Moscow he'd sent some money to Hewit, but it had never got through. Now he'd asked another former lover, the wealthy Peter Pollock, 'to help you at once'.[71]

Since both British and Soviet Intelligence had good reason to be interested in Burgess and not to trust him, he was effectively under surveillance on two fronts. The easiest way for them to do this was by intercepting as much of his post as they could lay their hands on. If there was ever any problem with his mail, he could never be quite sure which side had done it, but normally assumed it was the British. He said of one particular letter, 'I imagine MI5 would have it now'.[72] W. H. Auden, who had homes in both America and Europe, said of the letters Burgess sent him: 'I hope he doesn't send one to NY or the FBI will be around.'[73]

One of his tactics was to get letters hand-carried by somebody to Britain and posted there. He reassured one recipient, 'This letter is now going via a safe hand to England', though he also accepted that even that technique 'won't avoid MI5'. Forensic tests were regularly done on his letters by both MI5 and the *Daily Express*; somebody at the former noticed that one envelope addressed to his mother had been franked at the offices of *The Observer*. They assumed it was 'no doubt by hand of Mark Frankland', a former MI6 officer before he became a foreign correspondent.[74] Another suspected letter-carrier was also a former MI6 man turned *Observer* journalist, Edward Crankshaw.[75]

The fact that Burgess was well aware that the Western and Soviet security services and the Western press were reading at least some of his letters may help explain why in writing he showed such an unwavering commitment to the Soviet cause.

So 'no regrets' was a recurring theme in his correspondence with Roy Harrod, a man who in any case did not share his political views. On foreign policy: 'I regard present Western policy as even more criminally dangerous and ignorant in the real sense as that of Chamberlain. And now there is no Churchill to support.'[76] On his own situation: 'I'm completely at peace and am fully happy at work here ... I am v. well & happy & doing quite well. I now can't imagine living in the world of expense accounts & hate.'

But a very different version emerged 'off the record' when Burgess talked to Yuri Modin. The KGB man later recounted how every time he met Burgess after 1953 'it was only too painfully obvious that he was incapable of reconciling himself to life in the USSR. His impossible dream was to return some day to England.' But why had he not turned back at Prague in the first place when he had the chance? Modin had asked. Burgess gave no coherent answer but gave the impression that when he went to Moscow he was 'genuinely stunned' when the KGB told him he couldn't then go home.[77]

One reason letters to Burgess sometimes went astray was that for a time he kept his address secret, believing that his privacy at home was likely to be invaded by the Western reporters in Moscow. Although he developed social relationships with some of them, in order to prevent a wider knowledge of his whereabouts he adopted an alias. He gave himself the first name Jim, after Jim Lees, the former miner who'd been at Trinity with him. The surname he adopted was Eliot, apparently after the female author of *Middlemarch* known as George Eliot. To fit with the Russian style of having a patronymic as a middle name, he should have Russianised his father's name Malcolm, but it was easier to use a character from *War and Peace*, Andrei, and use Andreyvitch instead. Thus Guy Burgess was also 'Jim Andreyvitch Eliot', sometimes Elliot, and even Elliott.

Initially his friends had to write to him via 'Poste Restante', the international service where post is held until the recipient collects it, in this case at the Central Telegraph Agency in Moscow. But gradually Burgess got more relaxed, telling a friend that he was 'coming out of purdah' over his address. 'I think I'm no longer news and won't be besieged any more by journalists. Nor do I expect "C" to assassinate me'.[78]

The regular interception of Burgess's post by MI5 meant the Security Service was always up to speed with news, some good, some distressing, from the interlocking private lives of his friends. A HOW (Home Office Warrant) on all mail going to him in Moscow revealed, for example, that Peter Pollock wanted Burgess to share his excitement about 'a newish but very great friend Francis Bacon who is a very good painter'.[79]

Burgess seems to have genuinely shared Pollock's happiness with his new partner, Paul Danquah, the mixed-race son of one of the founders of Ghana and a white mother. Danquah was a lawyer who became an actor and a presenter of BBC's *Play School*.

When a senior official at MI5, Courtenay Young, spotted that one letter to Burgess was signed 'Sambo', he asked a colleague, 'From your past experience in Guy's boy friends can you identify Sambo? Is this Peter POLLOCK's black boy friend?'[80] In fact it was Sam Langford, boyfriend of Brian Howard, who'd written, 'My dear Guy, Why don't you write your old chums?'

Howard and Langford both became drug addicts. Burgess's former Foreign Office News Department colleague, Osbert Lancaster, who'd become a successful illustrator and designer, wrote to Moscow to say, 'I understand that Sam was liquidated by the explosion of a bathroom geyser and that poor B just turned his face to the wall and died.'[81]

Howard had committed suicide by a drug overdose. Burgess wrote to Pollock, 'I was rapidly going down Brian's path my last years in England and particularly that horrible year in America. Living and working here has saved me from that.'[82]

His longest-standing and most intimate correspondent, apart from his mother, was the man he'd first heard speak at Eton, who'd been a mentor, adviser and probably lover, and yet extraordinarily had hardly been questioned by MI5, despite them being told he'd heard Burgess was in the Comintern before the war.

'I have strained a muscle or ligament in my penis (not I assure you from overwork),' wrote the Honourable Sir Harold Nicolson, Knight Commander of the Royal Victorian Order. His neatly typed letters came either from Sissinghurst Castle, Cranbrook, Kent or The Albany, Piccadilly, London WI.

'It is hard to write seriously at this minute, Mark is kissing my friend who is playing my harmonium,' wrote Jim Andreyvitch Eliot in handwritten, hand-corrected, inky letters from Moscow and from the Sanatorium of the Council of Soviet Ministers in Sochi. In one letter, apologising for the 'vile ink', Burgess reported back on how he had been 'lying in hot mineral water (natural hot) in a Georgian bath … being scrubbed, washed in a way only Orientals wash (but I refused depiliation [sic]) by a youth … with apparently waterproof mascara around his eyes'.

'Gossip is, apart from the Reform Club, the streets of London and occasionally the English countryside, the only thing I really miss,' he told Harold Nicolson. 'The English colony here, tho' dears, are apt to gossip about rather different things, and Russian gossip, even in English, though penetrating, indiscreet and amusing is not about one's own parish and I moved rather late for it.' On another letter he added a simple postscript 'Gossip is what I crave.'[83]

Instead Nicolson provided updates on the streets of London, the 'vast ten decker biscuit box' being erected on the site of the Carlton Club and the 'number of black people from the West Indies who have come here in search of higher wages'.

Burgess thanked Nicolson for writing to his mother and told him how 'very touched, flattered and grateful' she was especially as she was 'a little bit of a snob'. Burgess went on: 'It is, as you say, hard not to be able to pay her a visit. But I took this into account as a possibility before I left.'[84]

Inevitably their own mortality became an increasingly regular theme in correspondence.

Burgess said he'd 'never absolutely recovered from having my skull cracked in three places by Fred Warner', and when Nicolson reported having had two strokes, he replied, 'I like to think that I approach dissolution in the same spirit as you. I pray I shall do so after two strokes.'

Nicolson always naively but loyally accepted Burgess's claim that he wasn't a spy, saying, 'All I care about is that you should not be exposed to unfounded suspicions and that you be allowed to follow your Slavic bent without opposition.'

* * *

In the autumn of 1956, two world-class crises erupted. One of them was Hungary, where Soviet military might was used to put down an uprising. The other involved the Suez Canal. Egypt wanted control of the canal; Britain and France, the only shareholders, plotted with Israel to respond.

Burgess played a role in how the Suez Crisis was read in Moscow. Tom Driberg, who was in Moscow, told him that Fleet Street thought Sir Anthony Eden's threats to invade Egypt were 'bluff'. The Russian leader, Nikita Khrushchev, heard about this from Burgess and subsequently had a meeting with Driberg, where he got it from the horse's mouth.

As the crisis developed, Burgess wrote background papers for the Soviet leadership about British diplomacy and the political personalities involved. He also spoke to another visiting Labour politician, the left-wing MP Konni Zilliacus, known to his friends as Zilly, who was confident that there would be no war. Burgess wrote up an account of their conversation and it was also sent to Khruschchev, who'd just had his own meeting with Zilliacus. Those papers were later opened up by the Kremlin's archive and show clearly that Burgess was giving advice to Khrushchev.[85]

Egypt seized control of the canal, and international moderation failed to defuse the situation. Ultimately an ill-judged covert collusion between Britain, France and Israel resulted in a short-lived invasion, followed by a humiliating withdrawal in the face of various threats and ultimatums made by the United States and Soviet Russia, which at one stage threatened a nuclear strike.

Burgess later told Harold Nicolson that he had read the crisis correctly, unlike many:

> As Tom may have told you, or you may have read in the column, I got
> Suez right in advance – what was going to be done. I was rather proud
> of doing so particularly as Tom, and Zilly also, fresh from England, who
> ought to have known more and to whom I said firmly when they were
> here that an attack would be made, did not agree.

After Suez Eden went to Jamaica with his wife to recover from his health problems. He never returned to political life. When Eden published his memoirs,

Burgess wrote that they 'have really saddened him for me; poor man how unhappy he must be to write such stuff and how pathetically transparent'.

Eden's successor was Harold Macmillan. It was common knowledge at Westminster that Macmillan's wife was having an affair with the bisexual Tory MP Bob Boothby, whose MI5 file was filling up because of improper financial dealings and a friendship with the East End gangster Ronnie Kray.

Guy Burgess, sitting in Moscow, would undoubtedly have enjoyed the gossip, but for him the appointment of Macmillan as Prime Minister raised a more intriguing personal prospect. After the 'unhappiness, disaster and worry I must have caused everyone', there was the very outside chance of some escape from the socialist 'paradise' he had condemned himself to.

CHAPTER 10

'I WOULD RATHER LIKE TO GO BACK TO ENGLAND'

DECLINE AND DEATH, 1956–63

Harold Macmillan was the third British Prime Minister in succession that Guy Burgess knew personally. The relationship was nowhere near as close as it had been at times with Churchill and Eden – he had never visited the family home as he had with Churchill and he'd never got personal notes that began 'My dear Burgess, Thank you so much for all your kindness' as he had from Eden – but Burgess would recount of the new PM how 'I had once spent an evening with him at the Reform and he had listened – as who could not it was my club – to my rantings'. He would also talk to reporters in Moscow about 'my friend Harold Macmillan'.[1]

Politically, he thought Macmillan was 'a man of some originality and imagination, quite prepared and possibly able to assist towards détente, and recalled 'his formative past and youth' and his 'role over the unemployed'. Burgess boasted how he'd predicted to the Kremlin how Macmillan, not R. A. Butler, would take over when Eden resigned.

Surely, Burgess reasoned to himself, the new Prime Minister could at least consider an Englishman's request to visit his elderly mother without being arrested and then return to Russia? After all, he'd never been accused of anything since that curious court case in Dublin when he'd been acquitted.

Burgess always realised it would be difficult to return for a visit. For the

British government, it would mean the prospect of a suspected Soviet spy walking the streets of London as a free man. In a letter to his mother in 1956 he wrote, 'I should probably be murdered not by the British but by the Americans ... More important , we should be persecuted by the Press.'[2] But that didn't stop him trying.

The saga started early in 1956, when Eden was still Prime Minister, and it ran for a full five years into Macmillan's term in Downing Street, during which time Guy Burgess tried to outmanoeuvre the massed ranks of British government ministers, intelligence agencies, civil servants and what today would be called 'spin doctors'. Occasionally working both for and against Burgess, but mostly against him, at this time was a very distinctive member of the British political class.

There are few people in the authoritative *Oxford Dictionary of National Biography* whose life story includes a line anything similar to 'Throughout adulthood Driberg had a consuming passion for fellating handsome, lean, intelligent working-class toughs.' Even the prestigious *London Review of Books* said the Labour MP had been 'indubitably the most consecrated blow-job artist ever to take his seat in either House'.

Among the similarities with the spy who whose life story he wrote, Tom Driberg was homosexual, joined the Communist Party when he was young (in his case aged fifteen), was educated at a public school and an Oxbridge college, worked for MI5 and the KGB, was a journalist for a time and had very left-wing views throughout his life.

Among the differences between the two men were that Driberg was married (although it's thought the marriage was never consummated), and was a High Anglican (while Burgess was an atheist). Most significantly, Driberg was a Labour MP from 1942 to 1955 when he lost his seat and from 1959 to 1974, having found a new, politically safer constituency. From 1957 to 1958, he was also chairman of the Labour Party.

Tom Driberg took on a range of roles on behalf of Guy Burgess. Some can be discovered in letters which were sent (rather brazenly) to 'Tom Driberg MP, House of Commons, London SW1'. Among these tasks, there was Driberg the fixer: one handwritten, twelve-page letter from Burgess covered everything from resolving a dispute over a payment for a shipment of art to Burgess's delight at furniture that Driberg had sent over; 'the flat is transformed' and 'a continuous joy and the admiration of all who see it'.

Then there was Driberg the sexual soulmate; the man who showed Burgess the Moscow public lavatory where homosexual men met for 'cottaging'. (According to one Soviet archive, on another visit to the lavatory, Driberg was photographed, blackmailed and recruited as a Soviet agent. He is said to have reported back to Moscow on Labour Party politics for a decade, copying in MI5.)

It was as Burgess's biographer that Driberg played his only public role in Burgess's life. During his out-of-parliament years, Driberg had developed his career as a journalist, writing sympathetically about Burgess in the left-wing newspaper *Reynolds News*. Resuming the connection from his time as a guest presenter on BBC's *Week in Westminster* in February 1956, Driberg sent cuttings of his article and a letter which began, 'My dear Guy':

> This letter is a very long shot, I am afraid, but I thought I might assume
> on our old friendship to write and ask you whether you thought that,
> if I came to Moscow, I could have a long talk with you and Donald
> Maclean, and really tell the whole story fully and in proportion to the
> Western press.

Burgess responded, saying he was touched and grateful for the article. He agreed to the plan. He also took the opportunity to put a marker down about the revelations by the KGB defector Petrov, telling Driberg he didn't want to get into a 'long screed about not having been an agent', but 'there is no evidence that I was; in fact I wasn't and that's that'.

Driberg travelled to Moscow twice, once to meet at the dacha and have lengthy conversations with Burgess and then a return visit by which time Burgess had moved to the flat. They went through what Driberg planned to write.

When Driberg returned from his second trip in mid-September, the *Daily Mail* headlined 'Burgess says he will come home'. Driberg was quoted as saying that 'Guy Burgess does not consider himself a traitor and intends to return to this country to try to prove it.'³ There were no further details and surprisingly no immediate follow-ups by the press, not even by the *Mail*.

MI5 had been preparing to make a move for two months. In July 1956, James Robertson had put a minute on file which began: 'I think we should be prepared for the possibility, remote though it may be, of BURGESS or MACLEAN turning up outside Russia.' He wanted to know what the legal case against the two men would be. This was an issue which would preoccupy MI5 for the next few years and to which there would not be a simple answer. But for now the priority was to see what was in Driberg's book. Copies of the draft were obtained and detailed commentaries were written comparing excerpts from the book with the official version of the truth.⁴ One of their first verdicts was that 'nearly all the facts as such are accurate though BUR-GESS has put his twist on them'. However, his claim that 'I never made any secret of the fact that I was a Communist' was noted to be 'patently untrue'.⁵

MI5's intermediary with the media was retired Rear-Admiral George Thomson, who had been Britain's wartime press censor. Now he was the Secretary of the Services, Press and Broadcasting Committee, better known as the 'D Notice Committee', which issued the 'advisory' D Notices when national security was at risk.

'Guy Burgess Tells All' was the *Daily Mail* front-page headline on 19 September 1956, above a story promoting their exclusive serialisation of the book. The Admiral told the *Daily Mail*:

> You may well feel, because the Russians already know what you are publishing in your 'Guy Burgess tells all' series, that there are no security considerations involved. Nor are there. But there are still the Official Secrets Acts! ... Might I suggest that you let me see the articles before they are published?

The *Mail* agreed and so did the book publishers.⁶

Of course, MI5 already had copies and were soon preparing a list of twenty-four 'passages in DRIBERG's articles as being potentially embarrassing to the Foreign Office, MI6 or this service'. These ranged from Burgess's visit to

Churchill in 1938, his friendship with Labour minister Hector McNeil and a reference by Burgess to 'MI5 inefficiency'. MI5 realised, however, that they were pushing their luck trying to get a phrase like that removed.[7]

Meanwhile, in Moscow, Burgess had been getting cold feet about one chapter in the book that, unlike the rest, was in a purely question and answer format. He told Driberg it might 'cheapen what we are trying to do'. Despite these concerns, however, the chapter stayed in.[8]

There were cases of cold feet too among friends and family in London. In a telephone call recorded and transcribed by MI5, Burgess's mother told Anthony Blunt that on her son's orders she had given Driberg the thank-you letter from Anthony Eden. Blunt replied, 'Oh, God', but accepted that Driberg wanted it to stay in the book.

Blunt's own priority was Lord Rothschild – 'If Victor's name can be kept out all the better' – and particularly a passage about an argument at Claridge's between Burgess, Rothschild and the Zionist leader Chaim Weizmann, eventually the first President of Israel. Blunt reminded Mrs Bassett 'do you remember the occasion ... when WEITZMAN [sic] was trying to turn VICTOR into a Zionist ... and Guy argued with VICTOR very strongly against it ... so to speak WEITZMAN and GUY wrestling for VICTOR's soul?' Tom Driberg agreed with Blunt to take this section out.[9]

The background to the Claridge's episode was later explained by Yuri Modin of the KGB, who wrote that in 1938 Burgess was 'working on' Rothschild on behalf of MI6, who were trying to divide the Zionists into warring camps and that Victor Rothschild later supported a rival Zionist movement.[10]

In her phone conversation with Blunt, Mrs Bassett revealed the financial deal between her son and the author:

Mrs Bassett: 'Guy won't take any money for the book.'

Blunt: 'Won't take any money for it, no.'

Mrs Bassett: 'But he's going to have a present.'

Blunt: 'Oh, good.'

Mrs Bassett: 'Some furniture, you see.'

The present was Burgess's Scandinavian furniture. Driberg had arranged the shipping to Moscow, but along the way everything got drenched, a 'terrible business' Burgess called it. The packers apparently hadn't realised the furniture would have to go on a long journey by goods train from the Baltic coast to Moscow. Eventually it dried out.[11]

Three weeks after the serialisation started, the author called in for a chat at the Foreign Office. Tom Driberg was 'completely co-operative', according to the official note of his meeting, with the head of the Security Department, Ian Samuel, and appeared happy to answer questions about Burgess's job, health, and home. He was 'after all on our side' recorded the man from the Foreign Office.

Driberg did mention one thing, though, which he thought was 'rather sinister'. Burgess had said that he had been asked by the Soviets for a list of homosexual ambassadors but would not give them one. Burgess had 'declared himself anxious to harm no one, except J. Edgar Hoover', the Director of the FBI whose sexuality has been much debated since his death in 1972.[12]

There was one other piece of business to be done before the book itself was published. A draft copy of page seventy-seven was taken round to 10 Downing Street, where Anthony Eden was in his final days as Prime Minister. It dealt with the visit to Washington where Eden was escorted by Burgess and included the letter of appreciation that Eden wrote to Burgess afterwards. Nobody seemed very keen to pass the news of the letter's inclusion to its author.

There was bad news about page seventy-seven on the way too for Mrs Eden, the former Clarissa Churchill, a woman Burgess once described to his mother as a 'former girlfriend' after his attempt to turn a friendship into something more romantic. He now sent her a letter of explanation and almost apology: 'Dear Clarissa,' Burgess wrote on 2 November 1956:

> I did in fact write but never posted for fear of embarrassing you a letter long ago to congratulate you on your marriage. Sir A. was very nice to me for the only week I knew him.
>
> This is not that letter but a note seizing opportunity of sending it by hand (Tom Driberg's).
>
> Its purpose is to say that I would <u>never</u> have given Tom your husband's letter to publish – or told him of it – if Goronwy Rees had not written

about it publicly, & of course first, in the *People*. The news today is too serious to make me want to say or make it seem likely that you will want to read more from your affectionate and quite unrepentant,

Guy Burgess.

He then wrote a PS about a mutual friend's latest books before signing off:

Look after both yourselves.

G.[13]

Over at MI5, their focus was on a very different element of the book, and one which they thought offered them a real opportunity. The legal director, Bernard Hill, representing not just MI5 but also MI6 and the Foreign Office, had been to see the Director of Public Prosecutions (DPP), Sir Theobald Mathew.

Hill floated an idea. Obviously, if Burgess ever came back to Britain and was arrested, it would be difficult to charge him for breaching the Official Secrets Act with any material in the book which had been through the official vetting process. But, presumably, they could charge him if material Burgess had given Driberg did not appear in the book because it could be said that this hadn't been through the vetting process. This might, for instance, include 'information acquired by him while serving in some way with M.I.5 and M.I.6'. Hill recorded that he put it to the DPP 'that if we got these items out of the text I did not think any difficulty would arise. The Director said he quite agreed.'

Hill and Admiral Thomson went off to make 'amendments in ink on the publishers' galley-proofs so there should be no mistake as to what we required to be deleted'.[14] The publishers accepted the deletions.

It was a cunning plan, to have material deleted in order to turn it into evidence for the prosecution. One might normally expect that MI5 would then have kept this material up their sleeves for the moment they could ever charge Burgess. But these were not normal times. Instead, MI5 set about using the deleted sentences in a way which they hoped meant they would never have to charge him and face all the awkward questions about his past roles for MI5 and MI6 that a trial would inevitably involve for them. Instead, they could try to ensure that he would never come back to Britain and embarrass them.

Bernard Hill sent an unusual request through Admiral Thomson to a *Daily Express* correspondent, Harry Chapman Pincher, who had already built a reputation for scoops in the areas of defence and security. They wanted him to write an article with a target audience of one – Guy Burgess.

Pincher was encouraged to give 'maximum prominence' to the possible consequences for Burgess of returning, if only for a visit. On 23 November a story duly appeared in the *Daily Express* headlined 'BURGESS BURNS HIS BOATS, NOW – AND ONLY NOW – THEY'VE GOT HIM'.

In his article, Pincher wrote:

> Burgess has unwittingly supplied evidence that he has committed a fel-
> ony under the Official Secrets Act – a crime which carries a maximum
> penalty of 14 years' imprisonment. Until he made this mistake he could
> not have been convicted of any crime if he returned to Britain. Burgess
> has played into the hands of the police by giving his life-story for use in
> a book to Mr Tom Driberg.

Pincher wrote that 'Burgess had given the names of other men in the department including some of the chiefs, a representative of Weidenfeld & Nicolson, the publishers of the book, told me. These were deleted because they contravened the Official Secrets Act'.[15]

When Driberg disputed this in a letter published in the next day's paper, Pincher got a quote from the Admiral confirming Burgess 'had committed a breach of the Official Secrets Act', something, MI5 duly pointed out, it was not Thomson's job to decide.[16]

Apart from this small hiccup, the MI5 plan had gone well. Pincher was well aware that the point of the exercise was to warn Burgess off but he had wondered why MI5 was going to so much trouble to do that. The official explanation was that the head of MI5, Sir Roger Hollis, thought a further chilling of Anglo-American relations might endanger what Macmillan had talked of as the 'great prize' – getting America to share with Britain its expertise on the atom bomb. The *Express* man came to a different conclusion; he later wrote, 'Apparently the home secretary had been prepared to allow Burgess to return on compassionate grounds, and Hollis wanted to ensure that he never did.'

Was it something Hollis had to hide? Pincher believed Hollis was himself an agent of the Russian military intelligence agency GRU, a claim dismissed by many other experts.[17]

There was one classically Burgess sidebar to this episode when one of his previous occasional employers, *The Spectator*, published a long letter from him, based on a textual analysis of an extract from the collected works of Lenin, to dispute what an anonymous reviewer had said about a serialisation of his book. It was all rather above even the readers of *The Spectator*.[18]

One of Burgess's other preoccupations in this period was money, and to try to improve his financial situation he played a typically bold card, a letter to somebody he knew from school and from his days at the BBC, the Chancellor of the Exchequer.

Peter Thorneycroft had not done as well academically at Eton as Burgess, and joined the army instead of going to university. When he entered Parliament in 1938, Thorneycroft renewed his acquaintance with Burgess as one of the MPs on *Week in Westminster*. His political career soon took off and he was appointed the youngest member of Churchill's 1951 Cabinet. When Macmillan succeeded Churchill, he promoted Thorneycroft to be Chancellor in January 1957.

On 4 September 1957 (for once he dated a letter), Burgess sat down and wrote to the 'Chancellor of the Exchequer at 11, Downing Street'. The envelope was typed, the letter handwritten on pages torn, rather roughly, out of a notebook. There were crossings out as Burgess changed his mind about what he wanted to write, seemed confused about when the first letter of a word should be a capital and couldn't be bothered to write out some words so abbreviated them. Not the way people would normally write to the Chancellor of the Exchequer.

The letter began 'My dear Peter':

> I have not seen you since I went to some trouble to include you more
> often than the then Chiefs of your Party liked in Broadcasts for the Week

in Westminster. You at that date were (& for all I know still are) a Tory Reformer.

What have you – or your department now done?

I have a small income in England administered (for yr information by the Royal Trust Company of Montreal, St James Square. Mr <u>Forman</u> in charge.

I left England in 1951. I qualify I am told for residence abroad. And did so for some time.

I am now told by my bank (Lloyd's, St James' Street) that all cheques whether paid in to me or paid out have to be vetted by your Treasury.

I imagine this bit of malicious & I am informed illegal Crichel (?) Downery was done without yr knowledge. Anyhow will you put it right. I do not, & cannot, believe that this measure is the only step so far taken to protect the pound. If it is, it ought to be announced. Zurich, with whom MI6 may tell you, I have some contact, is wobbly about your pounds. I think & tell them they may be wrong. But anyhow please issue instructions to free mine – and free your office from what looks like a very strange act.

Yrs

Guy Burgess

P.S. For the Treasury's information I shall be sending cheques to:

My grocers – Fortnum and Mason

My shirt-makers – New and Lingwood

My tailors – Tom Brown

My Booksellers – Messrs Collett or Nancy Rodd's.

The first internal response inside the Treasury was a typed note from an A. J. Collier about the letter 'which the Chancellor has received from a Mr Guy Burgess'. The 'security people' were asked to 'have a look at it'. Mr Collier wondered whether to reply. 'We would certainly not trouble the Chancellor with it but would write at Private Secretary level.'

This note had a handwritten P.S: 'The form of address used by Mr Burgess is a sign of impertinence – not acquaintance!'

This suggests that the civil servant did not realise that Burgess and Thorneycroft were acquainted, something the Chancellor freely accepted in later life. So, by the etiquette of the time, 'My dear Peter' was the appropriate greeting at the start of the letter.

The Treasury would probably have understood the phrase 'Crichel Downery' as a reference to the Crichel Down affair three years earlier when a minister resigned over a government land-ownership debacle, setting a new precedent for ministerial responsibility. Burgess may have used it as an implied threat to Thorneycroft.

The list of London shops by appointment to Mr Guy Burgess allowed Burgess to let it be known that he could still obtain what he needed. His choices were intriguing and he may have wanted to show off to Thorneycroft. The tailor he listed, Tom Brown, was – indeed still is – based in No. 1, Eton High Street. Burgess's main bookseller was, of course, Heywood Hill in Curzon Street, but he preferred to refer to it as Nancy Rodd's. She was better known as Nancy Mitford, the eldest of the famous Mitford girls who during the Second World War had worked at Heywood Hill helping to establish it as a centre of literary life and social gossip. Burgess could never resist name-dropping, especially that of a literary celebrity who'd just published an article entitled 'The English Aristocracy' on 'U' and 'non-U' usage of the English language.

For the Treasury, the main job at hand was not decoding Burgess's snobbery, however, but working out what to do next. In another note that day, Collier concluded 'the probability is that it is not a joke'. He thought Burgess was implying that 'this alleged action by the Treasury is part of a government plot to harry him'.

When Burgess and Maclean had gone to Moscow in 1951, their bank accounts were monitored but were reported to be 'inactive'. However, in June 1957, Burgess had begun to try to use his London account. It was then blocked so that payments could only be made with the permission of the Bank of England.

The Treasury considered that Burgess's letter now amounted to a request for 'redesignation', by which they meant that Burgess wanted no longer to be regarded as a British resident and all the ensuing controls over moving money abroad that went with that status in those days. Although he and Maclean never actually applied to be 'non-residents', thus avoiding those controls, the Bank of England advised the Treasury that he should be re-designated as an 'emigrant' and therefore a 'non-resident', thus releasing his account from exchange controls. It was pointed out that the funds were small and 'there was little interest in who was paying him or who he was paying'.[19] The Treasury might not have been interested but MI5 and MI6 certainly would be and now they could monitor the movement of that money. Peter Thorneycroft approved the proposal and Burgess began moving money to Moscow from his London account. Maclean soon applied for the same change of status and it was also granted. These decisions were not made public at the time.

As a result of a letter from one Old Etonian to another, the finances of two of the most infamous men of the period had been resolved, and their lives in Moscow were materially improved. No civil servant ever seems to have proposed a way of obstructing Burgess's request. Later, he would begin to wonder why that was.

While the Treasury were conducting a secret correspondence with Burgess, other parts of government had been in contact with him through Tom Driberg.

During the nine months since Driberg first mentioned the possibility of Burgess returning to a *Daily Mail* reporter, the Foreign Office had also been trying to work out what to do if he did. 'A satisfactory solution is by no means easy to find,' wrote the head of Foreign Office Security, Ian Samuel. So he had another meeting with Tom Driberg, who was now effectively an intermediary between Burgess and the British government. Driberg did not bring good news. 'Burgess still wishes to come to the United Kingdom and says that he has obtained Soviet permission to go to Yugoslavia. From there he hopes to go to Switzerland.' Samuel immediately decided he'd better 'warn Belgrade and Bern'. But Driberg had even worse news:

> What he would really like would be to spend a month or two every year
> in the United Kingdom and the rest of his time in Moscow. Apart from

wishing to be with his mother, another reason why Burgess wants to come to the United Kingdom, Mr Driberg said, is that he feels he is losing touch with this country and therefore cannot give the best advice to those high authorities in the Soviet Union who still, apparently, consult him.

So Burgess wanted to come to Britain partly so that he could be better briefed to advise the country Britain saw as its biggest potential enemy. At the end of the meeting, Driberg hoped that what he'd told Samuel 'was in strict confidence'. He would 'hate to find himself giving evidence, even in camera, against Burgess'.[20]

After seeing the account of the meeting with Driberg, Sir William Hayter, a former ambassador to Moscow, now back in London, wrote a note at the Foreign Office:

> My own hunch is that Burgess will not try to return unless and until there is a Labour Government here with which he would expect his friend Driberg to have influence. But in any case I very much doubt if the Russians when it came to the point, would let him out.

Foreign Office security also thought the most likely scenario was that 'Driberg might make an approach on the political level'.

Confirmation that something like this may indeed have been on Burgess's mind at some point came in a letter to Driberg about a visit to Russia the former Labour MP was planning to make with the leader of his party, Hugh Gaitskell. Burgess wanted to meet up with Driberg. He wrote that 'if you go to South', presumably a reference to a Black Sea resort:

> I might (??) come too. But of course this wld depend on yr companions & particularly of course Hugh Gaiters [...]
>
> So I think personally Gaiters might not object, as Isaiah did to meeting. But politically it might not be possible – unless he believes (what is true) that I can be trusted on important matters only not to leak anything.

British public schoolboys have a habit of shortening each other's names and adding '–ers' on the end. So 'Gaiters' was indeed Hugh Gaitskell. Burgess recalled, 'I have met him once and got drunk with him in the house of a great mutual friend I think, Dennis Proctor in, then Tryon Street, Chelsea.'

It is, of course, possible that Burgess was simply name-dropping, but we have confirmed that Dennis Proctor, the senior civil servant he'd known since Apostles days, was also a friend of Gaitskell. The two men were Whitehall civil servants during the war and there was correspondence between them in 1945. Proctor wrote to Gaitskell from 19 Tryon Street in Chelsea to congratulate Gaitskell on his CBE, to wish him luck in the forthcoming general election, where he was standing for a constituency in Leeds and to praise his work in the Treasury.[21]

To base the hope of a meeting between a suspected spy and the leader of the Labour Party on the memory of a shared drunken night in Chelsea seems optimism bordering on desperation. But Burgess apparently hoped that if Labour came to power, perhaps some sort of amnesty could be arranged for his return. One of Burgess's former BBC colleagues was sure Burgess 'expected to return from Moscow to a Titoesque government (perhaps Nye Bevan)'. In another letter, Burgess wrote, 'I unrepentantly pray that ... Labour wins the next election!' Labour was 'still our party!' As it was, Labour never took office again in Burgess's, Gaitskell's or Aneurin Bevan's lifetime.

Burgess was stuck with dealing with a Conservative government and they with him. As Christmas 1957 approached, there was another tip-off about Burgess's intentions, this time from *Daily Express* correspondent Terence Lancaster, who'd met him and whom Burgess liked.[22]

It was decided there ought to be 'a drill if Burgess landed at London Airport one morning with an out-of-date British passport', Samuel of Foreign Office Security told MI5. One was issued by Bernard Hill of the legal team the same day, an 'Instruction to Duty Officers during the Christmas Holiday'. If Burgess came home for Christmas, lots of DGs and DDGs should be told and the immigration men at the sharp end should 'delay as long as possible the identification of BURGESS, so to allow time for the Security Service to interrogate him before his status as a citizen of the UK and colonies is established'. Fortunately for them, MI5's Christmas was not disturbed. In later years, there would be extended debates about whether and how the Special Branch could follow Burgess to London if he arrived 'unheralded' at a port or airport and managed to get through immigration controls.[23]

The Security Service did have one setback around Christmas time 1957. They had continued to believe that what Burgess had told Driberg about his days in the intelligence services was enough to charge him if they ever had the chance. They had the material which they'd deliberately kept out of the book; they also had a letter which Burgess had written to Driberg describing a 'joint Secret Service–MI5 house party' he'd once attended.

Bernard Hill decided that 'BURGESS has disclosed information acquired by him in his official Foreign Office employment, contrary to the provisions of the Official Secrets Act'. But the Attorney General, Sir Reginald Manningham-Buller, was not convinced. Hill wrote to the Foreign Office with the bad news. The Attorney had advised that 'there was not at the moment sufficient evidence which would justify him granting a fiat for prosecution under Section 1'. Under the law of that time Section 1 covered a range of possible offences, the most serious of which was obtaining information which might be 'directly or indirectly useful to an enemy'.

Hill also passed on that 'the Attorney also stated that while there was a clear case for prosecution under Section 2, that is to say for retaining documents, he would not be prepared to proceed under Section 2 in a case of this kind'.[24]

Therefore there was not enough evidence to charge Burgess if the opportunity to arrest him arose. Sir Reginald also concluded that 'if Burgess returned to the United Kingdom, and was not prosecuted, Her Majesty's Government might be considerably embarrassed'. The 'general tenor' of the 1955 White Paper 'was that both men were spies' and 'this general impression was confirmed by ministerial statements'. On digging out Hansard from 1955, it was discovered that the Foreign Secretary had gone as far as to say that Burgess and Maclean had both committed 'the horrible crime of treachery' and were 'two traitors'. With hindsight, this did not sit easily with there being no evidence with which to prosecute him. The Petrov evidence couldn't be used in court because it was only hearsay from a KGB colleague. Even if the so-called VENONA evidence could have been used, and it couldn't because it was top secret, there was nothing specific in it against Burgess. This would be a weakness in the Crown's case which Burgess would thoroughly enjoy exploiting over the next few years.[25]

He discovered it when, two months later, *Reynolds News* headlined 'Burgess free to come back to Britain, he wouldn't be prosecuted'. A reporter called Harry Loftus wrote that the 'Director of Public Prosecutions and other Government legal experts have been asked, I understand, to study the legal implications of a possible visit to Britain by Burgess. They have now reported that there are no legal grounds that would prevent him from returning home.'

Burgess was soon on the phone to Driberg and followed up with a letter. He asked, 'How reliable do you think your friend's story was?' Burgess himself had received some confirmation of this, independently from 'sources close to sources'.

During this saga, months would often pass with nothing much happening and then there would be a sudden minor panic. Such as one in the summer of 1958 when Burgess wrote to his mother:

'You know I don't want to face the embarrassment of coming back from holiday while the Cold War is on – but if you're not well, I shall, after all due considerations.'

'Can you throw any light on the phrase "after all due considerations"?' Bernard Hill asked his MI5 colleagues. 'I am afraid we have no idea,' came the reply.[26]

It was in January 1959 that the 'Burgess to return' saga began to come to a head and it is probably no coincidence that this was the month before Harold Macmillan visited Moscow to meet the Soviet leader, Nikita Khrushchev. This would be the first visit by a British Prime Minister since Winston Churchill during World War Two. The trip had a wider geo-political significance as visits by Western leaders were rare during the Cold War and Washington would want a full briefing on the outcome of the talks.

Officials drafted a memorandum to members of the Cabinet, telling them they were 'faced with the situation that if Burgess wished to return to the

United Kingdom there is no means whereby Her Majesty's Government could stop him nor is there any action that they could take against him when he arrived'.

That paragraph was dropped from the final version – perhaps it was putting the problem a touch too bluntly. Ministers were told that his mother, Mrs Bassett, 'is over 70 and is undoubtedly in failing health'. It was a distinct possibility that her condition could suddenly deteriorate and they would be faced with a decision of whether to refuse permission for her son to come home to see his dying mother.[27] The previous year Anthony Blunt had given MI5 a full update on her health. She was suffering from arthritis and some as yet undiagnosed problem originally thought to have been cancer. Her husband, the 'unhappy Colonel', was struggling with the cooking, washing up and cleaning so, 'in order to prevent him from having a nervous breakdown', it had been decided to send his wife to the comfort of a nursing home and for the Colonel to 'live the life of a grass widower', a man who is effectively separated from his wife.[28]

Burgess sent a New Year letter that began 'Darlingest Mum'. In it he told her he was worried that 'your handwriting showed great signs of tiredness'. She had suggested that on her death some letters written by her late first husband should be sent to her son, Guy.

> Of course I should love to read Daddy's letters but can't bear to think of it the way you put it. I could and would love to read them <u>now</u>. But I don't think I could read them if as you suggest I get them after your death. They wouldn't I fear remind me of what you think, your happy life – which was as happy as anybodies [sic] ever – but of the unhappy parts, his shocking death so cruel, and then too of course your last sadness over me.[29]

As usual, the letter was intercepted, photographed, the original posted on and a copy placed in MI5 'Pf (Personal File) 604.529 (GUY BURGESS)'. Even the hard-nosed MI5 men reading it might have had a slight tinge of sympathy for Mrs Bassett, though probably not for Mr Burgess.

Burgess told friends he would love to visit his mother, 'who is I fear not far from the end' and who has 'behaved with incredible love and suffered a really terrible time'.[30] But he explained, 'My fear is not that I would be prevented from coming to England. My fear is that I would never get back to Russia.' Nowhere did Burgess mention the probability that the KGB wouldn't let him leave Russia in the first place. That trip to Yugoslavia and Switzerland had never come about, although he was allowed to travel to other parts of the Soviet Union such as Georgia.

On 17 February, the British Cabinet formally decided that the return of Burgess would be 'undesirable'. In a paper presented to the Cabinet an official wrote, 'We have no means of knowing whether the Soviet authorities would try to prevent his departure but I do not believe that they would.'[31] The Foreign Secretary, Selwyn Lloyd, and the Attorney General would arrange for Burgess to be 'dissuaded'. The ways in which he was to be 'dissuaded' would turn out to be rather unusual.

A few days later, on the 21st, Harold Macmillan left for Moscow with the prime ministerial press corps in attendance. Among the journalists was Randolph Churchill, son of Winston Churchill, who'd been at Eton with Burgess and now worked for the *London Evening Standard*. He was just settling into his hotel room when the telephone rang and, according to Churchill, 'a chap announces himself as Burgess and asks whether he can come and call on me'. Churchill initially thought it was a practical joke by another journalist but Burgess duly turned up, wearing his Old Etonian tie as usual. According to Churchill's account (he did go on to become a newspaper gossip diarist so a certain level of invention might be expected), Burgess announced, 'I am still a Communist and a homosexual,' to which Churchill replied, 'So I had always supposed.' Churchill told Burgess of long cherishing the hope that he was really a double agent and working on the British side. Burgess told him that if he was he wouldn't tell Churchill or anybody else.

In his report for the *Evening Standard*, Churchill wrote: 'Burgess further told me that he was thinking of coming back to England to see his aged mother to whom he speaks every week on the telephone. I warned him that the Attorney General Reginald Manningham-Buller might have a word or two to say about that.'[32] Burgess disputed Churchill's account of their meeting. In a fine example of the pot calling the kettle black, he told Harold Nicolson that Randolph was 'never in a fit state at any time to discuss anything'.

By coincidence or design, the first attempt to tell Burgess to stay away had been performed by the son of a former Prime Minister.

But, quite extraordinarily, it subsequently became known that whatever he said in his newspaper column Randolph Churchill had become convinced of the justness of Burgess's cause. Harold Macmillan's Press Secretary on the Moscow trip, (Sir) Harold Evans, revealed in his memoirs that Churchill had invited him to lunch in the royal suite of his Moscow hotel 'commandeered by Randolph on the grounds that his father had once stayed in it'. Evans arrived for lunch to find Churchill still in his pyjamas 'striding majestically around' dictating his latest dispatch to an assistant.

Over an omelette, whisky and black coffee, Churchill startled Evans by arguing the public relations benefit of allowing Burgess back to Britain. The Press Secretary agreed to pass the message on to his Prime Minister. At two o'clock in the morning Churchill phoned Evans demanding to know why nothing appeared to have been done. He threatened to write an article attacking Macmillan for inhumanity. Evans shouted back that 'the Prime Minister was not in Moscow to dish out favours to defectors', the 'British public didn't give a damn about Burgess' and Churchill could 'go to hell'. At this, the son of Britain's great war leader sounded the retreat.[33]

Robin Day, who was covering Macmillan's trip for Independent Television News (ITN), found time between visits to the Supreme Soviet and Moscow University on the 23 February and Macmillan's shooting expedition on the 25th to talk to Burgess and phone over an update to London:

Some minor matter – Mr Guy Burgess, one of the two ex-Foreign Office diplomats now working here, told me a moment ago on the telephone that he has not made any new appeal to return home. His hope was, he said, still as has been published some time ago, that he would like to come home for a month to see his mother but only if he could return to live in the Soviet Union.[34]

This was becoming a full-blooded Burgess campaign: a man who once didn't even want the press to know his address in Moscow had now spoken personally to two leading members of the prime ministerial press corps and through a third – George Hutchinson of the *London Evening Standard* – he sent a message directly to Harold Macmillan. He offered a deal to allow him to return to Moscow after a trip home:

> I will not make embarrassments for Her Majesty's Government if they don't make them for me. I will give no interviews without permission. I was grateful in the early days that Her Majesty's Government said nothing hostile to me. I for my part have never said a lot of things that I could have said.

The government decided to hold off replying while Macmillan was still in Russia and then tell Burgess there was no deal.[35]

Burgess then made an extraordinary decision for the times, to give a television interview in which he would, among other things, talk openly about wanting to come home for a holiday to see his mother.

He'd had requests before now. Robin Day of ITN had sent a message asking him for an on-camera interview, but Burgess said he'd always refused similar requests from the BBC. He agreed to talk to Day and consider his request but the best Day seems to have come up with was the one quote.[36]

The previous autumn, the ITV programme *This Week*, which had shown the first pictures of Burgess walking around Moscow with Driberg at the time of the publication of his book, had written to Burgess. They had asked if he would agree to be interviewed by the journalist Ludovic Kennedy and, 'of course, you would first approve the script'. Nothing came of this proposal.[37]

Burgess chose to give this world exclusive to a 28-year-old Canadian cameraman, Erik Durschmied, whose only claim to fame at the time was that he'd shot exclusive pictures of Fidel Castro in the mountains of Cuba, fighting to overthrow the American-supported government there.

By the next year, 1959, Castro was in power in Havana and Durschmied was in Moscow, shooting a documentary for the Canadian Broadcasting Corporation (CBC), but with another ambitious exclusive in mind – an interview with Guy Burgess or Donald Maclean. A few days later, wearing an Eton tie and a camel-hair coat, Burgess looked to Durschmied's camera and delivered what was effectively his appeal to be allowed home for a visit:

> I want to live in the Soviet Union because I am a socialist and this is a socialist country and I enjoy doing so. I cannot imagine living in England during the Cold War. On the other hand, naturally, everybody likes his own country best. If the Cold War were finished I don't know what I could do. Immediately, I would rather like to go back to England for a month to see my family, but I will never do that unless I can be quite certain that I can get out of England and come back to Russia, which is where I want to live. I don't want to be treated like Paul Robeson, to have my passport taken away and not be allowed to come back here. The British authorities are quite capable, eh no, I think not, no, I think the Americans are worse, but there would be a danger that I couldn't get back.

Asked how he came to be in Moscow, he replied: 'I will give you a very short answer – I went abroad as a tourist ... I simply went as a tourist. I and my friend approached the Russians, said could we come in? They kept us waiting in Prague for some weeks then agreed. That's all.'

And what had happened to that 'friend'?

> Donald Maclean is doing exactly what I am doing, that is, he is working in a publishing house, which is a traditional place where foreigners do work when they come here. We do not work in the same publishing house and therefore I don't see him very often. I last saw him a month ago. We were never close friends.

Was he a traitor?

It is no use me saying I'm not a traitor, that means nothing, of course I am not, but it is only I who know that … Before I left the British government states in its White Paper that they had no evidence at all that I was a traitor, up to the time of my leaving and for some years afterwards. There then came along a man called Petrov in Australia who had been a Russian spy in Australia. He sold information, cash on delivery, we say in England COD. The more information he sold – the more cash he got. His is the only evidence that has ever been quoted by the British government that I am a traitor. Of course its hearsay evidence, because he heard it from somebody else. It could never be used in a court of law.

And, finally, what was his political philosophy?

Since I was a student I have been a socialist, an extreme socialist. I am a Marxist. You asked my political philosophy, the strict answer is a Marxist. I am not actually a member of the Communist Party here, or in England. I was a member for some years. I resigned. They have a phrase in Russia which is a 'non-party Bolshevik'. I would be very proud indeed if I had earned such a title.

On camera, Burgess appeared cautious and careful about what he said, sometimes interrupting himself to correct or add facts. Off camera, according to Durschmied many years later, Burgess not only asked him to 'enquire for me with the British government' if it would be feasible to come back but also said, 'I wouldn't mind going to jail.' Durschmied's conclusion was that Burgess would rather face years in a British cell than in a Soviet flat.[38] The young Canadian sent his film by air back to Canada where it would be processed, edited and prepared for transmission later.

Soon afterwards came an even more unexpected development. For some time MI5 had been trying to worry Anthony Blunt about how he would be affected if Burgess returned. Since 1956 he had been Sir Anthony Blunt: in the same year Burgess and Maclean had appeared at a KGB-organised press conference in Moscow Blunt was at Buckingham Palace being knighted in recognition of his services to the Crown.

In January 1958, in a meeting at Sir Anthony's office at the Courtauld Institute of Art in London, Courtenay Young of MI5 told him Burgess would have to be tried, which

> would be obviously/extremely unpleasant for his friends, especially as some of them, including no doubt BLUNT, might well have to appear in the witness box (BLUNT agreed, and drained his glass of gin and French). I said that if the thought could be injected into the mind of Mrs BAS-SETT and BURGESS that if either of them thought he could come back here with impunity it was possibly wishful thinking.

Young finished his report by noting that 'we left amicably together in a taxi cab, accompanied by five fake Constables (pictures, not policemen)'.[39]

Now, one year later, Blunt 'appeared to be fussed by the possibility of BUR-GESS'S return'. MI5 decided to ask him to stress to Burgess's mother that her son 'would be arrested and prosecuted if he landed in the UK'. Blunt fell for that bluff. MI5 had one other scheme to let Burgess know of the 'great and hostile publicity' that would await him. They should 'suggest to Blunt that he himself might write to BURGESS'.[40]

As it turned out, they didn't need to persuade Sir Anthony; he had come to the same conclusion. He asked Courtenay Young to come to his flat at the Courtauld and told him that he had written a draft letter to BURGESS which he had composed that morning 'in the lavatory'.

Young was happy with the letter and gave Blunt the personal address of Burgess so that he could address the envelope himself. For the file, Young noted that Blunt was more relaxed than in previous talks but 'appears to me quite convinced that BURGESS would be prosecuted and that he, BLUNT, would be personally and intimately involved'. It would become clear from the letter itself that this was Blunt's primary purpose in writing. The MI5 man and the knighted ex-KGB spy 'parted extremely amicably, with me refusing an omelette'.[41]

On 25 February, Sir Anthony Blunt posted his letter in the West End of London to Guy Burgess in Moscow:

> Dear Guy,
>
> I am sorry to break a silence of seven and a half years with a letter which you will not, I fear, think friendly but it seems to me that you cannot have any idea of the effect your actions have on your friends here and on your mother who is, I know, too fond of you to tell you. But the fact is that when you make an announcement to the press or say anything that gets indirectly to the press in Moscow, the press here, headed by the *Daily Express*, is on the telephone and on the doorstep at Arlington House instantly and persistently.

He then focused on the reports of Burgess's return:

> The persecution is, of course, most violent when you talk of coming back to England. I cannot imagine that you are serious in this, though I can well imagine that you would like to do so. But what would happen if you did? You would be arrested on landing – that is certain – and put on trial. What the outcome of the trial would be is, of course, a matter of speculation, but on the way the story would be raked up again, many of your friends would certainly be called as witnesses, and mud would be slung in all directions. As regards myself I would certainly have to resign one of my jobs and might well lose another.

Then, suggesting that one particular trigger for writing seems to have been Randolph Churchill's quoting of Burgess as saying 'I am still a Communist and a homosexual', Blunt wrote:

> I can well understand your wanting to see people from England but why Randolph? One of your statements to him will have settled once and for all in the minds of people like my mother the question of queerness – I only hope she didn't see the article.

> I am sorry to be so direct but as I said at the beginning, I don't think
> you would do those things if you knew the trouble and pain they caused.
> Please don't answer this letter, but send a letter through your mother to
> acknowledge if you get it.
> Yours,
> Anthony.[42]

It was nearly two months before MI5 got any feedback on how the letter
had gone down. Sir Anthony wrote from New York to Courtenay Young:
'When I get back to England we might have a word about Guy's (not
very helpful or wholly intelligible) answer to my letter. I think he is really
crackers now.'

The Cabinet, unaware of whether their attempts at dissuading Burgess had
succeeded or not, were still in a cleft stick: embarrassed if they prosecuted
on flimsy grounds and lost in court, embarrassed if they didn't because they
had already publicly accused Burgess and Maclean of spying.

The note of one meeting summed up their worst fear: 'We shd. be ridi-
culed if we prosecuted.' The language around the Cabinet table got tougher.
The Home Secretary R. A. Butler talked about Burgess 'deteriorating – drink,
homosexuality, megalomania'.

The Prime Minister himself, Harold Macmillan, had a novel idea about
what should be done if Burgess suddenly turned up. It was noted down in
the minutes as: 'Instruct Embassy, if he applies, to require him to prove that
he is not R – Russian and not an impostor.'

The conclusion of the meeting was 'F.O. [Foreign Office] and H.O. [Home
Office] to concert means of keeping him away. . .'[43] In other words, the government wanted two of its biggest departments of state to try to find a way
of NOT arresting one of Britain's biggest traitors.

On 9 March, the Foreign Office went public on the issue for the first time
with a statement to the Commons that reported that Burgess wished to visit
the United Kingdom but feared that the British authorities would seize his
passport and prevent him from returning to the Soviet Union. He'd therefore
asked the Prime Minister for a commitment that he would be free to return

to Moscow but no reply had been sent to this message as the government had 'no power' to give Burgess the undertaking he wanted.

Two days later, CBC Canada transmitted their exclusive interview with Burgess. A nine-minute edited version was broadcast at 10 p.m. on a Wednesday night in a magazine programme. If Burgess had ever hoped that his appeal, delivered at some personal risk, would help to change the minds of the British public or government, he would have been bitterly disappointed.[44]

Burgess's interview, a scoop for CBC, seems to have fallen completely flat: our archival searches failed to find any mention of it at all. Strangely, the interview drew precious little coverage even in Canada itself. Only one Canadian newspaper – *The Ottawa Citizen* – seems to have mentioned it, and then only briefly in its television preview on page forty-four. Even though the issue of Burgess possibly returning home was topical enough at the time to have been mentioned in parliamentary questions just two days before, Burgess's interview passed everyone by in Britain too – in government, Parliament, Fleet Street and the media. Nevertheless, the MI5 files released to the National Archives in 2015 show that *somebody* realised the significance of what they were watching.

The Royal Canadian Mounted Police (RCMP)'s official motto is 'Defending the Law', but better known is the old adage 'the Mounties always get their man'. It is somewhat fitting, therefore, that it was a Mountie who tracked down the cameraman Erik Durschmied and asked him how he'd got the interview. According to the police note of the meeting that was sent to London, Durschmied said that in approaching Burgess he'd 'decided to work on the fact that he was reported to be homosexual'. He'd got Burgess on the phone and in the course of a conversation 'represented himself as a young Western correspondent, lonely for company'. Burgess invited him to visit his flat and to bring some drinks. Durschmied 'arrived with two bottles of champagne which Burgess drank in short order'.

When Durschmied brought the idea of a TV interview into the conversation, Burgess told him it was out of the question. The young cameraman was getting nowhere and decided to go back to his hotel. However, at 3 a.m. the phone rang in his hotel bedroom and he heard Burgess's voice saying, 'Let's do it. Why not?' Just in case Burgess had a change of heart, Durschmied went to the flat first thing the next morning, after which they had walked to one of Burgess's favourite spots near a monastery and filmed the interview.

The following morning, according to Durschmied's account, Burgess phoned 'begging him to burn the interview' and then went to the hotel to repeat his request. He said he had 'talked it over with the other boys' and they had urged him to get the film destroyed. Durschmied told him he would do his best to stop the interview going out but he knew that in fact it was already on its way out of Moscow, on the plane carrying Harold Macmillan and the British press corps back to London.[45]

Guy Burgess did not give up his campaign to be allowed home for a visit but may have begun to realise that, after many years of him outmanoeuvring the British establishment, perhaps they were now doing the same to him. Take, for instance, that decision by the British government back in 1957 to unfreeze his London bank account. Perhaps what had looked like a favour by an old friend might have had an ulterior motive. Peter Thorneycroft's decision as Chancellor of the Exchequer may, Burgess now concluded, 'have been to help keep me away, for, tho' Peter's a dear in some ways, I don't think he would have done that just to please my beautiful eyes'.[46]

In 1960, Burgess wrote to Roy Harrod wondering if there might be any help from another Eton school friend, Quintin Hogg, who'd since inherited his father's title Viscount Hailsham and become the leader of the House of Lords: 'He used to quite like me.' What about the Prime Minister himself, Harold Macmillan? 'I only just know him. He, I think, alone could help but I can't see why he should. I have caused some damage to the Establishment, which delights me but cannot prima facie appeal to it.'[47] Far from helping Burgess, however, the Prime Minister was at the heart of the establishment's plan to thwart him.

The prospect of Burgess returning had worried other people Burgess knew or 'just knew'. Stephen Spender found Tom Driberg 'in a state of great alarm at the prospect of Guy's return to England'. Roy Harrod tried hard to offer (rather unconvincing) reasons why Burgess should stay put: 'If you returned here you might, of course, be disappointed in your old friends, finding them faded, dried up, in a groove, lacking the vital spark that they had in the old days.'[48] As late as the summer of 1961, Harold Nicolson was writing to tell Burgess he would be arrested: 'I don't think you would be wise to come here, as it might entail proceedings. I can't imagine what they can have against you, but I gather that they have evidence and that there might be a case. Poor Guy.'

Burgess was getting similar advice in Moscow. Boris Piadyshev, his colleague at the Foreign Ministry's Information Committee, recalled that Burgess did once cheer up about the prospects of visiting his mother but 'the guarantees of his return to Moscow were somewhat vague'. Burgess decided to discuss the issue with his superiors. Piadyshev acted as interpreter as the head of the service said, 'Tell him (Burgess), that if he goes there, he'll be put behind bars.'[49]

On 18 April 1962, any remaining hope he ever had of returning without being arrested came to an end. The Chief Metropolitan Magistrate, Sir Robert Blundell, signed a warrant for the arrest of Burgess and Maclean. What had changed since the Attorney General's decision in 1957 that there wasn't enough evidence to charge Burgess was the arrest of an RAF Flying Officer, Anthony Wraight. He had defected to Moscow in 1956 but returned in 1959, was arrested for a breach of the Official Secrets Act and imprisoned for three years. The only secrets he had were some RAF technical documents. Government legal papers reveal that 'one of the objects ... of prosecuting Wraight under this section was to deter Burgess from returning to this country'.

Having been rejected once by the Attorney General, Bernard Hill of MI5 had not given up trying to find an offence to charge Burgess with. Some officials argued that Burgess and Maclean had broken a rule by not having permission to visit an Iron Curtain country. It turned out there was no such rule at the time.

But Hill saw a new possible route to prosecution with the precedent set when Flying Officer Wraight was 'convicted of putting himself (voluntarily) into such a position as to endanger classified information with which he may have been entrusted'. This offence had never been tested in court before. Not only that, but during the trial Hill had discussed the case with the Director of Public Prosecutions (DPP), who indicated to him informally that 'if he got the right decision on Wraight he thought we should be able to deal with Burgess'.

Now they were ready to go ahead in the unlikely event of ever getting their hands on Burgess. Only one small voice, an official called E. W. Battersby, dared to point out that 'the general public would take a dim view if Burgess were prosecuted only on such a minor charge'. All the more reason for the issuing of the warrant to send a clear warning signal to Burgess to stay away. The DPP even put it in writing to Hill: 'I am hoping that the Wraight case will be even more valuable as a deterrent to him than as an asset to us.'[50]

Scotland Yard's Press Bureau announced:

> There are grounds for supposing that Donald Maclean and Guy Burgess may be contemplating leaving – or may have left – the USSR for some other territory. In order that they may be arrested should they come within the jurisdiction of our courts, warrants have been applied for and issued for their arrest for offences under Section One of the Official Secrets Act.[51]

There was never any public explanation of how there was suddenly a case that would stand up in court. That didn't really matter, though, because neither Burgess nor Maclean were leaving Moscow. In truth the whole thing was a political plan to stop this 'Burgess to return' threat once and for all.

Unaware of this on the day, the British media was as excited as it was possible to be. The very thought that the two 'missing diplomats' may have left Moscow already and be on their way to who knows where created a media feeding frenzy. Then came an announcement at 6 p.m. by a Mr William Hatch, British European Airways (BEA) area manager for Amsterdam, that Burgess and Maclean would be on BEA flight 439, scheduled to land in London at 10 p.m. Surely, the press thought, BEA must have hard evidence to say that.

When the plane landed in London and the passengers began disembarking, the centre of attention was a man hurrying down the steps covering his head and shoulders with an overcoat. As cameramen surged towards him he took off the coat to reveal his identity. He was a *Daily Mail* reporter who'd got on the plane at Amsterdam, realised Burgess and Maclean weren't on board, and had decided to pull the legs of his colleagues.[52]

The *Daily Mail* itself had a very clear conclusion about the whole affair: 'B and M WARNED OFF'. The *Mail* believed that 'Scotland Yard's action in obtaining the arrest warrants yesterday was a move to keep Burgess and Maclean out of Britain'. If the government thought that the two men were going to get on that BEA plane, 'Why did they not keep their knowledge secret until the two runaways were back on British territory?'[53]

Official files reveal how Harold MacMillan's government planned the whole warrant affair. A week before, on 11 April, the Attorney General, Sir Reginald Manningham-Buller, had written to Macmillan at the Prime Minister's country home, Chequers. He said that the Foreign Office and MI5 thought Maclean 'may be in Cuba' and if he left Cuba 'it is possible that his plane might land at London Airport in transit or in another territory in which he might be apprehended. If he did so and was not arrested we should be much criticised.' He proposed a warrant should be obtained; the evidence available against Maclean was 'not entirely satisfactory' but enough for charges to be made. If they were doing this for Maclean they should get a warrant for Burgess too. This would be bound to leak and Manningham-Buller wrote, 'I do not think this would be a bad thing. It might well prevent Maclean returning here and causing us a great deal of embarrassment. Indeed I would welcome an inspired leak.'[54]

The next day an official wrote back confirming the Prime Minister's agreement with the plan and saying that news of the warrant 'should be leaked on the basis that they might enter the United Kingdom in transit'.[55]

Opposition MPs were soon asking awkward questions about the warrant and a government decision five years earlier. By now Peter Thorneycroft was out of government, but the Treasury's handling of the Burgess bank account letter was now public. When the issue came up in the House of Lords, fate decreed that it fell to another Eton contemporary of Burgess, Viscount Hailsham, to reply to an allegation that the government's decision amounted to 'a bribe for him (Burgess) to stay away'. That, Hailsham, replied, was 'certainly untrue'.[56]

The intelligence report that Maclean was in Cuba had been news to him sitting at his desk in Moscow, and the claim that Burgess would join him to fly back to London via Amsterdam came as something of a surprise to the man himself, who was on holiday in Yalta on the Black Sea coast. Burgess flew back to Moscow to clear up the confusion about his whereabouts. Reporters arriving at his home were told by his boyfriend Tolya that he was in somebody's room at the Ukraine Hotel and three reporters – from the *Express*, *Mail* and *New York Herald Tribune* – rushed up to a room on the twenty-seventh floor. They burst in and there was Burgess, lying on the bed, looking relaxed with his tie loosened, his shoes off and a glass of whisky in his hand. They went off to file their stories; after all, unlike their colleagues at London Airport, they had actually seen the real Guy Burgess. They told how he had laughed off the reports – 'What a splendid uproar about nothing' – that he was 'tanned and fit', 'chain-smoking', 'fingering his Old Etonian tie' and wearing 'in his lapel the red and white ribbon of the Order of the Red Banner'.

Burgess was quoted as saying, 'I am sure my decision to stay will be a tremendous relief to HMG.' He had heard from 'my confidential sources in England and from my many friends in the Establishment and even in MI5' that the government was terrified that he might go back. But, he said, 'I like living in the Soviet Union under socialism. I would not like to live in expense-account England.'[57]

Stephen Harper of the *Express* began his dispatch: 'Guy Burgess sat on the edge of a bed tonight and told me; I have no intention of returning to Britain to be arrested.'[58] What Harper didn't mention in his report was that the bed in question belonged to a reporter too, the Moscow correspondent of the *Daily Telegraph*. His name was Jeremy Wolfenden. Later, in an unpublished book, Harper provided more detail: 'We burst into room 2702 and found Burgess, then aged fifty, sitting on the edge of the bed in stockinged feet, a tumbler of Canadian Club whisky in his hand, and his flies undone. Wolfenden looked surprised and hastily put typewritten sheets into a desk drawer.'[59]

Burgess and Wolfenden had many things in common. Both had been to Eton, were described at some point as 'one of the most brilliant men' of their generations, worked on *The Times* for a period, were heavy drinkers, chain smokers and unashamedly homosexual. Their relationship in Moscow fascinated the other correspondents.

During Wolfenden's time at Eton he was the 'fag' – a kind of personal dogsbody – to a boy called Douglas Hurd, who became school captain and later British Foreign Secretary. As he grew older, Wolfenden talked and wrote freely of his sexual feelings for younger pupils and was almost expelled over one relationship. When his turn for National Service came round before going to university he went on a Royal Navy course in Russian at a camp in Surrey.[60] In 1952, while he was at the camp, he got involved in a correspondence with a boy still at Eton. His letters fell into the hands of a Master who objected strongly to the advice Wolfenden was offering the boy and reported the matter to Wolfenden's father.[61]

Thus it was that John 'Jack' Wolfenden, Vice-Chancellor of Reading University and well-known as a regular broadcaster on BBC Radio's *Any Questions* programme, learned of his own son's sexuality two years before agreeing to chair an official inquiry into the law which held all forms of male homosexual activity were illegal, whether in private or public.

When his appointment to this role was first announced, father is said to have told son, 'I have only two requests to make of you at the moment. 1) That we stay out of each other's way for the time being 2) That you wear rather less make-up.'[62]

Jeremy Wolfenden rationalised that, 'on mature consideration', being outed to his father was 'a good thing'. It forced him to distil what he wanted and, since his father had 'undermined' his home life, 'I am more of an emotional nomad, a nationless, mercenary, intelligence than ever. So be it.'[63]

After his national service, Wolfenden went to Magdalene College, Oxford, where his father had been a fellow, to study a course – Politics, Philosophy and Economics (PPE) – which his father had taught. He got a First and became a Prize Fellow at All Souls. According to his Eton school friend Neal Ascherson, Wolfenden was developing his own new philosophy, a very arrogant theory of 'deliberate under-achievement'. Giving of one's best was what everybody expected of you, he reasoned, so a truly individual 'existential act' would be to achieve less than one could.[64]

Magdalene College was a regular recruiting ground for the British security services and it was here that MI6 first made contact with Wolfenden. However, it is believed by some that while he was on a visit to Russia the KGB (presumably unaware of his theory of under-achievement) had spotted the potential in this student too, who not only spoke their language and had leftish views, but, as a reporter and editor on the student magazine *Isis*, was already getting some vacation work at *The Times*. They had also noticed his sexuality.

Wolfenden decided he would make journalism his career, got a full time job at *The Times*, progressed well and was made a correspondent in Paris. In 1960, he was poached by the newspaper which Fleet Street traditionally thought had even closer contacts with MI6, the *Daily Telegraph*. Their selling point to him, it appeared, was that he could work in Moscow – something he had always wanted to do.[65] It seems that everybody, the *Telegraph*, MI6, and certainly Wolfenden himself, was aware of the possibility, even probability, that a homosexual man, a heavy drinker, living alone in a hotel which was wired for sound and vision by the KGB, would be tempted into a sexual indiscretion. When the inevitable happened, he reported it to the British embassy. He was told to go along with the KGB but keep MI6 and MI5 informed. Indeed, it would be jolly useful, they thought, having somebody so close to the KGB.[66]

However, when it came to talking to Burgess, things seem to have got complicated between the embassy and Wolfenden. His biographer, Sebastian Faulks, wrote that the British embassy 'encouraged Wolfenden to keep in touch with Burgess'.[67] But MI5 files reveal that there was disquiet in the Foreign Office about these contacts: 'I am sorry to see that Burgess is in touch with Jeremy Wolfenden,' wrote the head of Foreign Office Security, Philip Adams, to MI5 in October 1961. 'I suppose it was inevitable that he should be. However, the Embassy are keeping in touch with Wolfenden and will do anything they can to keep him to the straight and narrow path.'[68] Evelyn McBarnet, who was MI5's long-standing Burgess and Maclean expert, agreed that 'it is indeed unfortunate about Jeremy WOLFENDEN. If his contact with BURGESS is, as would appear, a continuing one, he does not seem to have taken much notice of the warnings that have been given to him.'[69]

By contrast, a year later the Foreign Office wanted to use the opportunities arising from the Wolfenden–Burgess relationship. The *Daily Telegraph* correspondent had reported back to Howard Smith at the British embassy in Moscow on a conversation he'd had in his room with Burgess 'over large quantities of Canadian Club' whiskey. This was at the time when the warrant was taken out in London and Burgess 'seemed rather anxious for Wolfenden's view on whether he would, in fact, be brought to trial if he did return'. Wolfenden also reported back to the embassy that Burgess had told him that if he were brought to trial he would subpoena three senior diplomats whom he named.[70]

A Foreign Office colleague in London saw Smith's report on the conversation and wrote to him suggesting, 'I think it might be a good idea if you got the chance to encourage Wolfenden to let Burgess know that the Attorney General means business; in other words, there is no doubt that he would be brought to trial if he came to this country.'

Smith, who went on to become Director of MI5, made a note on the letter from London: 'A pretty frank admission that the warrant was issued in order to keep him out. I do not propose to "encourage Mr W..." since he would draw the obvious conclusion.'[71] One of the three senior diplomats Burgess threatened to subpoena was the British ambassador himself, Sir Frank Roberts. They had worked together in the Foreign Office in the late 1940s when Roberts was Private Secretary to the Foreign Secretary, Ernest Bevin. Roberts was very relaxed about Burgess's threat. He recalled that 'I found Guy Burgess's frequent interventions ... so consistently wrong-headed that my rule of thumb became "If Guy suggests X, do the opposite".'

Guy Burgess was twenty-three years older than Jeremy Wolfenden, but the age difference was probably an attraction for the former. Other British correspondents in the Soviet capital began noticing that if any of them were likely to get a good quote out of Burgess, to respond to some breaking news, it would be Wolfenden, especially after Burgess had opened a bottle of Armenian cognac.

For example, in April 1962, when the story of Burgess and Maclean's flight home turned out to be a very false alarm, Wolfenden got front-page stories two days running in the *Telegraph*. In one he reported Burgess 'pacing up and down my office' and saying he had cut short his holiday and flown back to Moscow because he was 'worried about the effect on my mother and the British government'.[72]

In July 1963, when it was finally admitted that Kim Philby was the 'third man', Burgess told Wolfenden that there *was* no 'third man'. He also gave Wolfenden a particularly pompous quote: 'The longer I stay in the Soviet Union and the more I read about the scandals in England the more glad I am to be here; and the more I believe that any civilised person like Philby might easily want to come here.'[73]

Wolfenden once wrote:

> In his own disreputable way Guy Burgess is very amusing but he has to be taken in small quantities ... apart from anything else, to spend 48 hours with him would involve being drunk for at least 47. He has a totally bizarre, and often completely perverse [idea] of the way the outside world works, but he makes up for this with a whole range of very funny, though libellous and patently untrue, stories about Isaiah Berlin, Maurice Bowra and Wystan Auden.

One man who knew Wolfenden from Oxford and by coincidence was in Moscow at the same time was an exchange student called Norman Dombey, who went on to become a leading physicist. He told us that there was something of an aura around Jeremy Wolfenden: 'He was very strange, brilliant, flagrant about his sexuality; well connected with intelligence circles ... I knew that at Oxford. The MI6 man in Moscow had encouraged him to keep in touch with Burgess so that the Embassy knew what was going on.'

Dombey remembered when one day Wolfenden asked him, 'Would you like to go and see Guy Burgess?' When he and Wolfenden got to the flat Burgess looked

> somewhat lost, couldn't speak the language, didn't go out, was clearly lonely, he was clearly questioning why he did it. We were talking about

life in Moscow, he said it was pretty awful or words to that effect and I said the Russian version of Communism is *passé*, the Chinese way is the way forward. Burgess was enthusiastic and he lent me the first volume of Joseph Needham's books on history of science in China.[74]

Was there a sexual relationship between Burgess and the man on whose hotel bed he was found with his flies apparently open? Sebastian Faulks, in his biography of Wolfenden *The Fatal Englishman*, concluded that Wolfenden had been close to Burgess, 'he may even have been his lover, though given the physical state of Burgess by the time they met no one could imagine much serious activity'.[75] Dombey also doubts there was a physical relationship – 'I don't think anything was going on – his boyfriend was there after all – he didn't need anyone else.'

But Anthony Purdy, a journalist who was regularly in Moscow to write a book about Burgess and Maclean, told MI5 in 1963 that he thought Wolfenden and Burgess were 'currently involved in a close homosexual relationship' and the *Daily Telegraph* correspondent would 'know more of Burgess's secrets than any other living person'. Purdy also said that Burgess was writing his own book 'to undermine the reputations of many of his erstwhile friends and acquaintances' and one secret Purdy had got from Burgess himself was that it was Blunt who in 1951 'had warned him that the security net was closing in on him'.[76]

There is an interesting reference to Wolfenden in a letter that Burgess sent to somebody in England who'd been in contact with Michael Berry, Burgess's friend since Eton who'd progressed up the family firm to become Editor-in-Chief of the *Daily Telegraph* and therefore Wolfenden's ultimate boss.

Burgess wrote:

Thanks for forwarding Michael Berry's letter. I imagine he sent it via you and not Jerome [*sic*] Wolfenden – a great pleasure to me here – out of caution. Don't repeat that please since Michael is a dear and nervous.[77]

Clearly Burgess didn't want the Editor of the *Telegraph* to know just how close his correspondent was to the story.

Burgess's health had been in decline for over a decade. When he defected in 1951 Goronwy Rees called him a 'sick man', blaming the incident two years earlier when Burgess fell down some stairs, fractured his skull, and having been in 'almost continuous pain ever since'.[78] Subsequently being beaten up on the streets of Kuybyshev can't have helped. In one letter Burgess wrote to Driberg, he told of the 'awful time' he'd had later in Moscow when he caught a chill that led to 'sinus and other head infection (in my broken skull) of a nature that made doctors and Professors gasp when they saw the X rays of my head'. There then followed a 'severe period of penicillin, shock waves, inhalations explanations, morphines for headaches etc etc and etc'. He wrote of answering a letter while 'under the influence of drugs for headaches' and fearing he may have been indiscreet.[79]

Burgess's other core health problem was a similar complaint to the one his father had suffered from. In 1961 he denied reports that he was seriously ill but admitted to undergoing treatment for 'slight hardening of the arteries'. He told a Reuters correspondent: 'I think it was Churchill who said nobody does any good work who had not had hardening of the arteries at 40 or 50.'[80]

In a letter to Driberg he listed his daily pains in his chest, in his arms, attacks first thing in the morning especially 'after my usual large breakfast', all of which left him feeling 'v.tired'.

Stephen Spender had found him 'florid, bright eyes, full mouth as before', but now 'thickset, chin receding, eyebrows with tufts ... a person I knew, who had added an unrecognisable mask to his familiar features'.[81]

By 1963, Burgess wrote to Harold Nicolson: 'I have been condemned to some months' inactivity because (this private and not for general circulation) of angina pectoris which first showed itself in the land of Colchis [western Georgia]. Not of course either fatal or even dangerous but painful & a bore.'

Angina pectoris, most often just known as angina, occurs when the heart muscle does not get enough blood and causes chest pain or discomfort. The cause of his angina was atherosclerosis, the hardening and narrowing of the arteries, and he was treated for this at the Sanatorium of the Council of Soviet Ministers in Sochi and at a sanatorium outside Moscow.

He wrote to Nicolson: 'Here I am taking what the Russians and my Grand-mother, but not my mother, call a "cure". Atherosclerosis and ulcers both threaten also arthritis which is the only one my mother knows about.' He appealed to Driberg: 'I beg you to say <u>nothing at all</u> to my mother.'

He'd earlier also had 'a minor but painful and complicated appendicitis' from which he'd convalesced in Georgia. The ailments were mounting up.

As things got worse, the Reuters correspondent John Miller discovered that Burgess seldom left his flat and spent most of the day lying on a chaise longue in pyjamas and dressing gown. 'Four times a day a nurse came to give him injections in his backside. Once when I called on him, she hadn't been, and the first thing he said, was, "I say, old boy would you give me an injection?"'[82] An art historian, Francis Haskell, was at Burgess's fifty-second birthday party in his flat. Haskell remembered Burgess shouting, 'Of course, we're bugged in here ... I know where it is ... it's up in that corner. I hate Russia. I simply loath [sic] Russia. I'm a Communist, of course, but I'm a British Communist, and I hate Russia.'[83]

Any thought of going home had long gone; indeed, he began to claim: 'I never had such plans. Chiefly because any return and any trial which they might have to bring, presumably would cause pain and troubles to dear friends.'[84]

During his years in Moscow Burgess was disappointed that, possibly because of this 'pain', his Washington embassy friend Esther Whitfield never wrote to him. He told his mother, 'I'm sorry about Esther but of course I quite understand anybody's fear of communicating with me – it is because of that, as I told you earlier, I have not so far written to people whom I otherwise would have written to precisely for that reason.'[85]

His mother was in regular correspondence with Miss Whitfield and would pass on her news to her son: 'Esther is going to Rhodesia in July to see her brother, she expects to be away a year and will take a job in Rhodesia. She has bought a dear little mews flat off the Fulham Road with a large garage and this she plans to let for 7 guineas a week.'[86]

Now, as Burgess began to face up to his own mortality, he wrote a letter that would effectively be his last will and testament in which he divided up his belongings between four people. One of them was Esther Whitfield and, it is said, he wanted the document entrusted to her.[87]

> Anything may happen at any operation. If anything happens to me – it's 99% against – I've sent this plan since everyone makes muddles and puts things off. There should be a balance to my account at Lloyds Bank, St James's Street, and Montreal Trust Company, St James's Square, but owing to me. It won't be much. But as a souvenir want to send a quarter each of total to these four – a quarter each to:
>
> 1. Sir Anthony Blunt
>
> 2. Miss Esther Whitfield
>
> 3. Tollya [sic] Borisovich Chishekov – Russian name and address is below
>
> 4. Kim Philby.
>
> If 1, 2 or 4 don't want this, send his/her share to Tollya. Mummy I'm sure would like her sofa table as a family thing to go to Nigel, which I have arranged. Other furniture, books, clothes here also disposed here – some books to nephews. Russian dining set to a Russian is arranged. Not family & it should stay here. Aunt Peggie's White Russian loot. Sorry brother. Guy not a worry really.

There was, noticeably, absolutely no mention of Donald Maclean.[88]

On 20 August 1963, Burgess was admitted to hospital, telling friends he would probably be 'out of touch for some time'. In the early hours of Sunday 1 September, Jeremy Wolfenden burst into John Miller's bedroom shouting, 'Guy's dead! Guy's dead!'[89]

This was not the result of an exclusive tip, some reward for Wolfenden's investment of many hours spent with Burgess. Instead, he had been phoned by his news desk in London, who had seen the first edition of the *Sunday Express* headlined: 'Guy Burgess dies. The vanishing diplomat has heart attack.' The *Express* said Burgess's mother had received the news in a cable from Melinda Maclean, wife of Donald Maclean.[90]

Burgess was fifty-two years old. Jeremy Wolfenden's first opportunity to report the death was – in this very pre-internet age – not in a *Telegraph* outlet, but on television, which by 1963 was beginning to establish itself as the medium by which most Britons got their news. He had been allowed by the *Telegraph* to send occasional audio reports from Moscow for ITN, which had started in 1955 as the news service of the ITV network but didn't yet have its own Moscow correspondent.

Wolfenden phoned over a one-minute, twenty-two-second audio report for the Sunday evening 6.05 p.m. news, crisply written and delivered, giving remarkable insights into the final hours of Burgess:

> To the two women doctors who received him ten days ago in the heart disease ward of the hospital here, he was just known as Jim Andreyvich Elliot, a 52-year-old intellectual in shocking condition. His sclerosis, which had forced him to take up to eight injections a day in the last year, was by then very serious indeed. All the same, in spite of a hospital rule they allowed him to chain-smoke his favourite cheap Russian Prima cigarettes.
>
> While he lay dying, he only seemed to have had one visitor apart from his faithful nagging maid Nadia Petrovya. This was a mysterious Englishman who has not yet been identified. It wasn't Donald Maclean who fled with him in 1951. Maclean has seen very little of Burgess during the last few years and they certainly aren't on close terms. It could well have been Harold Philby, the recent British defector who was a close friend of Burgess. The tragedy is that now Burgess is dead no one wants to know – unless his mother comes from England there is no one even to claim the body.[91]

Whether or not the viewers agreed that it amounted to a 'tragedy' that no one could claim Burgess's body, Wolfenden's knowledge of the detail would have impressed the ITN editors. It seems he got it right about Philby being the visitor, too. Philby's wife later confirmed there'd been a very brief farewell encounter as Burgess lay on his deathbed, the only time, she said, that Philby and Burgess were allowed to meet in Moscow.[92] Philby had to put aside his anger that, by defecting with Maclean, Burgess had put the spotlight on him.

He regarded Burgess as an 'out-and-out traitor, who had broken his word in the full knowledge that by doing so he was leaving a friend in desperate danger', according to Yuri Modin of the KGB.[93]

The precise cause of death, sclerosis, is different from the wording on his father's death certificate – 'atheroma of the aorta and valvular disease of aortic valve' – but the two conditions are essentially the same, and what would be known nowadays as coronary heart disease. Guy Burgess ticked at least three of the risk-factor boxes for that – family history, smoking, and being physically inactive – but seemed to do nothing to prevent it. He didn't, as many would suspect, actually drink himself to death, but it couldn't have helped.

Wolfenden said Burgess drank too much but that had never been the real problem, which was the advance of sclerosis over the previous year and a half. 'It made any journey into the outside world, even to lunch with friends, a dangerous adventure.'[94] In this, his first newspaper report on Burgess's death, Wolfenden wrote:

> My personal impression, from seeing him at home almost weekly over the last few years, is that the turning point was a day in April last year when a British warrant was issued for his arrest. This destroyed the dreams he had been nursing that he would eventually return to England.

The British government's plan had helped secure a surprisingly satisfactory outcome.

At the funeral at the Donskoi Crematorium, the tall figure of Donald Maclean stood out among the pall bearers on the left-hand side of the coffin. Across from him, on the right-hand side, was Jeremy Wolfenden. As the Associated Press wired over still pictures of the *Telegraph* correspondent carrying the coffin of one of Britain's greatest traitors, the reaction in Fleet Street must have been interesting, to say the least. The picture didn't appear in the paper. In the Editor-in-Chief's office, Michael Berry may have again been grateful that Burgess's defection meant that he died on the KGB's books in Moscow rather than the *Telegraph*'s staff in London.

In his own account of the funeral in the next day's *Telegraph*, Wolfenden wrote that three of the bearers of the coffin were British and named Maclean and Burgess's brother Nigel as two of them. He didn't mention that he was the third.[95]

Wolfenden's report went on:

> After two minutes' silence, broken only by the weeping of Nadezha Petrovna, Burgess's faithful housekeeper, the joyful brassy chords of the Internationale, the hymn of the International Communist Movement, struck up. Then the green doors under the coffin were opened.

The next short and final chapter of Wolfenden's own life was to be almost as bizarre as his time as Burgess's friend and possible lover. First, he swapped jobs with the *Telegraph*'s man in Washington. One theory had it that MI6 organised the move because a former Russian lover had moved to a Soviet post in Washington and they wanted Wolfenden to link up with this man again to get information.

He then married Martina Browne, who'd been a nanny at the home of MI6's station chief in Moscow. And, finally, he was found dead in 1965, aged thirty-one, in circumstances which were said to be mysterious. Some people claimed he'd been murdered by the CIA, but Sebastian Faulks concluded that he'd drunk himself to death, that his liver had killed him, not a plot by the security services.

Two years after Jeremy Wolfenden's death, the Sexual Offences Act of 1967 put into law a modified version of the reforms his father, by now Sir John Wolfenden, had recommended. It was the end of an old law, under which many men were jailed and many others like Jeremy Wolfenden lived with the threat of blackmail. It was the start of a new attitude in society which brought in more reforms leading to civil partnerships and eventually same-sex marriages from 2014.

But, deep in the heart of the English countryside, at West Meon in Hampshire, by 2014 there was no sign of changing attitudes to Guy Burgess. The man cutting the grass at the local church didn't even know that Burgess's ashes were interred in the grave of Malcolm Burgess and his wife Evelyn.

He'd never noticed the inscription 'In Loving Memory of Guy Francis De Moncy Burgess, died 30 August 1963'. The man who rented the old Burgess family home, West Lodge, didn't know Burgess had once lived there. The local pub is named, not after Burgess, but after Thomas Lord, founder of Lords Cricket Ground, who is buried in the same graveyard.

The Burgess family would have been pleased with this outcome. When Nigel Burgess brought back from Moscow a Russian urn containing his brother's ashes, it was agreed with the then vicar John Hurst that the only people at the interment would be the two of them and an undertaker. The conventional wisdom is that this was done after dark, but a local resident, Ray Stone, who went on to become the Church Warden, remembered it happening on a sunny morning on 5 October 1963. He told us that Nigel Burgess was anxious about the possible desecration of the family grave by vandals and made it clear he would be happy if the headstone became overgrown to mask the inscription about his brother's final resting place. Ray Stone also possessed an old copy of the *Southern Daily Echo* which had reported the 'secret buried in a Hampshire Graveyard'. Below a picture of Burgess and a hammer and sickle was one word in large type: 'TRAITOR'.

The year after Burgess died, his mother passed away too. She had just outlived her beloved son 'Guy boy'. During his relationship with Burgess, Micky Burn had got to know her and after her death wrote:

> She was a forthright wealthy lady, who had over-indulged him, coped in a brave and dignified way with the journalists who besieged her after his defection, went to see him in the USSR and made a *grande dame* best of a bad job with a comment, 'I think the discipline of Moscow will be good for Guy.'

In the records of the High Court of Justice, a symbol of the British legal system that Burgess, Maclean and Philby all managed to avoid but at a very human cost, there is a probate registry for Burgess, 'otherwise Jim Andreyevich Elliot'. It is a 'Grant of Letters of Administration', issued when a person dies without making a valid will.

The British authorities decided that Burgess's letter in which he left his belongings to Esther Whitfield and three other people was 'inadequately witnessed' and therefore invalid. The money reverted to his mother as his next of kin but she thought it should be shared out in the way he wanted, even if he hadn't filled the forms in properly. The High Court in London gave Nigel Burgess the power to sort out the money.

On 27 September 1963, he wrote to Donald Maclean enclosing a letter to Kim Philby. The tone of both letters from a former MI5 officer to two Soviet spies was very amicable, and was almost as if nothing untoward had happened in recent times other than his brother dying. Could Maclean help out because 'Guy's doctor wanted some stamps for his grand-daughter?' Nigel Burgess also wondered what had become of his brother's lover, Tolya Chishekov.[96]

In his letter to Kim Philby, Nigel Burgess wanted to know what could be done about sending back to Britain the sofa table his mother wanted him to have. He also asked what Philby wanted to do about the money Guy Burgess had left him.

There was only a only passing reference to the circumstances which had led to Philby and Maclean ending up in Moscow, a line in which Nigel Burgess made what sounds like a sarcastic commitment – 'Will give your love to the DG'– presumably a reference to the Director General of MI5 or MI6.[97]

Philby's reply, enclosing a letter for Burgess's mother, did not pick up on this offer but did ask for Philby's love to be passed on to a mutual friend from the days of Section D of MI6. On what was to be done with Burgess's money, Philby wanted it put in a trust fund for his children. He'd like to have 'Guy's books, plus the shelves to put them in', but apart from that he was 'very well equipped' and asked whether he and Donald Maclean should dispose of the other belongings as they thought fit. (Philby chose a wingback reading chair, which became one of his favourite pieces of furniture.)[98]

His final thought in the letter was: 'We are very much with you in your sadness.'

In a radio interview many years later, Nigel Burgess said he was sure his brother never wanted to live the rest of his life in Moscow. 'I mean, Christ's sake, who would? I mean, least of all Guy.' He thought Guy Burgess believed communism was a way forward to a better life for this country: 'I think he was tricked by Russia into believing this but I'm sure he believed it. In his way he was a patriot. But then' he added, 'you can twist anything to make anybody a patriot or a traitor really if you try hard enough.'[99]

The financial paperwork which Nigel Burgess went through to sort out his brother's money revealed the cash cost of Burgess's 'patriotism'. His estate, if one can call it that, was valued equal to about 5 per cent of the family wealth his mother had accumulated and left when she died just six months later. Micky Burn said Guy Burgess's life had come to 'a sad, lonely and paltry end'.[100]

CHAPTER 11

'BURGESS IS, OF COURSE, BRIGADIER BRILLIANT'

TOWARDS THE TRUTH, 1951–2016

In the twenty-first century it would be thought very odd if a government, faced with a public scandal over how it came to recruit a spy into its ranks, organised a committee of inquiry chaired by the very man who'd recruited the spy. But this was 1951, half a century ago, and the Cold War climate of secrecy and suspicion overrode any expectations of public accountability. Very few people knew the committee had even been set up; the members were shown just a handful of the relevant documents and their report was never published at the time.

It took until an autumn morning in 2015, when hundreds of documents comprising thousands of pages were made available to be read in the National Archives at Kew in West London, before it became possible to research the full story of how the British authorities had handled the Burgess and Maclean affair.

In 1951, Sir Alexander Cadogan was the top diplomat at the Foreign Office who in 1944 had written to the BBC Director General asking for the release of Guy Burgess. He'd also been Britain's representative at a United Nations conference in Paris in 1948 when Burgess was busy behind the scenes handing over secrets to the Soviet delegation. The former 'PUS' at the FO knew his loyalties lay with the Foreign Office.

In July 1951, in the wake of the defection of Burgess and Maclean, it had been a Labour government which in its final months in power had turned to Cadogan. He was asked to chair a committee to look into all aspects of the security arrangements in the Foreign Service: 'The security checks applied to members of the Foreign Service' plus the 'existing regulations and practice of the Foreign Service in regard to any matters which have a bearing on security'. Crucially, the committee was charged with reporting 'whether any alterations are called for'.[1]

One post-war anecdote illustrates how Sir Alexander's experience with Burgess conflicted with his task. At a meeting of the foreign ministers of Britain, Greece and Greece's neighbours, 'Burgess's appearance one evening, drunk and heavily painted and powdered for a night on the town, caused much outrage.' When this episode was mentioned by a young diplomat, Brian Urquhart, to the head of the British delegation, Sir Alexander, 'he replied icily that the Foreign Office traditionally tolerated innocent eccentricity'.[2] Now it would be down to Sir Alexander to decide if the Foreign Office should have realised the potential implications of Burgess's 'eccentricity'.

Patrick Reilly was the chairman of the Joint Intelligence Committee, the government committee that provided 'a co-ordinated intelligence service to policy makers'.[3] He'd obviously known about the defection before it was announced, but his reaction on hearing that the news was now public symbolised the shock throughout Whitehall. Shortly after the announcement, and 'exceedingly busy', he picked up an internal memo pressing him for action on some other issue which he'd left in his pending tray when this

> touched off a violent nerve storm. Within seconds I had demolished the solid wooden armchair in which I had been sitting. I stood for a long time looking aghast at its ruins. Then I collected the debris together, put my papers away in my safe, and went off to bed...[4]

The next day a new chair was waiting for him when he arrived in his office.

The Cabinet had first discussed the disappearance on 11 June 1951 and agreed 'that it might become necessary to hold a formal enquiry into the circumstances in which these two officers had left the country'. Days later, and following a decision taken by Labour Foreign Secretary Herbert Morrison, Sir William Strang, the Permanent Under-Secretary, contacted his old boss Cadogan and invited him in for a chat.

Cadogan met Strang on 29 June 1951 while on the way to his dentist. He wrote in his diary in an unpublished entry:

> [Strang] wants me to be Chairman of a Committee, the other members being Nevile Bland and Norman Brook, to consider FO security arrangements in the light of the disappearance of McLean [sic] and Burgess. We shall have nothing to do with the investigation of that case, but we shall learn what is known by MI5, who will give evidence.[5]

There was no danger that the Foreign Office was going to lose control of this inquiry. Former diplomat Sir Nevile Bland had just completed a review of the intelligence services for the government, and Sir Norman Brook was the Secretary to the Cabinet. All three members were insiders and were used to handling security and intelligence matters. Strang appointed his Private Secretary, Alan Campbell, as the Secretary to the Committee.

Cadogan's review was kept highly secret. There were no announcements that it was taking place and no publicity to proclaim its findings when it completed its work. The papers and the final report were to remain hush-hush for sixty-four years; a highly guarded secret until the day in September 2015 when the Foreign and Commonwealth Office decided to release its files to us, following our Freedom of Information request, in advance of the main release of documents the following month.

Alan Campbell was allowed no extra staff with which to service Cadogan's committee. He was also expected to carry out his normal duties as well, thus sending out a business-as-usual message to everyone. He later wrote: 'Looking back on it now, I think that the committee must have been somewhat amateurish in its administrative aspects.'[6] Indeed, the hand-drawn cover of the report looked more like a child's school essay. As neither Cadogan nor Bland had offices in Whitehall any longer, Campbell would frequently have to arrange with their domestic staff or trusted family members to send to their homes the highly sensitive paperwork locked into boxes. He confessed that the arrangements were only concluded through 'tiresome telephone negotiation'.[7]

The meetings were held in 'a large dignified room in the old India Office' where they were kept supplied with tea and biscuits. Bland always arrived early and was chatty; Cadogan was more focused and arrived with a minute to spare; whereas Brook always arrived late and out of breath.

Cadogan's committee soon got down to business. Brief career histories of both missing officials had been compiled and, very significantly, the committee saw a long and hastily prepared list of the possible files that Donald Maclean had – or might have – seen during his time as head of the American Department. They included NATO papers and Joint Intelligence Committee material as well as amendments to the war book.[8] The files show that, contrary to what has previously been published, even though Maclean had been under suspicion in the weeks before he had vanished, Foreign Office officials had not been able to establish exactly what he had and had not seen. Sensitive papers had clearly not been withheld from him, consistently, at any rate; and so it is unlikely that that would have tipped him off.

The initial list was coordinated by Maclean's deputy and later biographer Robert Cecil. He could not be sure if Maclean had been receiving top-secret material until the day that he disappeared. Robert Cecil wrote to Strang that it was quite impossible to know what was seen by Maclean because, crucially, '[some] papers were sent directly to Mr Maclean (mostly by PUS Dept.) without our knowledge ... the Department keeps no comprehensive record of other top secret and secret papers ... which may, or may not, have been seen by Mr Maclean'.[9]

We can only speculate how sharp the intake of breath was as each committee member read the list. The story put out to the press weeks earlier that neither of the diplomats had carried with them any confidential papers when they disappeared was laid bare as irrelevant to Cadogan and his colleagues. Maclean may have passed to Moscow countless numbers of papers while still unsuspected.

The committee met thirteen times, it interviewed ten witnesses and read a number of papers. But it also talked to people who remain anonymous because their contact wasn't recorded officially.[10]

The papers that survive reveal a process that was haphazard. Some papers and minutes are missing. Transcripts were never taken of any of the sessions. Fortunately, minutes of several of the key meetings do survive.[11]

What the committee members heard must have been uncomfortable for these good and great of British public life. Our research shows that some information that emerged at this time was not correct, some of what was given to the committee was inaccurate and many of the details were incomplete. The Cadogan Committee thus received a snapshot of a live investigation which provided a background, a context. Its job was to give Foreign Office security procedures a health check and put right whatever, if found, was wrong or broken.

Among the witnesses was Dick Goldsmith White of MI5. He told the committee what had been known about Burgess by MI5 since 'about 1939':

> His weaknesses, including his indiscretion and his homosexual tenden-
> cies, were all known to MI5 but they had not regarded him as a member
> of the Communist Party or as a possible Soviet agent since they did not
> think him capable of sustaining such a role. Burgess had given the strong
> impression to his large circle of acquaintances that he had been a Com-
> munist at one time but severed his connection with the Communists at
> the time of the German–Soviet pact of 1939.[12]

But, crucially, MI5 had not told anyone about Burgess because no one had asked, and MI5 didn't see it as its job to go around telling tales.

In its final report, the committee listed a whole series of earlier discoveries and allegations about Burgess's past, but 'none of this information, whether true or false, was available to the Foreign Office or to MI5 before the disappearance of the two men'.[13] This finding was never published, only a brief summary of the main recommendation that all members of the Foreign Service should be positively vetted as soon as possible.

Nor was there any public mention of an intriguing part of the report which began: 'We have given special consideration to the questions of homosexuality since Mr Burgess and, to a much lesser extent, Mr Maclean are alleged to have homosexual tendencies.' The committee 'recognised that in this and some other countries some forms of homosexuality involved offences under the criminal law. A practising homosexual is therefore especially liable to blackmail.' The working papers of the committee show how they pondered over what to do about this. On the one hand, there was the pressure from the Americans, who were much less tolerant of homosexuality in their Foreign Service, but on the other if the British went along with that, what would they do with the homosexuals they knew they already employed? Were they to be removed from their posts?

In the end a classic and some would say tolerant British compromise was reached: 'We doubt whether this is a matter for hard and fast rules: we think it preferable to leave it to the discretion of those responsible for the reputation and efficiency of the Service to deal with such cases as they may arise.' The committee specially noted that it would be 'distasteful' for members of the Service to be expected to have to watch colleagues and, 'in school parlance, to "blab" about them to the "Head"'.[14]

The overall conclusion was that 'we have not found anything radically wrong with the arrangements in the Foreign Service in the sphere covered by our terms of reference'. So, essentially, the biggest spy scandal in British Foreign Office history had occurred – but nothing much was wrong.

Copies were sent to the Foreign Secretary and King George VI. Guy Liddell of MI5 made a special point of noting in his diary for 12 June 1951 that the King's Private Secretary, Alan 'Tommy' Lascelles, 'asked me to go and see him in connection with the disappearance of BURGESS and MACLEAN, as the King was asking for information'.[15]

On 14 June, Lascelles sent a note to the Foreign Office acknowledging the receipt of 'the report sent with your Secret letter of yesterday. I have laid this before the King.'[16]

When we submitted a Freedom of Information Act (FOIA) request in 2015 to see the files, the Foreign Office informed us that 'some of the material is being withheld' under an exemption to the Act for 'communications with, or on behalf of, the Sovereign'.

As to what special interest the King might have had in the case, the most revealing mention in the files would appear to be in April 1956, after the Cadogan Report, when MI5 officers intercepted a letter between Burgess and his mother in which they said he 'plays upon his knowledge of the association between BLUNT and the British Royal Family'.[17]

Burgess wrote that Blunt had a system in which he kept 'the best letters etc he gets from his friends' in a black tin box, and said, 'I do not know if his Royal friends, from George VI onwards wrote to him,' but then remembered that

> the last <u>funny</u> joke made by the Royal Family was made by the
> <u>previous</u> dynasty with the possible exception of a joke George VI made
> to Anthony in Windsor Great Park while deciding to leap off a wet wall,
> on which he was sitting, against the advice of all. A. will remember what
> he said next. It can't be repeated by me since I don't like even faintly
> smoking room jokes.[18]

Understandably, a mention of a black box got MI5's attention and they would have been partly reassured when they confirmed that back in November 1951, nearly six months after the defection, Blunt had brought them a black box containing what he said was 'a certain amount of Burgess's property – letters etc. which Blunt said he had only just remembered'. So MI5 might have the black box (if that was the right black box), but it didn't mean they had any of the sensitive letters Blunt had possessed.[19]

The definitive biography of Blunt by Miranda Carter has a section on what she calls the 'sheer incongruity' of a 'Soviet spy looking after the royal family's art collection', and of how Blunt remarked that a day at Buckingham Palace had been 'rather a strain'.[20]

The senior Palace staff liked working with Blunt. 'He had lovely manners and treated everybody with respect – and was of course formidably intellectual,' one of them remembered. According to Miranda Carter, the King liked him too: 'He was polite, effective and, above all discreet. Over the years he divulged very little about his relations with the royal family.'[21]

Burgess's letter to his mother is evidence that at least some of Blunt's anecdotes had been passed on to Burgess. No wonder the King wanted to see the Cadogan Report, even if its terms of reference were focused more on the Foreign Office than Buckingham Palace at the other end of Birdcage Walk.

* * *

It is striking to compare the inadequacy of the Cadogan Report with the mass of detail which we know from the material released to the National Archives in 2015 was available at the time in 1951.

The files are not the full story. Over 20 per cent of the documents remain closed and many of those that were released have redactions where text has been covered up. In addition, MI5 personal files on key figures such as Goronwy Rees, Victor Rothschild and Harold Nicolson are still secret. The Secret Intelligence Service, MI6, has not opened up its files on Burgess and Maclean, so its documents are only visible when they were sent or copied to MI5 and released in its own files. But the October 2015 release was a great step forward in getting towards the truth.

Better briefed than Sir Alexander Cadogan, Sir Nevile Bland and Sir Norman Brook ever were, we have here been able to offer our own, hopefully more informed view of how Guy Burgess got away with being a KGB spy in a variety of great British institutions and, by looking back over all the different episodes in Burgess's career, attempt to detect some common theme, motive or strategy.

The Foreign Office line has often been that Burgess was a man 'who didn't fit in anywhere'. We now know that he fitted in wherever the KGB wanted him to, courtesy of MI5.

When, in 1952, Cyril Connolly wrote the first profiles of Burgess and Maclean in a series of articles in the *Sunday Times*, the literary critic in him couldn't resist colourful caricatures of the two men he'd known: 'With his black hat and his umbrella, his brief case under his arm', Donald Maclean was a 'terror of the unjust and hope of the weak'. Connolly's language about

Burgess, an acquaintance whom he believed was highly intelligent but a wasted talent and, moreover, a scoundrel, was even more sarcastic: 'Burgess is, of course, a power behind the scenes: a Brigadier in mufti, Brigadier Brilliant, DSO, FRS, the famous historian, with boyish grin and cold blue eyes, seconded now for special duties.'

The conventional, almost stereotypical picture of Burgess is that he was a heavy drinker whose lifestyle and habits were more significant than his espionage – that he was a burned out case by the time the KGB arranged his one-way ticket to Moscow. But, following the release of key documents into the National Archives, so much more is now known about Burgess the BBC producer, the Foreign Office official and the KGB spy. The detail supports the verdict of his first biographer Tom Driberg, who wrote of Burgess and Maclean back in 1956, that

> the circumstances of their birth and upbringing enabled them to tune in effortlessly, as it were, to the 'old boy network' and Guy at least, 'cynically and conscientiously' as he himself told me, exploited this advantage to the full – except that, as he also said, he could never bother to keep his fingernails clean.[22]

Burgess's appreciation that such irrelevancies as his dirty fingernails would convince MI5 that he was not 'capable of sustaining such a role' as a spy marks him out as someone who was, for the KGB, a 'Brigadier Brilliant', an accolade bestowed this time without a sarcastic subtext. His espionage work was prolonged and went undetected until he disappeared. In fact, for several days afterwards he probably could have come back to Britain and not been noticed. The Foreign Office desperately tried to work out why he had vanished with Maclean and whether he was anything more than an innocent dupe. Maclean was their main focus.

We have been struck by Burgess's strategic cunning in creating and maintaining his cover and in exploiting opportunities that presented themselves, or that he engineered, for the single objective of his espionage and for so long. He is one of the most unlikely and productive espionage agents of recent times. His spell working at the BBC and the Foreign Office apparently for MI5, but in reality for the KGB, was the most spectacular of his achievements for the Soviet Union.

He'd shown promise from the beginning as the novice KGB agent at the BBC the first time round. Whether he received help from his friends, or whether it was simply his talent that got him in, is irrelevant. Once inside, he began exploiting the bureaucratic machinery: he was an awkward employee and that led some people to keep him at arm's length while he kept them on the back foot. He was a little bolshie, particularly with the administrators, but he used his position to make connections: we have seen how he followed up the KGB's suggestion about MI6 officer David Footman, who was to be a key player in his later life. But many others – including Roger Fulford – proved useful to him too.

After unofficial introductions arranged by Footman with senior MI6 colleagues, Burgess had proved himself attractive enough to be formally approached by MI6 in autumn 1938, and recruited into the Section D organisation, doing a series of jobs, most of which are still shrouded in mystery. But neither historians nor, we now know, MI5's investigators have ever been able to assemble the fine-grain picture of what he did while working close to the heart of Britain's wartime intelligence establishment. For the two years – 1939 and 1940 – it is anybody's guess what he was up to for much of the time. Even discovering when Burgess stopped working for Section D is difficult, as we have seen. We have argued that the confusion of the early war years is something that Burgess utilised for his own ends: he was able to inveigle himself into a number of secret and semi-secret bodies and committees, doing a little bit here and there, that left only a few traces: his 'Kilroy was here' markers. But in this confusion, which he exploited ruthlessly, he engineered his way into gaining access to top-secret papers – including MI6 files – and highly classified information from insiders, including John Cairncross. It was only in October 1940 that his access to these sources was cut off, as Section D was being wound down and MI6 was beginning to fall out with the Special Operations Executive. All the while he was passing information to Moscow, albeit through what was at times a somewhat flaky connection.

For a significant part of his stay at Broadcasting House, parked there by MI5, he was protected both by MI5 and the BBC Director of Talks, Sir Richard Maconachie.

Burgess was able to spy on his BBC colleagues – if they were one of his targets – but, more importantly, he was also able to inform on MPs, other ministries that he came into contact with through working with John Hilton, as well as any other people he met. He would be able to influence and he would be able to do likewise with any speakers that his production responsibilities put his way – maybe with Sir Richard Maconachie's help. It is conceivable that Burgess's involvement with William Ridsdale in 1943 and the proposal to broadcast talks about foreign affairs was one manifestation of what Anthony Blunt had described to Guy Liddell in 1943 as this 'particularly delicate work'.

To keep MI5 happy, he also delivered valuable information from his agents – Eric Kessler (ORANGE) and Andrew Revai (TAFFY). This work was deemed valuable enough for MI5 to pay him £10 a month to treat them and it meant that he continued to avoid military service. Burgess in the BBC was much more useful to MI5 (and the KGB) than Burgess on the battlefield, after all.

Burgess was headhunted by the Foreign Office in 1944. Foreign Office documents released to us in 2013 gave a very strong hint that William Ridsdale, of the News Department, had approached Burgess, with support from 'Harold Nicolson among others'. He might even have played an active role in guiding this supporters club. Even though Ridsdale later distanced himself from this – indeed, his statement to MI5 in December 1952 is disingenuous on this point (and we think that MI5 knew it to be) – that was most likely because Ridsdale was appalled at the thought that he had introduced a spy into the Foreign Office and undoubtedly had an eye on protecting his personal position. That seems to have been MI5's conclusion, and we do not disagree. Ridsdale and Nicolson, Sir Alexander Cadogan and the other Foreign Office officials who helped recruit Burgess had all, we believe, been duped by 'Brigadier Brilliant'.

At the Foreign Office, Guy Burgess then pulled off another master stroke. As soon as he joined the News Department he told Ridsdale – and here we think that Ridsdale was being entirely candid – that he was carrying out work for MI5 and would need to continue doing so. Ridsdale told him that he had no objections, as long as his spying didn't interfere with his News Department work. Once accepted, it established a pretext for Burgess doing things that might not be explained in terms of his day-to-day workload, and about which Ridsdale may ask, but which Burgess could claim in reply Ridsdale was not cleared to hear.

Burgess's battle with the Foreign Office personnel department over his establishment not only sought to carve out a position for himself in the diplomatic stream, with all its promise of access to valuable policy-making discussions and papers, but it also crystallised his managers (and minister) into becoming his supporters. Meanwhile, it kept the administrators, as in the BBC, on the back foot. It was a war of attrition by memo.

That Burgess's work was good, if not distinguished, shows exactly that he knew how to play the game. Later published reports about his poor performance and behaviour during this phase of his career are not supported by contemporaneous documents in the files. The record that survives instead shows an employee who was not fantastically proficient at doing his job, but who was turning in a good performance and was considered by many to be highly intelligent, although still in need of greater experience before he could be considered for promotion. Later stories about poor performance and his 'disgrace' were exaggerated. Only after his disappearance did countless officials begin raising their doubts about his shortcomings and behaviour. Even if some of those later comments were made with an eye to avoiding any personal culpability, what they also reveal is that no one had had the reason, foresight or presence of mind to raise them before Guy Burgess disappeared.

We believe that this all points to the fact that Burgess, rather than being the disaster waiting to happen that some have argued, instead carefully cultivated and maintained that image and by doing so effectively threw everyone off the track. In short, he fooled the whole lot of them: some of the best brains in the country. That he used his class background to help maintain this mask, this persona, was yet another master stroke. He exploited the 'class blinkers', as he called them, utilised the sexual politics to manage his contacts, collect useful information and keep others away, and all the while he used it to mask what he was really up to.

It was Burgess's involvement with MI5 at this stage that established a justification for Burgess taking documents away with him, and meant also that not too many questions would be asked. In return for the measure of support from MI5, Burgess continued to run his two agents and presumably inform on any of his Foreign Office colleagues that were of particular interest to the security service.

There is also the possibility that Burgess might just have asked William Ridsdale if he could stagger his hours, or perhaps even take work and documents home with him sometimes. The department was one of the few in the Foreign Office then working to a near-24/7 routine. The files are silent on this, but it is conceivable that such arrangements would have been made by word of mouth and as the need arose. After a while, they would have become habit and soon after invisible.

Nevertheless, even if permission had never been sought, Sir Bernard Burrows's reflection about the laxity of security in the Foreign Office is relevant here. Would any doorkeeper who recognised Burgess as a member of staff really dare to ask to look inside his grip bag? But then for some of the time that Burgess was working in the News Department even that was less likely because it was housed inside the Ministry of Information's Senate House premises, not in Whitehall; and even after the Ministry was wound down it moved first to offices in Carlton House Terrace, not the main Foreign Office Building. So occasions would inevitably have arisen, therefore, when officials would have to carry documents between the Foreign Office and the department. It was yet another opportunity to be exploited; and it is likely to be one of the weaknesses that Burgess used to both his and the KGB's advantage.

Burgess's secondment to Hector McNeil's office at the end of 1946 – whether engineered by him or by Ridsdale: 'I was glad to get rid of him' – took him to another level of opportunity and yet another master stroke. Without clearly defined terms, Burgess was able to range relatively freely across a whole host of subjects unhindered by officials. All he had to say if challenged would be 'Hector asked'. It is unlikely that doubters would ring Hector to confirm that he really had asked, and we have seen how Burgess used McNeil's name to get hold of MI5's research on the history of Russian document forgeries in Britain. Burgess never returned the paper and McNeil was baffled when finally asked about it after Burgess's disappearance. Moreover, the minister's office also received highly prized and highly restricted Cabinet minutes and papers, and other secret policy documents.

All the while, Guy Burgess struck people such as Frank Roberts, Ernest Bevin's Private Secretary, as 'wrong-headed' and someone to be avoided. He appeared to others as a scruffy 'dirty don' type who smelled of garlic, alcohol and tobacco and who drank too much. Those who were useful were charmed by his brilliant, sparkling wit and his intellectual prowess, and they dropped their guard. Senior civil servant Sir Dennis Proctor said that he did not spy, but never withheld anything from Burgess because their relationship going back to the Apostles was based on trust. Burgess had no need to subvert him.

All the time this persona diverted attention from Burgess the KGB agent. If this was accidental, it was extremely fortuitous. But if it was partly deliberate, as we think (and suspect MI5 also came to the same conclusion), it was the perfect cover – if you could handle the alcohol. Dick Goldsmith White told the Cadogan Committee that Burgess's lifestyle had caused everyone to dismiss any thought that such a person could be a spy. No one ever entertained any suspicion – or almost no one.

For as long as Burgess continued to do work on the side for MI5, he would be able to rely on the agency's support if it became necessary. In 1948, he was still suggesting potential recruits to Guy Liddell. He would also be able to exploit that support by passing on information to Moscow about what he knew of MI5's activities and concerns.

It was only when Burgess began making mistakes that this carefully crafted house of cards and image began to collapse. We believe the origin lies with his head injury in 1949. It is clear that Burgess really did suffer a major trauma, and it is at this point that his behaviour began to change. His mother had written to him in Washington about how his happy demeanour had disappeared after the 'bad concussion' only to be replaced by 'awful depression'. She had suggested he try Veganin, a painkiller that included codeine, while acknowledging the dangers of mixing drink and painkillers. His KGB controller Yuri Modin remarked about it, his KGB file apparently refers to it, although, significantly, Burgess's Foreign Office file does not. Though neither are Burgess's sickness and annual leave records attached, nor any medical certificates. It is just possible that they have been withheld, but more probably, lost or destroyed – like the personnel file that contained all of the papers relating to his recruitment in 1944.

As a result of the injury, Burgess began taking painkillers, and maybe even cocaine, but certainly codeine, which can be addictive. Mixing drink with pills – and codeine in particular – has unforeseen side effects. In 1946 and 1947, when Burgess was put under considerable pressure by the Russians – Foreign Minister Molotov's unremitting demands, for instance – to deliver papers and insights into Foreign Office thinking on a number of subjects, he was able to cope. But, after his fall, reports about his drinking and unpredictable behaviour began to mount, certainly within his overlapping circles of friends. Peter Pollock told MI5 how, during what was Burgess's last weekend in Britain, he 'had been in an extremely bad physical state, taking drugs continuously and drinking hard'.[23]

Soon after the injury, Burgess had the car accident in Dublin and unwelcome coverage in the evening press. Months later, in Gibraltar and Tangier, he was manifestly uncontrollable and indiscreet. In January 1950, he was strongly suspected of having leaked information about Britain's recognition of the Chinese communists to the 'slippery' American journalist Freddie Kuh, who was believed to have close trading relationships with East European embassies and maybe even intelligence agencies, although nothing was ever proved. That same month Harold Nicolson's unpublished diary recorded two occasions when he experienced a drunken Burgess – on one being given probably the same information that Burgess had leaked to Kuh. Nicolson didn't like the new Burgess and moved to distance himself from his now troublesome friend. They never met again if Nicolson's unpublished diaries are candid.

Then there was the aftermath of the Tangier incident, when Burgess tried to dissemble and influence to get himself out of hot water. He saw that his days at the centre of Foreign Office power – access to documents and conversation

– were beginning to ebb away. His misjudged attempt to influence his friend Guy Liddell – in that remarkable 'Dear Guy … Luv Guy' letter – shows just how desperate he was to remain at the centre of power. That he also secured a meeting with David Footman about the allegations – much against Valentine Vivian's wishes – further points to this desperation. In the end, these two senior intelligence officers, and close friends, were unable, and by this stage probably unwilling, to save him. He had gone beyond the pale. His final conversation with George Middleton to halt being shipped across the Atlantic – 'I am a left-wing socialist' – fell on deaf ears. He was told to be professional and apolitical.

The failure of the KGB at this point was to spot early enough that Burgess had become so unreliable that he should have been retired on the grounds that he was becoming unusable – even if that would have meant having to manage his strong tantrums and protests for months afterwards. But its rapacious quest for information would never allow that; he was expendable just like all the other agents. Only too late did they realise that the Cambridge ring was too closely entwined.

Burgess's stay in Washington wrecked both his espionage career and his Foreign Office career. He no longer had the protection of MI5, and thus little excuse to pursue the fluid lifestyle that he had exploited for years while in London. He was also deprived of his London clubland contacts and gossip. He may have hoped that proving unsuitable for much of the work in the embassy would have given him a little elbow room for espionage activities, or provoke a recall to other duties in London, but he soon discovered that this just cut off his access to documents and conversations that would have been of continuing interest to Moscow. His only high point was his opportunity to spend some time with Anthony Eden. Just briefly he became an agent of influence.

The relatively strict supervision carried out by the embassy team was rather immune to his eccentric charms and wit. And, crucially, this time they did not look the other way. In attempting to stop wrecking his espionage career and get himself sent back home to the centre of power, he wrecked his Foreign Office career too.

The denouement in Washington is the point of collapse. His behaviour, his drinking – probably still influenced by a lethal mix of painkillers and alcohol – led to increasingly erratic behaviour. Kim Philby kept a watchful eye on him, but even he could not control the uncontrollable Burgess. Burgess's speeding offences show how out of control he was. Deprived of the comforting and moderating influences of his many London friends, his actions were reckless. When on holiday in Charleston a few weeks later, and under the calming influence of his mother, there were no reports of bad behaviour.

The Foreign Office was embarrassed that it had been duped by both Burgess and Mclean so completely and for so long. It had been blindsided. That it had never noticed that homosexuality was a 'problem' and in particular at that time a potential security risk in certain parts of the world, was another reason. It was humiliating that security procedures in the foreign service were really not fit for purpose. It was also clearly distressing that key departments didn't appear to talk to one another, irrespective of the daily tea parties that took place. George Carey-Foster never got to see Personnel Department files, and vice versa. So, when diplomats were considered for promotions, for example, no one from the Security Department was on hand to say whether there were any blots on someone's record. That was an embarrassment and until repaired was something to be guarded from hostile nations. But the Foreign Office Security Department itself, along with the Personnel Department – if it had known – was clearly mortified that it had ignored MI5's ultimate warning about Burgess. But, equally, security procedures were lax by today's standards. Procedures might have been in place, but they were frequently not followed. That was one reason why the ring of secrecy was maintained: don't let the Russians know that we are still decoding VENONA material because they will attack and we can't guarantee to keep their agents out.

Moreover, the Foreign Office was red-faced because 'everyone' had known about Guy Burgess's lifestyle and left-wing political views, but no one had thought to do or say anything about it to anyone else. They had all been blinded by him and their own public school values and class judgements. Their attention was diverted into other directions – how Burgess looked and behaved, how clean he was, how drunk, not what documents he might just have slipped under his jacket. In the case of Donald Maclean, his performance – apart from his nervous breakdown in Cairo – was outstanding; he was future 'PUS' material and that kept everyone off the trail. In Burgess's case, it was his very outrageousness that allowed him to hide in the spotlight, as it were, that seems to have been admitted by everyone only after the fact, but by no one before the disappearance. The system where no one blabbed to the 'Head' was both the Foreign Office's strength and its profound weakness. Guy Burgess saw it. He understood it and he exploited it. If, ultimately, that doesn't mark him out as a KGB 'Brigadier Brilliant', we don't know what would.

But there was also the Foreign Office's discomfort about hiding its failings in order to keep the Americans and Britain's other allies sweet and to convince them that it really *had* been on its guard when in fact it hadn't been. The list of documents to which Donald Maclean had possibly gained access was potentially explosive. If that had been shown to the American State Department, the CIA, or US military, relations with Britain would have been seriously ruptured and would have remained so for years. The decision of the British Joint Chiefs of Staff to supply the Americans with their plutonium air-sampling data – one of its key bargaining points in atomic policy matters, and which it readily admitted to Sir William Elliot in Washington would most likely be offered without any reciprocation – was a sign of initial desperation, if not panic in London. Joint atomic weapons testing with the Americans disappeared from the agenda forever. The timing of bringing Britain's testing facilities at Woomera and the Monte Bello Islands into operation was a testament to the impact of Burgess and Maclean's flight.

MI5 was embarrassed because it had known about Burgess's lifestyle 'since about 1939', but had essentially protected him and told no one else about him since what he did for them suited its purposes. The organisation had vetted Burgess three times and each time had found nothing that was exceptional. In 1937, it had vetted him for the BBC; in 1939 for Section D; in January 1950, for the Foreign Office, in the wake of the Tangier Incident. MI5's warning to George Carey-Foster that Burgess was 'undoubtedly unreliable and untrustworthy' was clearly not acted upon. Why is a mystery, but it was probably equally embarrassing to the Foreign Office as it was to MI5 for not insisting that it was an insurmountable impediment. Carey-Foster would later tell a Foreign Office legal adviser, Patrick Dean, 'I have kicked myself for not having made more of it and pressed for surveillance on BURGESS.'[24] MI5 was then no longer retaining Burgess's services, by all accounts, so why its legal adviser, Bernard Hill, fell short of insisting is not known. Maybe Guy Liddell persuaded him. The organisation proved that it could stop recruitment in the case of John Lehmann, whose one key difference with Guy Burgess was that he was not employed, part-time, by MI5, whereas Burgess was. Moreover, MI5 was also uncomfortable because if its registry clerks had checked their files more closely, they would have discovered Derek Blaikie's letter denouncing the turncoat Burgess in 1935, just around the time that the European Exchange programme was due to broadcast, and at least one of his vetting exercises would have thrown it up. The letter had been found within months of Burgess's disappearance and was used in Helenus Milmo's report on his investigation into Kim Philby, so it hadn't been destroyed in the war when MI5's card index was damaged.

MI6 was discomforted partly because the organisation had employed Burgess while he worked in Section D, and through his connections with David Footman. For some time after the defection occasional hints are evident in MI5's files that the organisation was a reluctant supplier of information to the investigation.

The BBC was disconcerted because it had employed a spy and more so if they ever discovered – or if W St John Pym remembered – that the Conservative Central Office had told Pym in 1935 that it had declined to employ Burgess on account of his communist activities at Cambridge.

The political establishment was greatly rattled because many of its members knew Guy Burgess – in some cases extremely well. Revelations emerging would damage careers and would earn public disapproval. Only when some were in their twilight years were they prepared to speak in positive terms about Guy Burgess: Lords Hailsham and Thorneycroft to name but two, whereas one, Lord (Christopher) Mayhew, could only speak ill of him. There is no sign so far of papers that support Mayhew's allegations that Hector McNeil foisted Burgess on his IRD for a few weeks until Mayhew was able to send him back with his tail between his legs. The absence of papers doesn't mean that it didn't happen, but it does raise questions why the placement hasn't been recorded when so many of IRD's files have been released to the archives. Perhaps we still don't know all the elements of the story.

Guy Burgess's friends and acquaintances fell into two distinct groups: those who immediately disowned him (sometimes out of fear for their own futures, or of what might emerge and whether they would be placed under the spotlight, some simply because they were horrified that he had betrayed his country). Others continued to keep in touch after he emerged from the shadows. Harold Nicolson, Peter Pollock, Tom Driberg, and, of course, his mother, fall into this camp. MI5's files reveal just how many letters he sent and received: if the 'safe hand' personal delivery service carried more than a few others, Guy Burgess's post bag was very well used.

Then there were the members of the gay community. They had perhaps most to fear through association with Burgess once details of his homosexuality emerged – they could face public opprobrium or worse, prosecution and vilification, as homosexual acts between men were still a criminal offence – although some still kept in touch with him. The other Cambridge spies were, of course, hoping not to be found out and had an interest in details of the spying and the investigation not leaking out. Anthony Blunt was keen to persuade Burgess to stay in Moscow, as was MI5. It was a rare confluence of interest between the two. One the suspected agent who didn't want him to return in case he shopped him, and the other – the security service – that didn't want him to return in case he shopped them and their political masters.

Each group had reasons for keeping the details of the investigation and those concerning Burgess, Maclean and, later, the other Cambridge spies secret. Each was a story of self-interest. Some were short term and some longer term. Many were intermeshed. Some were likely to prevail upon others. In this sense, there was a hierarchy of reasons and interests behind keeping the story secret for so many years. Moreover, and remarkably, the entire British establishment – all of the groups that we have mentioned above – had a common interest in keeping Donald Maclean and Guy Burgess firmly in Moscow and out of the country. Threats to return were met with obstacles. Instead of gladly allowing them, or Burgess at any rate, to return so that they could be given accommodation in Dartmoor, they planted whole fields of tank traps and barbed wire to keep them out. If any comparison is needed, there is the case of Flying Officer Wraight. He defected to Moscow in 1956 and by 1959 he wanted to redefect. He had no friends among the rich and powerful and, in Wraight's case, the Foreign Office managed his departure from Moscow, allowed him to return home to see his family, then, after Christmas 1959, arrested him, interrogated him for three weeks and ultimately imprisoned him for three years after a court case, thus providing a useful precedent for issuing a warrant to arrest Burgess. Wraight didn't know anyone powerful or pose the potential of public embarrassment.

In the final analysis, the cover up – because that is what there was – was to protect the guilty: to keep the institutional and individual failings from public view, including that of the country's allies. The political establishment, the friends, the intelligence services, the Foreign Office, to a lesser extent the BBC, and other government departments all found common cause in keeping a lid on the story. If there were weaknesses that were particularly embarrassing – we have found some – they point to a different country and a different time. A place where things were done differently, the pace of life was slower, more relaxed, and where personal freedoms were perhaps more highly prized. The system muddled through because enough people wanted it to work, but it was inherently weak and inefficient.

It was no match for someone like Guy Burgess. He was, we once wrote, a man on a mission. At that time, we thought he was a slightly risible character – a drunk and a slob. After having researched his life in much greater detail, however, we think we did him a disservice by thinking of him as such, and now want to revise our assessment.

He was a heavy drinker and a heavy smoker and a man you probably wouldn't invite to dinner – if he turned up at all he'd probably be late and draw insulting pictures of your guests. His triumph was to use his habits, his lifestyle and his contacts as a mask and as an entry point. And once in an institution, he was able to develop and exploit weaknesses further: if administrators needed to be kept at bay, he kept them on the hop. He challenged procedures and wore them down. If he needed to develop excuses for doing things outside normal duty to help him remove documents he would plead MI5; and there were undoubtedly times when he played one patron off against the other. All the while, he was keeping everyone under pressure, deflecting their gaze so that he could get what his friends in Moscow wanted. In this, he really was single-minded. He was also a considerable foreign policy brain, whose thinking on China was arguably years ahead of its time.

Burgess's very behaviour was his cover for his espionage and his sharp mind coupled with his undoubted charm were his weapons of choice. His talent was in understanding that his breeding, his contacts and his privileged background provided the very means by which he could create and exploit spying opportunities. His shield was his lifestyle and the drink. Occasionally he seemed to lose his grip, but even then we are not so sure that he actually lost it until the period after the head injury. All of it masked a sharp mind and it was his acute intellect that engineered the opportunities and kept the shield so highly polished that everyone was blinded whenever it caught the light. That he could hold his liquor was also something that a number of people in Gibraltar and Washington noted.

But the triumph of Guy Burgess was to look at British government, and the society that underlay it, and to work out ways that he could exploit it, in order to undermine it. He insinuated himself into the secret and official worlds and got to its foreign policy and intelligence heart. He penetrated the political establishment and reached close to its core too. And all the while, this slightly unkempt drinker, who had charm and wit, but if he didn't like you, could also be waspish, was calculating what his next move would be.

His legacy for British governments was that the Foreign Office reformed some of its procedures, Whitehall security was reviewed – and again after successive spy cases in the late 1950s and early 1960s. Western intelligence agencies sharpened up their acts and while there were still Russian triumphs and defections, there were a lot of Western successes, too.

For the KGB, there was one major irony in the story of Guy Burgess, the man who outmanoeuvred the British state for the first two-thirds of his adult life but was himself outsmarted in the final decade. So successful was he, so constant was the flow of information to Moscow that his masters there were never completely convinced he was for real. All those documents, the sensational insider briefing notes, they all looked just too good to be true and, as a result, many were never believed.

By the time of his death, there was probably nothing left to show for what he had achieved apart from the documents stored in his KGB file. Guy Burgess may have known everyone, but he had become a man trusted by no one.

BIBLIOGRAPHY

Acton, Harold, *More Memoirs of an Aesthete* (London: Faber & Faber, 2008)

Andrew, Christopher, *The Defence of the Realm: The Authorized History of MI5* (London: Penguin, 2010)

— — and David Dilks, *The Missing Dimension* (London: Macmillan, 1984)

— — and Oleg Gordievsky, *KGB: The Inside Story of its Foreign Operations from Lenin to Gorbachev* (London: Hodder & Stoughton, 1990, 1991)

— — and Vasili Mitrokhin, *The Mitrokhin Archive: The KGB in Europe and the West* (London: Penguin, 1999)

Annan, Noël, *Our Age: Portrait of a Generation* (London: Weidenfeld & Nicolson, 1990)

— —, *Our Age: The Generation That Made Post-War Britain* (London: Fontana, 1991)

Ashton, S. R., G. Bennett, K. Hamilton (eds), *Britain and China 1945–1950: Documents on British Policy Overseas, Series I, Volume VIII: Whitehall Histories* (London: Routledge, 2002)

Ashton-Gwatkin, Frank T., *The British Foreign Office* (New York: Syracuse University Press, 1950)

Ayer, A. J., *Part of My Life* (London: HarperCollins, 1977)

Barden, Ruth, *A History of Lockers Park: Lockers Park School, Hemel Hempstead 1874–1999* (Herefordshire: Sacombe Press, 2000)

Bloch, Michael, *Closet Queens: Some 20th Century British Politicians* (London: Little, Brown, 2015)

— —, *James Lees-Milne: The Life* (London: John Murray, 2010)

Borovik, Genrikh, *The Philby Files: The Secret Life of Master Spy Kim Philby* (London: Little, Brown, 1994)

Bower, Tom, *The Perfect English Spy* (London: Mandarin, 1996)

Boyle, Andrew, *The Climate of Treason* (London: Coronet, 1979, 1980 [rev.])

— —, *Poor Dear Brendan: The Quest for Brendan Bracken* (London: Hutchinson, 1974)

Briggs, Asa, *The History of Broadcasting in the United Kingdom, Volume I: The Birth of Broadcasting 1896–1927* (Oxford: Oxford University Press, 1961)

— —, *The History of Broadcasting in the United Kingdom, Volume II: The Golden Age of Wireless* (Oxford: Oxford University Press, 1995)

— —, *The History of Broadcasting in the United Kingdom, Volume IV: Sound and Vision* (Oxford: Oxford University Press, 1978)

Bristow, Bill, *My Father the Spy: Deceptions of an MI6 Officer* (Ross-on-Wye: WBML ePublishing and Media Company Ltd, 2012)

Brown, Andrew, *J. D. Bernal: The Sage of Science* (Oxford: Oxford University Press, 2005)

Burn, Michael, *The Debatable Land* (London: Hamish Hamilton, 1970)

Burrows, Sir Bernard, *Diplomat in a Changing World* (Durham: The Memoir Club, 2001)

Butler, D. and Butler, G., *Twentieth-Century British Political Facts 1900–2000*, 8th edn (London: Palgrave Macmillan, 2000)

Cairncross, John, *The Enigma Spy: An Autobiography* (London: Century, 1997)

Campbell, Alan, *Colleagues and Friends* (London: Michael Russell, 1988)

Carter, Miranda, *Anthony Blunt: His Lives* (London: Pan, 2001, 2002)

Cecil, Robert, *A Divided Life* (London: Coronet, 1988, 1990)

Churchill, Clarissa and Cate Haste, *Clarissa Eden: A Memoir: From Churchill to Eden* (London: Orion, 2007)

Clark, Jon, Margot Heinemann, David Margolies, Carole Snee (eds), *Culture and Crisis in Britain in the Thirties* (London: Lawrence & Wishart, 1979)

Coats, Peter, *Of Generals and Gardens* (London: Weidenfeld & Nicolson, 1976)

Cockett, Richard, *Twilight of Truth: Chamberlain, Appeasement and the Manipulation of the Press* (London: Weidenfeld & Nicolson, 1989)

— —, *David Astor and the Observer* (London: André Deutsch, 1991)

Collis, Rose, *Coral Browne: 'This Effing Lady'* (London: Oberon Books, 2007)

Cooper, Diana and Viscount John Julius Norwich (ed.), *Darling Monster: The Letters of Lady Diana Cooper to Her Son John Julius Norwich 1939–1952* (London: Chatto & Windus, 2013)

Costello, John and Oleg Tsarev, *Deadly Illusions* (New York: Crown, 1993)

Cruickshank, Charles, *SOE in Scandinavia* (Oxford: Oxford University Press, 1986)

Dallek, Robert, *Flawed Giant: Lyndon Johnson and His Times* (New York: Oxford University Press, 1998)

Damaskin, Igor with Geoffrey Elliott, *Kitty Harris: The Spy with Seventeen Names* (London: St Ermin's Press, 2001)

Deacon, Richard, *The Cambridge Apostles* (London: Robert Royce, 1985)

Driberg, Tom, *Guy Burgess: A Portrait with Background* (London: Weidenfeld & Nicolson, 1956)

— —, *Ruling Passions* (London: Jonathan Cape, 1977)

Durschmied, Erik, *Don't Shoot the Yanqui* (London: Grafton, 1990)

Evans, Harold, *Downing Street Diary: The Macmillan Years* (London: Hodder & Stoughton, 1981)

Faligot, Roger and Remi Kauffer, *Histoire mondiale du renseignement, Tome I: 1870–1939* (Paris: Editions Robert Laffont, 1993)

Faulks, Sebastian, *The Fatal Englishman: Three Short Lives* (London: Vintage, 1997)

Fraser, Antonia, *My History* (London: Weidenfeld & Nicolson, 2015)

Fursenko, Aleksandr and Timothy Naftali, *Khrushchev's Cold War: The Inside Story of an American Adversary* (New York: W. W. Norton & Company, 2010)

Gannon, Franklin Reid, *The British Press and Germany: 1936–1939* (Oxford: Oxford University Press, 1971)

Garnett, David and Andrew Roberts (notes by), *The Secret History of PWE: The Political Warfare Executive 1939–1945* (London: St Ermine's Press, 2002)

Gladwyn, Lord, *The Memoirs of Lord Gladwyn* (London: Weidenfeld & Nicolson, 1972)

Goodman, Michael S., *The Official History of the Joint Intelligence Committee* (London: Routledge, 2014)

Gorodetsky, Gabriel (ed.) and Ivan Maisky, *The Maisky Diaries: Red Ambassador to the Court of St James's, 1932–1943* (London: Yale University Press, 2015)

Grant Duff, Sheila, *The Parting of Ways: A Personal Account of the Thirties* (London: Peter Owen, 1982)

Greenhill, Denis, *More By Accident*, 2nd edn (York: Wilton 65, 1993)

Harrod, Roy, *The Life of John Maynard Keynes* (London: Norton, 1982)

Haslam, Jonathan, *Russia's Cold War: From the October Revolution to the Fall of the Wall* (New Haven: Yale University Press, 2011)

— —, *Near and Distant Neighbours: A New History of Soviet Intelligence* (Oxford: Oxford University Press, 2015)

Hastings, Selina, *Rosamond Lehmann: A Life* (London: Vintage Digital, 2012)

Hayes, John Earl and Harvey Klehr, *Venona: Decoding Soviet Espionage in America* (Yale: Yale University Press, 1999)

Herrera, Yoshiko M., *Imagined Economies: The Sources of Russian Regionalism,* (Cambridge: Cambridge University Press, 2004)

Higgins, Charlotte, *This New Noise: The Extraordinary Birth and Troubled Life of the BBC* (London: Guardian Faber Publishing, 2015)

Hobsbawm, Eric, *Interesting Times: A Twentieth-Century Life* (London: Allen Lane, 2002)

Hodgkin, Alan, *Chance and Design: Reminiscences of Science in Peace and War* (Cambridge: Cambridge University Press, 1992)

Holloway, Adrian, *From Dartmouth to War: A Midshipman in the Mediterranean 1940–1941* (Stroud: The History Press, 2012)

Holzman, Michael, *Guy Burgess: Revolutionary in an Old School Tie*, 2nd edn (CreateSpace Independent Publishing Platform, 2012)

Hopkins, James K., *Into the Heart of the Fire: The British in the Spanish Civil War* (Palo Alto: Stanford University Press, 2000)

Hughes, Richard, *Foreign Devil: Thirty Years of Reporting in the Far East* (London: André Deutsch, 1972)

Ignatieff, Michael, *Isaiah Berlin: A Life*, Kindle edn (London: Vintage, 2011)

Jeffery, Keith, *MI6: The History of the Secret Intelligence Service 1909–1949* (London: Bloomsbury, 2011)

Johnson, Gaynor, *The Foreign Office and British Diplomacy in the Twentieth Century* (London: Routledge, 2009)

Kerr, Sheila, *An Assessment of a Soviet Agent: Donald Maclean, 1940–1951*, unpublished PhD thesis (London: LSE, 1996)

Knightley, Phillip, *Philby: KGB Masterspy* (London: André Deutsch, 1988)

Leab, Daniel J., *Orwell Subverted: The CIA and the Filming of Animal Farm* (University Park: Pennsylvania State University Press, 2007)

Lees-Milne, James, *Harold Nicolson: A Biography, Vol. II: 1930–1968* (London: Chatto & Windus, 1981)

—— and Michael Bloch (ed.), *Diaries 1942–1970* (London: John Murray, 2007)

Lownie, Andrew, *Stalin's Englishman: The Lives of Guy Burgess* (London: Hodder & Stoughton, 2015)

Luke, Michael, *David Tennant and the Gargoyle Years* (London: Weidenfeld & Nicolson, 1991)

Lysaght, Charles Edward, *Brendan Bracken* (London: Allen Lane, 1979)

McDougall, Ian, *Foreign Correspondent* (London: Frederick Muller, 1980)

MacKenzie, William, *The Secret History of SOE: Special Operations Executive 1940–1945* (London: St Ermin's Press, 2000)

McLaine, Ian, *Ministry of Morale* (London: George Allen and Unwin, 1979)

Maclean, Alan, *No, I Tell a Lie, It Was the Tuesday* (London: Kyle Cathie Limited, 1997)

McNeish, James, *The Sixth Man: The Extraordinary Life of Paddy Costello* (London: Quartet Books, 2008)

Manser, José, *Mary Fedden and Julian Trevelyan: Life and Art by the River Thames* (London: Unicorn Press, 2012)

Mayhew, Christopher, *A War of Words: A Cold War Witness* (London: I. B. Tauris, 1998)

Miller, John, *All Them Cornfields and Ballet in the Evening* (London: Hodgson Press, 2010)

Milne, Tim, *Kim Philby: The Unknown Story of the KGB's Master Spy* (London: Biteback, 2014)

Modin, Yuri, *My Five Cambridge Friends* (London: Headline, 1994)

Morris, Jan, *Pleasures of a Tangled Life* (London: Barrie & Jenkins, 1989)

Muggeridge, Malcolm, *Chronicles of Wasted Time, Volume II: The Infernal Grove* (London: Fontana, 1981)

Murphy, David E., *What Stalin Knew: The Enigma of Barbarossa* (New Haven: Yale University Press, 2005)

Nagle, Thomas Wheeler, *A Study of British Public Opinion and the European Appeasement Policy: 1933–39* (Wiesbaden, Germany: Librairie Chmielorz, 1957)

Nicolson, Harold, *Why Britain is at War* (London: Penguin, 1939)

— —, *Diaries and Letters, Vol I: 1930–1939* (London: Collins, 1966)

— —, *Diaries and Letters, Vol II: 1939–1945* (London: Collins, 1967)

— —, *Diaries and Letters, Vol III: 1945–1962* (London: Collins, 1968)

Nicolson, Nigel, *Portrait of a Marriage* (London: Weidenfeld & Nicolson, 1973)

Newton, Verne, *The Butcher's Embrace* (London: Little, Brown, 1991)

Nixon, Edna, *John Hilton: The Story of His Life* (London: George Allen & Unwin, 1946)

Omand, Sir David, *Securing the State* (London: C. Hurst & Co., 2012)

Page, Bruce, David Leitch and Phillip Knightley, *Philby: The Spy Who Betrayed a Generation* (London: Sphere, 1969)

Pagnamenta, Peter, *The Hidden Hall: Portrait of a Cambridge College* (Cambridge: Third Millenium, 2004)

Panken, Shirley, *Virginia Woolf and the Lust of Creation: A Psychoanalytic Exploration* (New York: SUNY Press, 1987)

Penrose, Barry and Roger Freeman, *Conspiracy of Silence* (London: Grafton, 1986)

Philby, Kim, *My Silent War* (London: Granada, 1983; Arrow Books, 2003)

Philby, Rufina, *The Private Life of Kim Philby* (London: St Ermin's Press, 1999)

Pincher, Chapman, *Treachery: Betrayals, Blunders and Cover-Ups: Six Decades of Espionage* (New York: Random House, 2009)

Plokhy, S. M., *Yalta: The Price of Peace* (New York: Penguin, 2011)

Purdy, Anthony and Douglas Sutherland, *Burgess and Maclean* (London: Secker and Warburg, 1963

Purvis, Stewart and Jeff Hulbert, *When Reporters Cross the Line* (London: Biteback, 2013)

Redgrave, Michael, *In My Mind's Eye* (London: Weidenfeld & Nicolson, 1983)

Rees, Goronwy, *A Chapter of Accidents* (London: Chatto & Windus, 1972)

Rees, Jenny, *Looking for Mr Nobody: The Secret Life of Goronwy Rees* (London: Weidenfeld & Nicolson, 1994; Phoenix, 1997)

Roberts, Andrew, *The Holy Fox: The Life of Lord Halifax* (London: Phoenix, 1991, 1997)

Rothschild, Lord (Victor), *Meditations of a Broomstick* (London: Collins, 1977)

Rowse, A. L., *All Souls in My Time* (London: Gerald Duckworth, 1993)

Sackville-West, Vita, Harold Nicolson, Nigel Nicolson (ed.), *Vita and Harold: The Letters of Vita Sackville-West and Harold Nicolson, 1910-62*, re-issue edn (London: Weidenfeld & Nicolson, 2007)

Saville, John, *The Politics of Continuity* (London: Verso, 1993)

Seaman, Donald and John Mather, *The Great Spy Scandal: Inside Story of Burgess and Maclean* (London: Daily Express Publications, 1955)

Seaman, Mark, *Special Operations Executive: A New Instrument of War* (London: Routledge, 2005)

Seaton, Jean, *Pinkoes and Traitors* (Oxford: Oxford University Press, 2014)

Sewell, Brian, *The Outsider: Always Almost: Never Quite* (London: Quartet, 2011)

Skidelsky, Robert, *John Maynard Keynes: A Biography, Vol I: Hopes Betrayed, 1883–1920* (London: Macmillan, 1983; New York: Viking, 1986)

Sloan, Pat (ed.), *John Cornford: A Memoir* (London: Jonathan Cape, 1938)

Smith, Bradley F., *Sharing Secrets with Stalin: How the Allies Traded Intelligence* (Lawrence: University Press of Kansas, 1996)

Smith, James, *British Writers and MI5 Surveillance: 1930–1960* (Cambridge: Cambridge University Press, 2013)

Smith, Michael, *Foley: The Spy Who Saved 10,000 Jews* (London: Coronet, 1999)

— —, *The Secret Agent's Bedside Reader: A Compendium of Spy Writing* (London: Biteback, 2014)

Smolka, H. P., *Forty Thousand Against the Arctic: Russia's Polar Empire* (London: Hutchinson, 1937)

Spender, Stephen and John Goldsmith (ed.), *Journals 1939–1983* (London: Faber and Faber, 1985)

Stourton, Edward and John Lonsdale (eds), *Trinity: A Portrait* (London: Third Millennium Publishing, 2011)

Straight, Michael, *After Long Silence* (London: Collins, 1983)

Sweet, Matthew, *The West End Front: The Wartime Secrets of London's Grand Hotels* (London: Faber & Faber 2011)

Taylor, Philip, *British Propaganda in the 20th Century* (Edinburgh: Edinburgh University Press, 1999)

Thorpe, D. R., *Eden: The Life and Times of Anthony Eden, First Earl of Avon 1897–1977*, Kindle edn (Vintage Digital, 2011)

Urquhart, Brian, *A Life in Peace and War* (London: Weidenfeld & Nicolson, 1987)

Volodarsky, Boris, *Stalin's Agent: The Life and Death of Alexander Orlov*, Kindle edn (Oxford: Oxford University Press, 2015)

Weidenfeld, George, *Remembering My Good Friends: An Autobiography* (London: HarperCollins, 1995)

West, Nigel and Oleg Tsarev, *The Crown Jewels* (London: HarperCollins, 1999)

West, Nigel, *Venona: The Greatest Secret of the Cold War* (London: HarperCollins, 2000)

— — (ed.), *Guy Liddell Diaries, Volume II: 1942–1945* (London: Routledge, 2005)

— — (ed.), *Guy Liddell Diaries, Volume I: 1939–1942* (London: Taylor and Francis, 2007)

White, Terence De Vere, *A Fretful Midge* (London: Routledge and Kegan Paul, 1957)

Wright, Peter and Paul Greengrass, *Spycatcher* (Richmond, Victoria: Heinemann Australia, 1987)

ACKNOWLEDGEMENTS

Much of the content of this book is based on files which were only made public at the end of October 2015 and our Editor at Biteback, Victoria Godden, has had the unenviable task of getting us to the printers within six weeks. We are deeply grateful to her.

Michael Smith, Editor-at-Large at Biteback Publishing, provided us with documents from the KGB archive which help to fill an important gap in the literature on the Cambridge spies: what exactly did Burgess report back to the KGB?

Cherry Hughes, who worked on the original *Sunday Times* Insight team investigation into the Cambridge spies, has shown us her notes and been a constant adviser. Phillip Knightley, who led that *Sunday Times* team, has allowed us to publish his internal memos from that investigation. Michael Holzman, author of *Guy Burgess: Revolutionary in an Old School Tie*, has been a great help to us, and Michele Emrick and Katherine Ronan kindly gave us access to the papers of the man they knew as 'Uncle Jack', John Hunter. We are also grateful for the cooperation of Adrian Whitfield and Wendy Whitfield Guiffre.

Melissa Ellis of archivesearch.ca was our genealogical guide from Montreal to Moscow. James Dorrian and Nick Golding, the chief guardians of the late Michael Burn's archive, released to us his notes on his relationship with Burgess. FBI archivists found the audio recording of Burgess talking about Winston Churchill, and Greg Hobbs of CBC TV Toronto helped bring to light the discovery by his colleague, Arthur Schwartzel, of the only TV interview Burgess ever gave.

Our thanks also go to the staff at the Foreign Office Knowledge Management Centre, the National Archives at Kew in London, the BBC Written Archive Centre at Caversham, the British Library Newsroom, the Keep at Brighton, which houses the special collections of the University of Sussex, and the archivists at Churchill, King's, Trinity Hall and Trinity Colleges in Cambridge, Balliol and Christ Church Colleges in Oxford, the Bodleian Library, Princeton University, the University of Liverpool and City University London's Library. We are also grateful to the Countess of Avon and the Eden Papers and the Chamberlain Papers at the University of Birmingham.

Special thanks to Angela Frier who read our first draft and especially to Dominic Williams and Simon Clackson who helped us through the stressful but fascinating task of converting thousands of documents into what is hopefully a readable, enjoyable and logical book.

Finally, our publisher at Biteback, Olivia Beattie, made the toughest call of all and got it right: 'Let's wait for the files to be released.'

ENDNOTES

CHAPTER 1

1. http://www.oocities.org/layedwyer/guy.htm (accessed 20 December 2015)
2. E. H. Bensley, 'Robertson, William (1784–1844)', *Dictionary of Canadian Biography*, Vol. 7, University of Toronto/Université Laval, 2003 http://www.biographi.ca/en/bio/robertson_william_1784_1844_7E.html
3. http://archive.spectator.co.uk/article/10th-february-1866/3/alittle-war-has-broken---out-at---aden-the-british
4. *Montreal Gazette*, 20 January 1880, p. 4; Canadian genealogical research by Melissa Ellis of archivesearch@gmail.com
5. http://www.lockerspark.herts.sch.uk/about-us/history-of-lockers-park/ (accessed 20 December 2015)
6. Ruth Barden, *A History of Lockers Park: Lockers Park School, Hemel Hempstead 1874–1999* (Herefordshire: Sacombe Press, 2000), p. 126
7. Ibid., p. 112
8. Peter Coats, *Of Generals and Gardens* (London: Weidenfeld & Nicolson, 1976), p. 14
9. Andrew Boyle, *The Climate of Treason* (London: Coronet, 1980), p. 83
10. Michael Holzman, *Guy Burgess: Revolutionary in an Old School Tie*, 2nd edn (CreateSpace Independent Publishing Platform, 2012), p. 28
11. Authors' interview with Mrs Sheila Stone of West Meon, whose mother worked for the Burgess family
12. Nigel Burgess interviewed on BBC Radio 4, *Rebels*, 5 October 1984
13. Death certificate for Malcolm Kingsford De Moncy Burgess, 19 September 1924
14. Constance Burgess interviewed on BBC Radio 4, *Rebels*, 5 October 1984
15. Holzman, op. cit., p. 30
16. Adrian Holloway, *From Dartmouth to War: A Midshipman in the Mediterranean 1940–1941* (Stroud: The History Press, 2012), Chapter 1
17. Tom Driberg, *Guy Burgess: A Portrait with Background* (London: Weidenfeld & Nicolson, 1956), p. 13
18. Ibid., p. 10
19. 'Guy Was No Thief', *Daily Express*, 26 October 1955, p. 1
20. Donald Seaman and John Mather, *The Great Spy Scandal: Inside Story of Burgess and Maclean* (London: Daily Express Publications, 1955), p. 23
21. Sir Bernard Burrows, *Diplomat in a Changing World* (Durham: The Memoir Club, 2001), p. 10
22. Driberg, *Guy Burgess*, p. 14
23. Ibid., p. 15
24. Robert Birley quoted in Boyle, *The Climate of Treason*, p. 86

25.   Michael Berry quoted in Jenny Rees, *Looking for Mr Nobody: The Secret Life of Goronwy Rees* (London: Phoenix, 1997), p. 185

26.   A. J. Ayer, *Part of My Life* (London: HarperCollins, 1977), p. 47

27.   Letter from E. James to Andrew Boyle, 13 May 1977, Boyle Papers, University of Cambridge, Add 9429/1G/110 (ii)

28.   Michael Bloch, *James Lees-Milne: The Life* (London: John Murray, 2010), p. 20

29.   A. J. Ayer, op. cit., p. 59

30.   Board of Trade passenger list for *Patria* voyage from Southampton, 5 April 1929

31.   UK Incoming Passenger Lists 1878–1960, Arrival 17 September 1930

32.   Noël Annan, *Our Age: Portrait of a Generation* (London: Weidenfeld & Nicolson, 1990), p. 140

CHAPTER 2

1.   http://www.educationengland.org.uk/documents/hadow1926/hadow1926.html (accessed 20 December 2015)

2.   Constance Burgess interviewed on BBC Radio 4, *Rebels*, 5 October 1984

3.   Letter from Guy Burgess to George Rylands, August 1934, King's College Archive Centre, Cambridge, GHWR/3/37

4.   Papers of Rosamond Lehmann, Archive Centre, King's College, Cambridge, RNL/1/1/1/7

5.   Edward Stourton and John Lonsdale (eds), *Trinity: A Portrait* (London: Third Millennium Publishing, 2011), inside cover note

6.   Driberg, *Guy Burgess*, p. 15

7.   *Trinity Magazine*, Vols 10–11: 1928–33, Wren Library, Trinity College, Cambridge

8.   Driberg, *Guy Burgess*, p. 17

9.   Ibid.

10.   Holzman, op. cit., p. 35

11.   Michael Redgrave, *In My Mind's Eye* (London: Weidenfeld & Nicolson, 1983), p. 76

12.   https://www.adctheatre.com/about-us/history.aspx (accessed 20 December 2015)

13.   Miranda Carter, *Anthony Blunt: His Lives* (London: Pan, 2001), p. 79

14.   Letter from Dadie Rylands to Roy Harrod, January 1971, British Library Western Manuscripts Add MS 71181

15.   Letter from Dadie Rylands to Roy Harrod, 24 August 1960, British Library Western Manuscripts Add MS 71181

16.   Richard Deacon, *The Cambridge Apostles* (London: Robert Royce, 1985), p. 55

17.   http://www.theguardian.com/science/2015/may/02/turing-niece-demands-pardons-for-gay-men-outdated-laws (accessed 20 December 2015)

18.   Noël Annan, *Our Age: The Generation That Made Post-war Britain* (London, Fontana, 1991), p. 134

19.   Boyle, *The Climate of Treason*, p. 87

20.   Michael Burn, 'Guy Burgess: The Spy Who Loved Me and the Traitor I Almost Unmasked', *The Times*, 9 May 2003

21.   TNA KV2/4114 serial 673a

22.   Goronwy Rees, *A Chapter of Accidents* (London: Chatto & Windus, 1972), p. 114

23.   Noël Annan, *Our Age: The Generation That Made Post-war Britain*, p. 305

24.   Holzman, op. cit., p. 33

25.   Driberg, *Guy Burgess*, p. 17

26.   http://www.bbc.co.uk/programmes/b04xp4wq (accessed 20 December 2015)

27.   http://www.dmm.org.uk/news19/9300531j.htm (accessed 20 December 2015)

28. Driberg, *Guy Burgess*, p. 17
29. Phillip Knightley, *Philby: KGB Masterspy* (London: André Deutsch, 1988), p. 32
30. Andrew Brown, *J. D. Bernal: The Sage of Science* (Oxford, Oxford University Press, 2005), p. 109
31. TNA KV2/4102 serial 136z
32. Edward Stourton and John Lonsdale (eds), op. cit., p. 105
33. Driberg, *Guy Burgess*, p. 19
34. James Klugmann, 'Introduction', in Jon Clark, Margot Heinemann, David Margolies, Carole Snee (eds), *Culture and Crisis in Britain in the Thirties* (London: Lawrence & Wishart, 1979), p. 29
35. James McNeish, *The Sixth Man: The Extraordinary Life of Paddy Costello* (London: Quartet Books, 2008), p. 34
36. The National Archives [hereafter TNA] KV2/1996 serial 4a
37. TNA KV2/1996 serial 5a
38. 'The Inter-War Years', https://www.mi5.gov.uk/home/about-us/who-we-are/mi5-history/mi5-between-the-wars/the-inter-war-years.html (accessed 2 November 2015)
39. 'Empire and Anti-War by J. Cornford', Trinity magazine, May 1934
40. http://www.theguardian.com/politics/2011/oct/05/james-cornford-obituary (accessed 20 December 2015)
41. 'Cambridge Traveller', *The Times*, 25 May 1970
42. Deacon, op. cit., pp vii, 1–3
43. http://www.oxforddnb.com/view/article/30829 (accessed 20 December 2015)
44. From *The Strings are False* by Louis MacNeice, quoted by Richard Deacon, op. cit., p. 106
45. Deacon, op. cit., p. 106
46. Anthony Blunt Memoir, British Library, Add MS 88901 folio 13
47. 'Guy Burgess etc. some rather random notes', Private notes of Micky Burn, kindly made available by his literary estate
48. Quoted in Carter, op. cit., p. 105
49. John Cairncross, *The Enigma Spy: An Autobiography* (London: Century, 1997), p. 58
50. http://www.theguardian.com/books/2015/may/16/double-lives-a-history-of-sex-and-secrecy-at-westminster (accessed 20 December 2015)
51. Deacon, op. cit., p. 55
52. Quoted in Deacon, op. cit., p. 83
53. Roy Harrod, *The Life of John Maynard Keynes* (London: Norton, 1982), pp 72–3
54. Letter from George Barnes to Mr Roberts, 17 July 1930, Cambridge University Library, UA Pr A.B.194
55. Letters from Anne Barnes to George Rylands, Undated and 'Tuesday 1933', Papers of George Humphrey Wolferstan Rylands, 3/23/1, King's College Archive Centre, Cambridge University
56. Ibid., 9 July 1933
57. Ibid., 20 July 1933
58. Ibid., 'Tuesday 1933'
59. Ibid., 10 July 1933
60. Driberg, *Guy Burgess*, p. 16
61. Goronwy Rees, op. cit., p. 115
62. Carter, op. cit., p. 102
63. Margot Heinemann quoted in Holzman, op. cit., p. 46
64. Pat Sloan (ed.), *John Cornford: A Memoir* (London: Jonathan Cape, 1938), pp 99–100

65. Driberg, *Guy Burgess*, p. 18
66. Barry Penrose and Roger Freeman, *Conspiracy of Silence* (London: Grafton, 1986), p. 108
67. Robert Skidelsky, *John Maynard Keynes: A Biography, Vol I: Hopes Betrayed, 1883–1920* (London: Macmillan, 1983; New York: Viking, 1986), p. 528
68. http://www.lltjournal.ca/index.php/llt/article/viewFile/4818/5691 (accessed 20 December 2015)
69. James K. Hopkins, *Into the Heart of the Fire: The British in the Spanish Civil War* (Palo Alto: Stanford University Press, 2000), p. 29
70. Alan Hodgkin, *Chance and Design: Reminiscences of Science in Peace and War* (Cambridge: Cambridge University Press, 1992), p. 86
71. Driberg, *Guy Burgess*, p. 20
72. Jenny Rees, op. cit., p. 47
73. TNA KV2/4139 serial 1579b
74. Jenny Rees, op. cit., p. 71
75. Holzman, op. cit., p. 48
76. *London Gazette*, 19 December 1933, p. 8267
77. TNA KV2/4101 serial 1a
78. Driberg, *Guy Burgess*, p. 29
79. http://www.lrb.co.uk/v09/n12/vg-kiernan/vg-kiernan-on-treason, 25 June 1987 (accessed 20 December 2015)
80. Letter from Miriam Lane (née Rothschild) to Andrew Boyle, 15 September 1977, Boyle Papers, University of Cambridge, Add 9429/1G/152 (i) verso
81. TNA KV3/442 Minute Book of Cambridge University Labour Club/Socialist Society
82. *The Times*, 21 November 1981
83. Anthony Blunt, 'From Bloomsbury to Marxism', *Studio International*, 1973, p. 167
84. http://archive.spectator.co.uk/article/23rd-march-1934/34/the-seventeenth-century-synthesis (accessed 20 December 2015)
85. Christopher Andrew and Vasili Mitrokhin, *The Mitrokhin Archive: The KGB in Europe and the West* (London: Penguin, 1999), p. 75
86. Ibid.
87. Christopher Andrew and Oleg Gordievsky, *KGB: The Inside Story of its Foreign Operations from Lenin to Gorbachchev* (London: Hodder & Stoughton, 1991), p. 216
88. Knightley, *Philby: KGB Masterspy*, p. 36
89. TNA KV3/442 Minute Book of Cambridge University Labour Club/Socialist Society
90. Boris Volodarsky, *Stalin's Agent: The Life and Death of Alexander Orlov* (Oxford: Oxford University Press, 2015), Kindle loc. 2866
91. Ibid., Kindle loc. 2852
92. Nigel West and Oleg Tsarev, *The Crown Jewels* (London: HarperCollins, 1999), pp 132–3
93. Peter Pagnamenta, *The Hidden Hall: Portrait of a Cambridge College* (Cambridge: Third Millennium, 2004), p. 191
94. See Stewart Purvis and Jeff Hulbert, *When Reporters Cross the Line* (London: Biteback, 2013), Chapter 3
95. Ibid.
96. Ibid., p. 188
97. Robert Cecil, *A Divided Life* (London: Coronet, 1990), pp 170–72
98. John Costello and Oleg Tsarev, *Deadly Illusions* (New York: Crown, 1993), p. 456; S, or Synok, was another codename for Philby
99. Ibid., pp 226, 228–9

100. Rufina Philby, *The Private Life of Kim Philby* (London: St Ermin's Press, 1999), p. 230
101. Peter Pagnamenta, op. cit., p. 190
102. Ibid., p. 192
103. Andrew and Gordievsky, op. cit., p. 226
104. Eric Hobsbawm, *Interesting Times: A Twentieth-Century Life* (London: Allen Lane, 2002), p. 101
105. Goronwy Rees, op. cit., p. 115
106. TNA KV2/4117 serial 844
107. Miriam Lane (née Rothschild) to Boyle, 17 August 1977, Boyle Papers, University of Cambridge, Add 9429/1G/152 (ii)
108. The Papers of Julian Howard Bell, JHB/2/38A, Archive Centre, King's College, Cambridge
109. Costello and Tsarev, op. cit., p. 229
110. http://www.grahamstevenson.me.uk/index.php?option=com_content&view=articl e&id=250:david-guest&catid=7:g&Itemid=108 (accessed 20 December 2015)
111. Sloan (ed.), op. cit., pp 181–2
112. TNA KV2/1996 serial 23
113. 'Deaths in the Alps' and 'The Alpine Accident', *The Times*, 19 August 1933, p. 8; 21 August 1933, p. 10

CHAPTER 3

1. BBC Written Archives Centre [hereafter WAC] L1/68/1, Graves Controller (Programmes) to Controller (Administration), 5 December 1935
2. Ibid., Memorandum, Establishment Officer, 5 December 1935
3. Ibid., Director of Staff Administration (W. St John Pym) to Burgess, 28 July 1936
4. Elizabeth Bowes-Lyon was married to the Duke of York who, after the 1936 Abdication of Edward VIII, became King George VI
5. Alexander, Lord Dunglass, was to become Prime Minister Neville Chamberlain's Parliamentary Private Secretary and in the three decades after the end of the Second World War, as the Earl of Home, would hold a succession of government posts. This included Secretary of State for Commonwealth Relations, Lord President of the Council and Foreign Secretary under Anthony Eden and Harold Macmillan and (as Lord Home of the Hirsel) Prime Minister (1963–64) and Foreign Secretary under Edward Heath
6. In 1930, there were fewer than two million telephones in the country, including commercial, private and public call boxes; by 1940, the figure had increased to just fewer than 3.4 million. D. Butler and G. Butler, *Twentieth-Century British Political Facts 1900–2000*, 8th edn (London: Palgrave Macmillan, 2000), p. 375
7. Kevin Theakston, 'Proctor, Sir (Philip) Dennis (1905–1983)', *Oxford Dictionary of National Biography* (Oxford: Oxford University Press, 2004); online edition, May 2009 http://www.oxforddnb.com/view/article/60779 (accessed 1 June 2015); BBC WAC L1/68/1, Burgess to (W. St John) Pym. Like so many of Burgess's handwritten letters, this is undated
8. BBC WAC L1/68/1, Burnaby to Pym, 10 August 1936
9. BBC WAC L1/68/1, Proctor to Pym, 18 August 1936
10. BBC WAC L1/68/1, Published works are not specific as to the date; Driberg, *Guy Burgess*, p. 33; Barry Penrose and Roger Freeman, *Conspiracy of Silence* (London: Grafton, 1986), p. 207
11. BBC WAC L1/68/1, Special Report (signed Chief Instructor and Director of Administration), 21 December 1936

12. BBC WAC R51/150, European Exchange, 1935–37
13. Samuel Vyvyan Trerice Adams MP
14. That was when he was aged between twelve and fourteen years, and was his stint at Dartmouth College!
15. BBC WAC R51/150, European Exchange, 1935–37
16. A former Private Secretary to Prime Minister Stanley Baldwin and head of Conservative Party publicity from 1929 to 1939
17. BBC WAC R51/150 European Exchange, 1935–37
18. See Jean Seaton, *Pinkoes and Traitors* (Oxford: Oxford University Press, 2014), Chapter 12
19. BBC WAC R51/150, European Exchange, 1935–37, radio listing issued by the BBC
20. TNA KV2/4106 Letter from Derek Blaikie to Ralph Fox; TNA KV2/4016 serial 299, note for file
21. BBC WAC R51/150 European Exchange, 1935–37, Mary Adams to Director of Talks, Assistant Controller (Programmes) and Sir Stephen Tallents (Controller of Public Relations), 22 December 1935
22. BBC WAC R51/150 European Exchange, 1935–37, Mary Adams to Mr Spicer, 22 December 1935
23. 'Cancelled BBC Debate', *Manchester Guardian*, 28 December 1935
24. BBC WAC R51/150 European Exchange, 1935–37, Note by A. S. Martin, 22 December 1935
25. BBC WAC Talks: Goronwy Rees file 1, Mary Adams to Goronwy Rees, 19 November 1935. The programme, a scripted discussion between Pierre Millet and Geronwy [*sic*] Rees was aired in the BBC Regional programme on 7 December 1935
26. Letter from J. D. F. Green to Anthony Barnes, 21 July 1989, Barnes Papers, Kings College, Cambridge, GRB 4/2/1
27. By the time that Burgess took up his post, Adams had moved over to the Alexandra Palace television studios
28. Costello and Tsarev, op. cit., p. 232
29. The drug therapies available were Salvarsan, which was very tricky to administer, Neosalvarsan, which had potentially debilitating side effects, or Mapharsen, 'L Stamm, L. V. Antibiotic Resistance in Treponema pallidum subsp. pallidum, the Syphilis Agent', in M. Embers (ed.), *The Pathogenic Spirochetes: Strategies for Evasion of Host Immunity and Persistence* (New York: Springer, 2012). We are grateful to Dr Bashir Ahmed of the Department of Physiology, Anatomy and Genetics, Oxford University, for providing references
30. BBC WAC Left Staff file Burgess L1/68/1, D. H. Clarke to Burgess, 12 July 1937
31. TNA KV2/4101 [serial number unknown, but the unnumbered and unattached document is filed between serials 1b and 2a]
32. *Radio Times*, April–June 1937
33. BBC WAC RCont1 Guy Burgess source file. The programme was broadcast on the BBC's regional network, going on air at 12.30 p.m.
34. TNA KV2/2587 folio 33z, Burgess to Isherwood [undated], ('found at Courtauld Institute of Art, November 1951')
35. BBC WAC Left Staff file Burgess L1/68/1, note by S. D. Spicer, 24 March 1937
36. Ibid., 22 April 1937
37. British Library, Western Manuscripts, Add MS 71192; Letter from G. B. to Roy Harrod; handwritten on headed BBC notepaper (header crossed out), '9 Feb 1937' Burgess to Roy Harrod, Christ Church, Oxford
38. BBC WAC Left Staff file Burgess L1/68/1 note by Sir Richard Maconachie on

Burgess's annual staff assessment, 12 January 1938; Director of Staff Administration to Burgess, 1 April 1938

39. Genrikh Borovik, *The Philby Files: The Secret Life of Master Spy Kim Philby* (London: Little, Brown, 1994), pp 71–2

40. Burgess was sick in 1937 on the following days: three days in January, seven days in September, and one day in October. BBC WAC L1/68/1

41. The programme was broadcast on 2 August 1937

42. BBC WAC RCont 1 Roger Fulford 1937–62, file 1

43. BBC WAC RCont 1 David Footman, file 1 1937–62. Burgess to Christy & Moore, 25 May 1937

44. Ibid., Christy & Moore to Burgess, 31 May 1937

45. Ibid., Maconachie to Burgess, 5 August 1937

46. Costello and Tsarev, op. cit., p. 232

47. Ibid., p. 233

48. Ibid.

49. Igor Damaskin with Geoffrey Elliott, *Kitty Harris: The Spy with Seventeen Names* (London: St Ermin's Press, 2001), p. 151; Costello and Tsarev, op. cit., pp 232–3

50. KV2/4106 serial 317b, 20 May 1938

51. Ibid., 16 June 1938

52. Yuri Modin, *My Five Cambridge Friends* (London: Headline, 1994), p. 78

53. Costello and Tsarev, op. cit., p. 237

54. Ibid., p. 238

55. Ibid., p. 239

56. John Green interviewed on BBC Radio 4, *Rebels*, 5 October 1984

57. Goronwy Rees, op. cit., pp 127–8

58. http://genome.ch.bbc.co.uk/search/0/20?order=asc&q=harold+nicolson#search (accessed 20 December 2015)

59. Harold Nicolson, unpublished diary, 17 March 1936, the Vita Sackville-West and Harold Nicolson manuscripts, letters and diaries [microform]: from Sissinghurst Castle, Kent, the Huntington Library, California, and other libraries, reel 13

60. Michael Bloch, *Closet Queens: Some 20th Century British Politicians* (London: Little, Brown, 2015), p. 164

61. Nigel Nicolson, *Portrait of a Marriage* (London: Weidenfeld & Nicolson, 1973), p. 131

62. Goronwy Rees, op. cit., pp 113–14, 131. Whether due to memory lapse or avoidance of libel, Rees calls Jackie [Hewit] Jimmy; Norman Rose, *Harold Nicolson* (London: Jonathan Cape, 2005), p. 283 (sourced to 'Private information')

63. Reform Club Archive catalogue (NRA 43776): letter from Mr [D] Proctor nominating Guy Burgess and Anthony Blunt for membership of the club, 1937 (B41)

64. Court circular, 'Lady Dormer and Mrs Roderick Seagrave dance for their daughters', *The Times*, 8 June 1929, p. 17

65. TNA KV2/2588 folio 39a, Note of interview with Jack Hewit, 1 November 1952

66. Penrose and Freeman, op. cit., pp 216–17

67. Nicolson was first introduced to 'Micky Burn' in April 1938 and saw him intermittently as the year progressed. Harold Nicolson, unpublished diaries, Balliol College Archive, Oxford. See for instance the entry for 31 August when Burn was then writing for *The Times*

68. BBC WAC R Cont 1 Anthony Blunt Talks, file 1, contract dated 21 January 1938

69. BBC WAC R Cont 1 Anthony Blunt Talks, file 1, Blunt to Barnes (undated), Barnes to Blunt, 17 March 1938

70. BBC WAC L1/68/1 Dr Lansel, Medical Certificate

71. BBC WAC L1/68/1 Dr P. Lansel to Sir Richard Maconachie, Director Talks, 14 March 1938, and manuscript note, 15 March 1938

72. BBC WAC L1/68/1 Dr P. Lansel to Sir Richard Maconachie, Director Talks, 8 April 1938, and manuscript note, 15 March 1938

73. BBC WAC L1/68/1, Memoranda March–April 1938

74. Philby, Maclean and Burgess were apparently known to the KGB as 'the Three Musketeers'

75. Costello and Tsarev, op. cit., p. 212

76. Bruce Page, David Leitch and Phillip Knightley, *Philby: The Spy Who Betrayed a Generation* (London: Sphere, 1969), pp 99–100

77. Ibid.

78. Geoffrey Gorer, 'Maclean and Burgess' [a review of Cyril Connolly's *The Missing Diplomats*], *Sunday Times*, 18 January 1953, p. 5

79. Burgess to Rosamond Lehmann, 9 April 1938, King's College, Cambridge, The Papers of Rosamond Nina Lehmann, RNL/2/85

80. TNA KV2/4102 serial 136z, Statement made by Kim Philby, 12 June 1951, p. 2

81. Donald Lammers, 'Fascism, Communism, and the Foreign Office, 1937–39', *Journal of Contemporary History*, Vol. 6, No. 3 (1971), pp 66–86

82. Robert Cecil, 'The Cambridge Comintern', in Christopher Andrew and David Dilks, *The Missing Dimension* (London: Macmillan, 1984), p. 175

83. 'The Henlein Visit', *The Times*, 14 May 1938

84. James Lees-Milne, *Harold Nicolson: A Biography, Vol. II: 1930–1968* (London: Chatto & Windus, 1981), p. 104

85. Harold Nicolson, *Why Britain is at War* (London: Penguin, 1939), p. 78

86. Penrose and Freeman, op. cit., p. 223

87. TNA KV2/4117 serial 830b

88. Ball papers, Bodleian Library, Oxford, MS CEng C6656, pp 40–49

89. Costello and Tsarev, op. cit., pp 235–6

90. The 'four powers' were Germany, Italy, France and Great Britain

91. TNA Foreign Office [hereafter FO] 371/21709/C1431 Code and Cipher Telegram No. 61 to Sir Nevile Henderson, British Embassy, Berlin, from FO, London, 2 March 1938 9.20 p.m.

92. Andrew Roberts, *The Holy Fox: The Life of Lord Halifax* (London: Phoenix, 1991), p. 78; TNA FO 371/21709/1431 code cipher No. 60, 1 March 1938 and notes by Sir Orme Sargent and Sir Alexander Cadogan (same date)

93. TNA FO 371/21709/1431 note by Sir Alexander Cadogan, 1 March 1938

94. BBC WAC file C41. Internal memorandum about the Munich crisis. The memorandum says that Neville Chamberlain's No. 10 adviser, Sir Horace Wilson, asked the BBC to 'pay particular attention to opinions expressed in talks such as Harold Nicolson's "The Past Week".' During September, the memorandum records, 'Consultation between the BBC and Whitehall became extremely close and news bulletins as a whole inevitably fell into line with Government policy at this critical juncture.'

95. Roberts, *The Holy Fox*, pp 78–9. For a counterweight and details of government attempts to handle the press during appeasement, see Richard Cockett, *Twilight of Truth: Chamberlain, Appeasement and the Manipulation of the Press* (London: Weidenfeld & Nicolson, 1989). For the performance of the press during the Munich crisis, see Franklin Reid Gannon, *The British Press and Germany: 1936–1939* (Oxford: Oxford University Press, 1971); and Thomas Wheeler Nagle, *A Study of British Public Opinion and the European Appeasement Policy: 1933–39* (Wiesbaden, Germany: Librairie Chmielorz, 1957)

96. Roberts, *The Holy Fox*, pp 78–9; Richard Cockett, *Twilight of Truth*

97. Stewart Purvis and Jeff Hulbert, *When Reporters Cross the Line* (London: Biteback, 2013), Chapter 3

98. Driberg, *Guy Burgess*, p. 32

99. Goronwy Rees, op. cit., pp 131–2

100. Michael Straight, *After Long Silence* (London: Collins, 1983), p. 142

101. *Le Monde*, 23 July 1993

102. Goronwy Rees, op. cit., p. 144

103. New Paris evening newspaper, *The Times*, 26 September 1933, p. 13; Jean-Rene Maillot, *Jean Luchaire Et La Revue Notre Temps (1927–1940)* (Internationaler Verlag Der W: Peter Lang Gmbh, 6 November 2013); Court Circular, 'Reception for the Entente Internationale de Parties Radicaux, hosted at the National Liberal Club', *The Times*, 31 July 1935, p. 15; At Homes: Foreign Press Association, London, *The Times*, 10 May 1937, p. 17

104. Modin, op. cit., p. 79

105. 'Le taureau avec des cornes d'escargot', *Le Monde*, Hors Série 1940: La débâcle et le désespoir, May–June 2010, p. 23

106. Andrew and Gordievsky, op. cit., p. 236; Driberg, *Guy Burgess*, p. 40; TNA KV2/4117 serial 830b names Ball. Ball had earlier been named in an article by Driberg which had been published in the *Daily Mail*, prior to his book's publication. Ball's lawyers had pressed the book's publishers, Weidenfeld & Nicolson, to ensure that his name was omitted: see Ball papers, Bodleian Library, Oxford, MS CEng C6656, pp 40–49: 'a man of title' was the result

107. Peter Wright and Paul Greengrass, *Spycatcher* (Richmond, Victoria: Heinemann Australia, 1987), p. 228

108. TNA KV2/4106 serial 317b

109. BBC WAC L1/68/1

110. TNA KV2/4106 serial 317b

111. Driberg, *Guy Burgess*, p. 53

112. TNA KV2/4117 serial 830b carefully notes: 'nor is there anything in such information as has been passed to us by MI6' about the Chamberlain–Daladier communications

113. BBC WAC L1/68/1 absences 1938

114. Harold Nicolson, diary, 19 September 1938 (unpublished), The Vita Sackville-West and Harold Nicolson manuscripts, letters and diaries [microform]: from Sissinghurst Castle, Kent, the Huntington Library, California, and other libraries, reel 13

115. Volodarsky, op. cit., p. 555

116. Roger Faligot & Remi Kauffer, *Histoire mondiale du renseignement, Tome 1: 1870–1939* (Paris: Editions Robert Laffont, 1993), pp 432–8. After spending most of the 1950s working toward French decolonisation in North Africa, Pfeiffer retired to the Garonne valley, France and died in 1966, aged seventy-six

117. BBC WAC R51/317 The Mediterranean, 'Series of talks on the Mediterranean', undated

118. BBC WAC R51/317, NG Luker to Burgess and cc to Mr Gibson, 30 September 1938

119. Tom Driberg, *Guy Burgess*, pp 43–6

120. BBC WAC L1/68/1, Guy Burgess personnel file

121. https://www.city.ac.uk/cambridge-spies-the-guy-burgess-files (accessed 30 November 2015)

122. Ibid.

123. BBC WAC RCont1, Churchill, Talks file volume 1, 1926–39, Burgess to Maconachie, 4 October 1938

124. BBC WAC R73/374/1, Note by David Graham, 7 February 1980, p. 6
125. Gorodetsky, Gabriel (ed.) and Ivan Maisky, *The Maisky Diaries: Red Ambassador to the Court of St James's, 1932–43* (London: Yale University Press, 2015)
126. This detail appears in the entry for the following day, Friday 30 September 1938, but clearly refers to 29 September
127. BBC WAC RCont1, Churchill, Talks file volume 1, 1926–39
128. We are greatly indebted to Professor Gabriel Gorodetsky for confirming that Maisky's diaries do not mention Burgess. However, during the Munich crisis Professor Gorodetsky has pointed out Maisky's eagerness for the BBC to inform the public that the French were withholding information from the British government about the Soviet preparedness to activate the agreement with France and assist Czechoslovakia. That was the essence of Maisky's contacts with Churchill during the Munich crisis. Professor G. Gorodetsky email to Jeff Hulbert, 29 November 2015
129. BBC WAC R73/374, Guy Burgess and others
130. David Graham interviewed on BBC Radio 4, *Rebels*, 5 October 1984
131. Harold Nicolson, *Diaries and Letters, Vol I: 1930–39* (London: Collins, 1966), entry for 23 November 1938
132. BBC WAC R73/374/1, Note by David Graham, 7 February 1980, p. 1
133. Ibid., p. 2
134. BBC WAC R73/374/1, 4 February 1980
135. BBC WAC L1/68/1, Burgess to DSA (Director of Staff Administration) 'thru DT [Director of Talks]', 12 December 1938
136. Andrew and Gordievsky, op. cit., p. 237
137. TNA KV2/4104 serial 195y (MI6 to MI5, 21 June 1951)

CHAPTER 4

1. http://www.lrb.co.uk/v18/n16/basil-davidson/goodbye-to-some-of-that (accessed 20 December 2015)
2. William MacKenzie, *The Secret History of SOE: Special Operations Executive 1940–1945* (London: St Ermin's Press, 2000), p. 4; Seaman, *Special Operations Executive: A New Instrument of War* (London: Routledge, 2005), p. 10
3. Keith Jeffery, *MI6: The History of the Secret Intelligence Service 1909–1949* (London: Bloomsbury, 2011), p. 320
4. David Garnett (notes by Andrew Roberts), *The Secret History of PWE: The Political Warfare Executive 1939–1945* (London: St Ermine's Press, 2002), p. 6
5. Mark Seaman, op. cit., p. 11
6. Jeffery, op. cit., p. 322
7. According to a review of the organisation conducted in 1940 by Lord Hankey, Gladwyn Jebb and Sir Stewart Menzies ('C'), – see CAB 127/376, 'First report: Inquiry into the secret service (MI6)'; for loyalty to Grand, see Jeffery, op. cit., p. 352 and MacKenzie, op. cit., p. 13
8. Garnett, op. cit., p. 7
9. Ibid.
10. MacKenzie, op. cit., p. 33
11. Andrew Roberts, Introduction to David Garnett, op. cit., p. 1
12. TNA KV2/4104 serial 195y
13. MacKenzie, op. cit., p. 13
14. TNA KV2/4105 serial 245a
15. TNA KV2/4164110 serial 463a, p. 3

16.   Philby, op. cit., pp 9–10

17.   He was helped to overcome this by Guy Burgess, who interceded on Blunt's behalf by asking Burgess's friend (Sir) Roger Fulford, the historian whose talks Burgess had produced for the BBC, and whom in 1940 had taken up a non-executive post with MI5 (TBA)

18.   Jeffery, op. cit., p. 386. A romanticised version of the story was filmed in 1959 under the title *Operation Amsterdam*

19.   Jeffery, op. cit., p. 377. MI6 Swedish Station Chief Lt Cdr John Martin reports that operations suggested that a 'large portion of 22-Land [UK] S.I.S. composed of inexperienced amateurs'. The fiasco was known as the Rickman Affair, and is related in Charles Cruickshank, *SOE in Scandinavia* (Oxford: Oxford University Press, 1986)

20.   MacKenzie, op. cit., p. 35

21.   David Garnett, op. cit., p. 6

22.   TNA KV2/4106 serial 317b

23.   Note by Gerald Wellesley, 3 October 1938, Neville Chamberlain Papers, Cadbury Special Collection, University of Birmingham, NC L Add 1–43; and for a fuller description of the clandestine broadcasting, see Philip Taylor, *British Propaganda in the 20th Century* (Edinburgh: Edinburgh University Press, 1999), pp 123–6

24.   TNA CAB24/281, CP284(38), 8 December 1938

25.   BBC WACL1/68/1, DSA (Director of Staff Administration) to Talks Executive, 6 January 1939. The memo reminded the Talks Department management to tell Burgess that he did not need to report for work in the coming week

26.   David Garnett, op. cit., p. 6

27.   TNA KV2/4101 serial 2b, Note titled 'Gerald Hamilton'

28.   Costello and Tsarev, op. cit., p. 239

29.   Ibid.

30.   Charlotte Higgins, *This New Noise: The Extraordinary Birth and Troubled Life of the BBC* (London: Guardian Faber Publishing, 2015), p. 32

31.   TNA FO395/666, Hilda Matheson, Joint Broadcasting Committee Progress Report, 13 June 1939

32.   Ibid.

33.   The other board members were: Sir Frederick Whyte KCSI, A. V. Hambro MP, Lady Denman DBE, Professor Winifred Cullis CBE, Lady Maureen Stanley, Hon. Mrs Alfred Lyttleton GBE and H. B. Brenan

34.   Charlotte Higgins, op. cit., p. 20

35.   Shirley Panken, *Virginia Woolf and the Lust of Creation: A Psychoanalytic Exploration* (New York: SUNY Press, 1987), p. 190

36.   TNA BW 2/183

37.   MacKenzie, op. cit., p. 35

38.   Ibid., pp 35–6

39.   BBC WAC E2/374/2 Joint Broadcasting Committee, July–December 1939, Messrs Matheson, Benzie, Burgess and Turner represented JBC

40.   Tom Driberg, *Guy Burgess*, p. 52

41.   Anthony Blunt unpublished memoirs, British Library Add 88902/2

42.   Jonathan Haslam, *Near and Distant Neighbours: A New History of Soviet Intelligence* (Oxford: Oxford University Press, 2015), Kindle loc. 2350

43.   Costello and Tsarev, op. cit., p. 240

44.   TNA KV2/4169 serial 223c (but marked in red '364') is one of O'Neill's documents. Others are retained by the Foreign Office: TNA FCO158/15, Guy Burgess's private papers: C. D. W. O'Neill

45. Haslam, *Near and Distant Neighbours*, Kindle loc. 2350
46. Ibid., Kindle loc. 2364
47. Roberts, *The Holy Fox*, p. 168
48. Cairncross, op. cit., pp 75–6
49. Goronwy Rees, op. cit., pp 135–6
50. Anthony Blunt, unpublished memoir, British Library Add 88902/1, p. 40
51. Goronwy Rees, op. cit., p. 149
52. Ibid., p. 150
53. Anthony Blunt, unpublished memoir, British Library Add 88902/2, p. 41
54. Goronwy Rees, op. cit., p. 150
55. Jenny Rees, op. cit., p. 47
56. Andrew and Mitrokhin, op. cit., p. 105
57. TNA T162/858, part 4, appendix to Paper 82 (24 August 1939): 'I would submit that Mr Guy Burgess, who was detailed for liaison work with the FO, at their request, should be attached as JBC Liaison Officer to the Ministry of Information (both neutral and enemy sections) – wherever it may be established.'
58. TNA T162/858, part 4, appendix to Paper 82 (27 September 1939)
59. TNA KV2/4110 serial 463a, p. 8
60. TNA KV2/4105 serial 245a
61. TNA KV2/4110 serial 449a
62. TNA KV2/4110 serial 449a
63. TNA CAB 65/5, War Cabinet 11 (40), 4: Finland, 13 January 1940
64. TNA CAB 66/5/21, French Proposals for Allied Assistance to Finland: Report by the Chiefs of Staff, 2 February 1940
65. See: SECRET: WM (40) 38th Conclusions, Assistance to Finland: Note of points mentioned in discussion but not incorporated in the Minutes, TNA CAB/65/56, 10 February 1940. The Romanian government preference was for Romanian saboteurs to be used, although there was doubt that sabotage alone could produce a big enough bang
66. In October 1940, the British minister in Moscow, Sir Stafford Cripps, was both trying to prise Moscow away from the Ribbentrop–Molotov pact, while also trying to establish how benevolently neutral the country would be in the event of a German attack against either Turkey or Iran. London told Cripps that if the USSR refrained from help, Britain and its allies would refrain from taking action against Baku. Telegram sent to Cripps, TNA CAB/65/9/33, 15 October 1940
67. BBC WAC E2/374/3 JBC, January 1940–March 1941. Matheson to H. G. G. Welch (MoI), 23 December 1939
68. Imperial Calendar and Civil Service List, 1940
69. For instance: TNA FO898/5: Executive Committee, 8 February 1940 and 14 March 1940
70. TNA KV2/4105 serial 245a
71. Selina Hastings, *Rosamond Lehmann: A Life* (London: Vintage Digital, 2012), Kindle loc. 4328
72. TNA KV2/4106 serial 320b
73. SOE had, in fact, not yet been established by the time this memorandum was written. It should probably refer to Section D instead
74. TNA KV2/4110 serial 463a, p. 1
75. Holzman, op. cit., p. 96
76. TNA KV2/4117 serial 830b
77. TNA KV2/4105 serial 425a, p. 3
78. Harold Nicolson, diary, 1 June 1940, (unpublished), Balliol College Archive, Oxford

79. Information from SS *Antonia* manifest and *Border Crossings: From Canada to U.S., 1895–1956*: Berlin and Burgess Arrival: 19 July 1940 – Quebec, Canada

80. Straight, op. cit., pp 142–3

81. The saga is revealed in: Driberg, *Guy Burgess*, p. 59; Verne Newton, *The Butcher's Embrace* (London: Little, Brown, 1991), pp 19–20; Harold Nicolson, *Diaries and Letters, Vol II: 1939–1945* (London: Collins, 1967), entry for 17 June 1940 (and unpublished diary, June 1940); Modin, op. cit., p. 83; TNA FO 371/24847/N6063G, Telegram 1488, 'Burgess to "D" through "C", 24 July 1940'; TNA FO 371/24847/N6063G, Telegram 1683, FO to Lord Lothian (British Ambassador, Washington), 27 July 1940; Michael Ignatieff, *Isaiah Berlin: A Life* (London: Vintage, 2011), Kindle locs 1874–1916; Isaiah Berlin (ed. Henry Hardy), *Flourishing: Letters 1928–1946*, Kindle edn (Random House, 2012), Kindle locs 9371–509; and Michael Holzman, op. cit., Kindle locs 2498–550

82. TNA KV2/4115 serial 729b

83. TNA KV2/4118 serial 857c. Liddell saw James Robertson of MI5 on 24 October 1956, five months after Rothschild's meeting with Courtenay Young. Guy Liddell's diary is silent about both Rothschild and Burgess in this period: TNA KV4/186

84. Christopher Andrew, 'The fine art of lying to yourself', *The Times*, 17 November 2001, p. 12; Michael Evans, 'The meeting that nailed Kim Philby', *The Times*, 5 December 1986, p. 1

85. Harold Nicolson, unpublished diary, 19 August 1940, Balliol College Archives, Oxford

86. Costello and Tsarev, op. cit., p. 241

87. Cabinet Memorandum (40)271, TNA CAB 66/10, as modified by the War Cabinet 209(40), TNA CAB 65/8, 22 July 1940, Item 10

88. TNA HS8/321 Halifax to Dalton, 16 August 1940

89. TNA HS8/334

90. TNA KV2/4108 serial 388a

91. *Northern Daily Mail*, Tuesday 10 September 1940, p. 5

92. TNA KV2/4112 serial 608z

93. TNA KV2/4101 serial 2ea

94. TNA KV2/4112 serial 606a

95. Lord Gladwyn, *The Memoirs of Lord Gladwyn* (London: Weidenfeld & Nicolson, 1972), p. 101

CHAPTER 5

1. Asa Briggs, *The History of Broadcasting in the United Kingdom, Volume II: The Golden Age of Wireless* (Oxford: Oxford University Press, 1995), p. 139

2. Guy Burgess to Harold Nicolson, undated, Harold Nicolson Papers, Princeton, C0913, box 2

3. BBC WAC R154/35/1 – Burgess Formalities, DSA (Director of Staff Administration, D. H. Clarke, to A/C(A) [Acting Controller (Administration)]), cc to GEO [General Establishment Officer]

4. TNA KV2/4101 serial 6a, Blunt to Liddell, 30 April 1943

5. TNA KV2/4102 serial 115b

6. BBC WAC L1/68/1

7. Harold Nicolson, unpublished diary, 20 December 1940, Balliol College Archives, Oxford

8. David Bradshaw and James Smith, 'Ezra Pound, James Strachey Barnes ('The Italian Lord Haw-Haw') and Italian Fascism', *The Review of English Studies*, New Series, Vol. 64, No. 266, 2013, pp 672–93

9. BBC WAC L1/68/1 R. W. Baker (BBC) to G. D. Charles (Ministry of Information), 15 January 1941

10. BBC WAC L1/68/1 Barnes to Talks Ex[ecutive], 20 January 1941

11. BBC WAC, Aileen Furse papers

12. BBC WAC RCont 1, Smollett, Peter, file 2 1939–62. G. R. Barnes memo to Burgess (undated). An indent was a term used to describe an emergency change to a schedule caused by the need to make an urgent government broadcast

13. Andrew and Gordievsky, op. cit., p. 334; Sarah Gainham, 'Smolka "The Spy": a letter from Vienna', *Encounter*, December 1984, p. 79

14. TNA KV2/2254 folio 123a, note by Strong, C2 branch; other files include: Geoffrey Pyke, TNA KV2/3038 to KV2/3040 and Heinz Israel Kamnitzer, TNA KV2/2883; TNA KV2/4167, Smollett, Vol. 1

15. Andrew and Gordievsky, op. cit., p. 265. They suggest that Theodore Maly, an early KGB 'illegal' (unofficial) agent controller associated with the Cambridge spies, may have suggested that Smollett travel to London

16. H. P. Smolka, *Forty Thousand Against the Arctic: Russia's Polar Empire* (London: Hutchinson, 1937)

17. Andrew and Gordievsky, op. cit., p. 266

18. 'Contacts in Britain with the KGB during Cold War', Letter to the Editor from Sir John Lawrence, *The Times*, Tuesday 20 December 1994, p. 15

19. Borovik, op. cit., pp 55, 137; Boyle, *The Climate of Treason*, p. 144. The agency was called London Continental News Ltd

20. Borovik, op. cit., pp 55, 137

21. Garton Ash, op. cit.

22. TNA HO334/151, Smolka naturalisation (from 7 November 1938 he was known as Smollett by deed poll, according to an annotation on the file)

23. Weidenfeld, op. cit., p. 145

24. Andrew and Gordievsky, op. cit., p. 335 (attributed to information supplied by Gordievsky)

25. TNA KV2/4168 serials 110a, 111, 112a

26. TNA INF1/27, Establishment Officer to Smollett, 3 September 1939

27. Harold Nicolson MP, Parliamentary Secretary to the Ministry of Information, BBC Handbook, 1941

28. Andrew and Mitrokhin, op. cit., p. 158

29. Borovik, op. cit., p. 138

30. Their names appear in the 1940 Imperial Calendar and Civil Service List

31. TNA INF1/27, Smollett and Burgess to Carr, 14 March 1940. The memo shows that the pair had researched the question of producing an overseas radio bulletin, which would be 'a propaganda document'. The proposal envisaged the Ministry of Information's Foreign Press Division producing the bulletin. 'Mr Smollett and I have had detailed technical discussions … And think we have arrived at a satisfactory and workable arrangement.'

32. Purvis and Hulbert, op. cit., Chapter 4; Andrew and Gordievsky, op. cit.; West and Tsarev, op. cit.

33. West and Tsarev, op. cit., p. 157. Smolka is mistranslated as Henri in a KGB report by Philby, rather than either Hans or Harry

34. TNA FO898/5, Executive Committee Minutes, 9 February 1940 (Ministry of Information); Foreign Division Executive Minutes, 14 March 1940. Smollett and Burgess were at both meetings

35. The talk was broadcast on the Home Service, 14 March 1941 (21:20) and repeated on 9 April 1941 (13:15)

36. BBC WAC R51/115/1, *Week in Westminster* 1929–41, Barnes to Burgess, 14 September 1941

37. Peter Hill, 'Parliamentary Broadcasting – From TWIW to YIP', *British Journalism Review*, 01/1993; 4(4), pp 39–44

38. *Adventures in the BBC Archive*, Saturday 8 November 2008, BBC Radio 4 http://www.bbc.co.uk/archive/cambridgespies/7816.shtml (accessed 20 December 2015)

39. Harold Nicolson, unpublished diary, 6 May 1943, Harvester microform edition

40. Hailsham quotation taken from *Adventures in the BBC Archive* http://www.bbc.co.uk/archive/cambridgespies/7816.shtml (accessed 20 December 2015)

41. BBC WAC R51/115/1, *Week in Westminster* 1929–41, Barnes to Luker (cc Burgess), 16 October 1941

42. *Week in Westminster*, 11 December 1943; 22 January 1944; and 19 February 1944

43. BBC WAC R51/115/2; *Week in Westminster* (1942) File 1b, memoranda exchanged between DT (Barnes) and Burgess 12 and 17 June 1942

44. Both letters: BBC WAC R 51/115/3 *Week in Westminster*, file 2a, 1943–45

45. Hansard, HL Deb, 21 March 1989, Vol. 505, Cols 581–648

46. Costello and Tsarev, op. cit., p. 243

47. Andrew and Mitrokhin, op. cit., p. 120

48. BBC WAC L1/68/1, 28 March 1944

49. BBC WAC L1/68/1

50. The funeral service was for the broadcaster, John Hilton, whose programmes he had produced, and who had been the Director of Home Publicity at the Ministry of Information in 1940. Hilton's secretary and mistress, Edna Nixon, suggested that Hilton had been a heavy drinker and undoubtedly Burgess was a drinking chum. The pair would retire to either the refreshment room in the BBC or to local bars. After making what turned out to be his last broadcast, Hilton, who was already suffering from depression and exhaustion through overwork, went to the BBC refreshment room. Nixon wrote: 'He could not assuage his thirst that evening. His nerves were strong taut and he had to relieve the tension. He drank deeply, and when Guy had gone his way, his gaiety collapsed…' Hilton died weeks later and was buried in Cambridge, to where Burgess was travelling in his best suit [Edna Nixon, *John Hilton: The Story of His Life* (London: George Allen & Unwin, 1946), p. 337]

51. BBC WAC L1/68/1

52. TNA KV4/187, 11 April 1941

53. TNA KV2/4112 serial 621a

54. TNA KV2/4112 serial 622a (13 February 1956), D. G. White to Curry: 'I take it that the initiative was entirely on Footman's side? Don't bother to write again unless this is untrue.' There is no further letter from Curry on file

55. Carter, op. cit., p. 229

56. Quoted in Carter, op. cit., p. 283

57. TNA KV4/193, 8 March 1944

58. TNA KV4/195, 13 October 1944; TNA KV4/466, 20 November 1945

59. TNA KV2/4117 serial 830b

60. TNA KV4/188, Guy Liddell diary entry for 15 September 1941. William Codrington was Acting Assistant Under Secretary of State (unpaid)

61. Nigel West (ed.), *Guy Liddell Diaries, Volume I: 1939–1942* (London: Taylor and Francis, 2007), Kindle locs 2993–7

62. Costello and Tsarev, op. cit., p. 242; Andrew and Mitrokhin, op. cit., p. 110

63. Ibid.

64.   BBC WAC Russia 1A, 1929–41, Barnes to Maconachie, 9 July 1941

65.   TNA KV2/3941 folio 3a

66.   Andrew, *The Defence of the Realm*, pp 395–6

67.   Robert Dallek, *Flawed Giant: Lyndon Johnson and His Times* (New York: Oxford University Press, 1998), p. 254

68.   See Bradley F Smith, *Sharing Secrets with Stalin: How the Allies Traded Intelligence* (Lawrence: University Press of Kansas, 1996); but also see: TNA FO371/36920: N2876/9/38G and N2877/9/38G: NKVD Agents: 'Coffee Party'; N3581/9/38G: NKVD request for SOE assistance in dropping of Russian agents in France; N4570/9/G38: Relations between NKVD and SOE; TNA HS4/334: NKVD Collaboration; TNA HS4/335: SOE/NKVD cooperation in Moscow; TNA KV2/2827: Agents of the RIS [Russian Intelligence Service] Given SOE Facilities

69.   TNA FO371/29603 N6645, Sir Orme Sargent to Cyril Radcliffe, 24 November 1941

70.   It has been said that his career with the ministry flourished due to his acquaintance with the MP Brendan Bracken, a close confidant of Churchill. Bracken became the Minister of Information (MoI) in July 1941, just weeks after the Soviet Union had been attacked by Germany's military forces, and held on to the post for the duration, eventually helping to shut down the ministry as the end of the war loomed. Andrew and Gordievsky, op. cit., p. 335. See also Ian McLaine, *Ministry of Morale* (London: George Allen and Unwin, 1979), and the two biographies of Brendan Bracken: Andrew Boyle, *Poor Dear Brendan: The Quest for Brendan Bracken* (London, Hutchinson, 1974) and Charles Edward Lysaght, *Brendan Bracken* (London: Allen Lane, 1979)

71.   McLaine, op. cit., p. 201; TNA INF1/147 Grubb to Leigh Ashton, Stevens, 29 September 1941. Authorisation was given by Brendan Bracken: INF1/147 Director General to Minister if he can go ahead with the proposal 'Yes. BB', 22 August 1941

72.   TNA INF1/147 H. P. Smollett to Aynsley, 9 October 1941. Among other duties Smollett identified for the Russian Department were: '4. Liaison with the BBC and vetting of scripts projecting Russia to be used on the Home Service', '5. Liaison with the Soviet embassy and assistance to as well as control of their publicity activities', '6. vetting of files both ways...'

73.   TNA INF1/676 Bracken to Maisky, 31 October 1941, and Maisky to Bracken, 4 November 1941

74.   Daniel J. Leab, *Orwell Subverted: The CIA and the Filming of Animal Farm* (University Park: Pennsylvania State University Press, 2007), pp 143–4

75.   Sheila Kerr, 'An Assessment of a Soviet Agent: Donald Maclean, 1940–1951', unpublished PhD thesis, LSE, London, 1996, p. 92

76.   Andrew and Gordievsky, op. cit., p. 268; see also Andrew and Mitrokhin, op. cit., pp 158–9; McLaine, op. cit., pp 202–3; Christopher Andrew, 'Moscow's Literary Agents', *The Times*, 9 December 1994; Timothy Garton Ash, 'Orwell's list: Love, Death and Treachery', *The Guardian* (Saturday Review), 21 June 2003

77.   TNA CAB65/33, conclusions, CM(43)16 (25 January 1943) Item 8, USSR – Celebration of Red Army Day; TNA CAB66/33, CP(43)37, Red Army Day, Memorandum by the Minister of Information

78.   *Salute to the Red Army*, BBC Forces Programme, 21 February 1943, 1615–1700 hrs. It was produced by Basil Dean, later a doyen of British film production, and the Director of National Service Entertainment. The entire programme was written by a borrowed BBC official, Louis MacNeice, a close school friend of Anthony Blunt

79.   *The Times*, 22 February 1943, p. 2. Other gala ceremonies were held in Bristol (political address: A. V. Alexander), Newcastle upon Tyne (political address: Oliver

Lyttleton), Cardiff (political address: Clement Attlee), Sheffield (political address: Sir Stafford Cripps) and Brighton (political address: Herbert Morrison)

80. http://www.bbc.co.uk/archive/ussr/6726.shtml (accessed 20 December 2015)
81. TNA INF1/147, Smolka [Smollett] to Mrs Atkins, 2 August 1942
82. Clarissa Churchill and Cate Haste, *Clarissa Eden: A Memoir: From Churchill to Eden* (London: Orion, 2007)
83. Carter, op. cit., p. 457; Wright with Greengrass, op. cit., pp 242–3
84. George Orwell, *The Orwell Diaries* (Penguin Classics, 2010), Kindle locs 8033–68. Entry for 2 June 1942
85. Harold Nicolson, *Diaries and Letters, Vol II: 1939–1945*, entry for 9 September 1942
86. Violet Bonham Carter, unpublished diary, 9 September 1942, 'Harold bought [*sic*] a young man called Burgess to see me – very disturbed about Stafford Cripps position', Bodleian Library, Oxford, Bonham Carter, MS20
87. Harold Nicolson, *Diaries and Letters, Vol II: 1939–1945*, entry for 9 September 1942
88. Harold Nicolson, unpublished diary, 28 June 1940, Balliol College Archive, Oxford. Peter Montgomery was a cousin of General Bernard Montgomery
89. Harold Nicolson, unpublished diary, 27 December 1943, Balliol College Archive, Oxford
90. Wolf Rilla directed, among others, *Village of the Damned* (1961). Later active in the ACTT, the film technicians' union, as well as the Director's Guild, he became a hotelier in the south of France
91. Michael Luke, *David Tennant and the Gargoyle Years* (London: Weidenfeld & Nicolson, 1991), p. 148
92. Ibid., p. 177
93. Harold Acton, *Memoirs of an Aesthete* (London: Faber & Faber, 2008), p. 87
94. James Lees-Milne (ed. Michael Bloch), *Diaries 1942–1970* (London: John Murray, 2007), entry for 16 October 1943
95. Ibid., entry for 25 November 1944. Years later Fletcher Cooke was obliged to resign from Parliament over a homosexuality scandal
96. Lord (Victor) Rothschild, *Meditations of a Broomstick* (London: Collins, 1977), p. 16
97. Carter, op. cit., p. 262
98. Goronwy Rees, op. cit., p. 155
99. Ibid., p. 156
100. Ibid., p. 155
101. Malcolm Muggeridge, *Chronicles of Wasted Time, Volume II: The Infernal Grove* (London: Fontana, 1981), pp 114–15
102. Ibid., p. 241
103. Anthony Blunt, unpublished memoirs, British Library, Add 88902/2, folios 33–4
104. Richard Cockett, *David Astor and the Observer* (London: André Deutsch, 1991), p. 92
105. West and Tsarev, op. cit., p. 152
106. See Sir David Omand, *Securing the State* (London: C. Hurst & Co., 2012)
107. Alexander Vassiliev's Notebooks and Soviet Cables Deciphered by the National Security Agency's Venona Project White Notebook #3; File 58380 v.1 'Nigel', p. 13 http://digitalarchive.wilsoncenter.org/collection/86/Vassiliev-Notebooks (accessed 11 May 2015)
108. West and Tsarev, op. cit., p. 162
109. Ibid., p. 163, dated 25 October 1942
110. Modrzchinskaya KGB Report, (undated), SVR archives, Moscow

III. Identity of agent unknown

112. Sheila Grant Duff, *The Parting of Ways: A Personal Account of the Thirties* (London: Peter Owen, 1982)

113. Harold Nicolson, unpublished diary, 5 January 1944, Balliol College Archive, Oxford

114. BBC WAC R51/555 Signpost Series (1940–41), Burgess to Fisher, 31 January 1941

115. BBC WAC, Aileen Furse bundle

116. See, for instance, TNA FO366/1392, Ridsdale to Minister (Richard Law), 1 March 1944

117. BBC WAC R51/624/3, War Commentary 1943, File II

118. TNA FO954/23A folio 196, Ridsdale minute, 7 May 1943

119. TNA FO954/23A folio 200, Ridsdale to Harvey (Eden's Principal Private Secretary), 21 May 1943

120. BBC WAC R51/624/3, War Commentary 1943, File II

121. TNA FO954/23A folio 223

122. TNA FO954/23A folio 227

123. TNA FO954/23A folio 228

124. Harold Nicolson unpublished diary entries for 26 January 1944 and 2 February 1944, Balliol College Archive, Oxford

125. TNA FCO158/237

126. BBC WAC L1/68/1

127. Asa Briggs, *The History of Broadcasting in the United Kingdom, Volume IV: Sound and Vision* (Oxford: Oxford University Press, 1978), p. 620

CHAPTER 6

1. R. A. Butler quoted in Andrew Roberts, *The Holy Fox*, p. 87

2. See Frank T. Ashton-Gwatkin, *The British Foreign Office* (New York: Syracuse University Press, 1950), p. 15

3. John Saville, *The Politics of Continuity* (London: Verso, 1993), pp 10–12

4. See Frank T. Ashton-Gwatkin, op. cit., p. 24

5. Alan Maclean, *No, I Tell a Lie, It Was the Tuesday* (London: Kyle Cathie Limited, 1997), p. 68

6. 'Mr William Ridsdale's retirement', *The Times*, London, 25 November 1953, p. 7; William Ridsdale obituary, *The Times*, London, 26 November 1957, p. 13

7. Eden, when he became Foreign Secretary again in 1951, persuaded Ridsdale to stay on as head of the News Department for three years beyond the normal retirement age: 'Mr William Ridsdale's retirement', *The Times*, London, 25 November 1953, p. 7

8. TNA KV2/4109 serial 432a

9. TNA FO366/1739, E A Chapman Andrews [Head of Foreign Office Personnel Department] to [Ivone] Kirkpatrick [Assistant Under Secretary], [Roderick] Barclay [Assistant Head, Foreign Office and Diplomatic Service Branch A], Sir David Scott [Under Secretary], 29 March 1946

10. Maclean, *No, I Tell a Lie, It Was the Tuesday*, p. 69

11. Confirmed by the dearth of post-war News Department files held by the National Archives at Kew

12. Harold Nicolson, *Diaries and Letters, Vol II: 1939–1945*, 26 February 1945

13. Two KGB spies, Alger Hiss of the State Department and Harry Dexter White of the US Treasury, were part of the US Yalta team in the Crimea and passed messages to the Russians during the conference itself, giving Stalin almost real-time

insights into US and British thinking. The irony is that Stalin was paranoid enough not to allow himself to make full use of the material, fearing that some was being planted on him by US intelligence services. See, Andrew and Mitrokhin, op. cit., p. 176; S. M. Plokhy, *Yalta: The Price of Peace* (New York: Penguin, 2011), p. 78

14. The person to whom Volkov was alluding was actually Kim Philby, who was head of Section IX of MI6, which was responsible for anti-Soviet operations. See Tim Milne, *Kim Philby: The Unknown Story of the KGB's Master Spy* (London: Biteback, 2014), Chapter 10

15. Kessler, agent ORANGE, and Revai, agent TAFFY (TOFFEE)

16. Frank T. Ashton-Gwatkin, Foreign Office chief clerk.

17. Bertrand Russell, Letter to the Editor, *The Times*, 30 November 1948, p. 5, c. 7; 'A Philosopher's Letters: Love, Bertie', *The Economist*, 19 July 2001; and Ray Perkins, Jr., 'Bertrand Russell and Preventive War', *Russell: The Journal of the Bertrand Russell Archives*, 14 (Winter 1994–95): pp 135–53

18. 'A World of Two Blocs', *The Times*, 23 October 1947, p. 4

19. 'The Wallace Affair', *The Times*, 20 September 1946, p. 4; 'Mr Wallace's Letter', *The Times*, 27 September 1946, p. 3

20. See Marc Trachtenberg, 'Preventive War and US Foreign Policy', *Security Studies*, 2007, Vol. 16, No. 1, pp 1–31; Steven Casey, 'Selling NSC-68: The Truman Administration, Public Opinion, and the Politics of Mobilization, 1950–51', *Diplomatic History*, Vol. 29, No. 4, September 2005, pp 655–90; and Gian P. Gentile, 'Planning for Preventive War', *Joint Force Quarterly*, Spring 2000, pp 68–74

21. Jonathan Haslam, *Russia's Cold War: From the October Revolution to the Fall of the Wall* (Yale: Yale University Press, 2011), p. 74

22. *The Times*, 2 September 1950, p. 5. Anderson Commandant of the USAF's Air War College

23. Obituary of Hector McNeil, *The Times*, October 1955

24. Harold Nicolson Letters, Guy Burgess to Harold Nicolson, 9 April 1959, Princeton University, C0913, Box 2

25. Obituary of Hector McNeil, *The Times*, October 1955

26. Foreign Office List, 1948

27. TNA FCO158/9 and TNA FCO158/237, R. E. Barclay, 19 November 1946, et seq.

28. Ibid.

29. TNA FCO158/181, Jones to Burgess, 22 August 1947

30. Boyle, *The Climate of Treason*, p. 299

31. Ibid.

32. Ibid.

33. Ibid., undated draft, 'Secret: G F De M Burgess'

34. TNA PREM 8/1524, Burgess backgrounder, 13 June 1951

35. Guy Burgess, Letter to Moscow via London KGB controller, 9 December 1946. Michael Smith, *The Secret Agent's Bedside Reader: A Compendium of Spy Writing*, (London: Biteback, 2014), Kindle locs 4153–238. We have also seen a copy of the manuscript original: Madchen File No. 83792, Vol. 2. The authors are grateful to Michael Smith for providing them with this document

36. Boyle, *The Climate of Treason*, p. 300

37. TNA KV4/468

38. Ray Merrick, 'The Russia Committee of the British Foreign Office and the Cold War, 1946–47', *Journal of Contemporary History*, Vol. 20, No. 3, 1985, pp 453–68

39. For instance, TNA FO371/71687 shows Ridsdale or Nash attending meetings

40. Madchen File No. 83792, Vol. 2, Burgess letter to Max, 6 January 1947

41. John Vernon Rob was Hector McNeil's Private Secretary, and the Assistant Private

Secretary was Alan Bowes Horn. Both remained in the private office until 1 March 1948 when they took up new posts. Sources: Foreign Office Lists 1947 and 1948

42.   TNA CAB129/16, CP (47) 14, Proposed Intergovernmental Maritime Consultative Organisation (4 January 1947); TNA CAB129/18, CP (47) 114, United Nations Organisations: Report of Inter-Departmental Working Party (28 March 1947); TNA CAB129/18, CP (47) 117, Japanese Reparations (29 March 1947); TNA CAB129/18, CP (47) 125, Anglo-Iranian Oil Company (10 April 1947); TNA CAB129/18, CP (47) 140, The Submission of the Palestine Question to the Special Session of the United Nations Assembly (28 April 1947); TNA CAB129/19, CP (47) 162, Coal Imports (18 May 1947); TNACAB 129/19, CP (47) 166, Report on the Fourth Session of the Economic and Social Council (29 May 1947); TNA CAB129/21, CP (47) 256, Report on the Fifth Session of the Economic and Social Council (6 September 1947)

43.   Haslam, *Russia's Cold War*, pp 73–4

44.   Madchen File No. 83792, Vol. 2, Burgess letter to Max, 6 January 1947

45.   TNA FO371/71687, Jebb to Sargent, 16 January 1947: '... To my astonishment I found ... that although the Secretary [of State] had with great difficulty collected copies of these Cabinet Papers and Conclusions for my own temporary use, hardly any Member of the [Russia] Committee, except Sir I Kirkpatrick, had seen them at all ... I believe the difficulty is that the Private Secretaries are bound by very strict instructions as regards the circulation in the [Foreign] Office of Cabinet Papers and Cabinet Conclusions. I can see it is quite important to limit the distribution of such papers as these ... but if there is going to be any kind of Under-Secretarial coordination ... then all Under-Secretaries ... [or at least those] who are members of the Russia Committee, should at least be able to see Cabinet Papers on Foreign Policy and the Cabinet Conclusions on them...'

46.   Sir Bernard Burrows, op. cit., p. 21

47.   Goronwy Rees, op. cit., p. 167

48.   Ibid., p. 168

49.   On the use of material from 'Hicks' for the period 15 November 1947 to 15 May 1948, Signed Voronin, 17 May 1948, Madchen File No. 83792, Vol. 2. The authors are grateful to Michael Smith for providing them with this document

50.   Report on a meeting with 'Hicks', 4 March 1945, Madchen File No. 83792, Vol. 2

51.   Note on meeting with Hicks [one of Burgess's codenames], Madchen File No. 83792, Vol. 2

52.   Modin, op. cit., p. 143

53.   Note on meeting with Hicks [one of Burgess's codenames], 24 March 1945, Madchen File No. 83792, Vol. 2

54.   Pierson Dixon, a senior Foreign Office diplomat

55.   Madchen File No. 83792, Vol. 2, heavily censored report from Burgess, translated by Yuri Modin, 6 September 1946

56.   Madchen File No. 83792, Vol. 2, Burgess letter to Max, 6 January 1947

57.   Gaynor Johnson, *The Foreign Office and British Diplomacy in the Twentieth Century* (London: Routledge, 2009), p. 14

58.   Madchen File No. 83792, Vol. 2, Burgess letter to Max, 6 January 1947

59.   Ibid., No. 177, On meeting with Hicks, 4 March 1945

60.   Madchen File No. 83792, Vol. 2, heavily censored report from Burgess, translated by Yuri Modin, 6 September 1946

61.   Madchen File No. 83792 Vol 2. Report 77, information from 'M' on the Moscow three-power conference [words censored] on 23 October 1943 and the Department's evaluation of this material

62. Ashton-Gwatkin, op. cit.
63. Foreign Office Branches: these were the equivalent of staffing streams and while transfer upwards was possible it was unusual. There were four: A Branch comprised the diplomats – from vice consuls to ambassadors (around 750, of whom two-thirds were posted abroad); B Branch comprised executive and clerical staff (around 1,550, just over half of whom were posted overseas); Branch C comprised copy and shorthand typists (around 500); Branch D comprised chancery servants and office messengers (fewer than 100). Burgess was a temporary member of Branch B. Source: Frank T. Ashton-Gwatkin, op. cit., Chapter 2
64. TNA CSC11/68
65. TNA FCO158/166
66. TNA FCO158/181, Chapman-Andrews to Burgess, 29 April 1946
67. Harold Nicolson Letters, Burgess to Nicolson, undated, op. cit.
68. TNA FCO158/181; see, for instance: Burgess to McNeil (10 July 1947); Jones to Burgess (22 August 1947); McNeil to Caccia ([date uncertain] 1947, 4 December 1947, 12 February 1948); and Warner to Barclay (6 April 1948)
69. SVR (KGB) Archives, Document 316: Report to Molotov on Burgess from F. Kuznetsov, December 1947
70. West and Tsarev, op. cit., p. 178
71. Ibid., p. 177
72. Ibid.
73. Lord Gladwyn, op. cit., p. 205
74. Modin, op. cit., p. 167
75. Ibid.
76. West and Tsarev, op. cit., p. 178
77. Christopher Mayhew, *A War of Words: A Cold War Witness* (London: I. B. Tauris, 1998), p. 24
78. TNA FCO158/8, Roberts to Dean, 15 October 1955
79. TNA FCO158/181, file notes PGD Adams, 16 September 1948 and George Middleton, 18 September 1948
80. TNA KV2/4103 serial 183c
81. TNA KV2/4102 serial 188
82. British Pathé, UN Meet Over Berlin, Film ID: 2236.15S, canister: UN 2034, 1948
83. West and Tsarev, op. cit., p. 177
84. Ibid., p. 178
85. Andrew and Gordievsky, op. cit., p. 324: Mayhew, op. cit.; West and Tsarev, op. cit., p. 178
86. TNA PREM8/1524, Burgess backgrounder, 13 June 1951. This date may, or not be, accurate: reports to the Prime Minister did not mention Burgess's short stay in IRD, which is estimated to have lasted no more than three months
87. Foreign Office List, 1943
88. West and Tsarev, op. cit., p. 179
89. Ibid., pp 178–9
90. TNA FO371/75742/F3118
91. TNA FCO158/8 Roberts to Dean, 15 October 1955
92. S. R. Ashton, G. Bennett, K. Hamilton (eds), *Britain and China 1945–1950: Documents on British Policy Overseas, Series I, Volume VIII: Whitehall Histories* (London: Routledge, 2002), pp 155, 213, 317, 319, 320
93. TNA FO371/75742/F3120
94. TNA FO371/75745/F3953/1015/10, note by G Burgess, 18 March 1949

95. TNA FO371/75745/F3968/1015/10, 'GB 18.3' [1949]
96. TNA FO371/75761/F9335/1015/10
97. TNA FO371/83406/FC11991, Creda telegram No. 10 of 30 January from Hong Kong to Board of Trade; and Creda telegram No. 14, Board of Trade, 24 and 25 February 1950 (Burgess: 'see within', 18 February 1950)
98. TNA FO371/83410/FC11913/1, 'G Burgess 3/5', May 1950
99. Harold Nicolson, *Diaries and Letters, Vol III: 1945–1962* (London: Collins, 1968), entry for 29 January 1950
100. Harold Nicolson, unpublished diary, Thursday 12 January 1950, Balliol College Archives, Oxford

CHAPTER 7

1. http://bjhollingum.blogspot.co.uk/2010/08/life-and-times-of-dean.html (accessed 20 December 2015)
2. Bill Bristow, *My Father the Spy: Deceptions of an MI6 Officer* (Ross-on-Wye: WBML ePublishing and Media Company Ltd, 2012), Kindle loc. 3988
3. Bristow mistakenly dated it to late December 1949 and early January 1950
4. TNA KV2/4101 serial 20a
5. TNA KV2/4101 serial 21a
6. Dick Goldsmith White, then a senior MI5 officer and a future head of MI5 and then MI6
7. TNA KV4/472, 17 February 1950
8. The British economy, and the pound sterling, were under severe pressure and the British government had imposed strict limits on the amount of currency that travellers abroad could take out of the country with them. In 1949 that limit was set at £10. Contravention was a criminal offence
9. TNA KV4/472, 17 February 1950
10. That might have been one of the uses to which agent ORANGE, Eric Kessler, had been put
11. Andrew and Mitrokhin, op. cit., p. 202
12. TNA KV2/4101 serial 7a
13. TNA KV4/472, 16 February 1950
14. See Michael Smith, *Foley: The Spy Who Saved 10,000 Jews*; see also Keith Jeffery, op. cit.
15. TNA FCO158/182, Middleton file note, 3 March 1950, and Carey-Foster file note, 8 March 1950
16. TNA JV2/4101 serial 15a, 18 January 1950
17. TNA KV2/4101 serial 36a, Burgess to Liddell, 30 March 1950
18. TNA KV2/4101 serial 23a
19. TNA FCO158/182, Burgess to Ashley Clarke, 6 May 1950
20. TNA KV2/4101 serial 6c, 30 November 1949; TNA KV2/4101 serial 15a, 18 January 1950; see also TNA KV2/988 serial 1072b
21. TNA KV2/987 serials 1073b, 1076a, 1055a
22. TNA PREM8/1524, Herbert Morrison (Foreign Secretary) to Prime Minister, 51/39, 13 June 1951
23. TNA KV4/472, 23 January 1950
24. TNA KV4/472, 23 January 1950
25. 'Report Concerning the Disappearance of Two Former Foreign Office Officials', HM Stationary Office, 23 November 1955
26. *Sunday Dispatch*, 15 July 1951, quoted in Seaman and Mather, op. cit.
27. George Weidenfeld, *Remembering My Good Friends: An Autobiography* (London: HarperCollins, 1995), p. 157

28. TNA KV2/4103 serial 188, Warner statement
29. Terence De Vere White, *A Fretful Midge* (London: Routledge and Kegan Paul, 1957), pp 161–4
30. Cathal O'Flynn is the correct name. He was a Dublin District Judge appointed in October 1946 (*Irish Times*, 2 October 1946). He heard petty cases – such as driving offences – but also more substantial ones. In 1957 – the year White's book was published – O'Flynn struck a blow to censorship by refusing a Garda petition to close down Tennessee Williams's *The Rose Tattoo* (which was then being performed at the Pike Theatre in Dublin, starring Anna Magnani) on the grounds of obscenity. He challenged the Garda, saying that their storming of the theatre had been designed to close down the play without a petition. He ordered the play to reopen and continue while the proper process was run and the case proven
31. *Dublin Evening Herald*, 4 March 1949, p. 1
32. Ibid.
33. Ibid. and *Dublin Evening Mail*, 4 March 1949, p. 5
34. Modin, op. cit., p. 180
35. 'Death in 2am car crash', *Dublin Evening Herald*, 4 March 1949, p. 1
36. FCO 158/182, confidential telegram, 9 March 1950, London to Washington
37. FCO 158/182, confidential telegram, 14 March 1950, Sir Oliver Franks to Middleton
38. TNA KV2/4101 serial 32b, 1 March 1950, B. A. Hill file note
39. TNA KV2/4101 serial 34a, 3 March 1950, Carey-Foster to Hill
40. TNA FCO158/156, P. G. Adams file note, 9 March 1950: initialled as seen by G. Middleton, 9 March 1950
41. TNA KV2/4101 serial 37, 1 May 1950 (signed) G. Liddell
42. TNA KV2/4101 serial 38, B. A. Hill to DDG (Guy Liddell), 3 May 1950
43. TNA FCO158/182
44. TNA FCO158/182, Hoyer Millar to Middleton, 16 June 1950
45. TNA FCO158/182, Hoyer Millar to H. Ashley Clarke, 11 July 1950
46. TNA FCO158/182, Note to Middleton, 1 July 1950
47. TNA KV2/4112 serial 604a
48. TNA FCO158/182, Middleton to Hoyer Millar, 17 July 1950 and 26 July 1950
49. TNA FCO158/182, McKenzie to Carey-Foster, 19 July 1951
50. TNA PREM 8/1524, Herbert Morrison (Foreign Secretary) to Prime Minister, 51/39, 13 June 1951
51. 'Report Concerning the Disappearance of Two Former Foreign Office Officials', HM Stationary Office, 23 November 1955
52. TNA FCO158/182, Middleton file note, 12 July 1950
53. Professor Arnold Toynbee's son; Arnold Toynbee had originally provided a reference for Burgess to the BBC
54. See Cecil, op. cit., pp 147, 151–7
55. Diana Cooper, Viscount John Julius Norwich (ed.), *Darling Monster: The Letters of Lady Diana Cooper to Her Son John Julius Norwich 1939–1952* (London: Chatto & Windus, 2013)
56. TNA KV2/979 folio 77a, 15 November 1936
57. TNA KV2/981 folio 219a, 9 October 1950
58. TNA K 2/980 folio 107, withdrawal of work permit, 22 June 1940
59. Harold Nicolson Letters, Burgess to Nicolson, 15 April 1959, op. cit.
60. TNA KV2/980, folio 191a, dated 4 April 1950
61. Weidenfeld, op. cit.; Antonia Fraser, *My History* (London: Weidenfeld & Nicolson, 2015)

62. Weidenfeld, op. cit., p. 157
63. Ibid.
64. This is probably MI6 officer Tomas Harris, a colleague of Kim Philby's. During the war Harris had been the controller of GARBO [Juan Pujol], the double-cross spy who hoodwinked the Nazis
65. TNA KV2/980, folio 200z, 26 July 1950
66. Duff Cooper MP was a pre-war and wartime member of the Cabinet
67. Michael Evans and Magnus Linklater, 'Death-bed Confession of the Spy Who Got Away', *The Times*, 30 October 2004; Hamish MacGibbon, 'Diary', *London Review of Books*, Vol. 33 No. 12, 16 June 2011, pp 40–41; TNA KV2/1669–83 (15 files on MacGibbon and his wife covering 1938–53)
68. Salomea Halpern was the wife of Alexander Halpern, a lawyer who had served as Alexander Kerensky's Private Secretary in 1917. Kerensky was the chairman of the post-Tsarist government from July to November 1917, which was toppled by Lenin and the Bolsheviks in the 'October' revolution. Alexander Halpern served in MI6 during the Second World War and was based for some of it in Washington. Salomea was a former *Vogue* model
69. TNA KV2/980 serial 201a, note dated 15 August 1950, Mr B. A. Hill
70. Hansard, HC Deb, 18 June 1951, Vol. 489, Cols 30–33
71. See Nigel West, *Venona: The Greatest Secret of the Cold War* (London: HarperCollins, 2000); John Earl Hayes and Harvey Klehr, *Venona: Decoding Soviet Espionage in America* (Yale: Yale University Press, 1999)
72. The name VENONA dates from 1961. It is a meaningless name. The project's first name was BRIDE
73. Andrew and Mitrokhin, op. cit., p. 188
74. Andrew, *The Defence of the Realm*, p. 377
75. An alternative codename was REST
76. Andrew, *The Defence of the Realm*, p. 384; TNA KV4/471, Guy Liddell's diary, entry for 20 September 1949
77. 'Fuchs pleads guilty', *The Times*, 2 March 1950, p. 2
78. Andrew, *The Defence of the Realm*, p. 387
79. Ibid., p. 377
80. TNA CSC11/68 refers to Burgess being established in Branch A, but TNA PREM8/1524 refers to him only as belonging to Branch B
81. Kim Philby, *My Silent War* (London: Arrow Books, 2003), p. 165
82. Philby, *My Silent War* (London: Granada, 1983), p. 195
83. Madchen File No. 83792, Vol. 2, 249, note from Paul
84. Madchen File No. 83792, Vol. 2, 228, contact in US, partial document
85. TNA KV2/4103 serial 189b, Mrs E. Bassett to Guy Burgess, 29 January 1951
86. Goronwy Rees, op. cit., pp 188–90; Penrose and Freeman, op. cit., p. 352; Boyle, *The Climate of Treason*, p. 377
87. Penrose and Freeman, op. cit., p. 352; Boyle, *The Climate of Treason*, p. 377
88. We are very grateful to Svetlana Lokhova for telling us about Russian drinking habits. Burgess was probably the former, whereas Maclean was the latter
89. Ship's Manifest No. 47, SS *Caronia*
90. Denis Greenhill, *More By Accident*, 2nd edn (York: Wilton 65, 1993), p. 72
91. TNA FCO12/209. Greenhill's article was printed in *The Times*, 7 September 1977, p. 14, under the title, 'The day Kim Philby put in a good word for Guy Burgess'
92. Ibid.
93. TNA FO115/4483
94. TNA FO115/4483

95. Newton, op. cit., p. 274
96. Ibid.
97. TNA FO115/4483
98. Mary Pring (FCO) to Jeff Hulbert, 22 July 2015, 'I can confirm that the FCO is not holding any retained material for file FO 115/4483, and following searches, we have been unable to identify any further material which we hold for either 1950 or 1951.'
99. TNA FCO158/4 Burrows to Carey-Foster, 6 August 1951
100. Obtained from the Federal Bureau of Investigation through the Freedom of Information Act [hereafter FBI-FOIA], Philby 2a, pp 103–4
101. Ibid.
102. Ibid. p. 105
103. Greenhill, op. cit., p. 73
104. TNA FCO12/209. Greenhill's article was printed in *The Times*, 7 September 1977, p. 14, under the title, 'The day Kim Philby put in a good word for Guy Burgess'
105. *The Times*, 2 November 1950
106. FCO to Hulbert, 5 October 2015: 'Following a search I have identified the following entry in the 1950 subject index under the heading "Eden, Anthony: M.P." – "Visit to United States for unveiling of memorial to Field Marshall Sir John Dill. AU 1858/1-2-3." The reference AU 1858/1-2-3 is an original Foreign Office file reference. I have checked the National Archives (TNA) catalogue but could not find any evidence that the file had been selected for permanent preservation and transferred to TNA. I have been unable to identify any other information relevant to your request which we hold.'
107. D. R. Thorpe, *Eden: The Life and Times of Anthony Eden, First Earl of Avon 1897–1977* (London: Vintage Digital, 2011), Kindle loc. 8944
108. Tom Bower, *The Perfect English Spy* (London: Mandarin, 1996), p. 129
109. Thorpe, op. cit., Kindle loc. 8944
110. Ibid.
111. Ibid.
112. Driberg, *Guy Burgess*, p. 77
113. FBI-FOIA, Philby 2a, p. 94
114. FBI-FOIA, Philby 1b, pp 84–8
115. Newton, op. cit., p. 276
116. Driberg, *Guy Burgess*, p. 87
117. Newton, op. cit., p. 281. Newton cites a letter to him from Jebb confirming these details
118. Ibid.
119. Driberg, *Guy Burgess*, p. 84
120. Ibid., p. 87
121. FBI-FOIA, Philby 6c, p. 31
122. FBI-FOIA, Philby 1b, p. 111
123. Andrew and Mitrokhin, op. cit., p. 206
124. Thursday 23 November 1950
125. TNA FO115/4524, undated background note
126. TNA FO115/4524, Sir Roger Makins to Kit (Christopher) Steel, 2 February 1951, and Adams to Burrows, 13 February 1951
127. TNA FO155/4524, Lord Tedder (Chairman, British Joint Services Mission) to Lord Portal, ANCAM 454, February 1951
128. It has been said that Mann, who later became a US citizen, was a KGB spy who had been 'turned' into an American double agent at some time between the late

1940s and early 1950s. Some evidence for this is provided by recollections written by Sir Patrick Reilly, who was the secretary of the British Joint Intelligence Committee in 1951: Bodleian Library, Oxford: MS Eng c6920, 'Reflections on Burgess and Maclean'

129. Newton, op. cit., pp 305–11
130. FBI-FOIA, Philby 1a, pp 79–81, event programme
131. FBI-FOIA, Philby 1b, p. 89, 1–2 March 1951
132. FBI-FOIA, Philby 1c, p. 114
133. FBI-FOIA, Philby 1b, pp 57–9, statement by James A. Turck (identified by Newton in *The Butcher's Embrace*, op. cit.)
134. Newton, op. cit., p. 320
135. In some works called GOMER because the Cyrillic alphabet does not use the letter 'h'
136. Ibid.; Andrew, *The Defence of the Realm*, p. 423; Andrew and Mitrokhin, op. cit., p. 206
137. TNA KV6/145, master timeline
138. There might also have been other legal issues to be resolved, such as whether it would be considered to be admissible evidence in a legal process. Examination of that proposition could force a whole host of technical issues related to interception, decryption and interpretation to be examined by a court, which from a security point of view would have been highly undesirable
139. Harold Nicolson Letters, Burgess to Nicolson, 15 April 1959, op. cit.,
140. 'Report Concerning the Disappearance of Two Former Foreign Office Officials', HM Stationary Office, 23 November 1955
141. TNA FCO158/182, Sir Oliver Franks to Ashley Clark, 7 April 1951
142. TNA FCO12/209. Greenhill's article was printed in *The Times*, 7 September 1977, p. 14, under the title, 'The day Kim Philby put in a good word for Guy Burgess'
143. Donald Seaman and John Mather, op. cit., p. 63
144. FBI-FOIA, Philby 1b, p. 90
145. Modin, op. cit., p. 199; Andrew and Mitrokhin, op. cit., p. 206; Andrew, *The Defence of the Realm*, p. 424
146. Philby, *My Silent War* (London: Arrow Books, 2003), p. 171; Andrew, *The Defence of the Realm*, p. 424
147. FBI-FOIA, Philby 6c, p. 29
148. https://www.city.ac.uk/cambridge-spies-the-guy-burgess-files (accessed 20 December 2015)
149. TNA FCO158/6: Ridsdale to Talbot de Malahide, 1 November 1952; The *Daily Mirror*, 1 November 1952
150. TNA KV2/4106 serials 272b, 288b, 312z, 322a
151. Modin, op. cit., p. 200
152. Seaman and Mather, op. cit., p. 64
153. Driberg, *Guy Burgess*, p. 94; Penrose and Freeman, op. cit., p. 370
154. Penrose and Freeman, op. cit., p. 370
155. 'Report Concerning the Disappearance of Two Former Foreign Office Officials', HM Stationary Office, 23 November 1955
156. TNA FCO158/182, R. W. Hooper, Ashley Clarke and Joyce Gutteridge file notes, 9–23 May 1951
157. TNA FCO12/209. Greenhill's article was printed in *The Times*, 7 September 1977, p. 14, under the title, 'The day Kim Philby put in a good word for Guy Burgess'
158. A copy is filed in TNA FCO158/24
159. TNA FCO158/4 Jebb to Carey-Foster, 20 June 1951

160. TNA KV6/145
161. FBI-FOIA, Philby 1b, p. 76
162. Driberg, *Guy Burgess*, p. 93
163. TNA KV6/145
164. Driberg, *Guy Burgess*, p. 94
165. Ibid.
166. Anthony Blunt unpublished memoirs, British Library, MS Add 88902/2, folio 51
167. TNA KV6/145. All dates are taken from the master timeline
168. Brian Sewell, *The Outsider: Always Almost: Never Quite* (London: Quartet, 2011), pp 69–70
169. Birley letter to Andrew Boyle, 3 April 1977, ADD 9429/IG/14, Boyle papers, University of Cambridge
170. Seaman and Mather, op. cit., p. 65
171. *The Mysterious Affair at Styles* (1921) and *The Murder of Roger Ackroyd* (1926)
172. Anthony Blunt memoirs, British Library, MS Add 88901/2
173. TNA FCO158/3, record of action taken in the investigation into the Washington Leakage on 28 and 29 May 1951
174. TNA FCO158/3 folio 4
175. TNA FCO158/3, 30 May 1951, marked in pencil '2 Tels sent by 1915…', 31 May 1951
176. TNA FCO158/27 (undated, probably 1955) lists 16 names, plus 'S of S' (meaning by then Anthony Eden and Harold Macmillan), plus MI5 officers
177. TNA FCO158/26 Talbot de Malahide to Dean, 13 November 1953
178. TNA KV4/473, 12 June 1951
179. TNA KV2/4102 serial 117b, 10:20
180. Ibid., 14:25
181. Ibid., 15:03
182. TNA KV2/4102 serial 111b
183. TNA FCO158/4 and TNA FO115/4483
184. Ibid., 16:03
185. *Daily Mirror*, 8 June 1951
186. *The Times*, 8 June 1951, p. 4
187. *Daily Worker*, 8 June 1951, p. 1
188. '£9 day trip boat returned from France – minus two passengers', *Daily Mirror*, 8 June 1951
189. Alistair Cooke, 'US talks of lax security checks in Britain', *Manchester Guardian*, 8 June 1951, p. 7
190. *Daily Mirror*, 8 June 1951
191. Blunt: *Daily Mirror*, 8 June 1951; Rees: *Daily Graphic & Sketch*, 'Lost officials' trail to Paris', 8 June 1951, back page
192. Bill Greig, 'The nonsense of a hush-hush hunt', *Daily Mirror*, 8 June 1951
193. TNA FCO158/3, Makins file note, 7 June 1951
194. TNA CAB128/19, 42nd Conclusions, June 1951, item 3
195. TNA CAB195/9, Cabinet Secretary's notes of the discussion
196. TNA FCO 158/3 serial 58
197. TNA FO115/4524, Marten to Makins, 20 June 1951
198. TNA FO115/4524, Chiefs of Staff (Ministry of Defence) to Sir William Elliot, 20 June 1951
199. Vita Sackville-West, Harold Nicolson, Nigel Nicolson (ed.), *Vita and Harold: The Letters of Vita Sackville-West and Harold Nicolson, 1910-62*, re-issue edn (London: Weidenfeld & Nicolson, 2007), p. 399

CHAPTER 8

1. BBC WAC R13/447/2, SECRETARIAT: Library and NEWS_INFormation: Head of Secretariat's file, Stacy (night commissionaire) to Stacy copied to Farquarson, 19 September 1951
2. Maclean, *No, I Tell a Lie, It Was the Tuesday*, p. 103
3. TNA KV2/4105 serial 234
4. TNA KV2/4107 serial 344
5. TNA KV2/4102 serial 139a
6. Cynthia Jebb (Lady Gladwyn) to her mother (Celia, Lady Noble), 11 August 1951, Churchill College Cambridge, CGLA 1/1/6
7. TNA FCO158/3 serial 4
8. TNA FCO158/3, Gladwyn Jebb to William Strang, 4 June 1951
9. TNA FCO158/3, Strang to Jebb, 9 June 1951
10. TNA FCO158/182, Jebb to Strang, 8 June 1951
11. TNA FCO158/182, Jebb to Strang, 8 June 1951
12. TNA FCO158/3, handwritten note on 10 Downing Street notepaper
13. TNA FCO158/3, 'Tel sent by MI5 to their rep in W'ton 31/5'
14. TNA KV2/4107 serial 339a, G. T. D. Patterson 30 November 1951
15. TNA KV2/4112, message from SLO Australia to MI5, 8 March 1955
16. TNA KV 2/4102 serial 134
17. TNA KV2/4105, letter to 'James', 1 August 1951
18. TNA KV2/4105 serial 240, report by W. K. Skardon, 14 July 1951
19. TNA KV2/4106, doc. 315, note dated 23 October 1951
20. TNA KV2/4105, report from Special Branch Tanganyika
21. TNA KV2/4104, note by W. J. Skardon, 22 June 1951
22. TNA KV2/4105
23. TNA KV2/4106, note by G. T. D. Patterson, 28 September 1951
24. TNA KV2/4102 serial 135y
25. TNA KV2/4102 serial 116a. The colleague was Peter Matthews
26. TNA KV2/4108 serial 393
27. TNA KV2/4102 serial 115b
28. TNA KV2/4111 serials 512a and 609
29. TNA KV2/4102 serial 124a
30. TNA KV2/4106, doc. 301, Special Branch note headed 'Strictly Confidential'
31. TNA KV2 4104, letter from Brian Howard to Guy Burgess
32. TNA KV2/4104, letter from MI5, 14 June 1951
33. TNA KV2/4105, letter from R. T. Reed to Commander Special Branch
34. TNA KV2/4102 serial 101d
35. TNA KV2/2588, W. H. Auden file, f26c and 24b
36. TNA KV2/4104, note on 27 June 1951; TNA KV2/4106, note of 20 September 1951, Probate register 1949, p. 661, Wyllie, Thomas Hunter Steen. Wyllie's executor was H. L. A. Hart's cousin, Louis 'Boy' Hart
37. TNA KV2/4105, note by D. H. Whyte 15 August 1950; TNA KV2/4104, file notes on 21 and 29 June 1950
38. TNA KV2/4103 serial 188
39. TNA FCO158/6 serial 218a
40. TNA KV2/4107 serial 336a
41. TNA KV2 4102 serial 115
42. TNA KV2/4112 serial 607a
43. TNA KV2/4102 serial 101b
44. TNA KV2/4102 serial 111a

45. TNA KV2/4102 serial 101b
46. HC Deb, Oral Answers to Questions, Foreign Service (MR. Guy Burgess), 18 June 1951
47. TNA KV2/4104, doc. 225, Note of Further Action to be Taken
48. TNA KV2/4115 serial 701b
49. TNA KV2/4106, doc. 317; http://spartacus-educational.com/Theodore_Mally.htm (accessed 20 December 2015)
50. TNA KV2/4112 serial 616a
51. TNA KV2/4115 serial 690
52. TNA KV2/4106 serial 290b, 317b
53. TNA KV2/4103 serial 167z
54. TNA KV2/4103 serial 152a
55. TNA KV2/4113 serial 649
56. http://www.coldspur.com/some-diplomatic-incidents/ (accessed 20 December 2015)
57. TNA KV2/4102 serial 111b
58. TNA KV2/4105 serial 237
59. TNA KV2/4104 serial 203, note by W. J. Skardon, 26 June 1951
60. Carter, op. cit., p. 447
61. TNA KV2/2588 serial 31, W. H. Auden file
62. TNA KV2/2253, MI5 file on John Lehmann
63. TNA KV2/2254 and TNA KV2/2255
64. Hastings, op. cit.; Rosamond Lehmann, 'The Art of Fiction 88', interview in *The Paris Review*, Summer 1985, No. 96
65. James Smith, *British Writers and MI5 Surveillance: 1930–1960* (Cambridge: Cambridge University Press, 2013), p. 61–3
66. Stephen Spender, John Goldsmith (ed.), *Journals 1939–1983* (London: Faber & Faber, 1985), p. 96
67. But then, when he was the Parliamentary Under-Secretary at the Ministry of Information in the first year of the war, Nicolson had confided to his unpublished diary that MI5 was a 'a silly and hen-minded Gestapo' and was something that he could 'smash'. Harold Nicolson, unpublished diary, Balliol College Archive, Oxford, 13 July 1940
68. TNA KV2/2588 serial 29
69. TNA FCO158/26, Talbot to Dean, 23 September 1953
70. *The Missing Diplomats* by Cyril Connolly, *Sunday Times*, 21 September 1952
71. TNA KV2/2588 serial 25c, MI5 file on W. H. Auden
72. TNA KV2/3436 serial 33a, note from James Robertson to Geoffrey Patterson, British Embassy, Washington, 29 October 1952
73. TNA KV4/473, 18 June 1951
74. TNA KV2/3436
75. TNA KV2/4109 serial 432a
76. TNA KV2/4109 serial 432a
77. TNA KV2/4102 serial 101a
78. TNA KV2/4102 serial 111a
79. TNA KV4/473, 12 June 1951
80. TNA KV2/4108 serial 390a
81. TNA KV2/4102 serial 108a
82. TNA KV2/4102 serial 116f
83. TNA KV 2/4102 serial 136z
84. TNA FCO158/28, Milmo's report: findings
85. TNA FCO158/27, A. J. de la Mare, 10 January 1955

86. ITN Source References: BGY501210003 (1988); and 8 November 1955 (Story ref: 088239)

87. http://www.theguardian.com/uk-news/2015/oct/23/mi5-mi6-coverup-cambridge-spy-ring-archive-papers (accessed 20 December 2015)

88. Henry Fairlie, 'Political Commentary', *The Spectator*, 22 September 1955

89. Hansard, HL Debs, 22 November 1955, Vol. 194, cols 708–31

90. Anthony Blunt, unpublished memoirs, British Library, MS Add 88902/1

91. Carter, op. cit., p. 357

92. Jenny Rees, op. cit., p. 253

93. Margot Wittkower, Interview Transcript, *Interviews with art historians, 1991–2002*, Research Library, The Getty Research Institute, Accession no. 940109, p. 125

94. Carter, op. cit., p. 498

95. Cairncross, op. cit., p. 131

96. Dr Magnus Pyke, *Glasgow Herald*, 21 October 1992

97. TNA KV2/3040, documents found in Burgess's flat and the Courtauld Institute.

98. Email from A. Glees to the authors, 6 November 2014

99. BBC WAC R Cont 1, HP Smollett File 2, Smollett (Ministry of Information) to Mohammad Afzal (BBC), 7 October 1944

100. *London Gazette*, 10 June 1944, pp 26–9

101. TNA KV2/4169

102. TNA KV2/4170 serial 318

103. Note by Phillip Knightley of conversation with William Rees-Mogg, March 1979

104. 'Leading civil servant was Russian mole who recruited Oxford spies', *The Times*, 13 May 2009, p. 20

105. TNA KV2/4102 serial 116b

106. TNA KV2/4102 serial 111a

107. TNA KV2/1997 serial 96b

108. Harold Macmillan, Foreign Secretary, HC Deb, 7 November, 1955

109. TNA KV2/4102 serial 109a

110. TNA KV2/4102 serial 136z

111. TNA KV2/4102 serial 109a

112. http://www.express.co.uk/news/history/613881/Esther-Whitfield-spy-Cambridge-spy-ring (accessed 20 December 2015)

113. TNA KV2/4102 serial 136z

114. TNA KV2/4102 serial 133a. Copyright restrictions apply

115. TNA KV2/4102 minute sheet

116. TNA KV4/473, entry for 12 June 1951

117. TNA KV2/4103 serial 183c

CHAPTER 9

1. TNA KV2/4102 serials 116h and 136

2. British Government White Paper, 'Report Concerning the Disappearance of Two Former Foreign Office Officials', 23 November 1955

3. Driberg, *Guy Burgess*, p. 100

4. Yoshiko M. Herrera, *Imagined Economies: The Sources of Russian Regionalism*, (Cambridge: Cambridge University Press, 2004), p. 172

5. TNA KV2/4114 serial 678a

6. Stephen Spender, 'Brief Encounter', *The Observer*, 10 November 1985, p. 19

7. John Miller, *All Them Cornfields and Ballet in the Evening* (London: Hodgson Press, 2010), p. 52

8. TNA KV2/3440 serial 73a

9. TNA KV2/3440 serial 74a
10. TNA KV2/3442 serial 201a, telegram from SLO Australia to MI5, 5 May 1954
11. TNA KV2/4112 serial 598a
12. Richard Hughes, *Foreign Devil: Thirty Years of Reporting in the Far East* (London: André Deutsch, 1972), p. 127
13. Ibid., p. 130
14. http://www.bbc.co.uk/archive/cambridgespies/7817.shtml (accessed 20 December 2015)
15. 'Burgess and Maclean Appear in Moscow', *Sunday Times*, 12 February 1956, p. 1
16. 'Text of Statement Issued by Burgess and Maclean', *The Times*, 13 February 1956, p. 7
17. 'Hope of "New Era" from Russians' visit', *The Times*, 20 March 1956, p. 10
18. TNA FO371/122850, letter from Mrs Bassett to Sir William Hayter
19. TNA KV2/4115 serial 702a
20. TNA KV2/4111, letter from Mrs Bassett to Mr Eden, 6 September 1954
21. Ibid., 9 September 1954
22. TNA FO371/122850, letter from Sir William Hayter to Mrs Bassett
23. TNA KV2/4125 serial 1088
24. Quoted in Carter, op. cit., p. 402
25. 'Donation for Burgess Article Declined', *The Times*, 25 February 1956, p. 6
26. 'Guy Burgess Stripped Bare', *The People*, 11 March 1956, p. 3
27. 'London Day by Day', *Daily Telegraph*, 29 March 1956
28. 'Burgess One of the Nicest Men I Know', *Daily Mail*, 18 June 1951
29. TNA KV2/4118 serial 857c
30. Jenny Rees, op. cit.
31. Driberg, *Ruling Passions* (London: Jonathan Cape, 1977), p. 233
32. Letter from Roy Harrod to Guy Burgess, 24 October 1960, British Library Western Manuscripts Add MS 71610 f29
33. Letter from Roy Harrod to Goronwy Rees, 1 March 1972, British Library Western Manuscripts, Add MS 71610 f62–5
34. TNA KV2/4115 serial 702a
35. TNA KV2/4115 serial 703
36. Letter from Rees to Harrod, 3 February 1972, British Library Western Manuscripts, Add MS 71610 f20–21
37. Ibid., f56
38. Boyle, *The Climate of Treason*, p. 474
39. Guy Burgess interview with CBC TV, 11 March 1959
40. Driberg, *Guy Burgess*, p. 103
41. TNA KV2/3749 serial 413a
42. TNA KV2/3749 serial 410a
43. Harold Nicolson Papers, Burgess to Nicolson, op. cit., undated
44. TNA KV2/4116 serial 802
45. B. Piadyshev, Burgess, Guy Burgess, International Affairs, Moscow, Vol. 51, No. 2, 2005, p. 184
46. TNA KV2/4105, Letter from M. A. Jacobs & Sons
47. Miller, op. cit., p. 52
48. 'Burgess in the Crimea says I'm in Cuba', *Sunday Express*, 22 April 1962, p. 1
49. TNA KV2/4125 serial 314 and TNA KV2/4115 serial 732a
50. TNA KV2/4125 serial 109
51. Driberg, *Ruling Passions*, pp 230–36
52. Ian McDougall, *Foreign Correspondent* (London: Frederick Muller, 1980), p. 111

53. TNA KV2/4133 serial 1568
54. John Mossman, 'The last time I saw Burgess and Maclean', *Daily Mail*, 19 April 1962
55. Miller, op. cit., p. 56
56. TNA KV2/4112 serial 629z
57. Stephen Spender, 'Brief Encounter', *The Observer*, 10 November 1985, p. 19
58. Michael Redgrave, op. cit., pp 192–4
59. TNA KV2/3822, doc. 59a, source report
60. Rose Collis, *Coral Browne: 'This Effing Lady'* (London: Oberon Books, 2007), p. 121
61. TNA KV2/3822 folio 50a
62. Collis, op. cit., p. 123
63. Ibid., p. 122
64. Letter from Guy Burgess to Coral Browne quoted in Inigo Thomas, 'No Stripes Please' http://www.lrb.co.uk/blog/2015/03/11/inigo-thomas/no-stripes-please/ (accessed 20 December 2015)
65. Ibid.
66. Jan Morris, *Pleasures of a Tangled Life* (London: Barrie & Jenkins, 1989), p. 131
67. José Manser, *Mary Fedden and Julian Trevelyan: Life and Art by the River Thames* (London: Unicorn Press, 2012)
68. TNA KV2/4126 serial 1126a
69. TNA KV2/4127 serial 1143b
70. Harold Nicolson Letters, Burgess to Nicolson, 15 April, op. cit.
71. TNA KV2/4114 serials 665a, 670
72. Burgess letter to Tom Driberg from Moscow, begins 'My dear old fellow', no date visible, Driberg papers, B10, 1–39, Christ Church College, Oxford
73. Letter from W. H. Auden to Roy Harrod, British Library, Add MS 71192 f96
74. TNA KV2/4138 serial 552a
75. TNA KV2/4128 serial 1194
76. Letter from Guy Burgess to Roy Harrod, British Library Add MS 71192 f34
77. Modin, op. cit., pp 244–5
78. Harold Nicolson Letters, Burgess to Nicolson, 8 September 1958, op. cit.
79. TNA KV2/4117 serial 835b
80. TNA KV2/4117 serial 812c
81. TNA KV2/4134 serial 140a
82. TNA KV2/4115 serial 732a
83. Harold Nicolson Letters, Burgess to Nicolson, 'February 1st' (probably 1959), op. cit.
84. All extracts from the correspondence between Guy Burgess and Harold Nicolson, Princeton University.
85. Aleksandr Fursenko and Timothy Naftali, *Khrushchev's Cold War: The Inside Story of an American Adversary* (New York: W. W. Norton & Company, 2010), pp 108–9, 121

CHAPTER 10

1. Harold Nicolson Letters, Burgess to Nicolson, 'February 1st' (probably 1959), op. cit.
2. http://www.telegraph.co.uk/news/uknews/11949124/soviet-spy-guy-burgess-mi5-letters.html (accessed 20 December 2015)
3. 'Burgess says he will come home', *Daily Mail*, 15 September 1956, p. 1
4. TNA KV2/4116 serial 781
5. TNA KV2/4117 serial 814a
6. TNA KV2/4117 serial 817b

7. TNA KV2/4117 serial 824
8. TNA KV2/4118, Burgess to Driberg (undated)
9. TNA KV2/4117 serial 844
10. Modin, op. cit., pp 80–81; Costello and Tsarev, op. cit., pp 239–40
11. TNA KV2/4117 serial 844
12. TNA KV2/4117 serial 839
13. TNA KV2/4118 serial 870
14. TNA KV2/4117 serial 847
15. TNA KV2/4118; *Daily Express*, 23 November 1956
16. Ibid., 24 November 1956
17. Chapman Pincher, *Treachery: Betrayals, Blunders and Cover-Ups: Six Decades of Espionage* (New York: Random House, 2009), pp 411–13
18. 'Burgess on Pharos', *The Spectator*, 30 November 1956
19. TNA T326/1133
20. TNA KV2/4121 serial 998
21. UCL London Special Collections, Gaitskell F/1 to F/4, letter from Proctor to Gaitskell, 28 June 1945
22. TNA KV2/4122, J. B. Ure note of meeting, 3 December 1957
23. TNA KV2/4132 serial 1338
24. Pring (FCO) to Hulbert, 19 August 2015
25. TNA KV2/4128 serial 1170
26. TNA KV2/4126 serial 1105
27. TNA KV2/4117 serials 1172, 1168
28. TNA KV2/4123 serial 1037a
29. Letter from Guy Burgess to his mother, National Archives KV2/3822, Doc. 50a
30. Letter from Guy Burgess to Roy Harrod, 28 November 1960, British Library Add MS 71192 f31–3
31. TNA FCO158/178
32. Randolph Churchill, 'Old School Tie Burgess calls on me', *Evening Standard*, 23 February 1959, p. 7
33. Harold Evans, *Downing Street Diary: The Macmillan Years* (London: Hodder & Stoughton, 1981) pp 59–60
34. http://www.itnsource.com/en/shotlist/ITN/1959/02/24/T24025903/?s=Guy Burgess (accessed 20 December 2015)
35. TNA FCO 158/178
36. TNA KV2/4128 serial 1194
37. TNA KV2/4127 serial 1143
38. Erik Durschmied, *Don't Shoot the Yanqui* (London: Grafton, 1990), p. 227
39. TNA KV2/4123 serial 1037
40. TNA KV2/4128 serial 1198
41. TNA KV2/4128 serial 1199a
42. TNA KV2/4128 serial 1204
43. TNA CAB195/18/6
44. The British public finally got their first opportunity to see one of their most famous traitors talking on camera a full fifty-six years after the event. CBC finally transmitted the archive film and we prepared a version for simultaneous release on the BBC programme *Newsnight* on 23 February 2015
45. TNA KV2/4130 serial 1266
46. Letter from Guy Burgess to Roy Harrod, 28 November 1960, British Library Add MS 71610 f31–3
47. Ibid.

48. Letter from Roy Harrod to Guy Burgess, 24 October 1960, British Library Add MS 71610 f29
49. Piadyshev, op. cit., p. 185
50. TNA FCO158/118
51. Anthony Purdy and Douglas Sutherland, *Burgess and Maclean* (London: Secker and Warburg, 1963), p. 10
52. Ibid., p. 15
53. 'B and M Warned Off', *Daily Mail*, 19 April 1962, p. 1
54. TNA PREM 11/4461, note from Attorney General to Prime Minister, 11 April 1962
55. TNA PREM 11/4461, note from official to Attorney General, 12 April 1962
56. Parliamentary report, *The Times*, 11 May 1962
57. 'Many friends in the Establishment', *The Times*, 24 April 1962
58. 'I'm not going home either says Burgess', *Daily Express*, 23 April 1962, p. 1
59. Andrew Lownie, *Stalin's Englishman: The Lives of Guy Burgess* (London: Hodder & Stoughton, 2015), p. 311
60. Sebastian Faulks, *The Fatal Englishman: Three Short Lives* (London: Vintage, 1997), p. 235
61. Ibid., p. 238
62. Ibid., p. 255
63. Quoted in Faulks, op. cit., p. 239
64. http://www.independent.co.uk/voices/a-tale-of-two-arrogant-eton-boys-who-tried-hard-not-to-do-their-best-we-are-free-to-stay-out-of-the-game-but-doing-less-than-our-best-is-fatal-1345784.html (accessed 20 December 2015)
65. Quoted in Faulks, op. cit., p. 264
66. Faulks, op. cit., p. 284
67. Ibid., p. 269
68. TNA KV2/4135 serial 1450a
69. TNA KV2/4135 serial 1451a
70. TNA FO181/1154, letter from H. F. T. Smith to E. Youde, 26 April 1962
71. TNA FO181/1154, letter from P. G. D. Adams to H. F. T. Smith, 8 May 1962
72. '"Absurd", says Guy Burgess in Moscow', *Daily Telegraph*, 22 April 1962, p. 1
73. Jeremy Wolfenden, 'Car Accident was Warning says Burgess', *Daily Telegraph*, 1 July 1963, p. 1
74. Interview with the authors 4 March 2015
75. Faulks, op. cit., p. 294
76. TNA KV2/4139 serial 158b
77. Letter from Guy Burgess to Roy Harrod, 29 January 1963, British Library, Add MS 71610 f43–6
78. 'Burgess "One of the nicest men I know"', *Daily Mail*, 18 June 1951
79. Letter from Burgess to Tom Driberg from Moscow, begins 'My dear old fellow', no date visible, Christ Church College, Oxford
80. 'Guy Burgess to enter Moscow hospital', Reuters report in *The Times*, 11 October 1961, p. 9
81. Stephen Spender, 'Brief Encounter', *The Observer*, 10 November 1985, p. 19
82. Miller, op. cit., p. 55
83. Carter, op. cit., p. 441
84. Harold Nicolson Letters, Burgess to Nicolson, 23 May 1962, op. cit.
85. TNA KV2/4115 serial 702a
86. TNA KV2/4125, letter from Mrs Bassett to Guy Burgess intercepted 30 May 1956
87. http://www.express.co.uk/news/history/613881/Esther-Whitfield-spy-Cambridge-spy-ring (accessed 20 December 2015)

88. Lownie, op. cit., p. 313
89. Miller, op. cit., p. 57
90. 'Guy Burgess dies', *Sunday Express*, 1 September 1963, p. 1
91. http://www.itnsource.com/en/shotlist/ITN/1963/09/01/T01096301/?s=Guy Burgess dead (accessed 20 December 2015)
92. Boyle, *The Climate of Treason*, p. 473
93. Modin, op. cit., p. 256
94. 'Two day silence on Burgess', *Daily Telegraph*, 1 September 1963, p. 1 and back page
95. Jeremy Wolfenden, 'Burgess keeps double identity at funeral', *Daily Telegraph*, 5 September 1963
96. TNA KV2/4139
97. TNA KV2/4139 serial 1602
98. Rufina Philby, op. cit., p. 79
99. BBC Radio 4, *Rebels*, 5 October 1984
100. Michael Burn, *The Debatable Land* (London: Hamish Hamilton, 1970), p. 235

CHAPTER 11

1. TNA FCO 158/207, Cadogan Report, paragraph 1
2. Brian Urquhart, *A Life in Peace and War* (London: Weidenfeld & Nicolson, 1987), p. 117
3. Michael S. Goodman, *The Official History of the Joint Intelligence Committee* (London: Routledge, 2014), p. 173
4. Patrick Reilly papers, MS Ceng, 6920, Bodleian Library, Oxford
5. Cadogan Diaries, 29 June 1951, (unpublished entry), ACAD 1/22, Churchill College Cambridge archive centre. Reproduced with permission of the Master and Fellows of Churchill College, Cambridge
6. Alan Campbell, *Colleagues and Friends* (London: Michael Russell, 1988), p. 16
7. Ibid.
8. TNA FCO158/24: papers including '(signed by Maclean)' thus proving that he had seen them: 'Communist influence in South and South East Asia and the Far East' [JIC I 6],]; 'Procedure for obtaining information & certain facilities from French Authorities' [JIC (50) 67, 29 December 1950]; 'French requests for information' [JIC C365] – Chief of Staff papers (some signed by Maclean); minutes of the Permanent Under-Secretary's Committee, which also handled security and other issues (marked for Maclean's retention); minutes of the FO's Russia Committee, which was tasked with evaluating and countering communist propaganda worldwide (all marked for Maclean's retention). The list covers hundreds of papers and files and shows the sheer breadth of material to which he had been exposed
9. TNA FCO158/24, Cecil to Strang, 9 June 1951
10. Campbell, op. cit., p. 18. Campbell recounts the instance when an 'eminent neurologist' addressed the committee, although no record of that survives in the files
11. Dick Goldsmith White, a senior MI5 officer, and George Carey-Foster, the head of Foreign Office Security. Both appeared at the fourth meeting, 31 July 1951; Patrick Reilly, Secretary of the Joint Intelligence Committee (JIC), and 'C', the head of MI6. Both appeared at the sixth meeting, 8 August 1951; Roderick Barclay, Private Secretary to the Foreign Secretary and the former head of Foreign Office personnel when Burgess had been recruited and moved on to the permanent establishment, and John Winnifrith, a senior Treasury official who at the time of Burgess's recruitment had been responsible for Foreign Office pay and rations. Both appeared at the seventh meeting, 14 August 1951, and Assistant Commissioner R. M. Howe, the head of the Metropolitan Police CID, eighth meeting, 16 August

12. TNA FCO158/24, minutes fourth meeting of Cadogan Committee, 31 July 1951
13. TNA FCO158/207, Cadogan Report, paragraph 14, Box 9
14. TNA FCO158/205, Cadogan Report, paragraph 47
15. TNA KV4/473, 12 June 1951
16. TNA FCO158/3
17. TNA KV2/4115, MI5 commentary on serial 703
18. TNA KV2/4115 serial 703
19. TNA KV2/4115, MI5 commentary on serial 703
20. Carter, op. cit., p. 306
21. Ibid., p. 308–9
22. Driberg, *Guy Burgess*, p. 23
23. TNA KV2/4114 serial 675a
24. TNA KV2/4112 serial 619z, 3 February 1956

INDEX